German
vocabulary handbook

Joy Saunders

**Berlitz Publishing /
Apa Publications GmbH & Co. Verlag KG,
Singapore Branch, Singapore**

German Vocabulary Handbook

CONTACTING THE EDITORS
Every effort has been made fo provide accurate information in this publication, but changes are inevitable. The publisher cannot be responsible for any resulting loss, inconvenience, or injury. We would appreciate it if readers would call our attention to any errors or outdated information by contacting Berlitz Publishing, 95 Progress Street, Union, NJ 07083, USA. Fax: 1-908-206-1103. email: comments@berlitzbooks.com

Berlitz Trademark Reg. U.S. Patent Office and other countries. Marca Registrada.
Used under license from Berlitz Investment Corporation.

Printed in Singapore by Insight Print Services (Pte) Ltd., March 2005

Cover photo © Punchstock/Medioimages; inset photo © Photo Alto

Series Editor:

Christopher Wightwick is a former UK representative on the Council of Europe Modern Languages Project and principal inspector of Modern Languages for England.

CONTENTS

How to use this Handbook

A **Introduction**

    Word formation in German   2

    Conventions used in this Handbook   9

B **Vocabulary topics**

1   *Functional words*   12

2   *Where? – position & movement*   16
2a	Position	16
2b	Directions & location	18
2c	Movement	20

3   *When? – expressions of time*   22
3a	Past, present, & future	22
3b	The time, days, & dates	26

4   *How much? – expressions of quantity*   28
4a	Length & shape	28
4b	Measuring	30
4c	Numbers	32
4d	Calculations	34

5   *What sort of? – descriptions & judgements*   36
5a	Describing people	36
5b	The senses	38
5c	Describing things	40
5d	Evaluating things	42
5e	Comparisons	44
5f	Materials	45

6   *The human mind & character*   46
6a	Human character	46
6b	Feelings & emotions	48
6c	Thought processes	50
6d	Expressing views	52

7   *Human life & relationships*   56
7a	Family & friends	56
7b	Love, marriage, & children	58

7c	Life & death	60
8	*Daily life*	*62*
8a	The house	62
8b	The home	64
8c	Furnishings	66
8d	Daily routine	68
9	*Shopping*	*70*
9a	General expressions	70
9b	Household goods & toiletries	72
9c	Clothing	74
10	*Food & drink*	*76*
10a	Drinks & meals	76
10b	Fish & meat	78
10c	Vegetables, fruit, & desserts	80
10d	Cooking & eating	82
11	*Sickness & health*	*84*
11a	Accidents & emergencies	84
11b	Illness & disability	86
11c	Medical treatment	88
11d	Health & hygiene	90
12	*Social issues*	*92*
12a	Society	92
12b	Social services & poverty	94
12c	Housing & homelessness	96
12d	Addiction & violence	98
12e	Prejudice	100
13	*Religion*	*102*
13a	Ideas & doctrines	102
13b	Faith & practice	104
14	*Business & economics*	*106*
14a	Economic life	106
14b	At work	108
14c	Working conditions	110
14d	Finance & industry	112
14e	Banking & the economy	114
15	*Communicating with others*	*116*
15a	Meetings & greetings	116
15b	Approving, thanking, & disapproving	118

	15c	Permission, obligation, & clarification	120
	15d	Interjections, apologizing, & farewells	122
	15e	Post/Mail & telephone	124
	15f	Computers	126

16 Leisure & sport — 128

	16a	Leisure	128
	16b	Sporting activity	130
	16c	Sports & equipment	132

17 The arts — 134

	17a	Appreciation & criticism	134
	17b	Art & architecture	136
	17c	Literature	138
	17d	Music & dance	140
	17e	Theater & film/Theater & the movies	142

18 The media — 144

	18a	General terms	144
	18b	The Press	146
	18c	Television & radio	148
	18d	Advertising	150

19 Travel — 152

	19a	General terms	152
	19b	Going abroad & travel by boat	154
	19c	Travel by road	156
	19d	Travel by air	160
	19e	Travel by rail	162

20 Holidays/Vacation — 164

	20a	General terms	164
	20b	Accommodation & hotel	166
	20c	Camping & self-service	168

21 Language — 170

| | 21a | General terms | 170 |
| | 21b | Using language | 172 |

22 Education — 174

	22a	General terms	174
	22b	School	176
	22c	School subjects & examinations	178
	22d	Further & higher education	180

23 Science: the changing world — 182

| | 23a | Science & biology | 182 |
| | 23b | Physical sciences | 184 |

| | 23c | The earth & space | 186 |

24		*The environment: the natural world*	*188*
	24a	Geography	188
	24b	The animal world	190
	24c	Farming & gardening	192
	24d	Weather	194
	24e	Pollution	196

25		*Government & politics*	*198*
	25a	Political life	198
	25b	Elections & political ideology	200

26		*Crime & justice*	*202*
	26a	Crime	202
	26b	Trial	204
	26c	Punishment and crime prevention	206

27		*War & peace*	*208*
	27a	War	208
	27b	Military personnel & weaponry	210
	27c	Peace & international relations	212

| *C* | **Subject Index** | **215** |

| *D* | **Vocabulary Index** | **246** |

How to use this Handbook

This Handbook is a carefully ordered work of reference covering all areas of German vocabulary and phrasing. It is based on the thesaurus structure of the Council of Europe's Threshold Level, and expanded to include other major topics, especially in the fields of business, information technology, and education. Unlike a dictionary, it brings together words and phrases in related groups. It also illustrates their usage with contextualized example sentences, often in dialogue form. This enables learners and users of the language to:

* refresh and expand their general knowledge of vocabulary;
* organize systematically revision for public examinations, using the word groups to test their knowledge from German to English and vice versa;
* extend their knowledge of authentically German ways of saying things by studying the example sentences;
* support their speaking and writing on a given topic, as the logical arrangement of the sections will often prompt new ideas as well as supplying the means of expressing them.

The structure of the Handbook

The Handbook is divided into three parts:

A Introduction

The introduction is a concise account of the ways in which German creates compound words and phrases in order to express more complex ideas. (For a more extensive treatment of this topic, see the Berlitz *German Grammar Handbook*.)

B Vocabulary topics

There are 27 major areas of experience. Vocabulary samples are divided into a number of sections, so that words and phrases are gathered together into closely related groups. Almost all sections contain example sentences showing the vocabulary in use. Wherever it makes sense to do so, these sentences are linked together to form short narratives or dialogues that help to fix them in the memory.

Lists of specific terms such as the names of countries or musical instruments. These would simply clutter up the main Vocabularies, but they are linked to them by clear cross-references. Each

Appendix is numbered according to the Vocabulary to which it most closely relates.

C The subject index

An alphabetical index of topics and themes enables you to locate quickly the area you are interested in.

Locating the right section

The Handbook can be approached in two main ways:

• If you are not sure which topic will be best suited to your needs, start with the *List of Contents* on page iii. This will give you a general picture of the areas covered. You can then browse through the sections until you find the one you want.

• Alternatively, if you have a specific topic in mind, look it up in the *Subject Index* at the end of the book. This will take you directly to the relevant vocabulary section or appendix. To help you find what you are looking for, topics are often listed more than once, under different headings. Within most sections, there are cross-references to other, related areas.

A
INTRODUCTION

Word formation in German

Conventions used in this Handbook

Word formation in German

One of the great strengths of German is its ability to combine or modify words so as to express new meanings. A knowledge of how this is done helps the learner to understand new language and to build up a wide vocabulary.

1 *Nouns*

1a Many nouns are formed from the stem of strong verbs, using:

(a) the stem of the infinitive: **der Fall** "fall", **der Schlaf** "sleep";

(b) dropping the **-n** of the infinitive: **die Bitte** "request", **die Hilfe** "help", **die Lüge** "lie";

(c) the simple past: **der Griff** "grip", **der Klang** "sound";

(d) another vowel, often **-u-**: **der Schuss** "shot", **der Fluss** "river".

Sometimes the connection is not very easy to see, but it is worth noting the link: **ankommen - die Ankunft** 'arrival', **ziehen - der Zug** 'train', 'draft', **gehen - der Gang** 'corridor', 'gait'.

1b *Forming nouns with suffixes*

Nouns are often formed by adding suffixes to other words. Note that suffixes may cause the preceding vowel to take an Umlaut, particularly if the suffix has a short **i** in it.

(i) *Diminutives (with Umlaut):*

-chen	**das Kätzchen**	kitten
-lein	**das Entlein**	duck

(ii) *Other suffixes*

-e	**die Größe** 'size', **die Ferne** 'distance'
-ei	**die Metzgerei** 'butcher's shop', **die Angeberei** 'boasting'
-er, ler	**der Bäcker** 'baker', **der Sportler** 'sportsman'
-ie	**die Harmonie** 'harmony', **die Philosophie** 'philosophy'
-in	*(female form)* **die Ärztin** 'woman doctor', **die Sportlerin** 'sportswoman'

-nis	die Finsternis 'darkness', das Verhältnis 'relationship'
-schaft	die Eigenschaft 'quality', die Gesellschaft 'society'
-sal	das Schicksal 'fate'
-tum	der Reichtum 'wealth', das Christentum 'Christianity'
-ung	die Hoffnung 'hope', die Begegnung 'meeting'
-heit, -(ig)keit	die Schönheit 'beauty', die Tapferkeit 'bravery', die Tätigkeit 'activity'

1c   Nouns formed with prefixes

Erz-	der Erzbischof 'archbishop'
Miss-	das Missverständnis 'misunderstanding'
Un-	das Unglück 'misfortune'
Ur-	der Urgroßvater 'great-grandfather', der Urwald 'primeval forest'

1d   Compound nouns

Many nouns are formed by combining two or more words. With very few exceptions, they take the gender of the final part.

noun + noun	das Rathaus 'town hall'
noun + s + noun	die Landungsbrücke 'landing stage'
noun + (e)n + noun	das Studentenheim 'student hostel'
adjective + noun	das Schwarzbrot 'black bread'
verb stem + noun	das Schlafzimmer 'bedroom'
particle + noun	die Umwelt 'environment', das Abteil 'compartment' (but der Teil 'part')

1e   Adjectival nouns

Many adjectives and present and past participles can be used as nouns. They start with a capital letter, but otherwise behave just like adjectives:

der Deutsche 'the German', der Verletzte 'the injured man',
die Fremde 'the stranger' (female);
ein Beamter 'official' (male), eine Auszubildende 'trainee' (female);
Deutsche, 'Germans';
etwas Interessantes 'something interesting'.

1f   Verbal nouns

The infinitive is often used as a noun, usually with a meaning similar to the English form in '-ing': das Parken 'parking', das Schreiben 'writing'.

2 Genders & plurals

The gender and plural of a noun should be learned at the same time as the word.

The gender of nouns is shown in the word list by giving the definite article: **der** (masculine), **die** (feminine), or **das** (neuter). The article is given with most noun entries.

2a There are four common plural endings: **-e**, **-er**, **-(e)n**, **-s**, but some words take no plural ending. Words with a stem vowel in **a**, **o**, or **u**, and no ending or **-e** in the plural, sometimes have an umlaut on the stem vowel. Those with a plural in **-er** always take an umlaut. The plural form is given with every noun entry.

2b Other case endings are not shown, so remember to add:

(i) **-s** to the genitive singular of masculine and neuter nouns, e.g., **des Arms**;

(ii) **-(e)n** to the dative plural of all nouns not ending in **-n** or **-s**, e.g., **den Häusern**.

2c Weak masculine nouns

A few nouns, usually ending in **-e** in the nominative singular, add **-n** or **-en** in every other case of the singular and in the plural: **der Junge**, **den Jungen**, **des Jungen**, **dem Jungen**, **die Jungen**, etc.

Note that:

(i) many of these nouns refer to people or animals;

(ii) a large number of foreign nouns ending in **-and, -ant, -arch, -at, -ent, -ist, -krat, -loge,** and **-nom** are also weak: **der Student, den Studenten; der Demokrat, den Demokraten;**

(iii) **Herr** takes **-n** in the singular and **-en** in the plural: **den Herrn, die Herren;**

(iv) a few masculine nouns ending in **-e** add **-n** in every case and also **-s** in the genitive singular: **der Gedanke, des Gedankens;** others include: **der Glaube, der Wille.** One neuter noun, **das Herz,** follows this pattern but has no ending in the accusative singular.

2d *Useful short cuts*

(i) many masculine nouns add **-e** or **⸚e: der Stuhl**, *pl* **Stühle**

(ii) many feminine nouns add **-(e)n: die Frau**, *pl* **Frauen**

(iii) many neuter nouns, mostly one-syllable, add **⸚er: das Haus**, *pl* **Häuser**.

(iv) masculine and neuter nouns ending in **-el**, **-en**, or **-er** add no ending (other than the dative plural **-n** after **-el** and **-er**), but may take an umlaut: **der Garten**, *pl* **Gärten**.

Some suffixes always take the same plural ending and are almost always linked to a particular gender:

Feminine:

(i) add **-en**: words ending in **-anz**, **-ei**, **-enz**, **-heit**, **-ie**, **-ik**, **-ion**, **-keit**, **-schaft**, **-tät**, **-ung**, **-ur**;

(ii) add **-nen**: words ending in **-in**.

Masculine:

(i) add no plural ending: words ending in **-ler**, **-ner**, **-er** (words formed from verbs);

(ii) add **-e**: words ending in **-an**, **-än**, **-är**, **-eur**, **-ich**, **-ig**, **-ling**, stressed **-or**;

(iii) add **-en**: words ending in **-and**, **-ant**, **-ent**, **-et**, **-graph**, **-ist**, **-krat**, **-logen**, **-nom**, unstressed **-or**;

(iv) words with the ending **-ismus** change it to **-ismen**.

Neuter:

(i) add no plural ending: words ending in **-chen**, **-lein**, **-sel**, **-tel**;

(ii) add **⸚er**: words ending in **-tum**;

(iii) add **-e**: words ending in **-at**, **-ett**, **-il**, **-ment**;

(iv) words with the ending **-um:** change **-um** to **-en** or **-a**.

3 Adjectives

3a Forming adjectives with suffixes

-bar '-able, -ible'

berechenbar	predictable	**sichtbar**	visible

-en, -ern 'made of'

golden	golden	**hölzern**	wooden

-haft 'like a'

fehlerhaft	deficient	**vorteilhaft**	advantageous

-ig '-y'

staubig	dusty	**gütig**	kind

-isch '-ish',

identisch	identical	**kindisch**	childish

-lich '-ly, -able, -ish'

täglich	daily	**möglich**	possible
gelblich	yellowish		

-los '-less'

hilflos	helpless	**namenlos**	nameless
arbeitslos	unemployed		

-mäßig 'according to'

planmäßig	according to plan	**verhältnismäßig**	relatively

-sam 'having the quality of'

grausam	cruel	**ratsam**	advisable

-voll 'full'

sorgenvoll	anxious	**anspruchsvoll**	demanding
liebevoll	loving		

3b Adjectives formed with prefixes

The prefixes **un-** and **miss-** are used in the same way as with nouns:

unglücklich	unhappy	**missverstanden**	misunderstood

3c Compound adjectives

Adjectives, like nouns, can be formed of two or more words. Only the last part adds endings:

blutarm	anaemic
wasserdicht	watertight
schwarzweiß	black and white

4 Formation of verbs

4a Verbs formed from nouns

-(e)n (often with Umlaut) **der Trost - trösten** 'comfort', **der Gruß - grüßen** 'greet'

-ieren (common with new verbs) **marschieren** 'march', **konkurrieren** 'compete'

4b Verb families formed with prefixes and verbal particles

German uses prefixes and particles to extend the meaning of basic verbs. For any one verb there may be an immense range of compound verbs, and of nouns and adjectives formed from these compounds. It is worth studying these word families to enlarge your vocabulary, e.g.:

er fällt	he falls	**er fällt hin**	he falls down
er überfällt	he attacks	**es verfällt**	it decays
der Fall	the fall		

Sometimes compounds develop figurative meanings or meanings only loosely linked with each other or the basic verb:

der Fall	case	**der Zufall**	chance
die Abfälle _pl_	rubbish	**es fällt ihm ein**	it occurs to him

These prefixes are always attached to the verb stem:

be-, ent-, er-, ge-, hinter-, miss-, ver-, zer-.

Particles are always placed in the final part of the sentence and are therefore often separated from the verb stem, e.g.:

particles from prepositions: **ab, an, aus, ein, mit, nach, vor, zu**;

compound particles: **hinunter, vorbei, durcheinander, davon**;

particles from other verbs, adverbs, adjectives or nouns: **stehen, spazieren, statt, fern.**

The following can be used either as prefixes or as particles:

durch-, über-, um-, unter-, wider-, wieder-.

5 English cognates

German is rich in words that have a similar origin to English, or have been borrowed from English or other languages. Understanding can often be greatly helped by referring to the English.

5a Categories of words

(i) identical spelling and meaning: **die Hand, der Computer**

(ii) similar spelling, and identical meaning; note some common consonant changes:

offen	open	**helfen**	help
der Pfeffer	pepper	**das Pfund**	pound
lassen	let	**essen**	eat
sitzen	sit	**das Herz**	heart
gut	good	**tun**	do
dies	this	**der Bruder**	brother
machen	make	**suchen**	seek
kommen	to come	**der Keller**	cellar
leben	live	**lieben**	love
der Schnee	snow	**schlafen**	sleep
der Tag	day	**der Weg**	way

(iii) similar or identical spelling but a different meaning:

Lust haben	to want (to do something), but not in the sexual sense
aktuell	present, modern
das Gymnasium	Secondary School (US) or High School

(iv) loan translations from English or Latin stems:

der Buchmacher	bookmaker
das Mitleid	compassion
der Einfluss	influence

5b Sometimes a word derived from an English or common international source exists alongside a word of German origin: **der Hörfunk, das Radio; der Fernsprecher, das Telefon; der Mittelpunkt, das Zentrum.** With recent introductions, particularly those relating to technology, the English/international form is usually preferred, especially in speech.

Conventions used in this Handbook

(i) Noun plurals

The plural of almost every word is indicated in brackets (except for adjectival nouns, where the plural depends on the presence of the article:

Entry	*plural*
Arm(e)	**Arme**
Hand(̈e)	**Hände**
Haus(̈er)	**Häuser**
Garage(n)	**Garagen**
Auto(s)	**Autos**
Wagen(-)	**Wagen**
Garten(̈)	**Gärten**
Fluss (̈e)	**Flüsse**
Zentrum (-en)	**Zentren**
Praktikum (-a)	**Praktika**
Ministerium (-ien)	**Ministerien**

For some nouns the plural is shown in full in the bracket:

Firma   **(Firmen)**

(ii) Feminine forms

Feminine forms ending in **-in** are not given in full. They are freely formed, and where they are in normal use they are indicated after the masculine form by **[-in]**:
der Lehrer(-) [-in] = **der Lehrer**, *pl* **die Lehrer** male teacher, **die Lehrerin**, *pl* **die Lehrerinnen** female teacher.
Masculine nouns ending in **-e** drop this before adding **-in**:
der Zeuge, die Zeugin.

(iii) Cases

The cases taken by a preposition or verb are only indicated where there might be confusion.

(iv) Verbs

Verbs are given in the first or occasionally the third person in the word lists, so that the particle is always placed after the stem.
To avoid confusion, the particle is marked with an asterisk, e.g., **ich komme an*** 'I arrive'. To check the verb in a dictionary you need to find the infinitive, which will start with the particle, e.g., **ankommen**.

Where a verb is shown in the third person singular and there is a vowel change, the infinitive, without the particle, is shown in brackets, e.g., **es gibt** *(geben)*.

Abbreviations

acc	accusative
adj	adjective
adj/n	adjectival noun (plurals in **-e** or **-en**)
adv	adverb
conj	conjunction
dat	dative
etw.	**etwas**
fam	familiar form
gen	genitive
inf	infinitive
invar	invariable
jdn.	**jemanden** (accusative)
jdm.	**jemandem** (dative)
n	noun
pl	plural
pol	polite form
pop	popular form
sing	singular
sth	something
wk	weak masculine noun

Symbols

-	no ending: **Wagen(-)** = plural **Wagen**
( )	plural ending or a part of a word which is optional: **ich (ver)traue**
( )	the infinitive, where the third person singular entry shows a vowel change: **es gibt** *(geben)*
*	the particle is separable: **ich komme an***, infinitive **ankommen**
/	a) alternatives in adjective endings: **dieser/e/es** = **dieser, diese, dieses**, **mein/e/-** = **mein, meine, mein**
	b) alternative word: **erst als/wenn** = **erst als** or **erst wenn**
,	an alternative translation
➤	a cross-reference to a vocabulary topic or chapter

B

VOCABULARY TOPICS

1	Functional words	14	Business & economics
2	Where? – position & movement	15	Communicating with others
3	When? – expressions of time	16	Leisure & sport
4	How much? – expressions of quantity	17	The arts
5	What sort of? – descriptions & judgements	18	The media
		19	Travel
6	The human mind & character	20	Holidays/Vacation
		21	Language
7	Human life & relationships	22	Education
8	Daily life	23	Science: the changing world
9	Shopping	24	The environment: the natural world
10	Food & drink	25	Government & politics
11	Sickness & health	26	Crime & justice
12	Social issues	27	War & peace
13	Religion		

Functional words

Personal pronouns

	Nom	Acc	Gen	Dat
I	**ich**	**mich**	**meiner**	**mir**
you (fam)	**du**	**dich**	**deiner**	**dir**
he, it	**er**	**ihn**	**seiner**	**ihm**
she, it	**sie**	**sie**	**ihrer**	**ihr**
it	**es**	**es**	**seiner**	**ihm**
we	**wir**	**uns**	**unser**	**uns**
you (fam pl)	**ihr**	**euch**	**euer**	**euch**
you (pol)	**Sie**	**Sie**	**Ihrer**	**Ihnen**
they	**sie**	**sie**	**ihrer**	**ihnen**
one	**man**	**einen**	**seiner**	**einem**

Reflexive pronouns

	Acc	Dat
myself	**mich**	**mir**
yourself (fam)	**dich**	**dir**
himself	**sich**	**sich**
herself	**sich**	**sich**
itself	**sich**	**sich**
ourselves	**uns**	**uns**
yourselves (fam)	**euch**	**euch**
yourself/ves (pol)	**sich**	**sich**
themselves	**sich**	**sich**
oneself	**sich**	**sich**
each other	**sich**	**sich**

Interrogative pronouns

	Nom	Acc	Gen	Dat
who?	**wer**	**wen**	**wessen**	**wem**
which one?	**welcher/e/es**			
what?	**was**			

what sort of? (sing) **was für einer/e/es?**

what sort of? (pl) **was für welche?**

Relative pronouns who, that, which

	Masc	Fem	Neut	Plur
Nom	**der**	**die**	**das**	**die**
Acc	**den**	**die**	**das**	**die**
Gen	**dessen**	**der**	**dessen**	**deren**
Dat	**dem**	**der**	**dem**	**denen**

what you say is true **das, was du sagst, stimmt**

Demonstrative pronouns

Demonstrative adjective/pronouns this, this one, that one :

	Masc	Fem	Neut	Plur
Nom	**dieser**	**diese**	**dieses**	**diese**
Acc	**diesen**	**diese**	**dieses**	**diese**
Gen	**dieses**	**dieser**	**dieses**	**dieser**
Dat	**diesem**	**dieser**	**diesem**	**diesen**

this **dies** (invar)

this **dieser/e/es**

this **der/die/das** (stressed)

this one **der/die/das** (declined like relative pronoun)

this one **dieser/e/es**

these (ones) **diese**

that **das (hier)** (invar)

that **jener/e/es**

those (ones) **jene**

that one **der/die/das, derjenige/diejenige/dasjenige** (both parts decline)

the one, which **der(jenige), der**

the same one **derselbe, dieselbe, dasselbe** (both parts decline)

the red one **der/die/das Rote**

such a one **solch/so einer**
ones like that **solche**

Indefinite pronouns

anybody **irgendeiner**
both (people) **beide**
both (things) **beides**
each one **jeder/e/es**
everyone **jeder/e/es**
everything **alles**
everyone **alle**
one **einer/e/es**
one like that **so einer**
one which **einer, der**
none, not any **keiner/e/es**
nobody **keiner**
no-one **niemand, keiner/e/es**
not a single one **kein einziger**
nothing **nichts** *(invar)*
a lot **vieles**
quite a lot **manches**
not much **weniges**
someone/body **jemand**
something **etwas** *(invar)*
something else **etwas anderes**
something good **etwas Gutes**
some things **einiges**

Stressed pronouns

it's me **ich bin es, ich bin's**
it's us **wir sind es, wir sind's, etc.**
it's he who **er ist derjenige, der**
it's she who **sie ist diejenige, die,
    etc.**

*Possessive pronouns (declined
    like **dieser**)*

mine **meiner/e/es**
yours *(fam)* **deiner/e/es**
his **seiner/e/es**
hers **ihrer/e/es**
its **seiner/e/es**
ours **unserer/e/es**
yours *(fam)* **eu(e)rer/e/es**
yours *(pol)* **Ihrer/e/es**
theirs **ihrer/e/es**
ones **seiner/e/es**

this is mine **das ist
    meiner/meine/mein(e)s**
mine is better **meiner/meine/meines
    ist besser**

*Possessive adjectives (declined
    like **ein**)*

my **mein/e/-**
your *(fam)* **dein/e/-**
his/its **sein/e/-**
her/its **ihr/e**
its **sein/e/-**
our **unser/e/-**
your *(fam)* **euer/eu(e)re/euer**
your *(pol)* **Ihr/e/-**
their **ihr/e/-**
one's **sein/e/-**

Determiners

DEFINITE ARTICLE *the*

	Masc	Fem	Neut	Plur
Nom	der	die	das	die
Acc	den	die	das	die
Gen	des	der	des	der
Dat	dem	der	dem	den

INDEFINITE ARTICLE *a(n),* **kein** *not any*

	Masc	Fem	Neut	Plur
Nom	ein	eine	ein	keine
Acc	einen	eine	ein	keine
Gen	eines	einer	eines	keiner
Dat	einem	einer	einem	keinen

DEMONSTRATIVES

this, that **der/die/das**
this **dieser/e/es**
that **jener/e/es**
that **derjenige/diejenige/ dasjenige**
the same **derselbe, dieselbe,
    dasselbe**
such a **solcher/e/es, solch ein/e/-**

*Indefinite determiners (declined
    like **ein** or **dieser**)*

a few **wenige**
a couple/few **ein paar** *(invar)*
a little **ein bisschen, ein wenig**
    (invar)
all (of them) **alle**

FUNCTIONAL WORDS

all kinds of **allerlei, allerhand** *(invar)*
all sorts of **vielerlei** *(invar)*
all the same **einerlei** *(invar)*
any **irgendein/e/-**
any **irgendwelcher/e/es**
both **beide**
both (of them) **die beiden**
each **jeder/e (der beiden)**
every **jeder/e/es**
every child **alle Kinder**
many **viele**
many a **mancher/e/es, manch
ein/e/-**
no **kein/e/-**
not any **kein/e/-**
several **mehrere**
some (of them) **einige**
two kinds of **zweierlei, usw.** *(invar)*

Question forms

how many **wie viele?**
how **wie?**
how much **wie viel?**
how many **wie viele?**
what **was?**
what kind of **was für ein/e/-?**
when **wann?**
where **wo?**
which (one) **welcher/e/es?**
who **wer?**
whom **wen?**
to whom **wem?**
whose **wessen?**
why **warum?**

Logical relations

COORDINATING CONJUNCTIONS
as well as **sowie**
or **oder**
and **und**
both ... and **sowohl ... als/wie**
but **aber**
either ... or **entweder ... oder**
for (because) **denn**
neither ... nor **weder ... noch**
not only ... but also **nicht (nur) ...
sondern (auch)**

or alternatively **beziehungsweise**

SUBORDINATING CONJUNCTIONS
although **obgleich**
as **wie, da**
before **bevor, ehe**
after **nachdem**
especially as **zumal**
although **obwohl**
even though **trotzdem**
in case, if **falls**
unless **es sei denn, (dass)**
whenever **wenn**
as if **als ob**
as long as **solange**
as well as **sowohl**
as (since) **da**
because **weil**
even though **auch wenn**
if **wenn, ob**
in order that **damit**
not until **erst als/wenn**
provided that **wenn nur**
since *(time)* **seit(dem)**
since *(as)* **da**
so that **sodass, damit**
that **dass**
unless **wenn nicht**
until **bis**
when **als, wenn, wann**
whether **ob**
while/whereas **während**

(in order) to **um ... zu** +inf
instead of (doing) **(an)statt ... zu** +inf
without (doing) **ohne ... zu** +inf
apart from (doing) **außer ... zu** +inf

Adverbial expressions

about **etwa, ungefähr**
admittedly **allerdings**
again **wieder**
allegedly **angeblich**
almost **fast, beinahe**
also **auch**
by chance **zufällig**

certainly **bestimmt, doch**
entirely **ganz**
equally **gleich**
exactly **genau**
extremely **äußerst, höchst**
for that reason **darum, deshalb**
hardly **kaum**
hopefully **hoffentlich**
however **aber, jedoch**
in fact **zwar, tatsächlich**
in those days **damals**
just **eben, mal**
like **ähnlich**
merely **bloß**
naturally **natürlich**
naturally **selbstverständlich**
no longer **nicht mehr**
not at all **keineswegs**
not at all **gar nicht**
not either **auch nicht**
not even **nicht einmal**
not **nicht**
only **nur, erst**
perhaps **vielleicht**
possibly **möglicherweise**
probably **wohl, wahrscheinlich**
quite **ganz**
rather **lieber**
really **ja, recht**
relatively **verhältnismäßig**
so **so**
then **denn, dann**
therefore, consequently **deshalb**
to be sure **zwar**
too **auch**
totally **durchaus**
very **sehr**

Prepositions

WITH ACCUSATIVE
against **gegen**
along **entlang**
at about **gegen**
by *(time)* **schon um, bis**
for **für**
round **um**

through **durch**
until **bis**
without **ohne**

WITH DATIVE
according to **nach**
after **nach**
ago **vor**
along **an ... entlang**
at the house of **bei**
beside **außer**
except for **außer**
from **von**
opposite **gegenüber**
out of **aus**
since (time) **seit**
to **zu, nach**
towards **nach, entgegen**
with **mit**

WITH DATIVE OR ACCUSATIVE
across **über**
apart from **neben**
at **an**
behind **hinter**
between **zwischen**
in **in**
in front of **vor**
next to **neben**
on **auf**
over **über**
to **an**
under **unter**

WITH GENITIVE
above **oberhalb**
because of **wegen**
below **unterhalb**
during **während**
in spite of **trotz**
inside **innerhalb**
instead of **anstatt**
not far from **unweit**
on both sides of **beiderseits**
outside **außerhalb**
this side of **diesseits**

Where? – position & movement

2a Position

about **ungefähr, circa**
above **über** +acc/dat
    above *(adv)* **oben, nach oben**
across **über** +acc/dat
    across there **da drüben**
after **nach** +dat
against **gegen** +acc
ahead *(adv)* **vorne, nach vorne**
ahead of **vor** +acc/dat
along **entlang** +acc, **an** +dat
among **unter** +acc/dat
anywhere **irgendwo**
around **um** +acc
    around the tree **um den Baum herum**
around *(adv)* **umher/herum**
around in the garden **im Garten umher**
as far as **bis zu** +dat
at **an** +acc/dat
    at home **zu Hause**
    at school **in der Schule**
    at work **bei der Arbeit**
back **die hintere Seite(n)**
    at the back *(adv)* **hinten**
    at the back of **hinter** +acc/dat
    to the back **nach hinten**
backward **rückwärts, nach hinten**
before **vor** +acc/dat
    before *(adv)* **vorher**
behind **hinter** +acc/dat
    behind *(adv)* **hinten**
below **unter** +acc/dat
    below **unterhalb** +gen
    below *(adv)* **unten, (nach) unten**
beside **neben** +acc/dat
between **zwischen** +acc/dat
beyond **jenseits** +gen
bottom **der Grund, der Boden,**

der Fuß
    at the bottom (of) **unten (in** +dat**)**
center **die Mitte(n), das Zentrum (-en)**
    in the center **in der Mitte, mitten in** +acc/dat
direction **die Richtung(en)**
    in the direction of Bonn **Richtung Bonn**
distance **die Entfernung(en)**
    in the distance **in der Ferne**
distant **fern**
down **hinab, hinunter** +acc
    down there **dort unten**
    downstairs **(nach) unten**
edge **der Rand(ˉer)**
    at the edge **am Rande**
end **das Ende(n)**
    I end **ich beende**
    at the end **am Schluss**
everywhere **überall**
far **weit, fern**
    far away (from) **weit weg/entfernt (von** +dat**)**
first **erst**
    first (of all) **zuerst**
    I am first **ich komme als Erste(r)**
for **für** +acc
forward **vorwärts**
from **von** +dat
front **der vordere Teil(e)**
    at the front **vorn(e)**
    I am in front **ich stehe an der Spitze**
    in front of **vor** +acc/dat
    to the front **nach vorn**
here **hier**
    here and there **hier und da**

in **in** +acc/dat
  in there **da drinnen**
inside *(adv)* **drinnen**
  inside **innerhalb** +gen
into **in** +acc
last *(adj)* **der/die/das letzte**
  last of all **der/die/das allerletzte**
  last of all *(adv)* **zu allerletzt**
  I am last **ich stehe hinten**
left *(adj)* **der/die/das linke**
  the left **die linke Seite**
  on the left **links**
  to the left **nach links**
middle **die Mitte(n)**
  in the middle (of) **mitten (in**
  +acc/dat**)**
I move **ich bewege mich**
movement **die Bewegung(en)**
near **neben** +acc/dat
near(by) **in der Nähe, nebenbei**
neighborhood **die Nachbarschaft**
  in the neighborhood of **in der**
  Nähe von +dat
next *(adj)* **der/die/das nächste**
  next *(adv)* **daneben, zunächst,**
  dann
  next to **neben** +acc/dat, **dicht**
  bei +dat
nowhere **nirgendwo**
on **auf** +acc/dat
onto **auf** +acc
opposite **gegenüber** +dat
out of **aus** +dat
  out there **dort draußen**
outside *(adv)* **draußen**

outside **außerhalb** +gen
over **über** +acc/dat
  over there **dort drüben**
  over where **da drüben, wo**
past **an** +dat **vorbei**
right *(adj)* **der/die/das rechte**
  the right **die rechte Seite**
  on the right **rechts**
  to the right **nach rechts**
side **die Seite(n)**
  at the side **an der Seite**
  at both sides of **beiderseits**
  +gen/**von** +dat
I am situated **ich befinde mich**
somewhere **irgendwo**
there **dort, da**
  there, where **dort, wo**
to **zu** +dat, **an** +acc, **nach** +dat
top **die Spitze(n)**
  top *(of mountain)* **der Gipfel(-)**
  at the top **oben auf der**
  Spitze/dem Gipfel
  on top *(adv)* **oben**
  to the top **nach oben**
toward **nach** +dat, **auf** +acc, **zu**
  +dat
under **unter** +acc/dat
up **hinauf** +acc
  up here/there **hier/dort oben**
upstairs *(adv)* **(nach) oben**
where? **wo?**
where from? **woher?**
where to? **wohin?**
with **mit** +dat

We are going to London.	**Wir fahren nach London.**
He is going to work.	**Er geht zur Arbeit.**
We fly to the States.	**Wir fliegen in die USA.**
He walked to the front.	**Er ging nach vorne.**
She goes to school every day.	**Sie geht jeden Tag in die Schule.**
He went to the door.	**Er ging an die Tür.**
I am going home.	**Ich fahre nach Hause.**

2b Directions & location

Directions **Kompasse(e)**

atlas **der Atlas(se/Atlanten)**
compass **der Kompass(e)**
on the corner **an der Ecke**
east **der Osten**
   east *(adj)* **Ost-, östlich**
   in the east **im Osten**
   to the east **nach Osten**
   east of **östlich von**
first left **die erste links**
first right **die erste rechts**
floor **die Etage(n)**
on the first floor **in der ersten Etage**
the furthest *(adj)* **der/die/das am weitesten entfernte**
at the junction **an der Kreuzung**
Keep left **Links halten!**
Keep right **Rechts halten!**
latitude **die Breite(n)**
location **die Lage(n), die Positionsbestimmung(en)**
longitude **die Länge(n)**

map **die Karte(n)**
two miles from here **zwei Meilen von hier**
the nearest *(adj)* **die nächstgelegene/nächste**
north **der Norden**
   north *(adj)* **Nord-, nördlich**
   in the north **im Norden**
   to the north **nach Norden**
northeast **der Nordosten**
   northeast *(adj)* **nordöstlich**
northnortheast **der Nordnordosten**
northwest **der Nordwesten**
northnorthwest **der Nordnordwesten**
point of the compass **die Himmelsrichtung(en)**
second right **die zweite rechts**
south **der Süden**
   south *(adj)* **Süd-, südlich**
   in the south **im Süden**
   to the south **nach Süden**

Bonn is approximately 100 km north of here.

Bonn ist ungefähr 100 km nördlich von hier.

To the south of the woods you can see the church spire.

Südlich vom Wald sehen Sie den Kirchturm.

– Are you lost?

– Haben Sie sich verlaufen?

– Yes, I'm looking for the tourist office. Is it nearby?

– Ja, ich suche das Touristenbüro. Ist es hier in der Nähe?

Do you know your way around in the center of town?

Kennen Sie sich in der Stadtmitte aus?

Can you find your way?

Können Sie sich zurechtfinden?

southeast **der Südosten**
southsoutheast **der Südsüdosten**
southwest **der Südwesten**
southsouthwest **der Südsüdwesten**
straight ahead **gerade (da)vor, geradeaus**
third left **die dritte links**
this way **hier entlang**
west **der Westen**
    west *(adj)* **West-, westlich**
    in the west **im Westen**
    to the west **nach Westen**

Location & existence

I am **ich bin**

there is **es gibt** *(geben)* +acc
there isn't (any) **es gibt** *(geben)* **keinen/-e/-**
I become **ich werde**
I have got/I have **ich habe, ich besitze**
I exist **ich existiere, ich bestehe**
existence **die Existenz, das Dasein**
I possess **ich besitze**
possession **der Besitz** *(no pl)***, das Besitztum(¨er)**
present **anwesend**
    I am present **ich bin da/ zugegen**
    I am present at **ich bin bei** +dat

Some contracted forms

at the	**an das → ans**
at/by the	**an dem → am**
by the	**bei dem → beim**
from the	**von dem → vom**

in the	**in dem → im**
into the	**in das → ins**
onto the	**auf das → aus**
to the	**zu der → zur**
to the	**zu dem → zum**

The river is not very far from our house.

Der Fluss ist nicht sehr weit von unserem Haus.

Opposite the houses is the church and next to it are the shops/stores.

Den Häusern gegenüber befindet sich die Kirche und daneben sind die Geschäfte.

– Who's there? – It's me.

– Wer ist da? – Ich bin es/bin's.

My sister has five children.

Meine Schwester hat fünf Kinder.

Is there any cake? Are there still any biscuits/cookies?

Gibt's Kuchen? Sind noch Plätzchen da?

To get to the train station, you have to take the third left and then just go straight ahead.

Um zum Bahnhof zu gelangen, müssen Sie die dritte Straße links gehen und dann immer geradeaus.

2c Movement

I arrive	**ich komme an***
I bring	**ich bringe (mit*)**
by car	**mit dem Auto**
I carry	**ich trage**
I climb *(intr)*	**ich steige, ich klettere**
I climb *(tr)*	**ich besteige**
I come	**ich komme**
I come along	**ich komme mit***
I creep	**ich krieche**
I drive	**ich fahre**
I drive on the right	**ich fahre rechts**
I fall	**ich falle, ich stürze**
I fall down	**ich falle um***
I follow	**ich folge** +dat
I go	**ich gehe**
I go along	**ich gehe mit***
I go for a walk	**ich gehe spazieren**
I go (by vehicle)	**ich fahre**
I hike	**ich wandere**
I hurry	**ich eile**
I hurry up	**ich beeile mich**
I jump	**ich springe**
I leave	**ich fahre ab***
I leave sth	**ich verlasse etw.**
I march	**ich marschiere**
I move	**ich bewege mich**
on foot	**zu Fuß**

I pass	**ich gehe an** +dat **vorbei**
I pass *(in car)*	**ich überhole**
I pull	**ich ziehe**
I push	**ich stoße, schiebe**
I put (flat)	**ich lege**
I put (into)	**ich tue, ich stecke**
I put (onto)	**ich setze**
I put (upright)	**ich stelle**
I ride	**ich fahre**
I ride *(a horse)*	**ich reite**
I run	**ich laufe**
I run away	**ich laufe weg***
I rush	**ich stürze (mich)**
I sit up	**ich sitze aufrecht**
I slip	**ich rutsche aus***
I stand	**ich stehe**
I stand still	**ich bleibe stehen**
I step/come/go	**ich trete**
I stop	**ich halte, ich bleibe stehen**
straight	**gerade**
straight ahead	**geradeaus**
I stroll	**ich schlendere, ich bummele**
I take	**ich nehme, ich bringe**
I turn	**ich biege (ein*)**
I turn left	**ich biege nach links**
I turn off	**ich biege ab***
I turn around	**ich drehe mich um***
I turn to so	**ich wende mich an** +acc

Frank and I are going to the movies by car, but Susanne is walking to the theater.	**Frank und ich fahren mit dem Auto zum Kino, aber Susanne geht zu Fuß.**
Yesterday Annette's husband slipped on the ice in front of our house.	**Gestern ist Annettes Mann auf dem Eis vor unserem Haus ausgerutscht.**
We have to go down the hill, then along the river, and turn left by the inn.	**Wir müssen den Berg hinuntergehen, dann am Fluss entlang und am Gasthof links abbiegen.**

➤ TRAVEL 16a; POSITION 2a; DIRECTIONS 2b

walk   **der Gang(¨-e), der Spaziergang(¨-e)**
I walk   **ich gehe**
I wander   **ich wandere**
way   **der Weg(e)**

Here & there

Come here!   **Komm her!***
I go there   **ich gehe hin***
I rush there   **ich stürze hin***
I travel there   **ich fahre hin***

In & out

Come in!   **Herein!**
I come in   **ich komme herein***
I come here   **ich komme (hier)her***
I come out   **ich komme heraus***
I go in   **ich gehe hinein***
I go into the house   **ich gehe in das Haus (hinein)***
I go into the room   **ich betrete das Zimmer**
I come in (to the room)   **ich trete ein***
I get in   **ich steige ein***
I get out *(of vehicle)*   **ich steige aus***
Get out!   **Raus!**
I go out   **ich gehe hinaus***
Go out!   **Gehen Sie hinaus!***
I go out of the room   **ich gehe aus dem Zimmer (hinaus*)**

I go out (on an outing)   **ich gehe aus***
I get out (of vehicle)   **ich steige aus***

Up & down

I climb the mountain   **ich besteige den Berg**
I climb up the mountain   **ich klettere auf den Berg (hinauf*)**
I climb the stairs   **ich steige die Treppe hinauf***
I climb the wall   **ich steige auf die Mauer**
I come down   **ich komme herunter***
I come up   **ich komme herauf***
I fall down   **ich falle/stürze hin***
I get up   **ich stehe auf***
I go down the path   **ich gehe den Weg hinab*/hinunter***
I go up   **ich gehe hinauf***
I lie down   **ich lege mich hin**
Stand up!   **Stehen Sie auf*!**
Do sit down!   **Setzen Sie sich hin*!**

Around

I go around the town   **ich gehe um die Stadt (herum*)**
I run around in the garden   **ich laufe im Garten umher***
I run around   **ich laufe umher/herum***

– Where are you going? – To town. Are you coming? – No, I am going to my mother's.

Every evening our neighbors take a long walk.

Please go into the room. Mr. Schmidt will be here shortly.

– Wo gehen Sie hin? – In die Stadt. Kommen Sie mit? – Nein, ich gehe zu meiner Mutter.

Jeden Abend machen unsere Nachbarn einen langen Spaziergang.

Gehen Sie bitte in das Zimmer hinein. Herr Schmidt kommt gleich.

Note use of **hin** (movement away from the speaker) and **her** (movement toward the speaker) to make compound verbs expressing movement.

When? – expressions of time

3a Past, present, & future

about **gegen** +acc
after **nach** +dat
  after *(conj)* **nachdem**
  afterward **nachher, danach, hinterher**
again **nochmals, wieder**
  again and again **immer wieder**
ago **her** *(adv)*, **vor** +dat *(prep)*
  a short time ago **vor kurzem**
already **schon**
always **immer**
anniversary **der Jahrestag(e), der Hochzeitstag(e)**
annual **jährlich**
annually **jedes Jahr, jährlich**
as long as *(conj)* **solange**
as soon as *(conj)* **sobald**
at once **sofort, gerade, gleich**
before *(adj)* **vor** +acc/dat
  before *(conj)* **bevor, ehe**
  before, beforehand **vorher, davor**
I begin **ich beginne, ich fange an***
  it begins **es geht los***
beginning **der Anfang(-e)**
birthday **der Geburtstag(e)**
brief *(adj)* **kurz**
briefly **vorübergehend**
by (next month) **bis (nächsten Monat)**
calendar **der Kalender(-)**
centenary **der hundertste Geburtstag(e)**
century **das Jahrhundert(e)**
  in the twentieth century **im zwanzigsten Jahrhundert**
continuous(ly) **dauernd, ständig**
daily **täglich**
date **das Datum (-en)**
  date **der Termin(e)**

dawn **der Tagesanbruch(-e)**
  at dawn **bei Tagesanbruch**
day **der Tag(e)**
  by day **bei Tag**
  every day **jeden Tag**
decade **das Jahrzehnt(e)**
delay **die Verspätung(en)**
  delayed **verspätet**
during **während** +dat/gen
early **früh**
  I am early **ich bin früh dran**
  I am early **ich komme zu früh**
end **das Ende(n)**
  I end *(sth)* **ich beende etw.**
  it ends **es endet, es ist aus**
ever **je**
every **jeder/-e/-es**
  every time **jedes Mal**
  every day **jeden Tag**
exactly **genau, Punkt**
fast **schnell**
  my watch is fast **meine Uhr geht vor***
finally **schließlich**
I finish (reading) **ich (lese) zu Ende**
first *(adj)* **der/die/das erste**
  at first **zuerst**
firstly **erstens**
for **seit** +dat, **für** +acc, **auf** +acc
  for a day *(duration)* **einen Tag (lang)**
  (past continuous/progressive) **seit einem Tag**
  (future) **auf/für einen Tag**
for good/ever **auf immer**
formerly **früher**
fortnight/two weeks **vierzehn Tage**
frequent **häufig**
frequently **häufig, öfters**

from   **von +dat**
  as from (today)   **ab (heute)**
  from now on   **von nun an, von jetzt ab**
I go on (reading)   **ich (lese) weiter**
half   **die Hälfte(n)**
  half *(adj)*   **der/die/das halbe**
  one and a half   **anderthalb, eineinhalb** *(invar)*
  two and a half   **zweieinhalb** *(invar)*
it happens   **es ereignet sich**
holiday/vacation   **der Feiertag(e)**
I hurry up   **ich beeile mich, ich mache schnell**
  hurry   **die Eile**
  I am in a hurry   **ich habe es eilig**
instant   **der Moment(e)**
just   **gerade**
  just now   **gerade jetzt**
last *(final) (adj)*   **der/die/das letzte**
  last night   **gestern in der Nacht**
  last *(previous) (adj)*   **der/die/das vorige/vergangene**
  it lasts a long time   **es dauert lange**

last a short time   **es dauert kurze Zeit**
late   **spät**
  I am late   **ich komme zu spät**
  lately   **neulich**
  later (on)   **später**
long   **lang**
  long term   **langfristig**
  in the long term   **langfristig gesehen**
many   **viele**
  many times   **vielmals**
meanwhile   **unterdessen**
  in the meanwhile   **inzwischen**
middle   **die Mitte(n)**
moment   **der Augenblick(e)**
moment   **der Moment(e)**
  at the moment   **im Moment**
  at this moment   **in diesem Augenblick**
  at this moment *(right now)*   **zurzeit**
  in a moment   **in einem Augenblick**
month   **der Monat(e)**
  monthly   **monatlich, jeden Monat**
much   **viel**

The train from Frankfurt was delayed, and my girlfriend didn't arrive until eleven o'clock.

Der Zug aus Frankfurt hatte Verspätung, und meine Freundin ist erst um elf Uhr angekommen.

– Can you please tell me how often a bus goes to Würzburg?

– Können Sie mir bitte sagen, wie häufig ein Bus nach Würzburg fährt?

– From eight a.m. to five p.m., there's a bus every half hour. Every morning at dawn Stefan's mother takes her dog for a walk.

– Von acht bis siebzehn Uhr geht jede halbe Stunde ein Bus. Stefans Mutter führt jeden Morgen bei Tagesanbruch ihren Hund spazieren.

Jochen and Angelika recently celebrated their second anniversary.

Jochen und Angelika haben vor kurzem ihren zweiten Hochzeitstag gefeiert.

WHEN? – EXPRESSIONS OF TIME

never **nie**
next *(adj)* **nächst-, kommend-, folgend-**
   next *(adv)* **dann**
not till/until **erst (um)**
   not before **erst**
   not always **nicht immer**
now **jetzt**
   now *(next)* **nun**
nowadays **heutzutage**
occasionally **zufällig**
it occurs **es ereignet sich**
often **oft**
on and off **ab und zu**
once **einmal, mal**
   once upon a time **einmal**
   once in a while **ab und zu**
   once a day **einmal am Tag**
one day (when) **eines Tages (als/wo)**
only **nur**
   only when **erst als/wenn**
past **die Vergangenheit**
   past **nach** +dat
per (day) **pro (Tag)**
present **die Gegenwart**
   present *(adj)* **gegenwärtig**
   presently **bald**
   at present **zurzeit**

previous(ly) **früher**
prompt **pünktlich**
   promptly (at two) **Punkt (zwei Uhr)**
rare(ly) **selten**
recent **neu**
recently **kürzlich, neulich**
regular(ly) **regelmäßig**
I remain **ich bleibe**
right away **sofort**
Saint's day **der Namenstag(e)**
school term/semester **das Trimester(-), das Semester(-)**
season **die Jahreszeit(en)**
seldom **selten**
several **mehrere**
   several times **mehrmals**
short **kurz**
   short term **kurzfristig**
   in the short term **kurzfristig gesehen**
   shortly **in Kürze**
since *(conj)* **seit** +dat
slow **langsam**
   my watch is slow **meine Uhr geht nach**
some **einige**
   sometime **irgendwann**
   sometimes **manchmal**

– When are you going on vacation?
– Next month. We're staying in France for three weeks.

– Wann fahren Sie in Urlaub?
– Nächsten Monat. Wir bleiben drei Wochen in Frankreich.

My boss often makes short business trips to London.

Mein Chef macht oft kurzfristige Geschäftsreisen nach London.

This morning Peter and his colleague arrived in the office at the same time.

Heute Morgen sind Peter und sein Kollege gleichzeitig im Büro angekommen.

– How often do you see your parents?
– If possible, every weekend.

– Wie oft siehst du deine Eltern?

– Wenn möglich, jedes Wochenende.

soon **bald**
> sooner or later **früher oder später**
> the sooner the better **je eher desto besser**

I stay **ich bleibe**

still **noch**

I stop (doing) **ich höre auf* (zu ... tun)**

suddenly **plötzlich, auf einmal**

sunrise **der Sonnenaufgang(ᵉe)**
> at sunrise **bei Sonnenaufgang**

sunset **der Sonnenuntergang(ᵉe)**
> at sunset **bei Sonnenuntergang**

I take (an hour) **ich brauche (eine Stunde)**
> it takes (an hour) **es dauert (eine Stunde)**

then (next) **dann**
> then (at that time) **da, damals, dann**

thousand years **das Jahrtausend(e)**

till **bis** +acc

time (in general) **die Zeit(en)**

time (occasion) **das Mal(e)**
> at any time **jederzeit**
> at other times **zu anderen**

Zeiten
> at the same time **gleichzeitig**
> from time to time **von Zeit zu Zeit**
> for a long time **lange, lange Zeit**
> in good time **rechtzeitig**
> a long time ago **längst**
> the whole time **immer, die ganze Zeit**

time zone **die Zeitzone(n)**

twice **zweimal**

until **bis** +acc
> until **bis zu** +dat

usually **meistens**

I wait **ich warte auf** +acc

week **die Woche(n)**
> this week **diese Woche**
> weekly **jede Woche**
> weekday **der Werktag(e), der Wochentag(e)**
> weekend **das Wochenende(n)**

when **wann, wenn, als**

whenever **wenn**

while (conj) **während**

year **das Jahr(e)**
> yearly **jährlich, jedes Jahr**

yet **schon**
> not yet **noch nicht**

– I'll call you as soon as we get there.

– Ich werde dich anrufen, sobald wir ankommen.

– Hello Peter, John Brown here. I have been working on the project for a few days. We have to meet. What about tomorrow?

– Hallo Peter, John Brown hier. Ich arbeite seit einigen Tagen an dem Projekt. Wir müssen uns unbedingt treffen. Wie wäre es mit morgen?

– From time to time I get a letter from an old school friend.

Von Zeit zu Zeit bekomme ich einen Brief von einer alten Schulfreundin.

WHEN? – EXPRESSIONS OF TIME

3b Time, days, & date

Time of day

a.m. **vormittags**
morning **der Morgen(-), der Vormittag(e)**
in the morning **morgen früh**
in the mornings **vormittags**
early in the morning **frühmorgens**
this morning **heute Morgen**
noon **der Mittag(e)**
at noon **zu Mittag**
afternoon **der Nachmittag(e)**
in the afternoon **am Nachmittag**
in the afternoons **nachmittags**
this afternoon **heute Nachmittag**
p.m. **Nachmittags**
evening **der Abend(e)**
in the evening **am Abend**
in the evenings **abends**
this evening **heute Abend**
night **die Nacht(⁻e)**
at night **nachts**
midnight **die Mitternacht(⁻e)**
at midnight **um Mitternacht**
today **heute**
a week from today **heute in einer Woche**
tomorrow **morgen**
tomorrow morning **morgen früh**
tomorrow afternoon **morgen Nachmittag**
tomorrow evening **morgen Abend**
the day after tomorrow **übermorgen**
tonight **heute Abend/Nacht**
yesterday **gestern**
yesterday afternoon **gestern Nachmittag**
yesterday morning **gestern Vormittag**
yesterday evening **gestern Abend**
the day before yesterday **vorgestern**

Telling the time

second **die Sekunde(n)**
minute **die Minute(n)**
hour **die Stunde (n)**
half an hour **die halbe Stunde(n)**
in an hour's time **in einer Stunde**
hourly **jede Stunde**
quarter **das Viertel(-)**
quarter of an hour **die Viertelstunde(n)**
three quarters of an hour **drei Viertelstunden**
quarter past/after (two) **Viertel nach (zwei)**
quarter to/of (two) **Viertel vor (zwei)**
half past (two) **halb (drei)**
17:45 **siebzehn Uhr fünfundvierzig**
five past/after six **fünf nach sechs**
five to/of six **fünf vor sechs**
twenty five to/of six **fünfundzwanzig (Minuten) vor sechs**
twenty five to/of six **fünf nach halb sechs**
twenty five past/after five **fünfundzwanzig (Minuten) nach fünf**
twenty five past/after five **fünf vor halb sechs**
two a.m. **zwei Uhr nachts**
eight a.m. **acht Uhr vormittags**
two p.m. **zwei Uhr nachmittags**
eight p.m. **acht Uhr abends**
12:00 noon **zwölf Uhr mittags**
12:00 midnight **zwölf Uhr nachts**

The days of the week

Monday **der Montag(e)**
Tuesday **der Dienstag(e)**
Wednesday **der Mittwoch(e)**
Thursday **der Donnerstag(e)**
Friday **der Freitag(e)**
Saturday **der Samstag(e),
    Sonnabend(e)**
Sunday **der Sonntag(e)**

The months

January **der Januar(e)**
February **der Februar(e)**
March **der März(e)**
April **der April(-)**
May **der Mai(e)**
June **der Juni(s)**
July **der Juli(s)**
August **der August(e)**
September **der September(-)**
October **der Oktober(-)**
November **der November(-)**
December **der Dezember(-)**

The seasons

spring **der Frühling(e)**
summer **der Sommer(-)**
autumn/fall **der Herbst(e)**
winter **der Winter(-)**

The date

last Friday **letzten Freitag**
on Tuesday **am Dienstag**
on Tuesdays **dienstags**
by Friday **bis Freitag**
the first of January **der erste
    Januar**
on the third of January **am dritten
    Januar**
in (the year) 2000 **2000, im Jahre
    2000**
1st January/January 1st, 1994 **den
    ersten Januar 1994**
1/1/1994 **1.1.1994**
at the end of 1999 **Ende 1999**
by the end of 1999 **bis Ende 1999**
at the beginning (of July) **Anfang
    (Juli)**
by the beginning (of July) **bis
    Anfang (Juli)**
in December **im Dezember**
in mid/the middle of January **Mitte
    Januar**
at the end of March **Ende März**
in spring **im Frühling**

– I'm going shopping tomorrow morning. Would you like to come along?
– Yes, but I'd prefer to go in the afternoon. I always have a lot to do on Monday mornings.

– Okay. Let's meet at two thirty.

– What time does the movie start this evening?
– At 19:00 hours.
– And how long is it?
– One and a half hours. It will be over at 20:30 hours.

– **Ich gehe morgen früh einkaufen. Möchtest du mitkommen?**
– **Ja, aber ich würde lieber nachmittags gehen. Ich habe montagmorgens immer viel zu tun.**

– **In Ordnung. Treffen wir uns um halb drei.**

– **Wann beginnt der Film heute Abend?**
– **Um neunzehn Uhr.**
– **Und wie lange dauert er?**
– **Anderthalb Stunden. Er ist um zwanzig Uhr dreißig zu Ende.**

How much? – expressions of quantity

4a Length and shape

angle	**der Winkel**(-)
area	**die Fläche**(n)
big	**groß**
center	**die Mitte**(n)
concave	**konkav**
convex	**konvex**
curved	**gebogen**
deep	**tief**
degree	**der Grad** *(no pl)*
depth	**die Tiefe**(n)
diagonal	**schräg**
distance	**die Entfernung**(en)
I draw	**ich zeichne**
hectare	**das Hektar**(e)
height	**die Höhe**(n)
high	**hoch, hoh-**
horizontal	**waagerecht**
large	**breit**
length	**die Länge**(n)
line	**die Linie**(n)
long	**lang**
low	**niedrig**
it measures	**es beträgt**
narrow	**eng**
parallel	**parallel**
perpendicular	**senkrecht**
point	**der Punkt**(e)
room	**der Platz**(¨e)
round	**rund**
ruler	**das Lineal**(e)
shape	**die Form**(en)
short	**kurz**
size	**die Größe**(n)
small	**klein**
space	**der Raum**(¨e)
straight	**gerade**
tall	**groß, hoch**
thick	**dick**
thin	**dünn**
wide	**breit, weit**
width	**die Breite**(n)

Shapes

circle	**der Kreis**(e)
circular	**kreisförmig**
cube	**der Würfel**(-)
cubic	**Kubik-**
cylinder	**der Zylinder**(-)
pyramid	**die Pyramide**(n)
rectangle	**das Rechteck**(e)

You need a straight ruler and pencil.	**Sie brauchen ein gerades Lineal und einen Bleistift.**
Measure the space and then draw a plan.	**Messen Sie den Raum und machen Sie dann einen Entwurf.**
The driveway is too narrow for Alfred's new car.	**Die Einfahrt ist zu eng für Alfreds neuen Wagen.**
Leave room for some vegetables.	**Lassen Sie Platz für das Gemüse.**
The distance from the house to the fence is 12 meters.	**Die Entfernung vom Haus bis zum Zaun beträgt 12 Meter.**

rectangular **rechteckig**
sphere **die Kugel(n)**
 spherical **kugelförmig**
square **das Quadrat(e)**
 square **Quadrat-**
 square **quadratisch, viereckig**
triangle **das Dreieck(e)**
triangular **dreieckig**

Units of length

centimeter **der Zentimeter(-), cm**
foot **der Fuß** *(no pl)*
inch **der Zoll** *(no pl)*
kilometer **der Kilometer(-), km**
meter **der Meter(-), m**
mile **die Meile(n)**
millimeter **der Millimeter(-), mm**
yard **das Yard(s)**

Expressions of quantity

about **etwa, ungefähr**
almost **fast, beinahe**
approximate **ungefähr**
approximately **circa**
as much as **so viel**
at least **mindestens**
capacity **der Inhalt(e)**
 it contains **es enthält**
 (enthalten)
cubic capacity **das**
 Fassungsvermögen(-)
it decreases **es geht zurück***

difference **der Unterschied(e)**
empty **leer**
I empty **ich leere**
enough **genug**
it is enough **es reicht**
I fill **ich fülle**
full **voll**
full of **voll von** +dat, **voller** *(invar)*
I grow **ich wachse**
 growth **das Wachstum** *(no pl)*
hardly **kaum**
increase **die Vergrößerung(en)**
it increases **es nimmt zu***, **es**
 vermehrt sich
little **wenig** *(invar)*, **klein**
 a little **ein wenig, ein bisschen**
a lot (of) **viel**
I measure **ich messe**
measuring tape **das Bandmaß(e)**
more **mehr** *(invar)*
nearly **fast**
number **die Zahl(en)**
part **der Teil(e)**
quantity **die Menge(n)**
rarely **selten**
it suffices **es genügt**
sufficient **genügend**
too much **zu viel**
volume **das Volumen**
whole **ganz**
whole **das Ganze**

The garden is not wide enough for a pool.

Der Garten ist nicht breit genug für ein Schwimmbecken.

– How high is the tree? – About five meters.

– Wie hoch ist der Baum? – Ungefähr fünf Meter.

The shed will be at an angle of about 40 degrees to the house.

Der Schuppen wird in einem Winkel von 40 Grad zum Haus stehen.

The area of our garden/yard is 100 square meters.

Unser Garten misst 100 Quadratmeter.

➤ MATHEMATICAL & GEOMETRICAL TERMS App.4d

HOW MUCH? – EXPRESSIONS OF QUANTITY

4b Measuring

Expressions of volume

bag **die Tüte(n)**
bar **die Tafel(n)**
bottle **die Flasche(n)**
box **das Etui(s), die Dose(n)**
container **der Behälter(-)**
cup **die Tasse(n)**
gallon **die Gallone(n)**
glass **das Glas(¨er)**
liter **der Liter**
  centiliter **der Zentiliter**
  milliliter **der Milliliter**
pack **die Packung(en)**
  packet **das Paket(e)**
  packet *(small)* **die Schachtel(n)**
pair **das Paar(e)**

piece **das Stück(e)**
  a piece of cake **ein Stück Kuchen**
pint **das Pint(s), der halbe Liter(-)**
portion **die Portion(en)**
pot **das Glas(¨er)**
sack **der Sack(¨e)**
tube **die Tube(n)**

Temperature

it boils **es kocht**
I chill **ich kühle, ich stelle kalt**
cold **kalt**
  cold **die Kälte**
cool **kühl**
  I cool down **ich kühle mich ab**

Do you have this soda in liter bottles?

Haben Sie diesen Sprudel in Literflaschen?

– How many cubic meters of concrete do you need? – About two.

– Wie viel Kubikmeter Beton brauchen Sie? – Ungefähr zwei.

– Would you like a cup of tea?
– No, I would prefer a glass of water.

– Möchten Sie eine Tasse Tee?
– Nein, ich möchte lieber ein Glas Wasser.

– How much wood do you want?
– Enough for the whole fence. Give me a bag of cement too, please.

– Wie viel Holz brauchen Sie?
– Genug für den ganzen Zaun. Geben Sie mir bitte auch einen Sack Zement.

I need about a cup of flour, a quarter pound of butter and three eggs for this recipe.

Ich brauche ungefähr eine Tasse Mehl, ein viertel Pfund Butter und drei Eier für dieses Rezept.

You have to chill the cake for three hours before cutting it.

Sie müssen den Kuchen drei Stunden kalt stellen, bevor Sie ihn schneiden.

degree **der Grad** *(no pl)*
I freeze **ich friere**
heat **die Hitze**
  I heat **ich erhitze**
  I heat *(the house)* **ich heize**
hot **heiß**
temperature **die Temperatur(en)**
I warm (up) **ich wärme auf***
  warmth **die Wärme**

Weight & density

dense **dicht**
density **die Dichte(n)**

gram **das Gramm** *(no pl)*
heavy **schwer**
kilo **das Kilo(gramm)** *(no pl)*
light **leicht**
mass **die Masse(n)**
ounce **die Unze(n)**
pound (lb) **das Pfund** *(no pl)*
scales/balance **die Waage(n)**
ton(ne) **die Tonne(n)**
I weigh **ich wiege**
weight **das Gewicht(e)**

It's so hot! The temperature must be 30 degrees.

Es ist so heiß! Die Temperatur muss 30 Grad sein.

It's very hot today, and Michael just jumped into the pool to cool off.

Es ist heute sehr heiß, und Michael ist gerade ins Schwimmbecken gesprungen, um sich abzukühlen.

The fall and winter were very cold last year. We already had to put the heating on in September.

Der Herbst und Winter waren letztes Jahr sehr kalt. Wir mussten schon im September heizen.

If the temperature goes down further, we'll have to bring in our plants from the balcony.

Wenn die Temperatur noch weiter fällt, müssen wir unsere Pflanzen vom Balkon hereinbringen.

Would you please put the frozen vegetables into the boiling water?

Würdest du bitte das gefrorene Gemüse ins kochende Wasser tun?

Can you weigh the ingredients?

Können Sie die Zutaten wiegen?

How many grams of sugar do we need?

Wie viel Gramm Zucker brauchen wir?

The pizza can be warmed up in the oven.

Die Pizza kann im Ofen aufgewärmt werden.

HOW MUCH? – EXPRESSIONS OF QUANTITY

4c Numbers

Cardinal numbers

zero **null**
one **eins, einer/e/-**
two **zwei**
    two *(telephone)* **zwo**
three **drei**
four **vier**
five **fünf**
six **sechs**
seven **sieben**
eight **acht**
nine **neun**
ten **zehn**
eleven **elf**
twelve **zwölf**
thirteen **dreizehn**
fourteen **vierzehn**
fifteen **fünfzehn**
sixteen **sechzehn**
seventeen **siebzehn**
eighteen **achtzehn**
nineteen **neunzehn**
twenty **zwanzig**
twenty-one **einundzwanzig**
twenty-two **zweiundzwanzig**
twenty-nine **neunundzwanzig**
thirty **dreißig**
thirty-one **einunddreißig**
forty **vierzig**
fifty **fünfzig**
sixty **sechzig**
seventy **siebzig**

eighty **achtzig**
ninety **neunzig**
a hundred **hundert**
a hundred and one **hunderteins**
two hundred **zweihundert**
a thousand **(ein)tausend**
two thousand **zweitausend**
million **eine Million**
two million **zwei Millionen**
milliard/billion *(U.S.)* **die Milliarde(n)**

Ordinal numbers

first **der/die/das erste**
second **der/die/das zweite**
third **der/die/das dritte**
fourth **der/die/das vierte**
nineteenth **der/die/das neunzehnte**
twentieth **der/die/das zwanzigste**
twenty-first **der/die/das einunzwanzigste**
hundredth **der/die/das hundertste**

Nouns

zero **die Null(en)**
one **die Eins(en)**
    unit **der Einer(-)**
ten **die Zehn, der Zehner(-)**
dozen **das Dutzend(e)**
hundred **das Hundert(e)**
    hundreds of **Hunderte von**
million **die Million(en)**

Half of the house belongs to my brother.	**Die Hälfte des Hauses gehört meinem Bruder.**
– You cannot all have a bar of chocolate. There is only enough for a quarter each.	**– Ihr könnt nicht alle eine Tafel Schokolade haben. Es reicht nur für ein Viertel für jeden.**
– I don't want a quarter, I want a half.	**– Ich will kein Viertel haben, ich möchte die Hälfte.**

Writing numerals

1,000   **1.000**
1,500   **1.500**
1,000,000   **1 000 000**
1st   **1.**
2nd   **2.**
1.56   **1,56 (eins Komma fünf**
   sechs)
.05   **0,05 (null Komma null fünf)**

Fractions

half   **die Hälfte(n)**
   a half   **der/die/das halbe**
   one and a half   **eineinhalb**
   (invar)

two and a half   **zweieinhalb**
   (invar)
quarter   **das Viertel(-)**
   a quarter   **ein Viertel-**
   two and a quarter
   zweieinviertel
third   **das Drittel(-)**
fifth   **das Fünftel(-)**
five and five sixths
   fünffünfsechstel
tenth   **das Zehntel(-)**
sixth   **das Sechstel(-)**
hundredth   **das Hundertstel(-)**

---

double the price   **das Doppelte**
twice as much   **das Doppelte**
second best   **der/die/das**
   Zweitbeste
third from last   **der/die/das**
   Drittletzte
fourfold   **vierfach**
four times as much   **das**
   Vierfache

1,800,265   **eine Million**
   achthunderttausendzwei-
   hundertfünfundsechzig
1995   **im Jahre neunzehn-**
   hundertfünfundneunzig

telephone number 360542
   Telefon sechsunddreißig,
   null fünf, zwoundvierzig
area code 0482   **Vorwahl null**
   vier acht zwo

It was A1   **Es war eins a**
the 100 (bus)   **der Hunderter**
The Big Four   **die Vier**
We went in fours   **Wir sind zu**
   viert (vieren) gefahren
We make a foursome   **Wir haben**
   einen Vierer

Only a few people can remember the twenties.

Nur wenige Leute erinnern sich an die zwanziger Jahre.

Yesterday we celebrated Jörg's nineteenth birthday.

Wir haben gestern Jörgs neunzehnten Geburtstag gefeiert.

HOW MUCH? – EXPRESSIONS OF QUANTITY

4d Calculations

addition **die Addition(en)**
  I add **ich addiere, rechne zusammen***
  plus **plus, und**
  two plus two **zwei und/plus zwei**
average **der Durchschnitt(e)**
  I average out **ich nehme den Durchschnitt**
  on average **im Durchschnitt**
I calculate **ich berechne**
  calculation **die Berechnung(en)**
  calculator **der Taschenrechner(-)**
correct **richtig**
I count **ich zähle**
data **die Daten** *(pl)*
  piece of data **das Datum (-a/-en)**
decimal **die Dezimalzahl(en)**
  decimal point **das Komma(s)**
diameter **der Durchmesser(-)**
digit **die Ziffer(n)**

two digit **zweistellig**
I double **ich verdopple**
division **die Division(en)**
  I divide by **ich teile durch** +acc
  six divided by two **sechs geteilt durch zwei**
it equals **es gleicht**
equation **das Gleichnis(se)**
it is equivalent to **ist gleich**
I estimate **ich schätze**
even **gerade**
figure **die Ziffer(n)**
graph **der Graph(en), die Grafik(en)**
is greater than **ist größer als**
is less than **ist weniger als**
maximum **das Maximum(-a)**
  maximum **maximal, Maximal-**
  a maximum of **ein Maximum an** +dat
  up to a maximum of **bis zu maximal**

An inch is the same as 2.54 cm, and there are twelve inches in a foot, 36 in a yard. A mile is 1760 yards. A kilometre/kilometer is 1000 metres.

Ein Zoll ist gleich 2,54 Zentimeter, und es gibt 12 Zoll in einem Fuß, 36 in einem Yard. Eine Meile ist 1760 Yards. Ein Kilometer ist 1.000 Meter.

What is 14 plus 8? It equals 22. Did you get the right result?

Was macht 14 und 8? 14 plus 8 (ist) gleich 22. Hast du das richtige Ergebnis?

20 minus 5 is 15, 20 divided by 5 equals 4.

20 weniger 5 gleich 15, 20 geteilt durch 5 gleich 4.

Work out 12 times 22. That is an easy sum.

Rechnet 12 mal 22. Das ist eine leichte Aufgabe.

2 to the power of 3 is 8. Three squared equals 9.

Zwei hoch drei macht 8. Drei hoch zwei macht neun.

medium   die Mitte(n)
medium   **Mittel-, mittler-**
minimum   **das Minimum(-a)**
minimum   **Mindest-**
minus   **minus**
mistake/error   **der Fehler(-)**
multiplication   **die**
   Multiplikation(en)
   I multiply   **ich multipliziere**
   three times two   **drei mal zwei**
negative   **negativ**
number   **die Zahl(en)**
numeral   **die Ziffer(n)**
odd   **ungerade**
percent   **das Prozent(en)**
   by 10%   **um 10%**
   percentage   **der**
   Prozentsatz(ӫe)
positive   **positiv**
power   **die Potenz(en)**
   to the power of   **hoch**
   to the fifth   **hoch fünf**
problem   **die Aufgabe(n)**
quantity   **die Menge(n)**
ratio   **das Verhältnis(se)**

a ratio of 100:1   **im Verhältnis**
   100 zu 1
result   **das Ergebnis(se)**
similar   **ähnlich**
solution   **die Lösung(en)**
   I solve   **ich löse**
square   **die Quadratzahl(en)**
square root   **die zweite Wurzel(n)**
   three squared   **drei hoch zwei,**
   zum Quadrat
statistic   **die Statistik**
statistics   **die Statistik(en)**
statistical   **statistisch**
sum   **die Rechenaufgabe(n)**
subtraction   **die Subtraktion(en)**
   I subtract   **ich ziehe ab***
symbol   **das Symbol(e)**
take away   **weniger**
total   **die Endsumme(n),**
   Gesamtzahl(en)
   in total   **insgesamt**
I treble   **ich verdreifache**
triple   **dreifach**
I work out   **ich rechne aus***
wrong   **falsch**

Two negatives make a positive.   **Zweimal minus gibt plus.**

You have made a mistake there.   **Da hast du einen Fehler gemacht.**

– I estimate that we have about   **– Ich schätze, wir haben etwa**
500 visitors a year.   **500 Gäste im Jahr.**
– What percentage of visitors are   **– Welcher Prozentsatz kommt**
local? – 20% (percent).   **aus der Gegend? – 20 Prozent.**
– Have you got any statistics about   **– Haben Sie eine Statistik**
it?   **darüber?**

A snail travels at an average speed   **Eine Schnecke bewegt sich mit**
of 0.04 miles per hour.   **einer Durchschnittsgeschwindig-**
   keit von 0,06 Stundenkilometern.

Can you do me a graph?   **Würden Sie mir bitte eine Grafik**
   zeichnen?

What sort of? – descriptions & judgments

5a Describing people

appearance **das Aussehen**	figure **die Figur(en)**
attractive **attraktiv**	fit **fit**
average **mittel, mittelmäßig**	I frown **ich runzele die Stirn**
he is bald **er hat eine Glatze**	glasses **die Brille**
beard **der Bart(¨e)**	good-looking **gut aussehend**
bearded **bärtig**	I grow **ich wachse**
beautiful **schön**	hair **das Haar, die Haare**
beauty **die Schönheit(en)**	hairstyle **die Frisur(en)**
blond **blond**	handsome **gut aussehend**
broad **breit**	heavy **schwer**
build **der Körperbau** *(no pl)*	height **die Größe(n)**
chic **schick**	homosexual **homosexuell**
clean shaven **glatt rasiert**	large **breit, groß**
clumsy **ungeschickt**	I laugh **ich lache**
complexion **die Gesichtsfarbe(n)**	laugh **das Lachen**
curly **lockig**	I am left-handed **ich bin**
dark **dunkel**	**Linkshänder [-in]**
I describe **ich beschreibe**	light **leicht**
description **die Beschreibung(en)**	I look like **ich sehe aus* wie**
different (from) **anders (als)**	I look well **ich sehe gut aus***
elegant **elegant**	male **männlich**
energy **die Energie(n)**	masculine **männlich**
expression **der**	moustache **der Schnurrbart(¨e)**
Gesichtsausdruck(¨e)	near-sighted **kurzsichtig**
far-sighted **weitsichtig**	neat **ordentlich**
fat **dick**	neatness **die Sauberkeit**
feature **der Gesichtszug(¨e)**	obese **fettleibig**
female/feminine **weiblich**	overweight **übergewichtig,**
	korpulent

adolescence **die Pubertät**	old **alt**
adolescent **der/die Jugendliche**	older/elder **älter**
(adj/n)	teenager **der Teenager(-)**
age **das Alter**	young **jung**
elderly **ältlich, älter**	young person **der/die**
grown up **der/die Erwachsene**	**Jugendliche** *(adj/n)*
(adj/n)	young people **junge Leute**
grown up *(adj)* **erwachsen**	youth **die Jugend**
middle-aged **in den mittleren**	youthful **jugendlich**
Jahren	

part of body	**der Körperteil(e)**
paunch	**der Bauch(¨e)**
physical	**körperlich**
plump	**fett, pummelig**
pretty	**hübsch**
red-haired	**rothaarig**
I am right-handed	**ich bin Rechtshänder [-in]**
I scowl	**ich sehe jdn. finster an***
sex/gender	**das Geschlecht(er)**
short	**kurz, klein**
similar (to)	**ähnlich** +dat
similarity	**die Ähnlichkeit(en)**
size	**die Größe(n)**
slim/slender	**schlank**
small	**klein**
I smile	**ich lächele**
smile	**das Lächeln**

spot	**der Pickel(-)**
spotty	**pickelig**
stocky	**stämmig**
strength	**die Kraft(¨e)**
striking	**auffallend**
strong	**stark**
tall	**groß, lang**
thin	**mager, dünn**
tiny	**winzig**
trendy	**schick**
ugliness	**die Hässlichkeit**
ugly	**hässlich**
walk	**der Gang**
wavy	**gewellt**
I weigh	**ich wiege**
weight	**das Gewicht(e)**

– What a wonderful family photo! And that must be your uncle. You described him so well to me.

– He looks a lot like my father, but he wears glasses and has darker hair than him.

– Say, who's that tall, slim man over there?

– That's Beate's husband. He's a real exercise fanatic.

I almost didn't recognize my girlfriend's niece. She used to be a little plump, and had short, dark hair. Now she's very slim and her hair is long, wavy and blond.

– Little Ben has dark hair and is about one meter tall. He looks healthy, but he's very thin. He only weighs 16 kilos.

– **Was für ein schönes Familienfoto! Und das muss dein Onkel sein. Du hast ihn mir ja so gut beschrieben.**

– **Er sieht meinem Vater sehr ähnlich, aber er trägt eine Brille und hat dunkleres Haar als er.**

– **Sag mal, wer ist der große, schlanke Mann dort drüben?**

– **Das ist Beates Mann. Er ist ein echter Trimm-Dich-Fanatiker.**

Ich habe die Nichte meiner Freundin fast nicht erkannt. Sie war immer ein bisschen pummelig und hatte kurzes, dunkles Haar. Jetzt ist sie sehr schlank und ihr Haar ist lang, gewellt und blond.

– **Der kleine Ben hat dunkles Haar und ist ungefähr einen Meter groß. Er sieht gesund aus, aber er ist sehr mager. Er wiegt nur 16 Kilo.**

➤ PHYSICAL STATE 11d

WHAT SORT OF? – DESCRIPTIONS & JUDGMENTS

5b The senses

bitter **bitter**	I look at sth **ich sehe etw. an***
bright **hell**	loud **laut**
bright *(harsh)* **grell**	mouth **der Mund(-̈er)**
cold **kalt**	noise **der Lärm** *(no pl)*, **das**
cold **die Kälte**	**Geräusch(e)**
colorful **bunt**	noisy **laut, lärmend**
dark **dunkel**	nose **die Nase(n)**
darkness **das Dunkel, die**	odor **der Geruch(-̈e)**
Dunkelheit	opaque **trüb, undurchsichtig**
delicious **lecker**	perfume **das Parfüm(s)**
disgusting **ekelhaft**	perfumed **parfümiert**
dull **matt**	quiet **ruhig**
ear **das Ohr(en)**	rough **rau**
eye **das Auge(n)**	salty **salzig**
face **das Gesicht(er)**	I see **ich sehe**
I feel ... **ich fühle mich, mir ist ...**	sense **der Sinn(e)**
it feels **es fühlt sich an***	silence **die Stille**
I feel very cold **Mir ist sehr kalt**	silent **schweigend, still**
hand **die Hand(-̈e)**	I am silent **ich schweige**
I hear **ich höre**	smell **der Geruch(-̈e)**
hot **heiß**	I smell **ich rieche**
light *(color)* **hell**	it smells (of) **es riecht nach**
I listen **ich höre** +dat **zu***	+dat
I look **ich blicke**	smelly **stinkend**

– What kind of coat did you buy yesterday?	— Was für einen Mantel hast du gestern gekauft?
– A very chic, red woolcoat.	– Einen sehr schicken, roten Wollmantel.
– Dark or light red?	– Dunkel- oder hellrot?
– It's dark red, but actually more of a maroon than a true red.	– Er ist dunkelrot, aber eigentlich mehr rötlichbraun als ein echtes Rot.
The garage in our new house absolutely has to be painted. It's an ugly green now, and the floor has stains and smells of oil.	Die Garage in unserem neuen Haus muss unbedingt gestrichen werden. Sie ist jetzt in einem hässlichen Grün, und der Boden hat Flecken und riecht nach Öl.
The jam tastes of fruit but is very bitter.	Die Marmelade schmeckt nach Obst, aber sie ist sehr bitter.

soft *(sound)* **sanft, leise**
  soft *(texture)* **weich**
sound **der Klang(-̈e), das Geräusch(e)**
it sounds **es klingt**
  it sounds like **es hört sich an***
sour **sauer**
sticky **klebrig, schmutzig**
  it is sticky **es klebt**
stomach **der Magen(-)**
sweet **süß**

taste **der Geschmack**
I taste **ich schmecke**
it tastes (of) **es schmeckt nach** +dat
tepid **lauwarm**
tooth **der Zahn(-̈e)**
I touch **ich berühre**
transparent **durchsichtig**
visible (in-) **sichtbar (un-)**
warm **warm**
warmth **die Wärme**

Colors

beige **beige** *(invar)*
black **schwarz**
blue **blau**
brown **braun**
brownish **bräunlich**
cream *(adj)* **cremefarben**
gold **Gold-, golden**
green **grün**
grey/gray **grau**
maroon **rötlichbraun**
orange *(color)* **das Orange**

orange *(adj)* **Orangen-, orangenfarbig**
pink **rosa** *(invar)*, **rosarot**
purple **violett**
red **rot**
scarlet **hochrot, knallrot**
silver **Silber-, silbern**
turquoise *(color)* **das Türkis**
  turquoise *(adj)* **türkisfarben**
violet **lila** *(invar)*
white **weiß**
yellow **gelb**

– Please wash your hands before dinner. They're all sticky and dirty from playing.

– **Bitte wasch dir die Hände vor dem Essen. Sie sind ganz klebrig und schmutzig vom Spielen.**

– Our secretary has a terrible toothache. She can't eat anything, because she doesn't want anything to touch her tooth.

– **Unsere Sekretärin hat fürchterliche Zahnschmerzen. Sie kann nichts essen, weil sie nicht will, dass etwas ihren Zahn berührt.**

– I am very cold today, and it feels as if we're going to get snow.

– **Mir ist heute sehr kalt, und ich habe das Gefühl, als ob wir Schnee bekommen.**

NOTE: most colors can be used as neuter nouns, e.g., **das Blau**.

5c Describing things

big **groß**
broad **breit**
broken **kaputt, gebrochen**
appearance **die Erscheinung(en), das Aussehen**
clean **sauber**
closed **zu, geschlossen**
color **die Farbe(n)**
  colorful **bunt**
  colored **farbig**
damp **feucht**
deep **tief**
  depth **die Tiefe(n)**
dirt **der Schmutz**
dirty **schmutzig**
dry **trocken**
empty **leer**
enormous **ungeheuer**
fashionable **modisch**
fat **dick**
firm **fest**

flat **flach**
flexible **flexibel**
fresh **frisch**
full (of) **voll (von** +dat), **voller** *(invar)*
genuine/real **echt**
hard **hart**
hardness **die Härte**
height **die Größe(n)**
high **hoch**
kind **die Art(en)**
large **groß**
liquid **flüssig**
little **klein**
long **lang**
it looks like **es sieht aus* wie**
low **niedrig**
main **Haupt-**
material **der Stoff(e)**
it matches **es passt zu** +dat
matter **der Stoff(e)**

– What's that over there?
– That thing? It's a new kind of bottle opener.
– Does it work?
–Yes indeed. It's the best there is.

– I'm looking for something big to stand on.
– Does it matter what?
– Well, it must be something solid.

– What about this chair?

– That's too low. Is there nothing bigger?

I can't believe it. The refrigerator is empty again.

– **Was ist das da drüben?**
– **Das Ding dort? Es ist eine neue Art Flaschenöffner.**
– **Funktioniert er?**
– **Selbstverständlich. Das ist der beste, den es gibt.**

– **Ich suche etwas Großes, worauf ich stehen kann.**
– **Ist es egal, was?**
– **Na, es muss etwas Solides sein.**

– **Wie wäre es mit diesem Stuhl da?**
– **Der ist zu niedrig. Gibt es nichts Größeres?**

Es ist nicht zu glauben. Der Kühlschrank ist schon wieder leer.

moist **feucht**
moldy **modrig**
narrow **eng**
natural **natürlich**
new **neu**
open **auf, offen**
painted **bemalt**
pale **blass**
pattern **das Muster(-)**
plump **rundlich**
resistant **dicht**
rotten **morsch**
shade **der Farbton(ⁱe)**
shallow **flach, seicht**
shiny **glänzend**
short **kurz**
shut **zu, geschlossen**
small **klein**
smooth **glatt**
soft *(texture)* **weich**
softness **die Weichheit**
solid **solid**

soluble **wasserlöslich**
sort **die Sorte(n)**
spot **der Punkt(ⁱe)**
spotted **getupft**
stain **der Fleck(en)**
stained **fleckig**
stripe **der Streifen(-)**
striped **gestreift**
subsidiary **Neben-**
substance **die Substanz(en)**
synthetic **Kunst-, künstlich**
thick **dick**
thing **das Ding(e)**
thingamyjig **das Ding, das Dingsbums**
tint **der Ton(ⁱe)**
varied **variiert**
waterproof **wasserdicht, wasserfest**
wet **nass**
wide **weit, breit**
width **die Weite**

Ten questions

What's that? **Was ist das?**
What's it for? **Wozu dient es?**
What do you use it for? **.Wozu braucht man es?**
Can you see it? **Kannst du es sehen?**
What's it like? **Wie ist es?**
What does it look like? **Wie sieht es aus?**

What does it sound like? **Wie klingt es?**
What does it smell of? **Wonach riecht es?**
What color is it? **Welche Farbe hat es?**
What kind of thing is it? **Was für eine Sache ist das?**

– I am looking for a striped scarf, that matches my coat.

– **Ich suche einen gestreiften Schal, der zu meinem Mantel passt.**

– This is a genuine natural material, soft and thick. That is a synthetic material, it feels smooth but the colors are harsh.

– **Dies hier ist echte Naturfaser, weich und dicht. Das da ist Kunstfaser, es fühlt sich weich an, aber die Farben sind grell.**

5d Evaluating things

abnormal **anormal**
I adore **ich liebe sehr**
all right **okay**
    it is all right **es geht**
appalling **entsetzlich**
bad **schlecht**
beautiful **schön**
better/best **besser, best-**
cheap **billig**
correct **richtig**
it costs **es kostet**
delicious **köstlich**
I detest **ich hasse**
difficulty **die Schwierigkeit(en)**

difficult/hard **schwierig**
disgusting **ekelhaft**
I dislike **ich mag nicht**
I enjoy **ich genieße, es macht mir**
    Spaß
easy **leicht**
essential (in-) **(un)wesentlich**
excellent **ausgezeichnet**
expensive **teuer**
I fail **es ist mir nicht gelungen**
failure **der Misserfolg(e)**
    a total failure **eine totale Pleite**
false **falsch**
fine **schön**

– Would you like to try this wine? It's quite delicious.

– Möchten Sie diesen Wein probieren? Er schmeckt ausgezeichnet.

How do you like our neighbor's garden/yard? We do not like it at all.

Wie gefällt Ihnen der Nachbargarten? Wir mögen ihn gar nicht.

You cannot use the elevator today. It's momentarily out of order.

Sie können den Fahrstuhl heute nicht benutzen. Er ist zurzeit außer Betrieb.

The chef in this restaurant prepares very delicious meals, and he uses only top quality ingredients.

Der Küchenchef dieses Restaurants bereitet sehr köstliche Mahlzeiten zu, und er verwendet nur Zutaten bester Qualität.

Did you hear? The new play at the City Theater was a total failure.

Hast du gehört? Das neue Schauspiel im Stadttheater war eine totale Pleite.

My brother says that the new manager in his department is not very nice, and that last week he was particularly unpleasant.

Mein Bruder sagt, dass der neue Manager in seiner Abteilung nicht sehr nett ist und dass er letzte Woche besonders unangenehm war.

good **gut**
good value **preiswert**
great/terrific **großartig**
I hate **ich hasse**
high **hoch**
important (un-) **(un)wichtig**
incorrect **falsch**
interesting (un-) **(un)interessant**
I like **ich mag, es gefällt mir**
mediocre **mittelmäßig**
necessary (un-) **(un)nötig**
normal **normal**
order **die Ordnung**
  in order **in Ordnung**
  out of order **außer Betrieb**
out of date **veraltet**
ordinary **normal**
pleasant **angenehm**
poor **arm**
practical (im-) **(un)praktisch**
I prefer **ich ziehe vor***

quality **die Qualität(en)**
  top quality **beste Qualität**
  poor quality **schlechte Qualität**
right **richtig**
strange **seltsam**
I succeed **es gelingt mir**
success **der Erfolg(e)**
successful **erfolgreich**
true **wahr, echt**
I try **ich versuche**
ugly **hässlich**
unpleasant **unangenehm**
unsuccessful **erfolglos**
I use **ich verwende, ich benutze**
use **der Gebrauch**
useful **praktisch**
well **gut**
worse/worst **schlimm/schlimmst-**
I would rather **ich möchte lieber**
wrong **falsch**

---

a bit **ein bisschen**
enough **genug**
extremely **äußerst**
fairly **ziemlich**
hardly ... at all **kaum**
litte **wenig** *(invar)*
  a little **ein wenig**
a lot **viel, eine Menge**
much (better) **viel (besser)**

not at all **gar nicht**
particularly **besonders**
quite **ganz**
rather **ziemlich**
really **wirklich**
so **so**
too (good) **zu (gut)**
very **sehr**

– Do you enjoy going to the movie theater? – Yes, I particularly enjoyed last week's movie.

If you're looking for an elegant sweater to go with those wool pants, I would recommend this creme colored cashmere one.

Gehen Sie gern ins Kino? – Ja, der Film letzte Woche hat mir besonders gut gefallen.

Wenn Sie einen eleganten Pullover suchen, der zu dieser Wollhose passt, würde ich diesen cremefarbenen aus Kaschmirwolle vorschlagen.

5e Comparisons

Regular comparatives & superlatives

| small | **klein** | | smallest *(adj)* | **der kleinste** |
| small | **kleiner** | | smallest *(adv)* | **am kleinsten** |

Irregular comparatives & superlatives

big **groß, größer, größt-**
elderly **der/die/das ältere**
extremely **äußerst**
good **gut, besser, best-**
healthy **gesund, gesünder, gesündest-**
high **hoch, höher, höchst-**
　highly **höchst**
little **wenig, weniger, wenigst-**
　least of all **am wenigsten**
　at least **wenigstens**
　at the very least **mindestens**
much **viel, mehr, meist-**
　mostly **meistens**
near **nah, näher, nächst-**

soon **bald, eher, am ehesten**
willingly **gern, lieber, am liebsten**
acrylic **das Acryl**
brick **der Backstein(e)**
camel hair **das Kamelhaar**
cashmere **die Kaschmirwolle**
cement **der Zement**
china **das Porzellan**
concrete **der Beton**
corduroy **der Cord**
cotton **die Baumwolle**
denim **der Jeansstoff**

NOTE: some common one-syllable adjectives take an Umlaut, e.g., **stark, stärker, stärkst-**

Have you seen our newest products already? They are of the highest quality.

Haben Sie unsere neuesten Produkte schon gesehen? Sie sind von höchster Qualität.

I know you're very busy, but at least give me a call if you're coming home later.

Ich weiß, dass du sehr beschäftigt bist, aber ruf wenigstens an, wenn du später nach Hause kommst.

Look at our children! Peter, our eldest, is now the tallest. He loves playing soccer, because that's what he enjoys most.

Sehen Sie sich unsere Kinder an! Peter, unser Ältester, ist jetzt der größte. Er spielt am liebsten Fußball, weil ihm das am meisten Spaß macht.

If I were you, I would go to the gas station around the corner. You'll pay less for gas there.

An deiner Stelle würde ich zu der Tankstelle um die Ecke fahren. Da bezahlst du weniger für Benzin.

5f Materials

felt	**der Filz**
flannel	**der Flanell**
gas	**das Gas**
glass	**das Glas**
gold	**das Gold**
iron	**das Eisen**
iron *(adj)*	**eisern**
lace	**die Spitze**
leather	**das Leder**
leather *(adj)*	**ledern**
linen	**das Leinen**
material	**der Stoff(e)**
metal	**das Metall(e)**
mineral	**das Mineral(e/ien)**
nylon	**das Nylon**
oil	**das Öl(e)**
paper	**das Papier(e)**
plastic	**der Kunststoff(e)**
polyester	**der Polyester**
pottery	**die Keramik**
satin	**der Satin**

silk	**die Seide**
silk *(adj)*	**seiden**
silver	**das Silber**
steel	**der Stahl**
steel *(adj)*	**stählern**
stone	**der Stein(e)**
stone *(adj)*	**steinern**
suede	**das Wildleder**
terylene	**das Trevira, Diolen**
towelling	**das Frottee**
velvet	**der Samt**
viscose	**die Viskose**
wood	**das Holz**
wooden	**hölzern**
wool	**die Wolle**
woolen	**wollen**
worsted	**das Kammgarn**

NOTE: compound nouns are commonly used instead of adjectives, e.g., **das Backsteinhaus, der Wollpullover**.

– What do you think? Should I buy the green silk dress, or that one over there with the black lace?
– I like the lace dress the best.

– **Was meinst du? Soll ich das grüne Seidenkleid oder das mit der schwarzen Spitze kaufen?**
– **Mir gefällt das Spitzenkleid am besten.**

Next week all suede jackets and leather belts are on sale.

Nächste Woche sind alle Wildlederjacken und Ledergürtel im Angebot.

Nowadays many people prefer natural materials like cotton, linen and wool over synthetic ones.

Heutzutage ziehen viele Leute natürliche Stoffe, wie Baumwolle, Leinen und Wolle, den synthetischen vor.

– Did you succeed in finding something less expensive?
– Yes, this coat is particularly good value. And it's a very good quality.

– **Ist es Ihnen gelungen, etwas weniger Teueres zu finden?**
– **Ja, dieser Mantel ist besonders preiswert. Und die Qualität ist auch sehr gut.**

➤ CLOTHES 9c; MINERALS, CHEMICAL ELEMENTS App.23b   **45**

The human mind & character

6a Human characteristics*

active **aktiv**
I adapt **ich passe mich an***
I annoy **ich ärgere**
bad **schlecht**
bad-tempered **schlecht gelaunt**
I behave **ich benehme mich**
behavior **das Benehmen**
I boast **ich gebe an***
calm **ruhig**
care **die Vorsicht, die Sorge(n)**
careful **vorsichtig, sorgfältig**
careless **nachlässig**
character **der Charakter(e)**
characteristic **die Eigenschaft(en)**
characteristic **charakteristisch**
charming **charmant, anmutig**
cheerful **lustig, vergnügt**
clever **begabt, klug**
confident **voller Selbstvertrauen, selbstsicher**
discipline **die Disziplin**
dreadful **schrecklich**
evil **böse**
I forget **ich vergesse**

forgetful **vergesslich**
friendly (un-) **(un)freundlich**
fussy **anspruchsvoll**
generous **großzügig**
I get along with **ich verstehe mich gut mit** +dat
gifted **begabt**
good **gut**
good-tempered **gut gelaunt, gutmütig**
guilty **schuldig**
habit **die Gewohnheit(en)**
hard-working **fleißig**
help **die Hilfe**
I help **ich helfe**
helpful **hilfreich, hilfsbereit**
honest (dis-) **(un)ehrlich**
humor **der Humor**
humorous **humorvoll**
immorality **die Unsittlichkeit, die Unmoral**
innocent **unschuldig**
intelligence **die Intelligenz**
intelligent **intelligent**

Gerhard's oldest daughter used to be so shy and quiet. But she has turned into a very self-confident woman.

Gerhards älteste Tochter war immer so schüchtern und ruhig. Aber sie hat sich zu einer sehr selbstbewussten Frau entwickelt.

Sonja is always so serious. I think she has no sense of humor at all.

Sonja ist immer so ernst. Ich glaube sie hat überhaupt keinen Humor.

Mr. Schumann's wife is very pleasant, and she is always so helpful.

Herrn Schumanns Frau ist sehr nett, und sie ist immer so hilfsbereit.

kind (un-) **nett, lieb,
(un)freundlich**
kindness **die Liebenswürdigkeit,
die Freundlichkeit**
lazy **faul**
laziness **die Faulheit**
lively **temperamentvoll, lebhaft**
manners **die Manieren**
mental(ly) **geistig**
moral (im-) **(un)moralisch**
morality **die Moralität**
morals **die Moral**
nervous **nervös, ängstlich**
nice **nett, freundlich**
I obey **ich gehorche** +dat
optimistic **optimistisch**
patient (im-) **(un)geduldig**
personality **das Temperament(e)**
pessimistic **pessimistisch**
pleasant **lieb, angenehm, nett**
polite (im-) **(un)höflich**
popular **beliebt**
quality **die Eigenschaft(en)**
reason **die Vernunft**
reasonable (un-) **(un)vernünftig**
respect **der Respekt**
respectful **respektvoll**
rude **unhöflich, grob, rüde**
self-confidence **das
Selbstvertrauen**
self-esteem **die Selbstachtung**

sense **der Sinn(e)**
(common) sense **der gesunde
Menschenverstand**
good sense **die Vernunft**
sense of humor **der Sinn für
Humor**
sense of shame **das
Schamgefühl**
sensible **vernünftig**
serious **ernst**
shy **schüchtern**
skillful **geschickt**
sociable (un-) **(un)freundlich,
gesellig**
stupid **dumm**
stupidity **die Dummheit(en)**
suspicious **argwöhnisch,
misstrauisch**
sympathy **das Mitgefühl, das
Mitleid**
tact/tactful **der Takt, taktvoll**
tactless **taktlos**
talented **begabt**
temperament **das
Temperament(e)**
temperamental **launenhaft,
temperamentvoll**
I trust **ich traue** +dat
trusting **vertrauensvoll**
well-known **bekannt**
wit **der Witz(e)**
witty **geistreich**

The pupils in this school are hard-working and well-behaved.
We encourage self-confidence and discipline.
Bad behavior is punished.

Henrik is well known as a talented, charming, but very temperamental artist.

**Die Schüler in dieser Schule sind fleißig und benehmen sich gut.
Wir fördern Selbstvertrauen und Disziplin.
Schlechtes Benehmen wird bestraft.**

Henrik ist als ein begabter, charmanter, aber sehr temperamentvoller Künstler bekannt.

THOUGHT PROCESSES 6c; EXPRESSING VIEWS 6d

THE HUMAN MIND & CHARACTER

6b Feelings & emotions

I am afraid (of)   **ich habe Angst (vor** +dat**)**
I am amazed (at)   **ich staune (über** +acc**)**
amazement   **das Erstaunen**
I amuse   **ich amüsiere**
   I am amused by   **es amüsiert mich**
amusement   **das Vergnügen**
anger   **die Wut**
angry   **wütend**
I am annoyed (at/about)   **ich ärgere mich (über** +acc**)**
anxiety   **die Angst, Ängstlichkeit**
anxious   **ängstlich**
I approve (of)   **ich bewillige etw.**
I am ashamed (of)   **ich schäme mich (vor** +dat**)**
I am bored   **ich langweile mich**
boredom   **die Langeweile**
content (with)   **zufrieden (mit** +dat**)**
cross (with)   **böse (auf** +acc**)**
delighted (about)   **entzückt (über** +acc**)**
I dislike   **es gefällt mir nicht**
dissatisfaction   **die Unzufriedenheit(en)**

dissatisfied (with)   **unzufrieden (mit** +dat**)**
embarrassed (about)   **verlegen (wegen** +gen**)**
embarrassment   **die Verlegenheit(en)**
emotion   **das Gefühl(e)**
emotional(ly)   **emotional (emotionell)**
I enjoy ...   **... gefällt mir**
envy   **der Neid**
envious (of)   **neidisch (auf** +acc**)**
I feel   **ich fühle (mich)**
I forgive   **ich vergebe/verzeihe** +dat
forgiveness   **die Vergebung**
I am frightened (of)   **ich habe Angst (vor** +dat**)**
furious (about)   **wütend (über** +acc**)**
fussy   **pingelig**
grateful (to)   **dankbar (**+dat**)**
gratitude   **die Dankbarkeit**
happiness   **das Glück**
happy (about)   **glücklich (über** +acc**)**
hate   **der Hass**

My cousin is surprised how fast his son and his wife have adapted to country life. But their children are unhappy and are often bored.

The boss is in a bad mood today, because he's annoyed at a customer. I hope he's in a better mood tomorrow.

Mein Cousin ist überrascht, wie schnell sich sein Sohn und dessen Frau dem Landleben angepasst haben. Aber ihre Kinder sind unglücklich und haben oft Langeweile.

Der Chef ist heute schlecht gelaunt, weil er sich über einen Kunden ärgert. Hoffentlich ist er morgen wieder besserer Laune.

I hate **ich hasse**
I have a grudge against him **ich bin ihm böse**
hope **die Hoffnung(en)**
I hope (for) **ich hoffe (auf** +acc)
I hope that **hoffentlich**
hopeful **hoffnungsvoll**
idealism **der Idealismus**
indifference **die Gleichgültigkeit**
indifferent (to) **gleichgültig (gegenüber** +dat)
I am indifferent **es macht mir nichts aus***
interest **das Interesse(n)**
I am interested (in) **ich interessiere mich (für** +acc)
jealous **eifersüchtig auf** +acc
jealousy **die Eifersucht**
joy **die Freude(n)**
joyful **freudig**
I like **ich mag**
love **die Liebe(n)**
I love **ich liebe**
miserable (about) **miserabel, unglücklich (über** +acc)
misery **das Elend**

mood **die Laune(n)**
in a good/bad mood **gut/schlecht gelaunt**
I prefer **ich ziehe vor***
I regret **ich bedauere**
satisfaction **die Zufriedenheit**
satisfied (with) **zufrieden (mit** +dat)
surprise **die Überraschung(en)**
I am surprised (at) **ich bin überrascht/erstaunt (über** +acc)
thankful **dankbar**
unhappy **unglücklich**
unhappiness **die Traurigkeit, die Trauer**
I am upset (about) **aufgeregt (wegen** +dat)
I wonder (at) **ich wundere mich (über** +acc)
I wonder if **ich bin gespannt, ob**
worried (about) **besorgt (wegen** +gen)
worry **die Sorge(n)**
I worry (about) **ich mache mir Sorgen (über** +acc)
it worries me **es beunruhigt mich**

– I am really ashamed of my behavior. I was so upset and worried. Please forgive me.

– **Ich schäme mich wirklich wegen meines Benehmens. Ich war so aufgeregt und ängstlich. Bitte verzeihen Sie mir.**

– It's okay. I'm just glad that you're feeling better now.

— **Es ist schon gut. Ich bin nur froh, dass es Ihnen jetzt besser geht.**

I wonder if Eckhart suspects that we're giving him a party or if it will really be a surprise.

Ich bin gespannt, ob Eckhart ahnt, dass wir ihm eine Party geben, oder ob es wirklich eine Überraschung wird.

I'm very interested in tennis, but I also like golf.

Ich interessiere mich sehr für Tennis, aber ich mag auch Golf.

THE HUMAN MIND & CHARACTER

6c Thought processes

advantage   **der Vorteil(e)**
   disadvantage   **der Nachteil(e)**
against   **gegen** +acc
   I am against it   **ich bin dagegen**
I analyze   **ich analysiere**
analysis   **die Analyse(n)**
I assume   **ich nehme an***
assuming that ...   **angenommen,**
   dass ...
I base   **ich gründe**
basic   **Grund-**
basically   **im Grunde genommen**
basis   **die Grundlage(n)**
belief   **der Glaube(n)** (gen **-ns**)
I believe   **ich glaube** +dat
   I believe in   **ich glaube an** +acc
certainty   **die Sicherheit(en)**
certain/sure   **sicher**
I consider   **ich überlege**
   I consider ... (to be)   **ich halte ...**
   (für +acc**)**
consideration   **der Faktor(en)**
   I take into consideration   **ich**
   berücksichtige
   taking everything into

consideration   **alles in allem**
context   **der Zusammenhang(¨e)**
on the contrary   **im Gegenteil**
controversial   **umstritten**
I decide   **ich beschließe, ich**
   entschließe mich
decision   **der Entschluss (¨e)**
I determine   **ich stelle fest***
I disbelieve   **ich glaube nicht**
I distinguish   **ich unterscheide**
doubt   **der Zweifel(-)**
I doubt   **ich bezweifle, ich zweifle**
   an +dat
doubtful   **zweifelhaft**
doubtless/without a doubt   **ohne**
   Zweifel
exception   **die Ausnahme(n)**
evidence   **der Beweis(e)**
evidently   **offensichtlich**
fact   **die Tatsache(n)**
   in fact   **in der Tat, tatsächlich**
false   **falsch**
for   **für** +acc
   I am for it   **ich bin dafür**
I forbid   **ich verbiete**

– I suggest we try to analyze the problem carefully. But in my view, it will take some time. If you agree, I suggest we meet early on Thursday about it.

– **Ich schlage vor, wir versuchen das Problem genau zu analysieren. Aber meiner Ansicht nach wird es etwas dauern. Wenn Sie einverstanden sind, schlage ich vor, dass wir uns am Donnerstag früh treffen.**

– From the beginning I would like to make our position clear. On the one hand we need to do more research. On the other hand we must cut the budget.

– **Ich möchte unsere Lage von Anfang an klar machen. Auf der einen Seite müssen wir mehr Forschung betreiben. Auf der anderen Seite müssen wir den Etat kürzen.**

hypothesis die Hypothese(n)
implication die Bedeutung(en)
interesting interessant
issue die Frage(n)
I judge ich beurteile
judgement das Urteil(e)
justice die Gerechtigkeit
I justify ich rechtfertige
I know ich weiß
knowledge das Wissen, die
    Kenntnis(se)
logic die Logik
logical logisch
memory das Gedächtnis(se)
philosophy die Philosophie(n)
point of view der Gesichtspunkt(e)
I presume ich nehme an*
principle das Prinzip(ien), der
    Grundsatz(¨e)
    in/on principle im/aus Prinzip
problem das Problem(e)
proof der Beweis(e)
I prove ich beweise
I reason ich denke durch*
    I reason (conclude) ich
    schließe
reason (faculty) der Verstand

I recognize ich erkenne
I reflect ich denke nach*
relevant relevant
I remember ich erinnere mich +acc
right richtig
    I am right ich habe Recht
    it is right es stimmt
I see ich sehe
I solve ich löse
solution die Lösung(en)
I suppose ich vermute
theoretical theoretisch
theory die Theorie(n)
in theory theoretisch
I think ich denke, ich meine
thought der Gedanke(n) (gen -ns)
true wahr
truth die Wahrheit(en)
I understand ich verstehe
understanding das Verständnis
valid (in-) gültig (un-)
view die Ansicht
    in my view in/nach meiner
    Ansicht
wrong falsch
    I am wrong ich habe Unrecht
    it is wrong es stimmt nicht

– What do you think of the
speaker?
– In my opinion he did not consider
the basic problem. I would have
liked to ask more questions.

– In principle I agree with his
views. Firstly, he proved the need
for new housing. And secondly, he
discussed the problems of finding
a site.

– Was halten Sie vom
Referenten?
– Meiner Meinung nach hat er
das Hauptproblem nicht in
Betracht gezogen. Ich hätte gern
noch einige Fragen gestellt.
– Im Prinzip bin ich mit seinen
Ansichten einverstanden.
Erstens hat er den Bedarf an
neuen Häusern festgestellt. Und
zweitens hat er die Probleme
diskutiert, wie man ein
Grundstück findet.

6d Expressing views

I accept **ich nehme an***
I agree (with) **ich bin (mit** +dat)
einverstanden
I agree **ich stimme zu***
we agree (about) **wir sind uns**
einig über +acc
I answer **ich beantworte**
answer **die Antwort(en)**
I argue **ich diskutiere, ich streite**
argument **das Argument(e)**
I ask **ich frage**
I ask (a question) **ich stelle eine**
Frage
I contradict **ich widerspreche** +dat
I criticize **ich kritisiere**
I define **ich definiere**
definition **die Definition(en)**
I deny **ich leugne, ich bestreite**

I describe **ich beschreibe**
description **die Beschreibung(en)**
I disagree (with) **ich bin (mit** +dat)
nicht einverstanden
we disagree about **wir streiten**
uns über +dat
I discuss **ich bespreche, ich**
diskutiere
discussion **die Diskussion(en)**
I maintain **ich behaupte**
I mean **ich meine**
opinion **die Meinung(en)**
in my opinion **meiner Meinung**
nach
question **die Frage(n)**
I question **ich bezweifle**
a thorny question **eine heikle**
Frage

If I may quote my colleague. As is well known, these statements are contradictory. For example, we can not have total freedom of the press, and censorship.

Wenn ich meinen Kollegen zitieren darf. Wie bekannt ist, widersprechen sich diese Behauptungen. Wir können zum Beispiel nicht die totale Pressefreiheit und die Pressezensur haben.

Norbert had stated from the beginning that it wouldn't be possible to build this machine like that.
In my opinion he is asking too much.

Norbert hat von Anfang an behauptet, dass man diese Maschine nicht so bauen könne.

Meiner Meinung nach verlangt er zu viel.

Would you please explain the pros and cons of the new program? I would also like to hear how it stands in comparison to our present program.

Würden Sie bitte die Vor- und Nachteile des neuen Programms erklären? Ich möchte auch gern hören, wie es im Vergleich mit unserem jetzigen Programm abschneidet.

it is a question of **es handelt sich um** +acc

I say **ich sage, ich meine**

I state **ich behaupte**

statement **die Behauptung(en)**

suggestion **der Vorschlag(-̈e)**

I suggest **ich schlage vor***

I summarize **ich fasse zusammen***

summary **die Zusammenfassung(en)**

I think (of/about) **ich denke (an/über** +acc)

I think of **ich halte von** +dat

thought **der Gedanke**

I sum up **ich fasse zusammen***

Giving examples

as is known **wie bekannt**

etc./and so on **usw., und so weiter**

example **das Beispiel(e)**

for example **zum Beispiel**

I give an example **ich gebe ein Beispiel**

i.e. **das heißt, d.h.**

namely **und zwar**

I quote **ich zitiere**

such as **wie zum Beispiel**

Comparing & contrasting

advantage **der Vorteil(e)**

I compare **ich vergleiche**

comparison **der Vergleich(e)**

in comparison with **im Vergleich mit** +dat

I contrast **ich stelle** +dat **gegenüber***

it contrasts with **es unterscheidet sich von** +dat

contrast **der Gegensatz(-̈e)**

in contrast **im Gegensatz zu** +dat

I differ **ich unterscheide mich**

difference **der Unterschied(e)**

different **unterschiedlich**

different (from) *(adv)* **anders als**

disadvantage **der Nachteil(e)**

dissimilar **verschieden**

I distinguish **ich unterscheide**

pros and cons **die Vor- und Nachteile**

relatively **verhältnismäßig**

same **gleich, der/die/dasselbe**

similar **ähnlich**

---

beginning **der Anfang(-̈e)**

from the beginning **von Anfang an**

I am brief **ich fasse mich kurz**

in brief **kurz**

I conclude **ich schließe**

conclusion **der Schluss (-̈e)**

in conclusion **zum Schluss**

final **Schluss-**

finally **schließlich**

first **der/die/das erste**

firstly **erstens**

furthermore **weiter**

on the one hand **auf der einen Seite**

on the other hand **auf der anderen Seite**

initially **zu Anfang**

last **der/die/das letzte**

lastly **schließlich**

at last **endlich**

next **der/die/das nächste**

place **die Stelle(n)**

in the first place **an erster Stelle**

in the second place **an zweiter Stelle**

secondly **zweitens**

in short **kurz**

and so on **und so weiter, usw.**

THE HUMAN MIND & CHARACTER

Arguing a point

admittedly **zwar**
all the same **trotzdem**
although **obgleich**
anyway **auf jeden Fall**
apart from **abgesehen von** +dat
as for … **was … betrifft**
as I see it **nach meiner Ansicht**
as well **auch**
despite this **trotzdem**
in effect **in Wirklichkeit**
however **aber**
incidentally **übrigens**
instead **an seiner Stelle**
instead of **statt** +gen
just as important **genauso wichtig**
likewise **gleichfalls**
no matter whether **egal, ob**
that may be so **ich glaube schon**
nevertheless **trotzdem**
otherwise **sonst**
in reality **in Wirklichkeit**
in many respects **in vielerlei Hinsicht**
in return **dafür**
as a rule **meistens**
so to speak **gewissermaßen**
in spite of **trotz** +gen
still, … **dennoch**

to tell the truth **um ehrlich zu sein**
whereas **indem, während**
on the whole **im Großen und Ganzen, alles in allem**

Cause & effect

all the more (because) **um so mehr, (da)**
as **da**
because **weil**
cause **die Ursache(n)**
consequence **die Folge(n)**
consequently **infolgedessen**
effect **die Wirkung(en), die Auswirkung(en)**
it follows that **hieraus folgt, dass**
how? **wie?**
if **wenn**
reason **der Grund(¨e)**
for this reason **deshalb**
result **das Ergebnis(se)**
as a result **infolgedessen**
provided that **vorausgesetzt**
since **da**
so long as *(conj)* **solange**
that is why *(adv)* **deshalb**
therefore/so **so**
thus **so**
when(ever) **wenn**

In many respects things are not too bad.
As a rule people try to obey the law.
However, crime is still common, in spite of the efforts of the police.

In vielerlei Hinsicht ist die Lage nicht so schlimm.
Meistens versuchen die Leute dem Gesetz zu gehorchen.
Aber die Verbrechen sind immer noch weit verbreitet, trotz der Bemühungen der Polizei.

– He is not very ill, is he?
– Yes he is. His brother is not well either. Therefore we have to postpone our meeting.

– **Er ist nicht sehr krank, oder?**
– **Doch. Sein Bruder ist auch nicht gesund. Deshalb müssen wir unsere Besprechung verschieben.**

– I hope they will be better soon.

– **Hoffentlich sind sie bald wieder gesund.**

when *(past event)* **als**
whether **ob**
why? **warum?, wozu?**

Emphasizing

above all **vor allem**
in addition **dazu**
all the more **um so mehr**
also **auch**
certainly **sicher**
clearly **offensichtlich**
under no circumstances **unter keinen Umständen**
completely **völlig, ganz**
especially **besonders**
even (more) **noch (mehr)**
without exception **ohne Ausnahme**
I emphasize **ich betone**
extremely **höchst, äußerst**
far and away **bei weitem**
fortunately **zum Glück**
honestly **ehrlich**
just when **gerade wo**
mainly **hauptsächlich**
moreover **übrigens**
naturally **natürlich, selbstverständlich**
not at all **keineswegs**
not in the least **keineswegs**

both ... and **sowohl ... wie/als**
obviously **offensichtlich, ja**
in particular **insbesondere**
particularly **besonders**
in every respect **in jeder Hinsicht**
I stress **ich betone**
thanks to **dank** +dat
undeniably **unleugbar**
very **sehr**
and what is more **und dazu**

Expressing reservations

even if **auch wenn**
even so **selbst dann**
to some extent **gewissermaßen**
at first sight **beim ersten Blick**
hardly **kaum**
in general **im Allgemeinen**
in the main **zum größten Teil**
in part **zum Teil**
partly **teils, teilweise**
perhaps **vielleicht**
presumably **wohl, vermutlich**
probably **wahrscheinlich**
relatively **verhältnismäßig**
unfortunately **leider**
unusual(ly) **ungewöhnlich**
virtually **fast**
in a way **gewissermaßen**

Rolf is said to have gone abroad, in fact to the States.
Rolf is abroad, in fact he's in the States now. He'll probably be there for at least a week. So, unfortunately he won't attend our dinner.

Rolf soll ins Ausland gefahren sein, und zwar in die USA.
Rolf ist im Ausland, und zwar ist er gerade in den USA. Er wird wahrscheinlich mindestens eine Woche dort sein. Deshalb wird er leider nicht an unserem Essen teilnehmen.

Under no circumstances can we let the client wait for this shipment.
All the more, because the last one was delayed as well.

Unter keinen Umständen können wir den Kunden auf diese Lieferung warten lassen.
Um so mehr, da sich die letzte auch verzögert hatte.

Human life & relationships

7a Family & friends

Friendship

acquaintance   **der/die Bekannte**
   (adj/n)
boyfriend   **der Freund(e)**
chum   **der Kumpel(-)**
classmate   **der Klassenkamerad**
   (wk)
companion   **der Gefährte** *(wk)*, **die**
   Gefährtin(nen)
friend   **der Freund(e) [-in]**
   close friend   **der enge**
   Freund(e) [-in]
friendship   **die Freundschaft(en)**
gang   **die Gang(s)**
I get along/on with   **ich komme mit**
   jdm. gut zurecht*/aus*
we get together   **wir treffen uns**
girl friend   **die Freundin(nen)**
I get to know   **ich lerne kennen***
human relationships   **die mensch-**
   lichen Beziehungen *(pl)*
I introduce   **ich stelle . . . vor***
mate/buddy   **der Kamerad** *(wk)*

penfriend/pal   **der Brieffreund(e)**
   [-in]
relationship   **die**
   Verwandtschaft(en)
schoolfriend/pal   **der**
   Schulfreund(e) [-in]

The family & close relatives

adopted   **adoptiert, Adoptiv-**
ancestor   **der Vorfahr** *(wk)* **[-in]**
ancestry   **die Abstammung(en)**
aunt   **die Tante(n)**
baby   **das Baby(s)**
brother   **der Bruder(¨)**
brothers and sisters   **die**
   Geschwister *(pl)*
brother-in-law   **der Schwager(¨)**
child   **das Kind(er)**
close relative   **der/die enge**
   Verwandte *(adj/n)*
closely related   **nah verwandt mit**
   +dat

We're old school friends. We get along very well and do a lot together.

Wir sind alte Schulfreunde. Wir kommen sehr gut miteinander aus und unternehmen viel gemeinsam.

Helmut and Siegfried met each other during their vacation and quickly became close friends.

Helmut und Siegfried haben sich im Urlaub kennen gelernt und sind ganz schnell enge Freunde geworden.

I live with my grandparents.

Ich wohne bei meinen Großeltern.

common-law **eheähnlich**
common-law partner **der Partner(-) [-in]**
cousin **der Cousin(s), die Cousine(n)**
dad/daddy **der Vati(s)**
daughter **die Tochter(¨)**
daughter-in-law **die Schwiegertochter(¨)**
elder **älter**
eldest **der/die/das älteste**
family **die Familie(n)**
family-tree **der Familienstammbaum(¨e)**
father **der Vater(¨)**
father-in-law **der Schwiegervater(¨)**
fiance(e) **der/die Verlobte** *(adj/n)*
foster **Pflege-**
genealogy **die Genealogie(n)**
godmother **die Patin(nen)**
grandad **der Opa(s)**
grandchild **das Enkelkind(er)**
granddaughter **die Enkeltochter(¨)**
grandfather **der Großvater(¨)**
grandma **die Großmama(s)**
grandmother **die Großmutter(¨)**
grandpa **der Großpapa(s)**
grandparents **die Großeltern** *(pl)*
grandson **der Enkelsohn(¨e)**
granny **die Oma(s)**
guardian **der Vormund(¨er)**
half-brother **der Halbbruder(¨)**

half-sister **die Halbschwester(n)**
husband **der Ehemann(¨er)**
member of the family **der/die Familienangehörige** *(adj/n)*
mom **die Mutti(s)**
mother **die Mutter(¨)**
mother-in-law **die Schwiegermutter(¨)**
nephew **der Neffe(n)** *(wk)*
niece **die Nichte(n)**
only child **das Einzelkind(er)**
parents **die Eltern** *(pl)*
partner **der Partner(-) [-in]**
related **verwandt**
relation **der/die Verwandte** *(adj/n)*
sister **die Schwester(n)**
son **der Sohn(¨e)**
son-in-law **der Schwiegersohn(¨e)**
spouse **der Gatte** *(wk)*, **die Gattin(nen)**
step- **Stief-**
stepfather **der Stiefvater(¨)**
twin **der Zwilling(e)**
twin brother **der Zwillingsbruder(¨)**
twin sister **die Zwillingsschwester(n)**
uncle **der Onkel(-)**
wife **die Ehefrau(en)**
younger **jünger**
youngest *(adj)* **der/die/das jüngste**

– Do you have a big family?
– Yes. I have three brothers, four sisters, a sister-in-law and two brothers-in-law. My oldest sister has three children.

I have no close family. I am an only child.

Can you imagine, Lisa's grandpa is getting married again!

– **Hast du eine große Familie?**
– **Ja. Ich habe drei Brüder, vier Schwestern, eine Schwägerin und zwei Schwager. Meine älteste Schwester hat drei Kinder.**

Ich habe keine engen Verwandten. Ich bin (ein) Einzelkind.

Kannst du dir das vorstellen, Lisas Opa heiratet wieder!

➤ LOVE & CHILDREN 7b; LIFE & DEATH 7c

HUMAN LIFE & RELATIONSHIPS

7b Love, marriage, & children

Love & marriage

adultery der Ehebruch(¨e)
affair das Verhältnis(se)
I have an affair with ich habe ein
Verhältnis mit +dat
alimony die
Unterhaltszahlung(en)
bachelor der Junggeselle(n) *(wk)*
betrothal die Verlobung(en)
betrothed der/die Verlobte *(adj/n)*
breakdown der
Zusammenbruch(¨e)
bride die Braut(¨e)
bridegroom der Bräutigam(e)
bridesmaid die Brautjungfer(n)
I cheat on ich betrüge
couple das Paar(e)
married couple das Ehepaar(e)
I court ich mache jdm. den Hof
divorce die Scheidung(en)
divorced geschieden
I get divorced ich lasse mich
scheiden
divorcee der/die Geschiedene
(adj/n)
engaged verlobt
engagement die Verlobung(en)
I fall for ich bin in jdn. vernarrt
I fall in love (with) ich verliebe
mich (in +acc)
I get divorced (from) ich lasse

mich (von jdm.) scheiden
I get engaged to ich verlobe mich
mit +dat
I get married (to) ich verheirate
mich (mit +dat)
I go out with ich gehe mit +dat
we are incompatible wir passen
nicht zueinander
love die Liebe(n)
I love ich liebe
lover der/die Geliebte *(adj/n)*
marriage die Ehe(n), die
Heirat(en)
marriage guidance die
Eheberatung
married verheiratet
I marry ich heirate
matrimony der Ehestand *(no pl)*
mistress die Geliebte *(adj/n)*
newly-weds die Neuvermählten
(pl)
orgasm der Orgasmus (-en)
promiscuity die Promiskuität
he is promiscuous er wechselt
häufig seine Partnerin
relationship das Verhältnis(se)
we separate wir trennen uns
separation die Trennung(en)
sexual intercourse der
Geschlechtsverkehr *(no pl)*
we have sex wir haben Sex

– Are you married?
– No, but we are engaged.

Tell me, what do you buy an old
bachelor for his birthday?

I was surprised to hear that your
boss and his wife are separating
after so many years.

– Seid ihr verheiratet?
– Nein, aber wir sind verlobt.

Sag mal, was kauft man einem
alten Junggesellen zum
Geburtstag?

Ich war überrascht zu hören,
dass dein Chef und seine Frau
sich nach so vielen Jahren
trennen.

single **ledig**
single mother **die allein erziehende Mutter(⁻)**
unmarried **unverheiratet**
wedding **die Hochzeit(en)**
widow **die Witwe(n)**
widower **der Witwer(-)**

Birth & children

abortion **die Abtreibung(en)**
I have an abortion **ich lasse das Kind abtreiben**
I adopt **ich adoptiere**
adoption **die Adoption(en)**
baby **das Baby(s)**
babysitter **der Babysitter(-)**
baptism **die Taufe(n)**
I am baptized **ich werde/bin getauft**
birth **die Geburt(en)**
birth control **die Geburtenkontrolle**
birth rate **die Geburtsrate(n)**
birthday **der Geburtstag(e)**
I was born **ich wurde geboren**
boy **der Junge(n)** *(wk)*
I bring up **ich erziehe**
I breast feed **ich stille**
caesarian section **der Kaiserschnitt(e)**
child **das Kind(er)**
child maintenance **das Kindergeld**
child minder **der Kinderbetreuer(er) [-in]**
childhood **die Kindheit(en)**
christening **die Taufe(n)**
I conceive **ich empfange**
condom **das/der Kondom(e), das Präservativ(e)**
contraception **die Empfängnisverhütung**
contractions **die Wehen** *(pl)*
I deliver a baby **ich bringe ein Baby zur Welt**
I am expecting a baby **ich erwarte ein Baby**

family planning **die Familienplanung**
fertile (in-) **(un)fruchtbar**
fertility **die Fruchtbarkeit**
fertility drug **die Fruchtbarkeitspille(n)**
fetus **der Fötus (Foten/Fötusse)**
I give birth **Ich gebäre/bringe zur Welt**
girl **das Mädchen(-)**
infancy **die Kindheit(en)**
infant **das Kleinkind(er)**
infantile **kindlich**
insemination **die Befruchtung(en)**
artificial insemination **die künstliche Befruchtung**
lad **der Bursche(n), der Junge(n)** *(wk)*
lass **das Mädchen(-)**
he looks like his mother **er sieht wie seine Mutter aus***
I have a miscarriage **ich habe eine Fehlgeburt**
midwife **die Hebamme(n)**
nappy/diaper **die Windel(n)**
nanny **das Kindermädchen(-)**
new-born child **das neugeborene Kind(er)**
orphan **die Waise(n), das Waisenkind(er)**
ovary **der Eierstock(⁻e)**
pregnancy **die Schwangerschaft(en)**
I get pregnant **Ich werde schwanger**
period *(monthly)* **die Periode(n)**
I remind of **ich erinnere an** +acc
I spoil my child **ich verwöhne mein Kind**
stillbirth **die Totgeburt(en)**
teenage **Jugend-**
teenager **der Teenager(-)**
toddler **das Kleinkind(er)**
triplets **der Drilling(e)**

HUMAN LIFE & RELATIONSHIPS

Growing up

adolescent **der/die Jugendliche** (adj/n)

adolescence **die Jugend**

adult **der/die Erwachsene** (adj/n)

age **das Alter(-)**

aged **bejahrt**

centenarian **der/die Hundertjährige** (adj/n)

child **das Kind(er)**

I come from **ich stamme aus** +dat

early retirement **der Vorruhestand**

elder(ly) **älter**

elderly (adj) **der/die/das ältere**

eldest (adj) **der/die/das älteste**

female **die Frau(en)**

female (adj) **weiblich**

foreigner **der Ausländer(-) [-in]**

generation **die Generation(en)**

generation gap **das Generationsproblem(e)**

I grow old/older **ich werde größer**

grown-up **der/die Erwachsene** (adj/n)

I grow up **ich wachse auf***

life **das Leben(-)**

life insurance **die Lebensversicherung(en)**

male/man **der Mann("-er)**

male (adj) **männlich**

maturity **die Reife** (no pl)

menopause **die Wechseljahre** (pl)

middle age **das mittlere Lebensalter**

new **neu**

nickname **der Spitzname(n)** (wk)

old **alt**

old age **das hohe Alter**

old man/woman **der/die Alte** (adj/n)

old people's home **das Altenwohnheim(e)**

pension **die Rente(n)**

pensioner **der Rentner(-) [-in]**

people **die Leute** (pl)

person **die Person(en), der Mensch(en)** (wk)

in the prime of his/her life **in der Blüte seiner/ihrer Jahre**

puberty **die Pubertät** (no pl)

responsible for **verantwortlich für** +acc

I retire **ich gehe in den Ruhestand**

retired **pensioniert**

retirement **der Ruhestand**

senility **die Senilität** (no pl)

single **ledig**

stranger **der/die Fremde** (adj/n)

surname **der Familienname(n)** (wk)

I take after **ich bin jdm. ähnlich**

well brought up **wohlerzogen**

– When I grow up, I want to be an astronaut.
– And how old are you now?
– I'm ten.

– Wenn ich groß bin, möchte ich Astronaut werden.
– Und wie alt bist du jetzt?
– Ich bin zehn Jahre alt.

Werner respects his elders.

Werner respektiert ältere Menschen.

Young people often get into conflicts with their parents.

Junge Leute geraten oft in Konflikt mit ihren Eltern.

woman **die Frau(en)**
young **jung**
young person **der junge Mensch(en)** *(wk)*
younger **jünger**
youngest *(adj)* **der/die/das jüngste**
youth **die Jugend**
youth *(persons)* **der/die Jugendliche** *(adj/n)*

Death

afterlife **das Leben nach dem Tod**
angel **der Engel(-)**
ashes **die Asche** *(no pl)*
autopsy **die Autopsie(n)**
I bequeath **ich vererbe**
body/corpse **die Leiche(n)**
burial **das Begräbnis(se)**
I bury **ich begrabe**
he is cremated **er wird eingeäschert**
cremation **die Einäscherung(en)**
crematorium/crematory **das Krematorium (-ien)**
dead **tot**
death **der Tod(e), der Todesfall(-e)**
death certificate **die Sterbeurkunde(n)**
death rate **die Sterberate(n)**
I die **ich sterbe**
epitaph **die Grabinschrift(en)**
eulogy **die Lobesrede(n)**
fatal **tödlich**

funeral **die Beerdigung(en)**
grave **das Grab(-er)**
gravestone/tombstone **der Grabstein(e)**
graveyard/cemetery **der Friedhof(-e)**
heaven **der Himmel(-)**
he goes to heaven **er kommt in den Himmel**
hell **die Hölle**
I inherit **ich erbe**
inheritance **die Erbschaft(en)**
I kill **ich töte**
I am killed **ich komme um***
late *(dead)* **selig**
last rites **die Letzte Ölung**
I lose my life **ich komme ums Leben**
mortuary **die Leichenhalle(n)**
I mourn (for) **ich trauere um** +acc, **ich beklage**
mourning **die Trauer** *(no pl)*
obituary **der Nachruf(e)**
he passes away **er scheidet hin***
remains **die Überreste** *(pl)*
tomb **das Grab(-er), das Grabmal(-e)**
undertaker/mortician **der Leichenbestatter(-) [-in]**
will **der Wille** *(no pl) (gen des Willens) (wk)*
the last will and testament of … **der letzte Wille des/der …**

Mrs. Hansen went into retirement last August.
Frau Hansen ist letzten August in den Ruhestand gegangen.

It's a matter of life and death.
Es geht um Leben und Tod.

Aunt Gertrud bequeathed her entire estate to her nephew and his wife.
Tante Gertrud hat ihr ganzes Vermögen ihrem Neffen und seiner Frau vererbt.

SICKNESS 11; WAR 27a

Daily life

8a The house

amenities **die Einrichtung(en)**
apartment **die Wohnung(en)**
block of flats/apartment house **der Wohnblock(ˉe)**
I build **ich baue**
building **das Gebäude(-)**
building plot **das Grundstück(e)**
building site **die Baustelle(n), das Baugelände(-)**
building society/savings & loan association **die Bausparkasse(n)**
bungalow **der Bungalow(s)**
caretaker **der Hausmeister(-)**
chalet **das Chalet(s)**
condominium **die Eigentumswohnung(en)**
council flat **die Sozialwohnung(en)**
council/public housing **der soziale Wohnungsbau** *(no pl)*
detached house **das Einzelhaus(ˉer)**

I build an extension **ich baue ein Zimmer an***
apartment **die Wohnung(en)**
furnished (un-) **(un)möbliert**
home **die Wohnung(en), das Haus(ˉer)**
at home **zu Hause**
house **das Haus(ˉer)**
housing **die Wohnverhältnisse** *(pl)*
landlord **der Grundbesitzer(-), der (Haus)wirt(e)**
lease **der Mietvertrag(ˉe)**
leasehold property **der Pachtbesitz**
I let/rent out **ich vermiete**
I modernize **ich modernisiere**
mortgage **die Hypothek(en)**
mortgage rate **der Zinssatz(ˉe)**
I move (house) **ich ziehe um***
I occupy **ich bewohne**
I own **ich besitze**

Renate and Karl are buying a new detached house.
Renate und Karl kaufen ein neues Einfamilienhaus.

We are having a house built.
Wir lassen ein Haus bauen.

I live in a rented, furnished apartment.
Ich wohne in einer möblierten Mietwohnung.

My tenancy has two weeks to run.
Mein Mietvertrag läuft noch zwei Wochen.

We moved two years ago. Our house has a pleasant view
Wir sind vor zwei Jahren umgezogen. Unser Haus hat einen schönen Ausblick.

---

owner-occupied house **das Eigenheim**

penthouse **die Dachterrassenwohnung(en)**

prefabricated house **das Fertighaus(-̈er)**

I rent **ich miete**

rent **die Miete(n)**

semidetached house **das Zweifamilienhaus(-̈er)**

street lighting **die Straßenbeleuchtung** *(no pl)*

I take out a mortgage **ich nehme eine Hypothek auf***

tenancy **das Miet/Pachtverhältnis(se)**

tenant **der Mieter(-), der Pächter(-)**

Rooms

attic **die Dachstube(n), die Mansarde(n)**

balcony **der Balkon(s)**

basement **das Kellergeschoss(e)**

bathroom **das Badezimmer(-)**

bedroom **das Schlafzimmer(-)**

breakfast room **der Frühstücksraum(-̈e)**

cellar **der Keller(-)**

corridor **der Gang(-̈e)**

dining room **das Esszimmer(-)**

en suite **mit Bad**

garage **die Garage(n)**

ground floor **das Erdgeschoss(e)**

hall(way) **der Hausflur(e)**

kitchen **die Küche(n)**

landing **der Treppenabsatz(-̈e), der Flur(e)**

lavatory/bathroom **die Toilette(n)**

living room **das Wohnzimmer(-)**

loft **der Dachboden(-̈)**

lounge **das Wohnzimmer(-)**

mezzanine floor **das Zwischengeschoss(e)**

passage **der Korridor(e)**

room **das Zimmer(-)**

shower room **der Duschraum(-̈e)**

staircase **das Treppenhaus(-̈er)**

stairs **die Treppe(n)**

study **das Arbeitszimmer(-)**

sunroom **die Veranda (-en)**

terrace **die Terrasse(n)**

toilet **die Toilette(n)**

toilet/W.C. **das WC(s)**

upper floor **das obere Stockwerk(e)**

utility room **die Waschküche(n)**

verandah **die Veranda(s)**

Anke's penthouse is for rent.

Ankes Dachterrassenwohnung ist zu vermieten.

Let's go home.

Lass uns nach Hause gehen.

We are renting an apartment at the moment. The rent is very high and I do not like the estate/housing development.

Wir mieten zurzeit eine Wohnung. Die Miete ist sehr hoch, und ich mag die Wohnsiedlung nicht.

It's a large three-room apartment on the third floor.

Es ist eine geräumige Dreizimmerwohnung im dritten Stock.

8b The home

aerial **die Antenne(n)**
back door **die Hintertür(en)**
big **groß**
blind **das Rollo(s)**
button **der Knopf(ˉe)**
carpet **der Teppich(e)**
ceiling **die Decke(n)**
central **Zentral-**
central heating **die Zentralheizung(en)**
chimney/smokestack **der Schornstein(e)**
clean **sauber**
clothes hanger **der Kleiderbügel(-)**
comfortable (un-) **bequem**
cosy **gemütlich**
curtain **der Vorhang(ˉe), die Gardine(n)**
desk **der Schreibtisch(e)**
dirty **schmutzig**
door **die Tür(en)**
door handle **der Türgriff(e)**
door knob **der Türknauf(ˉe)**
door mat **die Fußmatte(n)**
downstairs **(nach) unten**
dusty **staubig**
dustbin/trash can **die Mülltonne(n)**
electric **elektrisch**
electric plug **der (elektrische) Stecker(-)**
electric socket **die Steckdose(n)**
electricity **der Strom, die Elektrizität**
filthy **dreckig**
fire alarm **der Feueralarm(e)**
fire extinguisher **der Feuerlöscher(-)**
fireplace **der offene Kamin(e)**
extension cord **das Verlängerungskabel(-)**
floor **der (Fuß)boden(ˉ)**
floor (storey/story) **der Stock, das Stockwerk(e)**
on the first (second Am.) floor **im ersten Stock**

front door **die Haustür(en)**
furnished **möbliert**
furniture **die Möbel** (pl)
item of furniture **das Möbelstück(e)**
gas **das Gas**
glass (material) **das Glas(ˉer)**
handle **der Griff(e)**
handle (of broom, pan) **der Stiel(e)**
handle (on jug) **der Henkel(-)**
hearth **der Kamin(e)**
hearth and home **Haus und Herd**
household **der Haushalt(e)**
included **inbegriffen**
key **der Schlüssel(-)**
keyhole **das Schlüsselloch(ˉer)**
lamp **die Lampe(n)**
lampshade **der Lampenschirm(e)**
letterbox **der Briefkasten(ˉ)**
lever **der Hebel(-)**
lift **der Lift(s), der Fahrstuhl(ˉe)**
light bulb **die Birne(n)**
light **das Licht(er)**
light switch **der Lichtschalter(-)**
lock **das Schloss (ˉer)**
mantelpiece **der Kaminsims(e)**
mat **die Matte(n)**
modern **modern**
new **neu**
nice **schön, nett**
off (switch) **aus**
off (tap/faucet) **zu**
old **alt**
on (switch, tap/faucet) **an**
own **eigen**
pipe **das Rohr(e)**
plaster **der Verputz** (no pl)
plumbing **die Leitungen** (pl)
price **der Preis(e)**
radiator **der Heizkörper(-), die Heizung** (no pl)
roof **das Dach(ˉer)**
rubbish/garbage **der Abfall(ˉe)**
shelf **das Regal(e)**

shutters **der Fensterladen(-)**
situation **die Lage(n)**
skylight **das (Dach)Fenster(-)**
small **klein**
step **die Stufe(n)**
switch **der Schalter(-)**
tile *(roof)* **der Dachziegel(-)**
   tile *(ceramic)* **die Fliese(n)**
upstairs **(nach) oben**
vase **die Vase(n)**
view **die Aussicht(en)**
wall **die Mauer(n)**
   (inside) **die Wand(-̈e)**
   (partition) **die Trennwand(-̈e)**
wastepaper basket **der Papierkorb(-̈e)**
water **das Wasser**
window **das Fenster(-)**
window sill **die Fensterbank(-̈e)**
wire/flex **das Kabel(-)**
wiring **die elektrischen Leitungen** *(pl)*
wood **das Holz**

Electrical items

blender **der Mixer(-)**
cassette deck **das Kassettendeck(s)**
cassette recorder **der Kassettenrecorder(-)**
coffee machine **die Kaffeemaschine(n)**
compact-disc player **der CD Spieler(-)**
chest freezer **die Tiefkühltruhe(n)**

dishwasher **der Geschirrspüler(-)**
electric appliance **das Elektrogerät(e)**
electric razor/shaver **der Rasierapparat(e)**
electric stove **der Elektroherd(e)**
food mixer/processor **die Küchenmaschine(n)**
fridge/refrigerator **der Kühlschrank(-̈e)**
freezer **der Tiefkühlschrank(-̈e)**
hairdryer **der Fön(e)®**
iron **das Bügeleisen(-)**
microwave oven **der Mikrowellenherd(e)**
radio **das Radio(s)**
refrigerator **der Kühlschrank(-̈e)**
stereo system **die Stereoanlage(n)**
television (TV) **das Fernsehen** *(no pl)*
tumble drier **der Wäschetrockner (-)**
TV set **der Fernseher(-)**
vacuum cleaner **der Staubsauger(-)**
video recorder **der Videorecorder(-)**
Walkman® **der Walkman(s)®**
washing machine **die Waschmaschine(n)**

Where did Alex put the toolbox? | **Wo hat Alex den Werkzeugkasten hingestellt?**

Careful, there's a step. | **Vorsicht, hier ist eine Stufe.**

If you're too cold, you can turn the heat up. | **Wenn es dir zu kalt ist, kannst du die Heizung höher stellen.**

We have rented a furnished apartment. | **Wir haben eine möblierte Wohnung gemietet.**

The electricity has been cut off. | **Der Strom ist abgestellt worden.**

8c Furnishings

Lounge

armchair   der Lehnstuhl(¨e)
ashtray   der Aschenbecher(-)
bookshelf   das Bücherregal(e)
bookcase   das Bücherregal(e), der
   Bücherschrank(¨e)
bureau   der Sekretär(e)
cupboard/closet   der Schrank(¨e)
cushion   das Kissen(-)
easy chair   der Sessel(-)
ornament   der Schmuck, der
   Ziergegenstand(¨e)
picture   das Bildnis(se), das
   Gemälde(-)
   picture (portrait)   das Porträt(s)
photo   das Foto(s)
poster   das Poster(-)
pouffe   der Puff(e)
rocking chair   der
   Schaukelstuhl(¨e)
rug   der Läufer(-)
settee   die Couch(en), das Sofa(s)
sofa   das Sofa(s)

Kitchen

bottle opener   der
   Flaschenöffner(-)
bowl   die Schüssel(n)
broom   der Besen(-)
cloth   der Stoff(e), das Tuch(¨er)
clothes line   die Wäscheleine(n)
clothes peg   die Wäscheklammer(n)
coffee pot   die Kaffeekanne(n)
crockery/dishes   das Geschirr (no
   pl)
cup   die Tasse(n)
cupboard   der Schrank(¨e)
   wall cupboard   der
   Wandschrank(¨e)
cutlery   das Besteck(e)
dish   die Schüssel(n)
dishrag   der Spüllappen(-)
dish washer   die Spülmaschine

dish washing liquid   das
   Spülmittel(-)
duster   das Staubtuch(¨er)
fork   die Gabel(n)
garbage can   der Mülleimer(-)
gas stove   der Gasherd(e)
glass   das Glas(¨er)
   wine glass   das Weinglas(¨er)
jug   der Krug(¨e), die Kanne(n)
knife   das Messer(-)
   carving knife   das
   Tranchiermesser(-)
leftovers   die Überreste (pl)
mug   der Becher(-)
oven   der Ofen
peppermill   die Pfeffermühle(n)   .
plate   der Teller(-)
rag   der Lappen
salt shaker   der Salzstreuer(-)
saucer   die Untertasse(n)
scouring pad   der Topfkratzer(-)
sink   das Spülbecken(-)
sink unit   die Spüle(n)
spoon   der Löffel(-)
stove   der Herd(e),
tap/faucet   der Wasserhahn(¨e)
teapot   die Teekanne(n)
tea towel   das Geschirrtuch(¨er)
tray   das Tablett(s)
washing powder   das Waschmittel(-)

Dining room

chair   der Stuhl(¨e)
candle   die Kerze(n)
candlestick   der Kerzenhalter(-)
chia cabinet   der
   Geschirrschrank(¨e)
hot warmer   die
   Warmhalteplatte(n)
place setting   das Gedeck(e)
serviette   die Serviette(n)
sideboard   das Büfett(s)

table **der Tisch(e)**
table cloth **die Tischdecke(n)**
table napkin/serviette **die Serviette(n)**

Bedroom

alarm clock **der Wecker(-)**
bed **das Bett(en)**
  bunk bed **das Etagenbett(en)**
  double bed **das Doppelbett(en)**
bedclothes **das Bettzeug** *(no pl)*
bedside table **der Nachttisch(e)**
bedspread **der Bettüberwurf(-̈e)**
blanket **die Decke(n)**
chest of drawers **die Kommode(n)**
duvet **das Federbett(en)**
pillow **das Kopfkissen(-)**
quilt **die Steppdecke(n)**
sheet **das Betttuch(-̈er)**
wardrobe **der Kleiderschrank(-̈e)**

Bathroom

basin **das (Wasch)becken(-)**
bath **das Bad(-̈er)**
bathplug **der Stöpsel(-)**
bath mat **die Bademasse(n)**
clothes brush **die Kleiderbürste(n)**
flannel **der Waschlappen(-)**
laundry basket **der Waschkorb(-̈e)**
mirror **der Spiegel(-)**
nail brush **die Nagelbürste(n)**
plug **der Stecker(-)**
shampoo **das Shampoo(s)**
shower **die Dusche(n)**
sink **das Waschbecken(-)**
soap **die Seife(n)**
tap **der Wasserhahn(-̈e)**
toilet **das Klo(s), die Toilette(n)**
toilet paper **das Toilettenpapier**
toothbrush **die Zahnbürste(n)**
toothpaste **die Zahnpasta(s)**
towel **das Handtuch(-̈er)**
towel rail **der Handtuchhalter(-)**
washbasin **das Waschbecken(-)**

The washing machine doesn't work! Can you repair it?

Die Waschmaschine funktioniert nicht. Können Sie sie reparieren?

Please come into the living room.

Bitte kommen Sie ins Wohnzimmer.

Would you please take the teapot out of the china cabinet?

Würdest du mal bitte die Teekanne aus dem Geschirrschrank nehmen?

Could we have some clean towels?

Könnten wir einige saubere Handtücher bekommen?

During the winter, our grandma likes to sit in her rocking chair by the fireplace.

Im Winter sitzt unsere Oma gerne in ihrem Schaukelstuhl am Kamin.

Tell your brother to clear the table and put the dishes in the sink.

Sag deinem Bruder, er soll den Tisch abräumen und das Geschirr ins Spülbecken stellen.

➤ GARDENING 24c; TOOLS App.8b; TOILETRIES 9b

DAILY LIFE

8d Daily routine

bath   **das Bad(¨er)**
bed   **das Bett(en)**
breakfast   **das Frühstück(e)**
clean   **sauber**
cleaner   **die Reinigungskraft (¨e)**
daily routine   **der Alltag** *(no pl)*
dinner *(evening)*   **das Abendessen(-)**
dirty dishes   **der Abwasch**
evening meal   **das Abendbrot(e)**
home   **das Heim(e), das Haus(¨er)**
   home *(at home)*   **zu Hause**
   home *(to one's home)*   **nach Hause**
housework   **die Hausarbeit(en)**
laundry   **die Wäsche**
lunch   **das Mittagessen(-)**
school   **die Schule(n)**
shop   **der Laden(¨)**
sleep   **der Schlaf** *(no pl)*
spare *(left over)*   **der Rest(e)**
   spare *(available)*   **übrig, frei**
spare time   **die Freizeit**
spring cleaning   **der Frühjahrsputz**
supper   **das Abendessen(-)**
time   **die Zeit(en)**
work   **die Arbeit(en)**

Actions

I break   **ich breche**
I bring   **ich bringe**
I buy   **ich kaufe**
I carry   **ich trage**
I change *(clothes)*   **ich ziehe mich um***
I chat   **ich plaudere**
I clean   **ich putze, ich mache sauber**
I clear away   **ich räume weg***
I clear the table   **ich räume/decke den Tisch ab***
I cook   **ich koche**
I close *(door)*   **ich mache zu***

I darn   **ich stopfe**
I dirty   **ich mache schmutzig**
I do   **ich tue, ich mache**
I drink   **ich trinke**
I drop   **ich lasse fallen**
I dry up   **ich trockne ab***
I dust   **ich wische Staub**
I eat   **ich esse**
I empty   **ich leere**
I enter   **ich betrete**
I extend   **ich baue aus*/an***
I fall   **ich falle**
I fasten   **ich verschließe**
   I fasten *(attach)*   **ich mache fest***
I fill   **ich fülle**
I get dressed   **ich ziehe mich an***
I get undressed   **ich ziehe mich aus***
I get up   **ich stehe auf***
I go to bed   **ich gehe ins Bett**
I go to sleep   **ich gehe schlafen**
I go to the toilet   **ich gehe zur Toilette**
I have breakfast   **ich frühstücke**
I have lunch   **ich esse zu Mittag**
I have tea/coffee   **ich trinke Tee/den Nachmittagskaffee**
I heat   **ich heize**
I iron   **ich bügele**
I knit   **ich stricke**
I knock   **ich klopfe, schlage**
I lay the table   **ich decke den Tisch**
I leave   **ich verlasse** +acc
I let *(allow)*   **ich erlaube**
I let/rent   **ich vermiete**
I live   **ich wohne**
I lock   **ich schließe ab***
I make   **ich mache**
I make wet/dampen   **ich befeuchte**
I mend   **ich repariere, flicke**
I move (house)   **ich ziehe um***
I move in   **ich ziehe ein***
I move out   **ich ziehe aus***
I move   **ich bewege mich**

it is on **es ist an**
it is off **es ist aus**
I paint **ich streiche an*, ich male an***
I pick up **ich hebe auf***
I polish **ich poliere**
I prepare **ich bereite vor***
I press *(button)* **ich drücke (den Knopf)**
I press *(iron)* **ich bügele**
I put on *(clothes)* **ich ziehe an***
I put on *(radio, TV)* **ich mache an***
I put away **ich räume weg***
I put right **ich stelle zurecht***
I repair/fix **ich repariere**
I rest **ich ruhe mich aus***
I ring *(telephone)* **ich telefoniere**
I ring *(doorbell)* **ich klingele**
I rinse **ich spüle**
I sew **ich nähe**
I share **ich teile**
I shine **ich poliere**
I shop **ich kaufe ein***
I shower **ich dusche**
I shut/close **ich schließe**
I sit down **ich setze mich (hin*)**

I sit **ich sitze**
I sleep **ich schlafe**
I speak **ich spreche**
I stand **ich stehe**
I stand up **ich stehe auf***
I start **ich beginne**
I stop **ich beende**
I sweep **ich kehre, ich fege**
I switch/turn off **ich schalte aus***
I switch/turn on **ich schalte ein***
I take off **ich ziehe aus***
I tear **ich zerreiße**
I throw away **ich werfe weg***
I tidy/straighten up **ich räume auf***
I tie **ich binde**
I unblock **ich schließe auf***
I undo **ich mache auf***
I use **ich benutze**
I wake up **ich wache auf***
I wake up someone **ich wecke jdn.**
I wallpaper **ich tapeziere**
I wash **ich wasche**
I wash up/wash dishes **ich wasche ab***
I watch TV **ich sehe fern***
I wear **ich trage**

I get up at seven o'clock, get dressed and go to work.

Ich stehe um sieben Uhr auf, ziehe mich an und gehe zur Arbeit.

Dinner will be at 9 p.m.

Das Abendessen ist um 9 Uhr.

Mrs. Fischer does the cleaning and dusting for us on Fridays.

Freitags macht Frau Fischer bei uns sauber und wischt Staub.

Shopping

9a General terms

article **der Artikel(-)**
assistant/sales clerk **der Verkäufer(-) [-in]**
automatic door **die automatische Tür(en)**
banknote **der Geldschein(e)**
bargain **das Sonderangebot(e)**
basement **das Untergeschoss(e)**
business **das Geschäft(e)**
cash desk/register **die Kasse(n)**
change *(coinage)* **das Wechselgeld(er)**
cheap **billig, preiswert**
checkout **die Kasse(n)**
choice **die Auswahl** *(no pl)*
closed **geschlossen, zu**
coin **die Münze(n)**
color **die Farbe(n)**
costly **kostspielig**
credit **der Kredit(e)**
credit card **die Kreditkarte(n)**
customer information **die Kundeninformation(en)**
customer service **der Kundendienst(e)**
day off/closed **am ... geschlossen**
dear **teuer**

department **die Abteilung(en)**
deposit **die Anzahlung(en)**
discount **der Rabatt(e)**
elevator **der Fahrstuhl(¨e)**
entrance **der Eingang(¨e)**
escalator **die Rolltreppe(n)**
exit **der Ausgang(¨e)**
expensive **teuer**
fashion **die Mode(n)**
fire door **die Feuertür(en)**
fire exit **der Notausgang(¨e)**
fitting room **die Ankleidekabine(n)**
free **frei, kostenlos**
free gift **das Werbegeschenk(e)**
it is good value **es ist preisgünstig**
handbag **die Handtasche(n)**
instructions for use **die Gebrauchsanweisung(en)**
item **die Ware(n), der Gegenstand(¨e)**
manager **der Manager(-), der Geschäftsführer(-) [-in]**
open **geöffnet, auf**
opening hours **die Öffnungszeiten** *(pl)*

packet **das Päckchen(-)**

Eight questions

Anything else?/Is that all?	**Sonst noch etwas?/Ist das alles?**
Are you being served?	**Werden Sie bedient?**
Can I help you?	**Kann ich Ihnen helfen?**
Do you want anything in particular?	**Möchten Sie etwas Bestimmtes?**
Sliced or whole?	**Geschnitten oder am Stück?**
What would you like?	**Was möchten Sie?**
Whose turn is it?	**Wer ist dran?**

I pay **ich bezahle**
pocket **die Tasche(n)**
I pull **ich ziehe**
purse **der Geldbeutel(-)**
I push **ich drücke**
quality **die Qualität(en)**
real/genuine **echt**
receipt **die Quittung(en)**
reduced **ermäßigt**
reduction **die Ermäßigung(en)**
refund **das Geld zurück**
sale **der Ausverkauf(¨e)**
security guard/store detective **der/ die Sicherheitsbeamte** *(adj/n)* **[-in]**
self-service **die Selbstbedienung(en)**
shop/store **der Laden(¨)**
shop assistant/sales person **der Verkäufer(-) [-in]**
shop keeper **der Geschäftsinhaber(-) [-in]**
shoplifter **der Ladendieb(e)**
shopping list **der Einkaufszettel(-)**
shopping basket **der Einkaufskorb(¨)**
shopping trolley/cart **der Einkaufswagen(-)**
shut **zu**
it shuts **es schließt**
special offer **das Sonderangebot(e)**
I spend **ich gebe aus***
summer sale **der Sommerschlussverkauf** *(no pl)*
till **die Kasse(n)**

till receipt **der Kassenbon(s)**
trader **der Händler(-)**
traveler's check **der Reisescheck(s)**
wallet **die Brieftasche(n)**
way in **der Eingang(¨e)**
way out **der Ausgang(¨e)**

Actions

I change **ich wechsle**
I choose **ich wähle**
I decide **ich entscheide**
I dress **ich ziehe mich an***
I exchange **ich tausche**
I have on/wear **ich trage**
I push in **ich drücke ein***
I put on **ich ziehe an***
line up **ich stehe an***
I select **ich sortiere aus***
I sell **ich verkaufe**
I serve **ich bediene**
I shop **ich kaufe ein***
I shoplift **ich stehle, ich klaue**
I show **ich zeige**
I spend (money) **ich gebe aus***
I steal **ich stehle**
I take off **ich ziehe aus***
I try on **ich probiere (an*)**
I wait **ich warte**
I wear **ich trage**
I weigh **ich wiege**
I wrap up **ich packe/wickle ein***

How much is it? Have you anything cheaper? | **Wie viel kostet das? Haben Sie (irgend)was Billigeres?**
Can I pay by check? | **Kann ich mit Scheck bezahlen?**
Do you take credit cards? | **Nehmen Sie Kreditkarten?**
I've no change. | **Ich habe kein Kleingeld.**
Can you change this note? | **Können Sie mir diesen (Geld)schein wechseln?**

– Is there a deposit on the bottle? | **– Ist auf der Flasche Pfand?**
– No, the bottle is nonreturnable. | **– Nein, es ist eine Einwegflasche.**

➤ HOUSEHOLD GOODS & TOILETRIES 9b; CLOTHING 9c

9b Household goods & toiletries

Toiletries

acne cream **die Aknesalbe(n)**
aftershave (lotion) **das After-shave/Rasierwasser**
antiperspirant **das Deospray**
bubble bath **das Schaumbad**
brush **die Bürste(n)**
cologne **das Kölnischwasser**
comb **der Kamm(-̈e)**
condom **das Kondom(e)**
cotton wool **die Watte**
cosmetics **das Kosmetikum (-a)**
deodorant **das (Deo-)spray(s)**
eye liner **der Eyeliner**
face cream **die (Haut)creme(s)**
foot powder **der/das Fußpuder(-)**
glasses **die Brille(n)**
hairbrush **die Haarbürste(n)**
dental floss **die Zahnseide(n)**
lipsalve **die Lippenpomade(n)**
lipstick **der Lippenstift(e)**
makeup **das Make-up**
makeup remover pad **die Abschminkwatte**
mascara **die Wimperntusche(-)**
mouthwash **das Mundwasser**
nail file **die Nagelfeile(n)**
paper handkercief **das Papiertaschentuch(-̈er)**
perfume **das Parfüm(e/s)**
razor **der Rasierapparat(e)**

razor blades **die Rasierklinge(n)**
sanitary towels **die Binde(n)**
shampoo **das Shampoo(s), das Haarwaschmittel(-)**
soap **die Seife(n)**
spray **das Spray(s)**
sunglasses **die Sonnenbrille(n)**
suntan lotion **das Sonnenöl(e)**
talcum powder **der/das Talkumpuder**
tampon **der Tampon(s)**
tissues **das Kosmetiktuch(-̈er)**
toilet paper **das Toilettenpapier**
toiletries **die Toilettenartikel** *(pl)*
toothpaste **die Zahnpasta(s)**
toothbrush **die Zahnbürste(n)**

Household items

bleach **das Bleichmittel(-)**
cellophane wrapping **die Frischhaltefolie**
clothes pegs **die Wäscheklammern(n)**
dishwashing liquid **das Spülmittel(-)**
fire lighter **der Feueranzünder(-)**
foil/aluminum foil **die (Aluminium)folie(n)**

Expressions of quantity

a bar of ...	**ein Stück/ein Riegel/eine Tafel...**
a bottle of ...	**eine Flasche ...**
a hundred gram(me)s of ...	**hundert Gramm ...**
a kilo of ...	**ein Kilo ...**
a liter of ...	**ein Liter ...**
a packet of ...	**ein Päckchen ...**
a slice of ...	**eine Scheibe ...**
a tin/can of ...	**eine Büchse/Dose ...**
half a pound of ...	**ein halbes Pfund ...**

insect spray **das Insektenbekämpfungsmittel(-)**
match **das Streichholz(-er)**
paper napkin/serviette **die Papierserviette(n)**
paper towel **das Papiertuch(-er), Küchentücher (von der Rolle)**
scouring pad **der Topfkratzer(-)**
string **die Schnur(-e)**
washing/wash powder **das Waschpulver(-)**

Basic foodstuffs

bacon **der Schinkenspeck**
beef **das Rindfleisch**
beer **das Bier(e)**
biscuit/cookie **der Keks(e)**
bread **das Brot(e)**
 black bread **das Schwarzbrot(e)**
 bread and butter **das Butterbrot(e)**
 rye bread **das Roggenbrot(e)**
 slice **die Scheibe(n)**
 sliced bread **das Brot in Scheiben**
 toast **der Toast(e)**
 white bread **das Weizenbrot(e)**
 wholemeal bread **das Vollkornbrot(e)**
butter **die Butter**
cakes **der Kuchen(-)**
cereal **das Getreide, die Getreideflocken**
cheese **der Käse**
chips/french fries **die Pommes frites**
chocolate spread **der Schokoladenaufstrich(e)**
cola **die Cola(s)**
coffee **der Kaffee(s)**
 instant coffee **der Pulverkaffee(s)**
crisps/chips *(US)* **die Chips**
custard **die Vanillesoße(n)**

egg **das Ei(er)**
fish **der Fisch(e)**
fruit **die Frucht(-e), das Obst**
ham **der Schinken**
jam **die Marmelade(n)**
juice **der Saft(-e)**
lemonade **die Limonade(n)**
loaf **das Brot(e), der Laib(e)**
macaroni **die Makkaroni(s)**
margarine **die Margarine**
marmalade **die Orangenmarmelade(n)**
mayonnaise **die Mayonnaise**
meat **das Fleisch**
milk **die Milch**
mustard **der Senf**
oil **das Öl(e)**
olive-oil **das Olivenöl(e)**
pasta **die Nudel(n)**
paté **die Pastete(n)**
peanut-butter **die Erdnussbutter**
pepper **der Pfeffer**
pizza **die Pizza(s)**
pork **das Schweinefleisch**
pudding **der Pudding(s)**
roll *(bread)* **die Semmel(n), das Brötchen**
salt **das Salz(e)**
sandwich **das Sandwich(es)**
 open sandwich **das belegte Brot(e)**
sardine **die Sardine(n)**
sauce **die Soße(n)**
sausage **die Wurst(-e)**
soup **die Suppe(n)**
spaghetti **die Spaghetti** *(pl)*
spice **das Gewürz(e)**
sugar **der Zucker**
 cube/lump sugar **der Würfelzucker**
sunflower oil **das Sonnenblumenöl(e)**
tea **der Tee(s)**
teabag **der Teebeutel(-)**
vegetables **das Gemüse(-)**
vinegar **der Essig**
wine **der Wein(e)**

➤ FOOD & DRINK 10; MEAT 10b; VEGETABLES 10c

9c Clothing

anorak/parka **der Anorak(s)**
beautiful **schön**
big **groß**
bikini **der Bikini(s)**
blouse **die Bluse(n)**
boot **der Stiefel(-)**
bra **der BH, der Büstenhalter(-)**
brand new **funkelnagelneu**
briefs **der Slip(s)**
cap **die Mütze(n)**
cardigan **die Strickjacke(n)**
check **kariert**
clothes **die Kleider** *(pl)*
clothing **die Kleidung**
coat **der Mantel(¨)**
colorfast **waschecht**
colorful **bunt**
cravate **die Krawatte(n)**
dress **das Kleid(er)**
elegant **elegant**
embroidered **bestickt**
fashion **die Mode(n)**
fashionable **modisch**
glove **der Handschuh(e)**
handkerchief **das Taschentuch(¨er)**
hat **der Hut(¨e)**
headscarf **das Kopftuch(¨er)**
heel **der Absatz(¨e)**
jacket **die Jacke(n)**
jeans **die Jeans** *(pl)*
jersey **der Pullover(-)**
jumper **der Pulli(s)**
knitted **gestrickt**
knitwear **die Strickware(n)**
ladies' wear **die Damenbekleidung**
the latest fashion **die neueste Mode**
linen **die Wäsche**
lingerie **die Damenunterwäsche**
long **lang**
long-sleeved **langärm(e)lig**
loose **locker, lose**

loud/brash **grell, schreiend**
low-heeled **mit flachem Absatz**
manmade fiber **die Kunstfaser(n)**
matching **passend zu** +dat
men's wear **die Herrenbekleidung**
non-iron **bügelfrei**
pair **das Paar(e)**
panties **der (Damen)slip(s)**
pants **die Hose(n)**
plain **einfach, schlicht**
printed **gedruckt, bedruckt**
pyjamas **der Schlafanzug(¨e)**
raincoat **der Regenmantel(¨)**
sandal **die Sandale(n)**
scarf **der Schal(s)**
shirt **das (Ober)hemd(e)**
shoe **der Schuh(en)**
shoelace **der Schnürsenkel(-)**
short sleeves **kurzärm(e)lig**
silky **seidig**
size **die Größe(n)**
skirt **der Rock(¨e)**
slip **der Unterrock(¨e)**
small **klein**
smart **elegant, schick**
sneakers **der Freizeitschuh(e)**
sock **die Socke(n)**
soft **weich**
stocking **der Strumpf(¨e)**
striped **gestreift**
suit **der Anzug(¨e)**
sweater **der Pullover(-)**
sweatshirt **das Sweatshirt(s)**
swimming trunks **die Badehose(n)**
swimsuit **der Badeanzug(¨e)**
T-shirt **das T-Shirt(s)**
tie **der Schlips(e)**
tight **eng**
tights **die Strumpfhose(n)**
trainers **der Sportschuh(e)**
ugly **hässlich**
umbrella **der Regenschirm(e)**
underpants **die Unterhose(n)**
underwear **die Unterwäsche**
unfashionable **unmodern**

vest die Weste(n), das Unterhemd(en)

Alterations & repairs

alteration die Änderung(en)
I alter ich ändere
belt der Gürtel(-)
buckle die Schnalle(n)
button der Knopf(-e)
collar der Kragen(-)
dressmaker der Damenschneider(-) [-in]
dressmaking das Schneidern
dry cleaning die chemische Reinigung
hem der Saum(-e)
I hem ich säume
I iron/press ich bügele
jewellery/jewelry der Schmuck
knitting machine die Strickmaschine(n)

knitting needle die Stricknadel(n)
material der Stoff(e)
needle die Nadel(n)
patch der Flicken(-)
pin die Stecknadel(n)
pocket die Tasche(n)
press stud/snap fastener der Druckknopf(-e)
I repair ich bessere aus*
safety pin die Sicherheitsnadel(n)
I sew ich nähe
sewing machine die Nähmaschine(n)
sleeve der Ärmel(-)
I stitch ich nähe
I take in/let out ich mache enger/weiter
tailor der Schneider(-) [-in]
tailored geschneidert
thread der Faden(-)
turn-up/cuff der Aufschlag(-e)
zip(per) der Reißverschluss(-e)

Expressions in clothes shops/stores

I'm next. Ich bin der /die Nächste.
I would like a ... Ich möchte ...
What color? Welche Farbe?
Do you have the same in red? Haben Sie das gleiche in Rot?
I would like it in brown. Ich hätte es gern in Braun.
I prefer ... Ich bevorzuge ...
I would rather have ... Ich würde lieber das ... nehmen/haben.
I take/wear size ... Ich trage Größe ...
I'd like it two sizes bigger. Ich hätte es gern zwei Größen größer.

Can I try it on? Kann ich es anprobieren?
That's not quite right. Das ist nicht ganz richtig/das Richtige.
They don't go together. Das passt nicht zusammen.
It suits me. Es passt/steht mir.
I like it. Mir gefällt es.
I'll take it. Ich nehme es.
I'll take the big one. Ich nehme das Große.
I bought it at the sale. Ich habe es im Schlussverkauf gekauft.
I would like to change it. Ich möchte es gern (um)tauschen.

Food & drink

10a Drinks & meals

Drinks

alcoholic **der Alkoholiker(-) [-in]**
alcoholic **alkoholisch**
aperitif **der Aperitif(s)**
beer **das Bier(e)**
black coffee **der schwarze Kaffee(s)**
brandy **der Weinbrand(̈-e), der Kognak(s)**
champagne **der Champagner(-), der Sekt(e)**
chocolate (drinking) **die (heiße) Schokolade(n)**
cider **der Apfelwein(e)**
cocktail **der Cocktail(s)**
coffee **der Kaffee(s)**
cola **die Cola(s)**
draught beer **das Bier(e) vom Fass**
drink **das Getränk(e)**
dry **herb**
fruit juice **der Fruchtsaft(̈-e)**
heavy **schwer**
juice **der Saft(̈-e)**
lemonade **die Limonade(n)**
light **leicht**
low alcohol **alkoholarm**
orange juice/squash **der Orangensaft(̈-e)**
milk **die Milch**
milkshake **das Milchmixgetränk(e)**
mineral water **das Mineralwasser(-)**
   fizzy **mit Kohlensäure**
   still **ohne Kohlensäure**
nonalcoholic **alkoholfrei**
punch **die Bowle(n)**
red wine **der Rotwein(e)**

sherry **der Sherry(s)**
sour **sauer**
sparkling wine **der Schaumwein(e)**
spirits **die Spirituosen** *(pl)*
sweet **süß**
tea **der Tee(s)**
water **das Wasser(-)**
whisky **der Whisky(s)**
white coffee **der Kaffee (mit Sahne)**
white wine **der Weißwein(e)**
wine **der Wein(e)**

Drinking out

bar **die Bar(s)**
barman/barmaid **der Kellner(-) [-in]**
beer hall **die Bierhalle(n)**
bottle **die Flasche(n)**
cafe **das Café(s)**
coffee bar **die Kaffeebar(s)**
cellar **der Keller(-)**
coffee shop **der Kaffeeladen(̈-)**
counter/bar **der Ladentisch(e), die Theke(n)**
I drink **ich trinke**
I get drunk **ich betrinke mich**
pub **die Kneipe(n)**
public house **das Lokal(e)**
refreshments **die Erfrischungen** *(pl)*
saucer **die Untertasse(n)**
sip **das Schlückchen(s)**
straw **der Trinkhalm(e)**
teaspoon **der Teelöffel(-)**
wine cellar **der Weinkeller(-)**
wine glass **das Weinglas(̈-er)**
wine tasting **die Weinprobe(n)**

Meals

appetizer/starter **die Vorspeise(n)**
breakfast **das Frühstück(e)**
course **der Gang(ᵈe)**
dessert **der Nachtisch** *(no pl)*
I dine **ich speise**
dinner **das Mittag-/Abendessen**
dish **das Gericht(e)**
I eat **ich esse**
I have/take **ich nehme**
I have a snack **ich esse eine Kleinigkeit**
I have breakfast **ich frühstücke**
I have dinner **ich esse zu Abend**
I have lunch **ich esse zu Mittag**
lunch **das Mittagessen(-)**
main **Haupt-**
meal **das Essen(-), die Mahlzeit(en)**
snack **der Imbiss(e)**
supper **das Abendessen(-)**

Eating out

I add up the bill **ich mache die Rechnung**
bill/check **die Rechnung(en)**
bowl **die Schüssel(n)**
charge **der Preis(e)**
I charge **ich verlange**
cheap **billig, preiswert**
I choose **ich wähle**
it costs **es kostet**
cup **die Tasse(n)**
I decide **ich entscheide mich**
dessert **der Nachtisch(e)**

expensive **teuer**
first course **der erste Gang(ᵈe)**
fixed price **der Festpreis(e)**
fork **die Gabel(n)**
glass **das Glas(ᵈer)**
inclusive **inklusiv, einschließlich**
knife **das Messer(-)**
main course **das Hauptgericht(e)**
menu **die Speisekarte(n)**
menu of day **das Tagesangebot(e), das Tagesmenü(s)**
napkin **die Serviette(n)**
I order **ich bestelle**
order **die Bestellung(en)**
place setting **das Gedeck(e)**
plate **der Teller(-)**
portion **die Portion(en)**
reservation **die Reservierung(en)**
I serve **ich bediene**
service **die Bedienung**
set menu **die Tageskarte(n)**
side-dish **die Beilage(n)**
spoon **der Löffel(-)**
table **der Tisch(e)**
tablecloth **die Tischdecke(n)**
I take away/out **ich nehme mit***
tip/gratuity **das Trinkgeld(er)**
I tip **ich gebe ein Trinkgeld**
toothpick **der Zahnstocher(-)**
tourist menu **das Touristenmenü(s)**
tray **das Tablett(s)**
waiter/waitress **der Kellner(-) [-in]**
wine list **die Weinkarte(n)**

---

cafeteria **das Selbstbedienungsrestaurant(s)**
canteen **die Kantine(n)**
hot-dog stall **die Wurstbude(n)**
ice-cream parlor **die Eisdiele(n)**
pizza parlor **die Pizzeria(s)**

pub/inn **das Wirtshaus(ᵈer)**
restaurant **das Restaurant(s)**
self-service **die Selbstbedienung(en)**
snack bar **die Imbissstube(n)**
take-away/out **zum Mitnehmen**

➤ COOKING, EATING 10d; BASIC FOODSTUFFS 9b

10b Fish & meat

Fish & seafood

anchovy **die Sardelle(n)**
carp **der Karpfen(-)**
clam **die Venusmuschel(n)**
cockle **die Herzmuschel(n)**
cod **der Kabeljau(e)**
crab **der Krebs(e)**
crayfish/crawfish **die Languste(n)**
eel **der Aal(e)**
fish **der Fisch(e)**
hake **der Seehecht(e)**
herring **der Hering(e)**
langouste **die Languste(n)**
lobster **der Hummer(-)**
mussels **die Miesmuschel(n)**
octopus **der Tintenfisch(e)**
oyster **die Auster(n)**
perch **der Flussbarsch(e)**
pike **der Hecht(e)**

plaice **die Scholle(n)**
prawn **die Krabbe(n)**
salmon **der Lachs(e)**
sardine **die Sardine(n)**
scampi **die Scampi** *(pl)*
seafood **die Meeresfrüchte** *(pl)*
shell **die Muschel(n)**
shellfish **die Meeresfrüchte** *(pl)*
shrimp **die Krabbe(n), die Garnele(n)**
snails **die Schnecke(n)**
sole **die Seezunge(n)**
squid **der Tintenfisch(e)**
sturgeon **der Stör(e)**
trout **die Forelle(n)**
tuna/tunny **der Thunfisch(e)**
turbot **der Steinbutt(e)**
whitebait **der Breitling(e)**

Where can we get a drink around here?	**Wo können wir hier in der Nähe etwas zu trinken bekommen?**
I would like a white wine with soda.	**Ich möchte einen Weißwein gespritzt.**
Two white coffees, please.	**Zweimal Kaffee mit Sahne bitte.**
I'd like a pot of coffee, please.	**Ich hätte gerne ein Kännchen Kaffee.**
Can I have a mineral water, please?	**Könnte ich bitte ein Mineralwasser bekommen?**
I'd rather have tuna than crab.	**Ich nehme lieber den Thunfisch als den Krebs.**
Would you prefer cod or sole?	**Möchtest du lieber Kabeljau oder Seezunge?**
One trout with boiled potatoes.	**Einmal Forelle mit Salzkartoffeln.**
Shall we try the chicken?	**Wollen wir das Hühnchen probieren?**
I'll have a rare steak with french fries and salad, please.	**Ich möchte bitte ein leicht durchgebratenes Steak mit Pommes frites und Salat.**

Meat & meat products

bacon **der Schweinespeck**
beef **das Rindfleisch**
beefburger **der Beefburger(-)**
bolognese **die Bolognese**
chop **das Kotelett(s)**
cold meats **der Aufschnitt** *(no pl)*
cold table **das kalte Büfett(s)**
cutlet **der/das Schnitzel(-)**
escalope **das Schnitzel(-)**
ham **der Schinken**
hamburger **der Hamburger(-)**
hare **der Hase(n)**
hotdog **der Hot-Dog(s)** *(wk)*, **das heiße Würstchen(-)**
kidney **die Niere(n)**
lamb **das Lammfleisch**
liver **die Leber**
liver sausage **die Leberwurst(-̈e)**
meat **das Fleisch**
meatball **der Fleischklops(-̈e)**
mixed grill **gemischte Grillplatte(n)**
mutton **das Hammelfleisch**
pate **die Pastete(n)**
pork **das Schweinefleisch**
rissole **die Frikadelle(n)**

salami **die Salami(s)**
sausage **die Wurst(-̈e)**
sirloin **das Rindfleischfilet(s)**
steak **das Steak(s)**
stew **der Eintopf(-̈e)**
veal **das Kalbfleisch**
venison **das Reh(e), das Wild** *(no pl)*

Poultry

chicken **das Hühnchen(-)**
duck **die Ente(n)**
goose **die Gans(-̈e)**
partridge **das Rebhuhn(-̈er)**
pheasant **der Fasan(e)**
pigeon **die Taube(n)**
poultry **das Geflügel**
quail **die Wachtel(n)**
turkey **die Pute(n)**

Egg dishes

egg **das Ei(er)**
boiled egg **das gekochte Ei(er)**
fried egg **das Spiegelei(er)**
omelette **das Omelett(s)**
poached egg **das pochierte Ei(er)**
scrambled egg **das Rührei(er)**

Traditional German dishes

die Gulaschsuppe beef soup
die Leberknödelsuppe liver dumpling soup
eingelegte Heringe pickled herrings
Forelle in Mandelbutter trout in almond butter
der Heringsalat herring salad
Lachs vom Grill grilled salmon
der Matjes young herring
der Rollmops(-̈e) pickled herring
der Salzhering(e) salted herring

der Aufschnitt cold, sliced meat
die Blutwurst blood sausage
die Bockwurst boiled sausage

das Eisbein mit Sauerkraut pork knuckle with sauerkraut
das Geschnetzelte meat cut in strips and stewed
der/das Gulasch beef stew
der Hasenpfeffer jugged hare
der Sauerbraten braised beef (marinaded in vinegar)
das Schweinekotelett(s) pork chop
die Thüringer Rostbratwurst fried sausage
das Wiener Schnitzel veal schnitzel
das Zigeunerschnitzel(-) veal in spicy sauce

FOOD & DRINK

10c Vegetables, fruit, & dessert

Vegetables

artichoke **die Artischocke(n)**
asparagus **der Spargel**
avocado **die Avocado(s)**
beans **die Bohne(n)**
beetroot **die Rote Bete(n)**
broccoli **der Brokkoli** *(pl)*
Brussels sprout **der Rosenkohl**
  (no pl)
cabbage **der Kohl** *(no pl)*, **der**
  Kohlkopf(-̈e)
carrot **die Mohrrübe(n)**
cauliflower **der Blumenkohl**
celeriac **der Knollensellerie**
celery **der Sellerie**
chickpea **die Kichererbse(n)**
chicory/endive **der Endivensalat**
corn **der Mais**
corn on the cob **der Maiskolben(-)**
cucumber **die Gurke(n)**
eggplant **die Aubergine(n)**
French bean **die Brechbohne(n)**
gherkin **die saure Gurke(n)**
haricot bean **die Gartenbohne(n)**
herb **das Kraut(-̈er)**
leek **der Lauch(e), der Porree(s)**
lentil **die Linse(n)**
lettuce **der Kopfsalat(e)**
marrow **der Kürbis(e)**
mushroom **der Pilz(e), der**
  Champignon(s)
onion **die Zwiebel(n)**
parsnip **die Pastinake(n)**
pea **die Erbse(n)**
pepper **die Paprikaschote(n)**

potato **die Kartoffel(n)**
  boiled **die Salzkartoffel(n)**
  jacket **die Pellkartoffel(n)**
  mashed **der Kartoffelbrei**
  roast **die Röstkartoffel(n)**
pumpkin **der Kürbis(e)**
radish **das Radieschen(-)**
rice **der Reis**
salad **der Salat(e)**
spinach **der Spinat**
sweetcorn **der Mais**
tomato **die Tomate(n)**
turnip **die Steckrübe(n)**
vegetable **das Gemüse(-)**
watercress **die Kresse(n)**
zucchini **die Zucchini** *(pl)*

Fruit

apple **der Apfel(-̈)**
apricot **die Aprikose(n)**
banana **die Banane(n)**
berry **die Beere(n)**
bilberry **die Heidelbeere(n)**
blackberry **die Brombeere(n)**
blackcurrant **die schwarze**
  Johannesbeere(n)
cherry **die Kirsche(n)**
chestnut **die Kastanie(n)**
coconut **die Kokosnuss(-̈e)**
currant **die Korinthe(n)**
date **die Dattel(n)**
fig **die Feige(n)**
fruit **die Frucht(-̈e), das Obst** *(no*
  pl)
fruit pie **die Obsttorte(n)**
gooseberry **die Stachelbeere(n)**

I want a tomato salad.
Does it have garlic in it?

Ich möchte einen Tomatensalat.
Ist da Knoblauch drin?

grape **die Weintraube(n)**
  bunch of grapes **die Weintraube(n)**
grapefuit **die Pampelmuse**
hazelnut **die Haselnuss(¨e)**
kiwifruit **die Kiwi(s)**
lemon **die Zitrone(n)**
lime **die Limone(n)**
melon **die Melone(n)**
nut **die Nuss(¨e)**
olive **die Olive(n)**
orange **die Orange(n)**
passion fruit **die Passionsfrucht(¨e)**
peach **der Pfirsich(e)**
peanut **die Erdnuss(¨e)**
pear **die Birne(n)**
peel **die Schale(n)**
I peel **ich schäle**
piece of fruit **das Obststück(e)**
pineapple **die Ananas(se)**
pip **der Kern(e)**
plum **die Pflaume(n)**
pomegranate **der Granatapfel(¨)**
prune **die Backpflaume(n)**
raisin **die Rosine(n)**
raspberry **die Himbeere(n)**
redcurrant **die rote Johannisbeere(n)**
rhubarb **der Rhabarber** *(no pl)*
stone **der Kern(e)**
strawberry **die Erdbeere(n)**
sultana **die Sultanine(n)**

tangerine **die Mandarine(n)**
walnut **die Walnuss(¨e)**

Dessert

biscuit/cookie **der Keks(e)**
blancmange **der Pudding(s)**
caramel **die Karamelle(n)**
chocolate **die Schokolade(n)**
chocolates **die Praline(n)**
cake **der Kuchen(-)**
cream **die Sahne, die Creme**
creme caramel **die Karamelcreme**
custard **die Vanillesoße(n)**
dessert **der Nachtisch**
flour **das Mehl**
fresh fruit **das Frischobst** *(no pl)*
fruit of the day/season **die Früchte der Saison**
fruit salad **der Fruchtsalat(e)**
gateau **die Torte(n)**
ice cream **das Eis**
mousse **die Mousse**
pancake **der Pfannkuchen(-)**
pastry **der Blätterteig(e)**
pie **die Pastete(n)**
pudding **der Pudding(s)**
stewed apple **das Apfelmus**
stewed fruit **das Kompott(e)**
sweet **der Nachtisch**
tart **das Obsttörtchen(-)**
vanilla **die Vanille**
whipped cream **die Schlagsahne**
yoghurt **der Joghurt(s)**

Traditional dishes

Bratkartoffeln fried potatoes
Butterreis fried rice
Himmel und Erde potato and apples with black pudding
Kartoffelklöße/knödel potato dumplings
Kartoffelpuffer(-) potato pancake
Sauerkraut pickled cabbage

Spätzle Swabian noodles
der Kaiserschmarrn pancake with raisins
die rote Grütze red fruit pudding
Salzburger Nockerln sweet soufle
Schwarzwälder Kirschtorte Black Forest Gateau
Zwetschenknödel plum dumplings

FOOD & DRINK

10d Cooking & eating

Food preparation

I bake **ich backe**
I beat **ich schlage**
I boil **ich koche**
bone **der Knochen(-)**
   bone *(of fish)* **die Gräte(n)**
I bone **ich entferne die Knochen/Gräten**
I braise **ich schmore**
in breadcrumbs **paniert**
breast **die Brust(¨e)**
I carve **ich tranchiere**
I chop **ich hacke**
I clear the table **ich räume den Tisch ab***
I cook **ich koche**
cooking/cuisine **die Küche, die Kochkunst**
creamed **-püree**
I cut **ich schneide**
I dice **ich schneide in Würfel**
diced **gehackt**
I dry up **ich trockne ab***
flavoring **der Geschmack** *(no pl)*
I fry **ich brate**

I garnish with **ich garniere mit** +dat
I grate **ich reibe**
gravy **die Bratensoße(n)**
I grill **ich grille**
grilled **vom Grill**
with ice **mit Eis**
ingredients **die Zutaten** *(pl)*
large **groß**
leg **die Keule(n)**
I lay/set the table **ich decke den Tisch**
I marinate **ich mariniere**
I mix **ich mixe**
I mix in **ich mische unter***
I peel **ich schäle**
I pour **ich gieße**
preparation **die Vorbereitung(en)**
I prepare **ich bereite vor***
rare **leicht durchgebraten**
recipe **das Rezept(e)**
roast **der Braten**
I roast **ich brate**
roasted **gebraten**
in sauce **in Soße(n)**

Potato cakes
Peel and grate 1 kg raw potatoes.

Add a grated onion, 50g flour and salt to the potatoes. Mix into a dough.

Heat plenty of cooking oil in a frying pan.
Put spoonfuls of the mixture into the hot pan and make about 4 cakes.
Fry golden brown on both sides and serve with stewed apples.

Kartoffelpuffer
1 kg rohe Kartoffeln schälen und grob reiben.

Eine geriebene Zwiebel, 50g Mehl, Salz unter den rohen Kartoffelbrei mischen und zu einem Teig verrühren.

In einer Pfanne reichlich Öl erhitzen.
Mit einem Löffel den Teig in die heiße Pfanne geben und etwa 4 Küchlein daraus formen. Die Reibekuchen auf beiden Seiten goldgelb backen und mit Apfelmus servieren.

I sift/sieve **ich siebe durch***
sliced **in Scheiben**
I spread **ich streiche**
stewed **gedämpft**
I stir **ich verrühre**
stuffed **gefüllt**
I toast **ich toaste**
toasted **getoastet, überbacken**
I wash up **ich wasche ab***
I weigh **ich wiege**
well done **durchgebraten**
I whip/whisk **ich schlage**

Eating

additive **der Zusatz(-̈e)**
appetite **der Appetit**
appetizing **appetitanregend**
bad **schlecht**
I bite **ich beiße**
bitter **bitter**
calorie **die Kalorie(n)**
  low-calorie **kalorienarm**
I chew **ich kaue**
cold **kalt**
delicious **lecker**
diet **die Diät**
  I'm on a diet **ich mache eine Schlankheitskur**
fatty/oily **fett**
food **die Lebensmittel** *(pl)*
fresh(ly) **frisch**
healthy **gesund**
I help myself **ich bediene mich**
hot **heiß**
hunger **der Hunger**

hungry **hungrig**
  I am hungry **ich bin hungrig, ich habe Hunger**
I like **ich mag**
mild **mild**
I offer **ich biete**
I pass (the salt) **ich reiche jdm. (das Salz)**
piece **das Stück(e)**
I provide **ich versorge (jdn.) mit** +dat, **ich besorge (etw.)**
salty **salzig**
I serve **ich serviere, ich trage auf***
serving **die Portion(en)**
sharp **scharf**
I smell **ich rieche**
soft **weich**
sour **sauer**
spicy **pikant, würzig**
stale *(bread)* **altbacken**
strong **stark, fest**
I swallow **ich (ver)schlucke**
sweet **süß**
taste **der Geschmack**
  it tastes of **es schmeckt nach** +dat
tasty **schmackhaft**
thirst **der Durst**
thirsty **durstig**
  I am thirsty **ich habe Durst**
I try **ich probiere, ich versuche**
vegan **der radikale Vegetarier(-) [-in]**
vegetarian **der Vegetarier(-) [-in]**
  vegetarian *(adj)* **vegetarisch**

Enjoy your meal!	**Guten Appetit!**
Did you enjoy it?	**Hat's geschmeckt?**
Dinner is served.	**Darf ich zu Tisch bitten?**
It tastes of lemon.	**Es schmeckt nach Zitrone.**
Pour the wine.	**Schenk' den Wein ein!**
Pass the salt, please.	**Reich` (mir) bitte das Salz rüber.**

➤ HOUSEHOLD ITEMS, BASIC FOODSTUFFS 9b

Sickness & health

11a Accidents & emergencies

accident **der Unfall(-̈e)**
alive **am Leben**
ambulance **der Krankenwagen(-)**
black eye **das blaue Auge**
bomb **die Bombe(n)**
break **der Bruch(-̈e)**
I break **ich breche**
I break my arm **ich breche mir den Arm**
I have broken my leg **ich habe mir ein Bein gebrochen**
break **die Bruchstelle(n)**
breakage **der Bruch(-̈e)**
broken **gebrochen**
bruise **der blaue Fleck(e/en)**
I bruise **ich bekomme einen blauen Fleck**
burn **die Verbrennung(en)**
I burn **ich verbrenne (mich)**

casualty **der/die Verunglückte (adj/n)**
casualty department **die Unfallstation(en)**
it catches fire **es fängt Feuer**
I collide **ich stoße zusammen***
collision **der Zusammenstoß(-̈e)**
I have cut my finger **ich habe mich in den Finger geschnitten**
I crash (into) **ich knalle (gegen +acc)**
I crush **ich quetsche**
dead **tot**
death **der Tod, der Todesfall(-̈e)**
I die **ich sterbe**
emergency **der Notfall(-̈e)**
emergency department **die Notaufnahme(en)**
emergency exit **der Notausgang(-̈e)**

– What's happened? | – **Was ist los?**

– There has been an accident! We need an ambulance quickly! | – **Es ist ein Unfall passiert! Wir brauchen schnellstens einen Krankenwagen!**

Call the fire department! | **Rufen Sie die Feuerwehr!**

It was his fault, not mine! | **Es war seine Schuld, nicht meine!**

My friend is injured! Are you a doctor? Where's the nearest hospital? | **Mein Freund ist verletzt! Sind Sie Arzt? Wo befindet sich das nächste Krankenhaus?**

Calm down! | **Beruhigen Sie sich!**

emergency services **der Notdienst(e)**

it explodes **es explodiert**

explosion **die Explosion(en)**

I extinguish **ich lösche**

I fasten my seatbelt **ich schnalle mich an***

fatal **tödlich**

fire **der Brand(-̈e)**

fire brigade **die Feuerwehr**

fire engine **das Feuerwehrauto(s)**

fire extinguisher **der Feuerlöscher(-)**

fireman **der Feuerwehrmann(-̈er)**

first aid **die erste Hilfe**

graze **die Schramme(n)**

I graze **ich schramme mich**

I have an accident **ich habe einen Unfall**

hospital **das Krankenhaus(-̈er)**

impact **der Zusammenprall(-̈e)**

incident **der Vor-/Zwischenfall(-̈e)**

I injure **ich verletze**

injury **die Verletzung(en)**

injured **verletzt**

insurance **die Versicherung(en)**

I insure **ich versichere**

I kill **ich töte**

killed **getötet**

life belt **der Rettungsgurt(e)**

life jacket **die Schwimmweste(n)**

oxygen **der Sauerstoff**

paramedic **der Sanitäter(-) [-in]**

I recover consciousness **ich komme wieder zu mir**

I rescue **ich rette**

rescue **die Rettung(en)**

rescue services **der Rettungsdienst(e)**

I run over **ich überfahre**

I rush **ich renne, ich eile**

safe **sicher**

safe and sound **gesund und wohlbehalten**

safety belt **der Sicherheitsgurt(e)**

I save **ich rette**

seat belt **der Sitzgurt(e)**

terrorist attack **das Terroristenattentat(e)**

third party **die dritte Person(en)**

witness **der Zeuge(n)** *(wk)* **[-in]**

Fasten safety belts.	**Bitte anschnallen!**
I think I have broken my arm. It hurts a lot.	**Ich glaube, ich habe mir den Arm gebrochen. Es tut sehr weh.**
Sylvia has cut her hand badly.	**Sylvia hat sich tief in die Hand geschnitten.**
Statistics show that the most likely place for accidents is in the home.	**Laut Statistik sollen die meisten Unfälle zu Hause passieren.**

➤ MEDICAL TREATMENT 11c

11b Illness & disability

arthritis   **die Arthritis**
I am asleep   **ich schlafe**
asthma   **das Asthma**
awake   **wach**
bacillus   **der Bazillus (-en)**
bacteria   **die Bakterie(n)**
I bleed   **ich blute**
blind   **blind**
blood   **das Blut**
breath   **der Atem, der Atemzug(̈-e)**
I breathe   **ich atme**
breathless   **atemlos**
catarrh   **der Katarrh(e)**
I catch a cold   **ich erkälte mich**
circulatory problem   **die Kreislaufstörung(en)**
constipated   **verstopft**
constipation   **die Verstopfung(en)**
convalescence   **die Genesung**
I am convalescing   **ich genese**
cough   **der Husten**
I cough   **ich huste**
I cry   **ich weine**
I cut   **ich schneide**
dead   **tot**
deaf   **taub**

deafness   **die Taubheit**
death   **der Tod(̈-e)**
depressed   **deprimiert**
depression   **die Depression(en)**
diarrhea   **der Durchfall**
I die   **ich sterbe**
diet   **die Diät**
disabled   **behindert**
disease   **die Krankheit(en)**
dizziness   **das Schwindelgefühl(e)**
dizzy   **schwindelig**
Down's syndrome   **das Down-Syndrom**
drug   **die Droge(n), die Arznei(en)**
drugged   **betäubt**
drunk   **betrunken**
dumb   **stumm**
earache   **die Ohrenschmerzen** *(pl)*
I fall   **ich falle**
I feel   **ich fühle mich, mir ist ...**
fever   **das Fieber**
I'm feverish   **ich habe Fieber**
flu   **die Grippe(n)**
I got better   **mir geht es besser**
I have an operation   **ich habe eine Operation**

I don't feel well. I think I've got the flu.

Ich fühle mich nicht wohl. Ich glaube, ich habe eine Grippe.

I've had a sore throat since yesterday, and now I have a headache.

Seit gestern tut mir der Hals weh, und jetzt habe ich Kopfschmerzen.

Your boss must be sick too. He's been sneezing all morning.

Ihr Chef muss auch krank sein. Er niest schon den ganzen Morgen.

If you have a fever, you should stay in bed.

Wenn Sie Fieber haben, sollten Sie im Bett bleiben.

I have a cold **ich habe eine Erkältung**

I have a temperature **ich habe Fieber**

headache **die Kopfschmerzen** *(pl)*

health **die Gesundheit**

healthy **gesund**

heart attack **der Herzanfall(ᐨe), der Herzinfarkt(e)**

high blood pressure **der Bluthochdruck**

hurt **der Schmerz(en)**

hurt *(adj)* **verletzt**

I hurt **es tut mir weh**

it hurts **es schmerzt**

I am ill/sick **ich bin krank**

illness **die Krankheit(en)**

I live **ich lebe**

I look ill **Ich sehe krank aus***

mental illness **die Geisteskrankheit(en)**

mentally sick **geisteskrank**

microbe **die Mikrobe(n)**

migraine **die Migräne(n)**

nervous breakdown **der Nervenzusammenbruch(ᐨe)**

overdose **die Überdosis (-en)**

pain **der Schmerz(en)**

painful **schmerzhaft**

pale **blass, bleich**

pregnancy **die Schwangerschaft(en)**

I recover/get well **ich erhole mich**

recovery **die Erholung(en)**

rheumatism **der Rheumatismus**

I sneeze **ich niese**

sore throat **die Halsschmerzen** *(pl)*

sting **der Stich(e)**

it stings **es sticht**

stomach **der Magen(-ᐨ)**

stomach ache **die Magen-/ Bauchschmerzen** *(pl)*

stomach upset **die Magenverstimmung(en)**

I take drugs **ich nehme Medikamente**

temperature **die Temperatur(en)**

I vomit **ich übergebe mich**

Where does it hurt? **Wo tut es weh?**

I wound **ich verletze**

wounded **verletzt**

My children have diarrhea.

Meine Kinder haben Durchfall.

I don't know what was wrong with Max last week. He looked very ill, but he seems to have recovered.

Ich weiß nicht, was letzte Woche mit Max los war. Er sah sehr krank aus, aber er scheint sich wieder erholt zu haben.

I can't breathe very well

Ich kann nur schwer atmen.

My husband suffers from high blood-pressure.

Mein Mann leidet an Bluthochdruck.

➤ PARTS OF THE BODY App.5a

11c Medical treatment

antibiotic **das Antibiotikum (-a)**
appointment **der Termin(e)**
bandage **der Verband(ᵋe)**
blood **das Blut**
blood test **die Blutprobe(n)**
blood pressure **der Blutdruck**
capsule **die Kapsel(n)**
chemotherapy **die Chemotherapie(n)**
cure **die Heilung(en)**
danger to life **die Lebensgefahr(en)**
dangerous **gefährlich**
death **der Tod(e)**
I diet **ich halte eine Diät**
doctor (Dr.) **der Arzt(ᵋe), die Ärztin(nen)**
dressing **der Verband(ᵋe)**
drop **der Tropfen(-)**
drug **die Arznei(en)**
I examine **ich untersuche**
examination **die Untersuchung(en)**
I fill **ich fülle**
I have **ich habe**
heating **die Heizung(en)**
hospital **das Krankenhaus(ᵋer)**
I improve **ich erhole mich**
I inject **ich spritze**
injection **die Spritze(n)**

insurance certificate **der Krankenschein(e)**
intensive care **die Intensivpflege(n)**
I look after **ich pflege**
medical **medizinisch**
medicine **die Medizin, das Medikament(e), das Mittel(-)**
alternative medicine **die alternative Medizin**
midwife **die Hebamme(n)**
nurse **die Krankenschwester(n), der Krankenpfleger(-)**
I nurse **ich pflege**
I operate **ich operiere**
operation **die Operation(en)**
I have an operation **ich lasse mich operieren**
operating theater/room **der Operationsaal (-säle)**
pastille **die Pastille(n)**
patient **der Patient(en)** *(wk)* **[-in]**
pharmacist **der Apotheker(-) [-in]**
physiotherapy **die Physiotherapie(n)**
physiotherapist **der Physiotherapeut(en)** *(wk)* **[-in]**
pill **die Tablette(n), die Pille(n)**
plaster (of Paris) **der Gipsverband(ᵋe)**

Call a doctor! This man needs help immediately!

Rufen Sie einen Arzt! Dieser Mann braucht sofort Hilfe!

Lisas mother is having an operation next week, and afterwards she has to go to physiotherapy.

Lisas Mutter lässt sich nächste Woche operieren, und danach muss sie zur Physiotherapie gehen.

I'll prescribe an antibiotic for you that you have to take twice a day for five days.

Ich verschreibe Ihnen ein Antibiotikum, das Sie fünf Tage zweimal täglich nehmen müssen.

Ernst has never had an X-ray.

Ernst wurde noch nie geröntgt.

I prescribe **ich verschreibe**
prescription **das Rezept(e)**
radio therapy **die Röntgentherapie(n)**
service **der Dienst(e)**
I set *(in plaster)* **ich richte ein*, ich gipse**
smear test **der Abstrich(e)**
spa resort **der Kur- und Erholungsort(e)**
specialist **der Facharzt(-̈e)**
stitch **der Faden(-̈)**
sticking plaster/Bandaid® **das Heftpflaster(-)**
surgery **die Chirurgie**
syringe **die Spritze(n)**
tablet **die Tablette(n)**
therapeutic **therapeutisch**
therapy **die Therapie(n)**
therapist **der Therapeut(en)** *(wk)* [-in]
thermometer **das Thermometer(-)**
transfusion **die Transfusion(en)**
I treat **ich behandle**
treatment **die Behandlung(en)**
ward **die (Kranken)station(en)**
wound **die Wunde(n)**
X-ray **die Röntgenaufnahme(n)**
I X-ray **ich röntge**

Dentist & optician

abscess **der Abszess(e)**
bifocals **die Bifokalbrille(n)**

contact lens **die Kontaktlinse(n)**
    hard/soft lenses **harte/weiche Linsen**
contact lens fluid **die Flüssigkeit für Kontaktlinsen**
crown **die Krone(n)**
dental treatment **die zahnärtliche Behandlung(en)**
dentist **der Zahnarzt(-̈e) [-in]**
dentures **das Gebiss(e)**
I drill **ich bohre**
I extract **ich ziehe heraus***
eye **das Auge(n)**
eyesight **die Sehkraft**
eye test **der Augentest(e)**
false teeth **das künstliche Gebiss**
far-sighted **weitsichtig**
I fill **ich plombiere**
filling **die Plombe(n)**
frame **das Gestell(e)**
glasses **die Brille(n)**
gum **das Zahnfleisch** *(no pl)*
lens **die Linse(n)**
near-sighted **kurzsichtig**
optician **der Optiker(-)**
pupil **die Pupille(n)**
spectacle case **das Brillenetui(s)**
stye **das Gerstenkorn(-̈er)**
sunglasses **die Sonnenbrille(n)**
tinted **dunkel**
tooth **der Zahn(-̈e)**
toothache **die Zahnschmerzen** *(pl)*

In order to determine what's wrong with you, we have to take a blood test.

Wir müssen Ihnen Blut abnehmen, um festzustellen was mit Ihnen nicht in Ordnung ist.

I have a terrible toothache, and I urgently need an appointment with Dr. Brenner.

Ich habe fürchterliche Zahnschmerzen, und ich brauche dringend einen Termin bei Herrn Dr. Brenner.

Detlef has been working in the city hospital as a nurse since last year.

Detlef arbeitet seit letztem Jahr im städtischen Krankenhaus als Krankenpfleger.

➤ DISEASES & ILLNESSES App.11b; PARTS OF THE BODY App.5b

SICKNESS & HEALTH

11d Health & hygiene

Physical state

ache der Schmerz(en)
aching schmerzen
  aching (adj) schmerzend
all right/OK in Ordnung
I am asleep ich schlafe
awake wach
blister die Blase(n)
boil das Furunkel(-)
bruise der blaue Fleck(en)
I am cold mir ist kalt
comfort der Trost
I comfort ich tröste
comfortable (un-) (un)bequem
corn das Hühnerauge(n)
discomfort die Beschwerden (pl)
drowsiness die Schläfrigkeit
drowsy schläfrig
faint ohnmächtig
I faint ich falle in Ohnmacht
I feel ich fühle mich, mir ist …
I am hot mir ist warm
I get fat ich werde dick, ich
  nehme zu*
I get fit ich trimme mich
I get thin ich werde mager/dünn
hunger der Hunger
hungry hungrig
  I am hungry ich habe Hunger
it hurts es tut weh
ill/sick krank
I lie down ich lege mich hin*
I look ich sehe, ich gucke
I lose weight ich nehme ab*
I put on weight ich nehme zu*
queasy übel, schlecht
I relax ich ruhe mich aus*
I rest/have a rest ich mache eine
  Pause
I sleep ich schlafe
sleepy schläfrig
I slim ich mache eine
  Schlanksheitskur
strange komisch, sonderbar
thirst der Durst

thirsty durstig
I am thirsty ich bin durstig, ich
  habe Durst
tired müde
I am tired ich bin müde
tiredness die Müdigkeit
under the weather angeschlagen
unwell nicht wohl
I wake up ich wache auf*
well wohl
well-being das Wohlbefinden

Beauty & hygiene

acne die Akne
bath das Bad(¨er)
beauty die Schönheit
beauty contest der
  Schönheitswettbewerb
beauty queen die
  Schönheitskönigin(nen)
beauty salon/parlor der
  Schönheitssalon(s)
beauty specialist der
  Kosmetiker(-) [-in]
beauty treatment die kosmetische
  Behandlung
body odor der (üble)
  Körpergeruch
I burp/belch ich rülpse
I brush ich bürste
brush die Bürste(n)
I clean ich putze
clean sauber
I clean my teeth ich putze mir die
  Zähne
comb der Kamm(¨e)
I comb my hair ich kämme meine
  Haare
complexion der Teint
condom das Kondom(e)
contraceptive das
  Verhütungsmittel(-)
contraception die
  Empfängnisverhütung(en)
cosmetics die Kosmetika (pl)

cosmetic/plastic surgery **die Schönheitsoperation(en)**
I cut **ich schneide**
dandruff **die Schuppen** *(pl)*
dirty **schmutzig**
electric razor **der elektrische Rasierapparat(e)**
I exercise **ich bewege mich**
exercise bike **der Heimtrainer(-)**
face-lift **das Facelift(s)**
face-pack **die Gesichtspackung(en)**
fit (un-) **(nicht) gesund**
fitness **die Fitness**
flea **der Floh(ˉe)**
hair **das Haar(e)**
  unwanted hair **das unerwünschte Haar**
hairbrush **die Haarbürste(n)**
haircut **der Haarschnitt(e)**
I have my hair cut **ich lasse mir die Haare schneiden**
hairdo **die Frisur(en)**
hairdryer **der Fön(e)®**
head lice **die Kopfläuse** *(pl)*
healthy *(person)* **gesund**
hygiene **die Hygiene**
hygienic **hygienisch**
laundry *(establishment)* **die Wäscherei(en)**
  laundry *(linen)* **die Wäsche**
I'm losing my hair **die Haare fallen mir aus***
I make up **ich schminke mich**
I menstruate **ich menstruiere**
menstruation **die Menstruation(en)**

mole **der Leberfleck(e)**
nailbrush **die Nagelbürste(n)**
period **die Periode(n)**
period pains **die Menstruationsschmerzen** *(pl)*
permanent wave **die Dauerwelle(n)**
pill **die Pille(n)**
razor **der Rasierer(-)**
I remove unwanted hair **ich enthaare**
sanitary **hygienisch**
sanitary towel **die Monatsbinde(n)**
scissors **die Schere(n)**
shampoo **das Shampoo(s)**
I shave **ich rasiere mich**
shower **die Dusche(n)**
soap **die Seife(n)**
spot **der Fleck(en)**
spotty **fleckig**
smell *(odor)* **der Geruch(ˉe)**
I smell (bad) **ich rieche (übel)**
sweat **der Schweiß**
I sweat **ich schwitze**
I take a bath **ich nehme ein Bad**
I take a shower **ich dusche (mich)**
tampon **der Tampon(s)**
toothbrush **die Zahnbürste(n)**
toothpaste **die Zahnpasta(s)**
towel **das Handtuch(ˉer)**
wart **die Warze(n)**
I wash **ich wasche mich**
washcloth **der Waschlappen(-)**
wig **die Perücke(n)**

I need a haircut. But please don't cut it too short, just a little shorter in the back and on the sides.

Ich brauche einen Haarschnitt. Aber bitte schneiden Sie es nicht zu kurz, nur hinten und an den Seiten etwas kürzer.

Rainer bought an exercise bike, because he really wants to lose weight now.

Rainer hat sich einen Heimtrainer gekauft, weil er jetzt unbedingt abnehmen will.

➤ TOILETRIES 9b

12 Social issues

12a Society

abnormal **anormal, abnormal**
alternative **alternativ**
amenity **die Unterhaltungsmöglichkeit(en)**
anonymous **anonym**
attitude **die Einstellung(en)**
available **verfügbar**
   it is available **es steht zur Verfügung**
basic **grundlegend**
basis **die Grundlage(n)**
burden **die Last(en)**
campaign **die Initiative(n)**
care **die Sorge, die Fürsorge**
cause **die Ursache(n)**
change **der Wandel(-)**
circumstance **der Umstand(ˉe)**
community **die Gemeinde(n), die Gemeinschaft(en)**
compulsory **Pflicht-**
contribution **der Beitrag(ˉe)**
cost **die Kosten** *(pl)***, die Unkosten** *(pl)*
I counsel **ich berate**
counselling **die (soziale) Beratung**
criterion **das Kriterium (-ien)**
dependence **die Abhängigkeit**
dependent **abhängig**
depressed **deprimiert**
depression **die Depression(en)**
deprived **benachteiligt, depriviert**
difficulty **die Schwierigkeit(en)**
effect **die Auswirkung(en)**
effective **wirksam**
fact **die Tatsache(n)**
finance **die Finanzen** *(pl)*
financial **finanziell**
frustrated **frustriert**
frustration **die Frustration(en)**
guidance **die Orientierung(en)**

increase **die Zunahme**
inner city **die Innenstadt(ˉe)**
institution **die Anstalt(en)**
loneliness **die Einsamkeit**
lonely **einsam**
long-term **langfristig**
measure **die Maßnahme(n)**
negative **negativ**
normal **normal**
policy **die Politik**
   policies **die Politik**
positive **positiv**
power **die Macht(ˉe)**
prestige **das Prestige** *(no pl)*
problem **das Problem(e)**
protest movement **die Protestbewegung(en)**
I provide (with) **ich versorge jdn. (mit** +dat)
provision **die Versorgung**
psychological **psychologisch**
quality of life **die Lebensqualität**
question/issue **die Frage(n)**
rate **die Rate(n), die Quote(n)**
responsibility **die Verantwortung(en)**
responsible (ir-) **(un)verantwortlich**
result **die Folge(n)**
right **das Recht(e)**
role **die Rolle(n)**
rural **ländlich**
scarcity **der Mangel(ˉ)**
scheme **die Maßnahme(n)**
I belong on the scrap heap **ich gehöre zum alten Eisen**
secure (in-) **(un)sicher**
security (in-) **die (Un)sicherheit(en)**
self-esteem **die Selbstachtung**

short-term **kurzfristig**
situation **die Lage(n)**
social **sozial**
society **die Gesellschaft(en)**
stable (un-) **(in)stabil**
stability (in-) **die (In-)Stabilität**
statistics **die Statistik(en)**
status **der Status**
stigma **das Brandmal(e)**
stress **der Stress (no pl.)**
stressful **stressig**
structure **die Struktur(en), der Aufbau**
superfluous **überflüssig**
support **die Unterstützung(en)**
urban **Stadt-**
urge to conform **der Anpassungsdruck**
value **der Wert(e)**

Some useful verbs

I adapt/conform **ich passe mich +dat an***
it affects **es beeinflusst**
I afford **ich leiste mir (etw.)**
I alienate **ich entfremde**
I am ashamed **ich schäme mich**
I break down **ich breche zusammen***
I campaign **ich kämpfe**
I care for **ich sorge für +acc**
I cause **ich verursache**
it changes **es wandelt sich**

I contribute **ich trage zu +dat bei***
I cope **ich komme gut zurecht***
I depend on **ich hänge von +dat ab***
I deprive **ich benachteilige**
I discourage **ich entmutige**
I dominate **ich beherrsche, ich dominiere**
I encourage **ich ermutige**
I help **ich helfe +dat**
I increase **ich vergrößere**
I lack **es mangelt mir an +dat**
I look after **ich kümmere mich um +acc**
I need **ich brauche**
I neglect **ich vernachlässige**
I owe **ich bin jdm. etw. schuldig**
I protest **ich protestiere**
I provide for **ich versorge jdn. mit +dat**
I put up with **ich finde mich ab mit +dat**
I rely on **ich bin auf jdn. angewiesen.**
I respect **ich achte, respektiere**
I share **ich teile**
I solve **ich löse**
I suffer from **ich leide an +dat**
I support **ich unterstütze**
I tackle **ich befasse mich mit +dat**
I value **ich schätze**

There are immense social problems in the inner city.	**Es gibt ungeheuere Sozialprobleme der Innerstadt.**
Since our cousin lost his job, he's financially dependent on his father.	**Seitdem unser Cousin seine Stelle verloren hat, ist er finanziell von seinem Vater abhängig.**
What measure did the police take against the demonstrations in the city?	**Welche Maßnahmen hat die Polizei gegen die Demonstrationen in der Stadt ergriffen?**

➤ ADDICTION & VIOLENCE 12d; PREJUDICE 12e

SOCIAL ISSUES

12b Social services & poverty

Social services

aid   die Sozialhilfe
agency   die Agentur(en)
authority   die Gemeinde(n)
benefit   die Unterstützung(en)
I benefit   ich profitiere
charity   die
   Wohlfahrtsorganisation(en)
   I give to charity   ich spende
claim   der Anspruch(-̈e), der
   Antrag(-̈e)
I claim   ich beantrage
claimant   der Antragsteller(-)
disability   die Arbeitsunfähigkeit
disabled   arbeitsunfähig
eligible (for)   berechtigt zu +dat
I am eligible for   ich habe
   Anspruch auf +acc
frail   schwach
frailty   die Schwäche(n)
grant   der Zuschuss(-̈e)
handicap   die Behinderung(en)
handicapped   behindert
ill health   die schlechte Gesundheit
income support   die Beihilfe(n)
loan   die Anleihe(n)
maintenance   die finanzielle
   Unterstützung(en)
official   amtlich, offiziell
reception center   das
   Aufnahmelager(-)

Red Cross   das Rote Kreuz
refuge   der Zufluchtsort(e)
refugee   der Flüchtling(e)
I register   ich melde mich an*
registration   die Anmeldung(en)
Salvation Army   die Heilsarmee
service   der Dienst(e)
social security   die soziale
   Sicherheit
social service   der Sozialdienst(e)
social worker   der Sozialarbeiter(-)
   [-in]
support   die Hilfe
I support   ich unterstütze
welfare   die Wohlfahrt

Wealth & poverty

I beg   ich bettele
beggar   der Bettler(-) [-in]
I am broke   ich bin abgebrannt
debt   die Schuld(en)
   I am in debt   ich habe Schulden
deprivation   die Benachteiligung
deprived   benachteiligt
destitute   mittellos
living standards   der
   Lebensstandard(s)
millionaire   der Millionär(e)
need   die Not(-̈e)
   those in need   die
   Notleidenden (adj/n) (pl)

The physically handicapped can
apply for help.

**Die körperlich Behinderten
können einen Antrag auf Hilfe
stellen.**

Not everyone gets unemployment
benefits.

**Nicht jeder bekommt
Arbeitslosenunterstützung.**

Mr. Karsten is eligible for his
pension beginning January 1.

**Herr Karsten kann ab 1. Januar
seine Rente beziehen.**

---

nutrition **die Ernährung**
poor **arm**
poverty **die Armut**
rich **reich**
subsistence **der Lebensunterhalt**
tramp/vagrant **der Landstreicher(-) [-in]**
wealth **der Reichtum(¨-er), der Wohlstand**
well off **wohlhabend**

Unemployment

I cut back *(on jobs)* **ich baue ab***
I dismiss **ich entlasse**
dole/unemployment benefits **das Arbeitslosengeld**
I employ **ich beschäftige**
employee **der Arbeitnehmer(-) [-in]**
employer **der Arbeitgeber(-) [-in]**
employment **die Arbeit**
employment office **das Arbeitsamt(¨-er)**
full-time **Vollzeit-**
I give notice **ich kündige jdm.**
income support **die Sozialhilfe**
job **der Job(s), die Arbeit, der Arbeitsplatz(¨-e)**
job/workplace **die Arbeitsstelle(n)**
job-sharing **das Jobsharing**
job creation scheme **die Arbeits-beschaffungsmaßnahme(n)**

long-term unemployed **der/die Langzeitarbeitslose** *(adj/n)*
occupation **der Beruf(e)**
occupational **beruflich**
part-time **Teilzeit-**
qualification **die Qualifikation(en)**
qualified **qualifiziert**
redundancy/layoff **die Entlassung(en)**
redundant/laid off **arbeitslos**
I am made redundant/I was layed off **mir wird/wurde gekündigt**
retraining **die Umschulung(en)**
I am retrained **ich lasse mich umschulen**
short-time work **die Kurzarbeit**
skill **die Fertigkeit(en)**
staffing **die Arbeitskräfte** *(pl)*
I take on **ich stelle an***
training scheme/program **die Ausbildungsmaßnahme(n)**
unemployed **arbeitslos**
unemployment figure **die Arbeitslosenzahl(en)**
unemployment rate **die Arbeitslosenrate(n)**
unskilled worker **der Hilfsarbeiter(-)**
vacancy **die freie/offene Stelle(n)**
wage costs **die Lohnkosten** *(pl)*

– How high is the level of unemployment? – In the South it is about 15%.
– Can people retrain or work part-time?

– Some yes, but many retire early.

My brother was laid off some months ago. Now he has to report every two weeks to the job centre/employment office.

– **Wie hoch ist die Arbeitslosenrate? – Im Süden ist sie ungefähr 15%.**
– **Können die Leute umgeschult werden oder Teilzeitarbeit machen?**
Manche ja, aber viele treten vorzeitig in den Ruhestand.
Mein Bruder hat vor einigen Monaten seine Arbeitsstelle verloren. Jetzt muss er sich alle zwei Wochen beim Arbeitsamt melden.

➤ JOB APPLICATION 14c

12c Housing & homelessness

accommodation **die Unterkunft**
apartment **die Wohnung(en)**
apartment share **die Wohngemeinschaft(en)**
I build **ich baue**
building **das Gebäude(-)**
comfortable/homey **gemütlich**
I commute **ich pendle**
commuter **der Pendler(-)**
delapidated **baufällig**
I demolish **ich reiße ab***
demolition **der Abbruch**
it deteriorates **es verfällt**
digs/unfurnished rooms **die Bude(n)**
drab **trist, traurig**
estate/real estate agent **der Immobilienmakler(-)**
it falls down **es stürzt ab***
house **das Haus(-̈er)**

council house **die Sozialwohnung(en)**
housing **die Wohnungen** *(pl)*
housing association **die Wohnungsbaugesellschaft(en)**
housing policy **die Wohnungspolitik**
inner city **die Innenstadt(-̈e)**
landlord **der Vermieter(-)**
I let/rent out **ich vermiete**
I maintain **ich halte instand**
I modernize **ich modernisiere**
I move (house) **ich ziehe um***
own **eigen**
public housing **die Sozialwohnung(en)**
redevelopment **die Sanierung**
I renovate **ich saniere**
I rent **ich miete**
rent **die Miete(n)**

– Will the downtown area really be redeveloped?

—**Wird die Stadtmitte wirklich saniert?**

– Yes, some of the old houses will be torn down. But most of them will be restored or renovated.

—**Ja, einige der alten Hauser werden abgerissen. Aber die meisten werden restauriert oder renoviert.**

– Are you going to buy your own home soon?

—**Wollen Sie bald ein Eigenheim kaufen?**

– Yes, we are trying to get a mortgage. We have found an older property that we want to modernize.

—**Ja, wir versuchen eine Hypothek aufsunehmen. Wir haben ein alteres Haus gefunden, das wir modernisieren wollen.**

At the moment we are renting an apartment.

Zur Zeit mieten wir eine Wohnung.

It is impossible to find a furnished apartment to rent.

Es ist unmoglich, eine moblierte Mietwohnung zu finden.

I repair   **ich repariere**
repair   **die Reparatur(en)**
shelter   **die Unterkunft(⁻e)**
speculator   **der Spekulant(en)** *(wk)*
squalid   **elend**
squatter   **der Hausbesetzer(-) [-in]**
suburb   **der Vorort(e)**
tenant   **der Mieter(-) [-in]**
town planning   **die Stadtplanung**
urban   **städtisch**
urban renewal   **die Stadterneuerung**

Housing shortage

camp   **das Lager(-)**
container town   **die Containerstadt(⁻e)**
delapidated   **verfallen**
I evict   **ich zwinge jmdn. zur Räumung**

homeless   **obdachlos**
homelessness   **die Obdachlosigkeit**
hostel   **das Wohnheim(e)**
housing shortage   **die Wohnungsnot**
living conditions   **die Wohnverhältnisse** *(pl)*
overcrowded   **überfüllt**
overcrowding   **die Überfüllung**
I pull down   **ich reiße ab***
shanty town   **das Armenviertel(-)**
I sleep rough   **ich übernachte im Freien**
slum   **die Baracke(n)**
slum clearance   **die Slumsanierung(en)**
squalid   **dreckig**
I squat   **ich besetze ein Haus**
it stands empty   **es steht leer**
wasteland   **das Ödland**

There's such a housing shortage that they've built a container town on the outskirts.

Wir haben solch eine Wohnungsnot, dass man eine Containerstadt am Stadtrand gebaut hat.

– Is the municipality still building public housing?–

–Baut die Stadtbehörde immer noch Sozialwohnungen?

SOCIAL ISSUES

12d Addiction & violence

abuse **der Missbrauch(¨e)**
I abuse **ich missbrauche**
act of violence **die Gewalttat(en)**
addict **der/die Abhängige** *(adj/n)*
addiction **die (Drogen)Abhängigkeit**
addictive **zur Abhängigkeit führend**
aggression **die Aggression(en), die Aggressivität(en)**
aggressive **aggressiv**
alcohol **der Alkohol**
alcoholic **der Alkoholiker(-) [-in]**
alcoholism **der Alkoholismus**
anger **die Wut**
angry **wütend**
I attack **ich greife an***
attack **der Angriff(e), das Attentat(e)**
I beat up **ich verprügele, ich schlage zusammen***
I bully **ich tyrannisiere**
bully **der Schlägertyp(en)**
consumption **der Konsum**
I cure, I dry out **ich entwöhne mich**
dangerous **gefährlich**
I drink **ich trinke**
I get drunk **ich betrinke mich**

drunk **betrunken**
drunken driving **die Trunkenheit am Steuer**
effect **die Wirkung(en)**
fatal **tödlich**
fear **die Angst(¨e)**
I fear **ich habe Angst (vor** +dat)
force **die Gewalt**
gang **die Bande(n)**
I harass **ich schikaniere, ich belästige**
hooligan **der Rowdy (-ies)**
hostile **feindlich**
hostility **die Feindseligkeit(en)**
insult **die Beleidigung(en)**
I insult **ich beleidige**
intoxication **der Rausch**
legal (il-) **(il)legal**
I legalize **ich gebe frei***
I mug **ich überfalle**
mugger **der Straßenräuber(-)**
nervous **ängstlich**
nervousness **die Ängstlichkeit**
pimp **der Zuhälter(-)**
porno **der Porno(s)**
pornography **die Porno(graphie)**
prostitution **die Prostitution**
punk **der Punk(s)**

Many alcoholics meet in the inner city and are often aggressive.

Viele Alkoholiker treffen sich in der Innenstadt und verhalten sich oft sehr aggressiv.

Older people and women are sometimes afraid to go out alone.

Ältere Leute und Frauen haben manchmal Angst, allein auszugehen.

Some young people have a drug problem. They start by sniffing solvents, or by taking soft drugs.

Einige Jugendliche haben ein Drogenproblem. Es fängt damit an, dass sie schnüffeln oder weiche Drogen nehmen.

rehabilitation **die Rehabilitation**
I revert **ich falle zurück***
rocker **der Rocker(-)**
I seduce **ich verführe**
sexual harassment **die sexuelle Belästigung(en)**
skinhead **der Skinhead(s)**
I smoke **ich rauche**
stimulant **das Anregungsmittel(-)**
stimulation **der Rausch**
I terrorize **ich terrorisiere**
I threaten **ich bedrohe**
thug **der Schlägertyp(en)**
vandal **der Vandale(n)** *(wk)*
vandalism **der Vandalismus**
victim **das Opfer(-)**
violent **gewalttätig**
act of violence **die Gewalttat(en)**

Drugs

addicted to drugs **süchtig**
cannabis **das Marihuana**
cocaine **das Kokain**
crack **das Crack**
I deal **ich handle**
dealer **der Dealer(-)**
drug **das Rauschmittel(-), die Droge(n)**

drug scene **die Drogenszene**
drug traffic **der Drogenhandel**
I get infected **ich infiziere mich**
glue **der Klebstoff(e)**
hard drug **die harte Droge(n)**
hashish **das Haschisch, das Heu**
I have a fix **ich setze mir einen Schuss**
heroin **das Heroin**
I inject **ich spritze**
junkie **der Fixer(-)**
I kick *(the habit)* **ich komme los von** (+ dative)
LSD **das LSD**
narcotic **das Rauschgift(e)**
pusher **der Dealer(-)**
I sniff **ich schnüffele**
soft drugs **weiche Drogen**
solvent **das Lösungsmittel(-)**
stimulant **das Anregungsmittel(-)**
syringe **die Spritze(n)**
I take drugs/a fix **ich nehme ein***
tranquilizer **das Betäubungsmittel(-) /Beruhigungsmittel(-)**
withdrawal **die Entwöhnung**

Cannabis is the most common. It gives a feeling of intoxication. People become psychologically dependent. Then they go onto hard drugs.

Marihuana wird am häufigsten gebraucht. Es erzeugt einen Rausch. Die Leute werden psychologisch abhängig. Dann greifen sie zu harten Drogen.

All drugs are dangerous, but injecting them brings risks of AIDS.

Alle Drogen sind gefährlich, aber das Spritzen birgt das Risiko, dass man sich mit AIDS infiziert.

Junkies inject or smoke drugs.

Die Fixer spritzen oder rauchen die Drogen.

SOCIAL ISSUES

12e Prejudice

asylum seeker **der Asylant(en)** *(wk)*
I call names **ich beschimpfe**
citizenship **die Staatsangehörigkeit(en)**
country of origin **das Geburtsland(-̈er)**
cultural **kulturell**
culture **die Kultur(en)**
I discriminate **ich diskriminiere**
discrimination **die Diskriminierung**
dual nationality **die doppelte Staatsangehörigkeit**
emigrant **der Auswanderer(-)**
emigration **die Auswanderung**
equal (un-) **gleich (un-)**
equal opportunities **die Chancengleichheit**
equal pay **der gleiche Lohn(-̈e)**
equal rights **die Gleichberechtigung**
equality (in-) **die (Un)gleichheit**
ethnic **ethnisch**
far-right (adj.) **rechtsradikal**
fascism **der Faschismus**
fascist **der Faschist(en)** *(wk)* **[-in]**, **der/die Rechtsradikale** *(adj/n)*
foreign **fremd, ausländisch**

foreign worker **der Gastarbeiter(-)**
freedom **die Freiheit**
  freedom of movement **die Bewegungsfreiheit**
  freedom of speech **die Redefreiheit**
ghetto **das Ghetto(s)**
I immigrate **ich wandere ein***
immigrant (from Eastern block) **der Aussiedler(-) [-in]**
immigration **die Einwanderung**
I integrate **ich integriere mich**
integration **die Integration**
intolerance **die Intoleranz**
intolerant **intolerant**
majority **die Mehrheit(en)**
minority **die Minderheit(en)**
mother tongue **die Muttersprache(n)**
I persecute **ich verfolge**
persecution **die Verfolgung**
prejudice **das Vorurteil(e)**
prejudiced **voreingenommen gegenüber** +dat
rabid **rabiat**
race riot **der Rassenkrawall(e)**
racism **der Rassismus**
racist **der Rassist(en) [-in]**
  racist *(adj)* **rassistisch**

Unfortunately, many people are prejudiced against foreigners.

Leider sind viele Leute gegen Ausländer voreingenommen.

In recent years many immigrants from the former Eastern block countries have come to Germany.

In den letzten Jahren sind viele Einwanderer aus den ehemaligen Ostblockstaaten nach Deutschland gekommen.

refugee **der Flüchtling(e)**
I repatriate **ich sende in das Heimatland zurück***
residence permit **die Aufenthaltserlaubnis(se)**
right **das Recht(e)**
  right to asylum **das Asylrecht**
  right to residence **das Wohnrecht**
second language **die zweite Sprache(n)**
stereotypical **stereotypisch**
tolerance **die Toleranz**
tolerant **tolerant**
I tolerate **ich toleriere**
work permit **die Arbeitserlaubnis(se)**

Sexuality

female **weiblich**
feminine **weiblich**
feminism **der Feminismus**
feminist **feministisch**
gay **schwul**
heterosexual **der Hetero(s)**
  heterosexual *(adj)* **heterosexuell**
homophobic **homophobisch**
homosexual **der/die Homosexuelle** *(adj/n)*
  homosexual *(adj)* **homosexuell**
homosexuality **die Homosexualität**
lesbian **die Lesbierin(nen), die Lesbe(n)**
lesbian **lesbisch**
male **männlich**
sexual **sexuell**
sexuality **die Sexualität**
women's lib **die Frauenbewegung(en)**
women's libber **die Frauenrechtlerin(nen)**
women's rights **die Frauenrechte**

– What about the ethnic minority population resident here?

– Was ist mit den ethnischen Minderheiten, die hier sesshaft sind?

– Many have no right to citizenship.

– Viele haben kein Recht auf Staatsangehörigkeit.

The feminist movement is still demanding equal rights for women.

Die Frauenbewegung verlangt immer noch die Gleichberechtigung der Frauen.

➤ HUMAN RELATIONSHIPS 7; LOVE 7b

Religion

13a Ideas & doctrines

agnostic **der Agnostiker(-) [-in]**
anglican **der Anglikaner(-) [-in]**
anti-Semitism **der Antisemitismus**
apostle **der Apostel(-)**
atheism **der Atheismus**
atheist **der Atheist(en)** *(wk)* **[-in]**
atheistic **atheistisch**
authority **die Autorität(en)**
belief **der Glaube** *(gen* **-ns)** *(wk)*
I believe (in) **ich glaube (an** +acc)
believer **der/die Gläubige** *(adj/n)*
Bible **die Bibel(n)**
biblical **biblisch**
blessed **gesegnet**
Buddha **der Buddha(s)**
Buddhism **der Buddhismus**
Buddhist **der Buddhist(en)** *(wk)* **[-in]**
Calvinist **der Calvinist(en)** *(wk)* **[-in]**
cantor **der Kantor(en)** *(wk)* **[-in]**
Catholic **der Katholik(en)** *(wk)* **[-in]**
catholic *(adj)* **katholisch**
charismatic **charismatisch**
charity **die Nächstenliebe**
charity *(adj)* **karitativ**
charity organization **die Wohlfahrtsorganisation(en)**
Christ **Christus**
Christian *(adj)* **christlich**
all Christians **alle Christen**
Christianity **die Christenheit**
church **die Kirche(n)**
commentary **der Kommentar(e)**
consciousness **das Bewusstsein**
covenant **der Bund(¨e)**
disciple **der Jünger(-)**
divine **göttlich**
doctrine **die Lehre(n)**

duty **die Aufgabe(n), die Pflicht(en)**
ecumenicism **der Ökumenismus**
ethical **ethisch**
evil **das Böse** *(adj/n)*
evil *(adj)* **böse, übel**
I forgive **ich vergebe** +dat
forgiveness **die Vergebung(en)**
free will **der freie Wille** *(gen* **-ns)** *(wk)*
fundamentalism **der Fundamentalismus**
fundamentalist **der Fundamentalist(en)** *(wk)* **[-in]**
god **der Gott(¨er)**
goddess **die Göttin(nen)**
Gospel **das Evangelium (-ien)**
grace **die Gnade**
heaven **der Himmel(-)**
Hebrew **der Hebräer(-)**
hell **die Hölle(n)**
heretical **ketzerisch**
Hindu **der Hindu(s)**
Hinduism **der Hinduismus**
holiness **die Heiligkeit**
holy **heilig**
Holy Spirit **der Heilige Geist**
hope **die Hoffnung(en)**
human **menschlich**
human being **der Mensch(en)** *(wk)*
humanism **der Humanismus**
humanity **die Menschheit, die Menschlichkeit**
infallibility **die Unfehlbarkeit**
infallible **unfehlbar**
Islam **der Islam**
Islamic **islamisch**
Jesus **Jesus**

Jew **der Jude(n)** *(wk)*, **die Jüdin(nen)**
Jewish **jüdisch**
Judaic **judäisch**
Judaism **der Judaismus**
Lord **der Herr(en)** *(wk)*
merciful **gnadenvoll**
mercy **die Gnade(n)**
Messiah **der Messias**
Mohammed **Mohammed**
moral **moralisch**
morality **die Moral, die Moralität**
Muslim **der Moslem(s)**
    Muslim *(adj)* **moslemisch**
myth **der Mythos (-en)**
New Testament **das Neue Testament**
nirvana **das Nirwana**
Old Testament **das Alte Testament**
orthodox **orthodox**
pagan **der Heide(n)** *(wk)* **[-in]**
parish **die Gemeinde(n)**
prophet **der Prophet(en)** *(wk)* **[-in]**
Q'uran/Koran **der Koran**
redemption **die Erlösung**
religion **die Religion(en)**

Roman Catholic **römisch-katholisch**
sacred **heilig**
saint **der/die Heilige** *(adj/n)*
Saint Peter **Sankt Peter, der Heilige Petrus**
Salvation Army **die Heilsarmee**
he sanctifies **er heiligt**
Satan **der Satan**
he saves **er rettet**
scripture **die Heilige Schrift(en)**
service **der Gottesdienst(e)**
Sikh **der Sikh(s)**
Sikhism **der Sikhismus**
sin **die Sünde(n)**
sinful **sündig**
soul **die Seele(n)**
spirit **der Geist(er)**
spiritual **geistlich**
spirituality **die Geistlichkeit**
Talmud **der Talmud**
Taoism **der Taoismus**
theological **theologisch**
theology **die Theologie(n)**
traditional **traditionell**
Trinity **die Trinität, die Dreifaltigkeit**
true **wahr**
truth **die Wahrheit(en)**

Religious fundamentalism can lead to fanaticism and intolerance in any religion.

Religiöser Fundamentalismus kann in jeder Religion zu Fanatismus und Intoleranz führen.

Freedom of faith, of conscience and freedom of religious and ideological belief are inviolable. (Article 4 of the German constitution)

Die Freiheit des Glaubens, des Gewissens und die Freiheit des religiösen und weltanschaulichen Bekenntnisses sind unverletzlich. (Artikel 4 des Grundgesetzes)

There is considerable disagreement about the ordination of women to the priesthood.

Es bestehen beträchtliche Differenzen über die Ordination von Frauen ins Priesteramt.

13b Faith & practice

archbishop **der Erzbischof(-̈e)**
baptism **die Taufe(n)**
I baptise **ich taufe**
bar mitzvah **das Bar-Mizvah**
I bear witness to **ich bekenne**
bishop **der Bischof(-̈e)**
bishopric/see **das Bistum(-̈er)**
he canonises **er spricht heilig**
cathedral **die Kathedrale(n)**
I celebrate **ich feiere**
chapel **die Kapelle(n)**
christening **die Taufe(n)**
clergy **der Klerus**
clergyman **der Geistliche(n)**
 (adj/n), **der Pfarrer(-)**
communion *(catholic)* **die**
 Kommunion
 holy communion **die heilige**
 Kommunion
 communion *(protestant)* **das**
 Abendmahl
community **die Gemeinde(n)**
I confess *(faith)* **ich bekenne mich**
 zu +dat

I confess *(sins)* **ich beichte**
confession **die Beichte(n)**
confirmation **die Konfirmation**
congregation **die Gemeinde(n)**
 (of cardinals) **die**
 Kongregation
conversion **die Bekehrung(en)**
convent **das Kloster(-̈)**
I convert *(others)* **ich bekehre**
I convert *(self)* **ich konvertiere**
Eucharist **die Eucharistie**
evangelical **evangelisch**
evangelist **der Evangelist(en)** *(wk)*
faith **der Glaube (***gen* -ns**)** *(wk)*
faithful **treu, gläubig**
the faithful **die Gläubigen** *(pl)*
I give alms **ich gebe Almosen, ich**
 spende
I give thanks **ich sage Dank**
Imam **der Imam**
intercession **die Fürsprache(n)**
laity **der Laienstand** *(no pl)*
lay **Laien-**
layperson **der Laie(n)** *(wk)*

Those who are called to ministry must demonstrate their vocation before being accepted in theological colleges.

Wer Pfarrer werden will, muss seine Berufung demonstrieren, bevor er in eine theologische Fakultät aufgenommen wird.

The sacrament of Holy Communion will be celebrated on Sunday at nine o'clock.

Das Sakrament der heiligen Kommunion wird am Sonntag um neun Uhr gefeiert.

We work for charity.

Wir arbeiten für eine Wohlfahrtsorganization.

Aunt Anna always contributes to the Red Cross.

Tante Anna spendet für das Rote Kreuz.

The Baptist tradition is very strong in the American South.

Die baptistische Tradition ist sehr stark im Süden der USA.

the Lord's Supper **das Abendmahl**
Mass **die Messe**
I meditate **ich meditiere**
meditation **die Meditation**
minister **der Pfarrer(-)**
I minister to the parish **ich diene der Gemeinde**
ministry **das geistliche Amt(-̈er)**
mission **die Mission(en)**
missionary **der Missionar(e) [-in]**
monastery **das Kloster(-̈)**
monk **der Mönch(e)**
mosque **die Moschee(n)**
mullah **der Mullah(s)**
nun **die Nonne(n)**
parish **die Gemeinde(n)**
parishioner **das Gemeindemitglied(er)**
pastor **der Pastor(en)** *(wk)*
pastoral **seelsorgerisch**
Pope **der Papst(-̈e)**
I praise **ich lobe**
I pray (for) **ich bete (für +acc)**

prayer **das Gebet(e)**
morning prayer **die Morgenandacht**
prayerful **fromm**
priest **der Priester(-)**
rabbi **der Rabbi(s)**
I repent **ich empfinde Reue**
repentance **die Reue**
repentant **reuevoll**
I revere **ich verehre**
reverence **die Verehrung(en)**
reverent **ehrfürchtig**
rite **der Ritus (Riten)**
ritual **das Ritual(e)**
sacrament **das Sakrament(e)**
sermon **die Predigt(en)**
synagogue **die Synagoge(n)**
synod **die Synode(n)**
temple **der Tempel(-)**
vision **die Vision(en)**
vocation **die Berufung(en)**
witness **der Zeuge(n)** *(wk)* **[-in]**
I witness **ich bezeuge**
I worship **ich bete an*, ich verehre**

About 85% of the population belongs to one of the Christian faiths.
The Protestants predominate in the north, the Catholics in the south of Germany.

In England there is an Established Church. In Germany state and church are separate.

Bishops in the Church of England are not afraid to speak about social problems.

Etwa 85% der Bevölkerung **bekennen sich zu einer der christlichen Konfessionen.**
Die Evangelischen überwiegen im Norden, die Katholiken im Süden Deutschlands.

In England gibt es eine Staatskirche. In Deutschland sind Staat und Kirche getrennt.

Die Bischöfe der anglikanischen Kirche scheuen sich nicht, über soziale Probleme zu sprechen.

➤ RELIGIOUS FESTIVALS 13b

14 Business & economics

14a Economic life

I administer **ich verwalte**
we agree (to) **wir beschließen (zu +inf)**
agreement **die Übereinkunft(¨e)**
bureaucracy **die Bürokratie(n)**
business **das Geschäft(e), die Unternehmung(en)**
a business **ein Geschäft(e)**
capacity *(industrial)* **die Kapazität(en)**
commerce **der Kommerz, der Handel**
commercial **kommerziell**
company **die (Handels)gesellschaft(en)**
competition **die Konkurrenz**
competitive **konkurrenzfähig**
deal **das Geschäft(e)**
I deliver **ich liefere**
demand **die Nachfrage(n)**
in demand **gefragt**
development **die Entwicklung(en)**
I dismiss **ich kündige**
I earn (a living) **ich verdiene**
economy **die Wirtschaft(en), die Konjunktur** *(no pl)*
I employ **ich beschäftige**
employee **der Arbeitnehmer(-)**
employer **der Arbeitgeber(-)**
employment **die Arbeit**
executive **der Geschäftsführer(-) [-in]**
I export **ich exportiere**
export(s) **der Export(e)**
it falls **es sinkt, es fällt**
firm **die Firma (Firmen), der Betrieb(e)**
goods **die Ware(n)**
it grows **es wächst**
I import **ich importiere**

I increase **ich erhöhe, ich erweitere**
increase **der Anstieg, die Zunahme**
industrial **industriell**
industrial output **die Produktion(en)**
industry **die Industrie(n), der Industriebetrieb(e)**
I invest **ich investiere**
investment **die Investition(en)**
job **der Arbeitsplatz(¨e)**
job creation scheme **die Arbeitsbeschaffungsmaßnahme(n)**
lay off **die Entlassung(en)**
living standards **der Lebensstandard(s)**
I manage **ich leite**
management **das Management(s), die Leitung(en)**
multinational **multinational**
I negotiate **ich verhandle**
priority **die Priorität(en)**
I produce **ich produziere, ich stelle her***
producer **der Hersteller(-)**
product **der Produkt(e)**
production line **das Fließband(¨er)**
productivity **die Produktivität(en)**
public company **die Aktiengesellschaft(en)**
quality **die Qualität(en)**
I raise (prices) **ich erhöhe (die Preise)**
reliability **die Zuverlässigkeit**
rise **der Anstieg(e)**
wage rise/raise **die Gehaltserhöhung(en)**
semiskilled **angelernt**
service **der Service**

service industry **der Dienstleistungsbetrieb(e)**

I set (priorities) **ich setze (Prioritäten)**

I am on sick leave **ich bin krankgeschrieben**

sick pay **das Krankengeld(er)**

I sign (contracts) **ich unterzeichne (Verträge)**

skilled labor **der Facharbeiter(-) [-in]**

I strengthen **ich stärke**

supply **das Angebot(e)**

trade-unionism **das Gewerkschaftswesen**

turnover **der Umsatz(-̈e)**

unemployment **die Arbeitslosigkeit(en)**

unemployment benefit **das Arbeitslosengeld(er)**

unskilled labor **der ungelernte Arbeiter(-)**

work **die Arbeit(en)**

worker **der Arbeiter(-) [-in]**

work ethic **die Arbeitsmoral** *(no pl)*

workforce **die Arbeitskräfte** *(pl)*

working week **die Arbeitswoche(n)**

workplace **der Arbeitsplatz(-̈e)**

working conditions **die Arbeitsbedingungen** *(pl)*

Industrial/Labor dispute

ballot **die Abstimmung(en)**

I boycott **ich boykottiere**

demonstration **die Demonstration(en)**

dispute **der Streit(e), die Auseinandersetzung(en)**

I go slow/slow down **ich mache einen Bummelstreik**

industrial/labor dispute **der Arbeitskonflikt(e)**

industrial relations **die Beziehungen zwischen Arbeitgebern und Gewerkschaften**

I lock out **ich sperre aus***

lockout **die Aussperrung(en)**

minimum wage **der Mindestlohn**

I picket **ich stelle Streikposten auf***

picket **der Streikposten(-)**

productivity bonus **die Prämie(n)**

I resume work **ich nehme die Arbeit wieder auf***

social unrest **die soziale Not/Unruhe(n)**

stoppage **der Stopp(s)**

strike **der Streik(s)**

unofficial strike **der wilde Streik(s)**

I am on strike **ich streike**

I go on strike **ich trete in den Streik**

striker **der Streikende(n)**

strikebreaker **der Streikbrecher(-)**

trade union **die Gewerkschaft(en)**

unfair dismissal **die ungerechtfertigte Entlassung(en)**

unrest **die Unruhe(n)**

wage costs **die Lohnkosten** *(pl)*

wage demand **die Lohnforderung(en)**

wage settlement **das Lohnabkommen(-)**

The unions called for a reduction in working hours.

Die Gewerkschaften forderten eine Verkürzung der Arbeitszeit.

Unemployment is rising to 12%.

Die Arbeitslosenquote steigt auf 12 Prozent an.

➤ AT WORK 14b; UNEMPLOYMENT 12c; JOBS & PROFESSIONS.14b

14b At Work

agenda **die Tagesordnung(en)**
on the agenda **auf dem Programm**
on business **geschäftlich**
boring **langweilig**
business lunch **das Geschäftsessen(-)**
business meeting **das Treffen(-), die Konferenz(en), die Besprechung(en)**
business trip **die Geschäftsreise(n)**
I buy **ich kaufe**
canteen **die Kantine(n)**
career **der Beruf(e)**
I chair a meeting **ich führe den Vorsitz**
computer **der Computer(-)**
I delegate **ich delegiere**
disciplinary proceeding **das Disziplinarverfahren(-)**
I do **ich mache**
I follow a training course **ich lasse mich ausbilden**
free **kostenlos**
grant **das Stipendium (-ien)**
holiday/vacation **die Ferien** (pl), **der Urlaub(e)**
job **der Job(s)**

I have job satisfaction **ich bin mit meiner Arbeit zufrieden**
I market **ich bringe ... auf den Markt, ich vermarkte**
meal **die Mahlzeit(en)**
meeting **die Sitzung(en)**
misconduct **das Vergehen(-)**
occupation **die Beschäftigung(en), der Beruf(e)**
I'm absent **ich fehle**
I pay taxes **ich zahle Steuern**
post **die Stelle(n), die Stellung(en)**
profession **der Beruf(e)**
professional **der Fachmann(-̈er)**
professional (adj) **beruflich, professionell**
publicity **die Öffentlichkeit**
I qualify **ich qualifiziere**
I report to **ich unterstehe jdm.**
research **ich forsche**
I am responsible for **ich bin für +acc verantwortlich**
I sell **ich verkaufe**
I teach **ich lehre**
I toil **ich schufte**
training **die Ausbildung(en)**

Please tell Mrs. Weber in reception that I'm expecting Mr. Hartmann at 10 o'clock.

Bitte sagen Sie Frau Weber am Empfang, dass ich Herrn Hartmann um 10 Uhr erwarte.

– What kind of work does your daughter do?

– Was macht Ihre Tochter beruflich?

– She took a training course as a computer programmer and is now looking for a job.

– Sie hat sich zur Computerprogrammiererin ausbilden lassen und sucht jetzt eine Stelle.

Our meeting will be in the conference room next to my office.

Unsere Besprechung findet im Konferenzzimmer neben meinem Büro statt.

training course **das Ausbildungsprogramm(e)**
I transfer **ich werde versetzt**
unskilled **ungelernt**
vocation **die Berufung(en)**
warning *(verbal)* **die Verwarnung(en)**
written warning **die schriftliche Warnung(en)/Abmahnung(en)**
I work as ... **ich arbeite als ...**

In the office

computer **der Computer(-)**
conference room **der Konferenzsaal (-säle)**
desk **der Schreibtisch(e)**
I dictate **ich diktiere**
dictating machine **das Diktiergerät(e)**
electronic mail **die elektronische Post**
extension **der Apparat(e)**
fax **das Fax**
fax machine **das Faxgerät(e)**
I fax **ich faxe**
file **die Akte(n)**
I file **ich ordne/lege Akten an***
filing cabinet **der Aktenschrank(ᴗe)**
intercom **die Sprechanlage(n)**
memorandum **die Mitteilung(en)**
open plan **offen angelegt**
photocopier **der Fotokopierer(-)**
photocopy **die Kopie(n)**
I photocopy **ich kopiere**
pigeonhole **das Fach(ᴗer)**
reception **die Rezeption(en)**
receptionist **der Herr/die Dame am Empfang**
swivel chair **der Drehstuhl(ᴗe)**
telephone **das Telefon(e)**
typing pool **die Schreibzentrale(n)**
wastebasket **der Papierkorb(ᴗe)**
work station **die Arbeitssplatz(ᴗe)**

At the factory & on site

automation **die Automatisierung**
blue-collar worker **der Arbeiter(-) [-in]**
bulldozer **die Planierraupe(n)**
car/automobile industry **die Autoindustrie(n)**
component **der Bestandteil(e)**
concrete **der Beton**
construction industry **die Bauindustrie(n)**
crane **der Kran(ᴗe)**
forklift truck **der Gabelstapler(-)**
I forge **ich schmiede**
industry **die Industrie(n)**
heavy industry **die Schwerindustrie(n)**
light industry **die Leichtindustrie(n)**
I manufacture **ich stelle her***
manufacture **das Herstellen**
mass production **die Massenproduktion**
mining **der Bergbau**
power industry **die Energieindustrie(n)**
precision tool **das Präzisionswerkzeug(e)**
prefabricated **vorgefertigt**
process **der Prozess(e)**
I process **ich verarbeite**
product **das Produkt(e)**
on the production line **am Fließband**
raw materials **der rohe Werkstoff(e)**
road building **der Straßenbau**
robot **der Roboter(-)**
scaffolding **das Gerüst(e)**
shipbuilding **der Schiffbau**
I smelt **ich schmelze**
steamroller **die Dampfwalze(n)**
steel smelting **das Stahlschmelzen**
textile industry **die Textilindustrie(n)**

➤ WORKING CONDITIONS 14c; COMPUTERS 15f; STATIONERY 22b

BUSINESS & ECONOMICS

14c Working conditions

I am employed **ich bin angestellt**
apprenticeship **die Lehre(n), die Lehrzeit(en)**
benefit **der Nutzen(-)**
bonus **die Prämie(n), der Zuschlag(¨e)**
I clock (in/out) **ich stemple (beim Kommen/Gehen)**
commission **die Kommission(en)**
on commission **auf Provision**
company car **der Firmenwagen(-)**
conditions of employment **die Arbeitsbedingungen** *(pl)*
contract **der Vertrag(¨e)**
expenses **die Spesen** *(pl)*
expense account **das Spesenkonto (-en)**
flextime **die flexible Arbeitszeit(en)**
freelance **freiberuflich**
I work freelance **ich arbeite freiberuflich**
full-time **ganztägig, ganztags**
full-time job **die Ganztagsstelle(n)**

income **das Einkommen**
overtime **die Überstunde(n)**
overworked **überfordert**
part-time **Teilzeit-**
pay **der Lohn(¨e)**
payday **der Zahltag(e)**
pay raise **die Gehaltserhöhung(en)**
payslip **die Lohnabrechnung(en)**
pension **die Rente(n), die Pension(en)**
perk **die Vergünstigung(en)**
permanent **permanent**
professional association **die Berufsgenossenschaft(en)**
remuneration **die Vergütung(en)**
I retire **ich trete in den Ruhestand**
retirement **der Ruhestand**
salary **das Gehalt(¨er)**
self-employed **selbstständig**
shift **die Schicht(en)**
day shift **die Tagesschicht(en)**
night shift **die Nachtschicht(en)**
shiftworking **die Schichtarbeit**

The conditions in this office are intolerable. The place is cold, badly lit, and poorly ventilated.

Die Zustände in diesem Büro sind unerträglich. Der Raum ist kalt, schlecht beleuchtet und nicht ausreichend gelüftet.

Many people who are in part-time work choose not to work full-time because of family commitments.

Viele Leute, die in Teilzeitjobs beschäftigt sind, wählen diese, um Familienverpflichtungen nachzukommen.

Our policy is to create more part-time jobs, and to protect the rights of the part-time workers.

Unsere Geschäftspolitik sieht vor, mehr Teilzeitstellen zu schaffen und die Rechte der Teilzeitkräfte zu stärken.

temporary **für kurze Zeit, befristet**
trial period **die Probezeit(en)**
working-hours **die Arbeitsstunden**
wage **der Lohn(-e)**

Job application

I advertise the position **ich inseriere die Stelle**
advertisement **die Anzeige(n)**
I apply for a job **Ich bewerbe mich um eine Stelle**
classified ad **die Kleinanzeige(n)**
curriculum vitae/resumé **der Lebenslauf(-e)**
discrimination **die Diskriminierung(en)**
racial discrimination **die Rassendiskriminierung(en)**
sexual discrimination **die sexuelle Diskriminierung(en)**
employment agency **die Arbeitsvermittlungsagentur(en)**
job centre/employment office **die Agentur für Arbeit**
I find a job **ich finde einen Job**
interesting **interessant**

interview **das Einstellungsgespräch(e)**
I interview **ich führe ein Einstellungsgespräch**
job application **die Bewerbung(en)**
job offer **das Stellenangebot(e)**
I look for **ich suche**
opening **die freie Stelle(n)**
vacant positions **die Stellenangebote** *(pl)*
I promote (someone) **ich befördere (jdn.)**
I am promoted **ich werde befördert**
promotion **die Beförderung(en)**
qualification **die Qualifikation(en)**
qualified **qualifiziert, ausgebildet**
I start work (for) **Ich fange (bei +dat) zu arbeiten an***
I take on *(employee)* **ich stelle ein***
vacancy **die offene Stelle(n)**
wage **der Lohn(-e), die Bezahlung(en)**
work experience **das Praktikum(-a)**

– Hello. Could I speak to the personnel manager, please.
– Speaking. What can I do for you?
– I saw your advertisement in the local paper for a sales executive.

How many references do you require?
– Two, including your present or last employer.

– Hallo, könnte ich bitte den **Personalchef sprechen.**
– Am Apparat. Was kann ich für **Sie tun?**
– Ich habe Ihre Anzeige für **einen Verkaufsleiter in der Lokalzeitung gesehen.**
Wie viele Arbeitszeugnisse **benötigen Sie?**
– Zwei, einschließlich das Ihres **jetzigen oder letzten Arbeitgebers.**

➤ UNEMPLOYMENT 12c

14d Finance & industry

account **die Rechnung(en), das Konto (-en)**

advance **der Vorschuss(-̈e)**

I audit **ich prüfe**

bill **die Rechnung(en)**

bond **die Staatsanleihe(n)**

branch *(of company)* **die Zweigstelle(n)**

budget **das Budget(s), der Haushalt(e), der Etat(s)**

capital **das Kapital**

capital expenditure **die Kapitalaufwendungen** *(pl)*

chamber of commerce **die Handelskammer(n)**

collateral **die Sicherheit(en)**

company **die Gesellschaft(en)**

competition **die Konkurrenz**

I consume *(resources)* **ich verbrauche**

consumer goods **die Konsumgüter** *(pl)*

consumer protection **der Verbraucherschutz**

consumer spending **die Verbraucherausgaben** *(pl)*

cost of living **die Lebenshaltungskosten** *(pl)*

costing **die Kostenberechnung(en)**

costs **die Kosten** *(pl)*

credit **der Kredit(e)**

debit **die Abhebung(en)**

deflation **die Deflation**

economic **wirtschaftlich**

economy **die Wirtschaft(en)**

government spending **die öffentlichen Ausgaben** *(pl)*

income **das Einkommen**

income tax **die Einkommenssteuer(n)**

installment **die Rate(n)**

interest rate **die Zinsrate(n)**

I invest in **ich investiere in** +acc

investment **die Investition(en)**

invoice **die Rechnung(en)**

labour/labor costs **die Arbeitskosten** *(pl)*

liability **die Verpflichtung(en)**

limited liability company **Gesellschaft mit beschränkter Haftung (GmbH)**

loan **der Kredit(e)**

manufacturing industry **die herstellende Industrie(n)**

market **der Markt(-̈e)**

market economy **die Marktwirtschaft**

marketing **das Marketing**

merchandise **die Güter** *(pl)*

national debt **die Staatsschulden** *(pl)*

I nationalize **ich verstaatliche**

output **die Leistung(en), die Produktion(en)**

pay **der Lohn(-̈e)**

price **der Preis(e)**

private sector **der Privatsektor(en)**

I privatize **ich privatisiere**

product **das Produkt(e)**

production **die Produktion(en)**

public sector **der öffentliche Sektor(en)**

quota **die Quote(n)**

rate (going) **der Kurs(e)**

real estate/realty **die Immobilien** *(pl)*

retail sales **der Einzelhandelsverkauf** *(no pl)*

retail trade **der Einzelhandel** *(no pl)*

salaries **das Gehalt(-̈er)**

sales tax **die Verkaufssteuer(n)**

service sector **der Dienstleistungssektor(en)**

share **die Aktie(n)**

shares are going up/down **die Aktien fallen/steigen**

share index **der Aktienindex(e)**

statistics **die Statistik(en)**
stock exchange **die Börse(n)**
I subsidize **ich subventioniere**
subsidy **der Zuschuss(-̈e)**
supply and demand **Angebot und Nachfrage**
supply costs **die Lieferkosten** *(pl)*
I tax **ich versteuere**
tax **die Steuer(n)**
  after tax **nach Abzug der Steuern**
tax cut **die Steuersenkung(en)**
tax relief **die Steuerbegünstigung(en)**
tax increase **die Steuererhöhung(en)**
taxation **die Steuern** *(pl)*
taxation level **das Steuerniveau(s)**
turnover **der Umsatz(-̈e)**
VAT/sales tax **die Mehrwertsteuer, MwSt**
viable **rentabel**
wage(s) **der Lohn(-̈e)**

Financial personnel

accountant **der Wirtschaftsprüfer(-) [-in]**
actuary **der Versicherungsmathematiker(-) [-in]**
auditor **der Wirtschaftsprüfer(-) [-in]**
banker **der Banker(-)**
  investment banker **der Investmentbanker(-)**
  merchant banker **der Handelsbanker(-)**
bank manager **der Bankmanager(-) [-in]**
broker **der Makler(-) [-in]**
  insurance broker **der Versicherungsmakler(-) [-in**
consumer **der Verbraucher(-) [-in]**
investor **der Investor(en)**
speculator **der Spekulant(en)** *(wk)*
stockbroker **der Börsenmakler(-) [-in]**
trader *(Wall St.)* **der Händler(-) [-in], der Makler(-) [-in]**

Industry is recovering.	**Die Industrie erholt sich.**
In spite of the increase in the value of the euro, there is an export surplus.	**Trotz der Euro- Kursanstiegs gibt es einen Ausfuhrüberschuss.**
Inflation is slowing down.	**Die Inflation nimmt ab.**
A stable economy, free trade and an organized monetary system are important for the EU/European Union.	**Eine stabile Wirtschaft, freier Handel und ein geordnetes Währungssystem sind wichtig für die EU.**
We have to pay for the import of raw materials.	**Wir müssen die Einfuhr von Rohstoffen bezahlen.**
The fall in value of the dollar is the cause of the recession.	**Der Rückgang des Dollarkurses ist Ursache der Rezession.**
I have overdrawn my account.	**Ich habe mein Konto überzogen.**

BUSINESS & ECONOMICS

14e Banking & the economy

Banking & personal finance

account das Konto (-en)
automatic teller/cash point der
    Geldautomat(en) (wk)
bank die Bank(en)
I bank (money) ich zahle Geld ein*
banking das Bankwesen
bank loan das Bankdarlehen(-)
bank charge die Bankgebühr(en)
bank statement der
    Kontoauszug(¨e)
building society/savings and loan
    association die
    Bausparkasse(n)
cash das Bargeld(er)
I cash a cheque/check ich löse
    einen Scheck ein*
cashcard die Scheckkarte(n)
cashdesk die Kasse(n)
I change ich wechsle
cheque/check der Scheck(s)
credit card die Kreditkarte(n)
I'm in credit ich habe Geld auf
    dem Konto
currency die Währung(en)
deficit das Defizit(e)
deposit (in a bank) die
    Einzahlung(en)
deposit (returnable) die Kaution(en)

I deposit ich zahle ... ein*
direct debit die Einzugs-
    ermächtigung(en)
down payment/deposit die
    Anzahlung(en)
exchange rate der Wechselkurs(e)
hire purchase/installment plan der
    Teilzahlungskauf(¨e)
I invest ich lege an*
I lend ich leihe
loan das Darlehen(-)
mortgage die Hypothek(en)
I mortgage ich nehme eine
    Hypothek auf*
I open an account ich eröffne ein
    Konto
overdraft der
    Überziehungskredit(e)
I overdraw ich überziehe
I pay cash ich bezahle bar
in the red in den roten Zahlen
repayment die Zurückzahlung(en)
I save ich spare
savings die Ersparnisse (pl)
savings bank die Sparkasse(n)
standing order der Dauerauftrag(¨e)
I transfer (to) ich überweise auf
    +acc

I have opened an account at the
(savings) bank. You only need an
identity card and an initial deposit.
Now I have my salary
automatically transferred into my
account.

Ich habe bei der Sparkasse ein
Konto eröffnet. Man braucht nur
einen Personalausweis und eine
erste Einzahlung. Jetzt lasse ich
mein Gehalt automatisch auf
das Konto überweisen.

I pay my rent by standing order.

Ich begleiche meine Miete per
Dauerauftrag.

Gas and electricity are withdrawn
from my account by direct debit.

Gas und Strom werden durch
Einzugsermächtigungen von
meinem Konto abgebucht.

travellers' cheque/traveler's check
  der Reisecheck(s)
I withdraw **ich hebe ab***

Growth

appreciation **die
  Wertsteigerung(en)**
asset **der Aktivposten(-)**
assurance **die Versicherung(en)**
auction **die Auktion(en)**
boom **die Hochkunjunktur, der
  Boom(s), der Aufschwung(-̈e)**
I diversify **ich diversifiziere**
economic miracle **das
  Wirtschaftswunder(-)**
efficiency **die Wirtschaftlichkeit**
I grow/expand **ich wachse**
growth **das Wachstum**
it increases **es steigt**
joint venture **das
  Gemeinschaftsunternehmen(-)**
they merge **sie fusionieren**
we merge **wir schließen uns
  zusammen***
merger **die Fusion(en)**
plan **der Plan(-̈e)**
profit **der Gewinn(e)**
profitable **rentabel**
progress **der Fortschritt(e)**
prosperity **der Wohlstand** *(no pl)*
prosperous **wohlhabend**

recovery **der neue Aufschwung**
takeover **die Übernahme(n)**
takeover bid **das
  Übernahmeangebot(e)**

Decline

bankrupt **bankrott, pleite**
I go bankrupt **ich mache bankrott**
credit squeeze **die
  Kreditbeschränkung(en)**
debt **die Schuld(en)**
it is declining **es fällt, es geht
  zurück**
deficit **das Defizit(e)**
depreciation **der
  Kaufkraftverlust(e)**
I dump **ich verkaufe zu
  Dumpingpreisen**
inflation **die Inflation(en)**
inflation rate **die Inflationsrate(n)**
loss **der Verlust(e)**
no-growth economy **die
  stagnierende Wirtschaft**
recession **die Rezession(en)**
it slows down **es geht zurück**
slump **der Rückgang(-̈e)**
it slumps **es stürzt**
spending cuts **die Kürzungen im
  Etat**
stagnant **stagnierend**
stagnation **die Stagnation(en)**

Nobody accepts a check today
without a check card. The bank
guarantees that every check is
honored.

**Niemand nimmt heutzutage
einen Scheck ohne Scheckkarte
an. Die Bank garantiert, dass
jeder Scheck eingelöst wird.**

We have a record surplus of 8
million euros.

**Wir haben einen
Rekordüberschuss von 8 Millionen
Euro.**

The cost of oil imports is rising
steeply.

**Die Kosten der Öleinfuhren
steigen enorm.**

15 Communicating with others

15a Meetings & greetings

Meetings

I accept (invitation) **ich nehme an***
appointment **die Verabredung(en), der Termin(e)**
at home **zu Hause**
ball **der Ball(-e)**
banquet **das Bankett(e)**
I bump into **ich begegne jdm.**
I'm busy **ich habe keine Zeit**
I celebrate **ich begehe, ich feiere**
celebration **die Feier(n) , die Gedenkfeier(n)**
club **der Klub(s), der Club(s)**
dance **der Tanz(-e)**
date (appointment) **die Verabredung(en), das Rendezvous(-)**
diary/datebook **der (Termin)kalender(-)**
I drop in **ich komme vorbei**
I'm expecting … for dinner **ich erwarte +acc zum Abendessen**
I greet **ich begrüße**
guest **der Gast(-e)**

I have guests **ich habe Besuch**
handshake **der Händedruck(-e)**
I invite **ich lade ein***
invitation **die Einladung(en)**
I join **ich trete +dat bei***
we meet **wir treffen uns**
meeting **die Begegnung(en), das Treffen(-)**
party **die Party(s), die Feier(n), das Fest(e)**
    I throw a party **ich gebe eine Party**
reception **der Empfang(-e)**
I shake hands with (someone) **ich gebe (jdm.) die Hand**
social life **das gesellschaftliche Leben**
I socialize **ich komme viel unter die Leute**
I spend (an evening) **ich verbringe**
I take part **ich mache mit***
I talk to someone **ich unterhalte mich mit jdm.**

– Please come in and take a seat.

– I'm delighted you were able to come. How are you?

– Very well thank you, and you?
– Excellent.

– Hello, Otto! May I introduce my cousin Martina?
– I'm delighted to meet you.

– **Kommen Sie bitte herein und nehmen Sie Platz.**
– **Ich freue mich, dass Sie kommen konnten. Wie geht es Ihnen?**
– **Sehr gut, danke, und Ihnen?**
– **Ausgezeichnet.**

– **Hallo, Otto! Darf ich dir meine Cousine Martina vorstellen?**
– **Es freut mich dich kennen zu lernen.**

I visit *(someone)* **ich besuche**
visit **der Besuch(e)**

Greetings

Good day **Guten Tag!**
Good morning! **Guten Morgen!**
Good evening! **Guten Abend!**
Hello! **Guten Tag! Grüß Gott!**
  Hello! *(fam)* **Hallo!**
Hey you! **Heh! Du!**
Doctor Braun, ... **Herr Doktor
  Braun, ...**
greetings to you all **ich begrüße
  Sie alle**
I say, did you know? **Du, weißt du
  schon?**
welcome to our home! **herzlich
  willkommen bei uns!**
what is it? **was ist?**
what's up? **was gibt's?**
yes? **ja, bitte?**

Introductions

I am called ... **ich heiße ...**
can I introduce you? **darf ich (Sie)
  bekannt machen?**
delighted to meet you **es freut
  mich, Sie kennen zu lernen**
do you know Doctor Schmidt?
  **kennen Sie schon Herrn Doktor
  Schmidt?**
I am a friend of Peter's **ich bin ein
  Freund von Peter**
how do you do! **angenehm! freut
  mich!**
may I introduce my friend Peter?
  **darf ich meinen Freund Peter
  vorstellen?**
my name is ... **mein Name ist ...**

what are you called? **wie heißt
  du?**
what's your surname? **wie heißt
  du mit Nachnamen?**

Congratulations

all the best! **alles Gute!**
cheers! **zum Wohl! prost!**
congratulations! **herzlichen
  Glückwunsch!**
merry Christmas! **frohe
  Weihnachten!**
happy Easter! **frohe Ostern!**
happy New Year! **ein gutes neues
  Jahr!, einen guten Rutsch ins
  neue Jahr!**
I congratulate you on **ich
  gratuliere (Ihnen) zu** +dat
I wish you ... **ich wünsche
  Ihnen ...**
my deepest sympathy! **mein
  herzliches Beileid!**
thank you so much! **ich bedanke
  mich (sehr)!**
to your good health! **auf Ihr Wohl!**

Pleasantries

I address *(someone)* **ich rede
  (jdn.) an*, ich spreche zu** +dat
I address as "du" **ich duze**
I address as "Sie" **ich sieze**
may I come in? **darf ich
  reinkommen?**
come in! **herein!**
am I disturbing you? **störe ich?**
am I in your way? **störe ich?**
not at all! **nein, keineswegs!**

We were so lucky with the
weather.

**Wir haben wirklich Glück mit
dem Wetter gehabt.**

Mrs. Eilers, best wishes on your
birthday!

**Frau Eilers, recht herzlichen
Glückwunsch zum Geburtstag!**

➤ FAREWELLS 15d; POST/MAIL, TELEPHONE 15e; COMPUTERS 15f **117**

COMMUNICATING WITH OTHERS

15b Approving, thanking, & disapproving

Approval

all right   **in Ordnung**
that's all right   **es ist ganz in Ordnung**
all right by me!   **meinetwegen!**
that's all right by me!   **von mir aus!**
fabulous   **fabelhaft**
fantastic   **phantastisch**
I'm in favor of   **ich bin (wäre) dafür**
delighted   **erfreut**
I'm delighted   **das freut mich**
I enjoy   **ich genieße**
exactly   **genau**
I feel   **ich fühle mich**
I feel like (doing)   **ich habe Lust, zu** +inf
fun   **der Spaß(-e)**
that's fun   **das macht Spaß**
fine!   **schön!, prima!, gut!**
I am fond of him   **ich habe ihn sehr gern**
glad   **froh**
I'm glad   **ich bin froh, ich freue mich**
great!   **toll!, prima!, phantastisch!, klasse!**
that would be great   **das wäre gut/prima!**
interesting   **interessant**
it interests me   **das interessiert mich**

I am interested in   **ich interessiere mich für** +acc
just so!   **so ist das einfach/eben**
I like it a lot   **ich mag es sehr**
I like reading   **ich lese gern**
I like it   **es gefällt mir**
I really like you   **ich mag dich wirklich gern**
I like her   **ich kann sie gut leiden**
I would like   **ich würde gern, ich möchte**
I look forward to   **ich freue mich auf** +acc
I love   **ich liebe**
lovely   **schön**
marvellous   **herrlich**
I don't mind   **das ist (mir) egal/gleich**
nice   **nett, schön, sympathisch**
how nice!   **wie schön!**
pleased   **zufrieden**
with pleasure   **mit Vergnügen**
rather   **lieber**
I would rather   **ich möchte lieber**
right   **korrekt**
that's right   **das stimmt**
I want   **ich will/möchte**
wonderful   **großartig, wunderbar**
it works out   **es klappt**

I am really looking forward to my vacation. It is exactly what I need.

Ich freue mich sehr auf meine Ferien. Es ist genau das, was ich brauche.

I really like it in Bavaria. I feel great there.

Es gefällt mir sehr gut in Bayern. Ich fühle mich dort sehr wohl.

Last year I spent two marvelous weeks at the Chiemsee. This summer I would like to go to Reit-im-Winkl.

Letztes Jahr habe ich zwei herrliche Wochen am Chiemsee verbracht. Diesen Sommer möchte ich nach Reit-im-Winkl.

Thanking

please! **bitte!**
I thank **ich danke** +dat
thank you! **danke!**
many thanks! **vielen Dank!, danke sehr!**
thank you very much! **danke schön!**
thank you very much indeed! **herzlichen Dank!**
thanks a lot! **schönen Dank auch!**
don't mention it! **nichts zu danken!**
glad to help! **gern geschehen!**
no need to thank me! **keine Ursache!**
not at all! **bitte!, bitte schön!**
it was the least I could do! **das ist doch selbstverständlich!**

Disapproval

I annoy **ich störe**
you're annoying me! **du störst mich!**
bad **schlecht**
that's too bad! **das geht zu weit**
bad luck **das Pech**
we had bad luck **wir hatten Pech**
what bad luck! **so ein Mist!**
damn! **verdammt!**
dreadful **schrecklich, furchtbar**
fed up **sauer**

furious **wütend**
how dreadful! **wie schrecklich!**
I hate doing **ich hasse es, zu** +inf
it hurts! **das tut weh!**
impossible **unmöglich**
that's impossible **das geht (doch) nicht, unmöglich!**
leave me in peace! **lass mich in Ruhe!**
are you mad? **bist du verrückt?**
I mind a lot **es macht mir viel aus***
miserable **miserabel**
nonsense! **Quatsch!, (das ist) Unsinn!**
it's nothing to do with me **das geht mich nichts an***
ouch! **au!**
there's no point! **das hat keinen Zweck/Sinn**
rubbish **Quatsch!**
shit! **Scheiße!**
I can't stand him **ich kann ihn nicht leiden**
stop that! **lass das!, hör doch auf!**
stupid **dumm**
that's stupid! **das ist zu dumm!**
that won't do **das geht nicht**
that's enough **das genügt**

The weather was dreadful. **Das Wetter war schrecklich.**
Such bad luck! **So ein Pech!**

– Thanks a lot for your help, Willi. **– Vielen Dank für deine Hilfe, Willi.**

– Don't mention it. Glad to help. **– Nichts zu danken. Gern geschehen.**

There's no point planning a picnic for Sunday. It's supposed to rain. **Es hat keinen Zweck ein Picknick für Sonntag zu planen. Es soll regnen.**

I have to concentrate on my work. Please leave me in peace! **Ich muss mich auf meine Arbeit konzentrieren. Bitte lass mich in Ruhe!**

➤ INTERJECTIONS, APOLOGIZING, & FAREWELLS 15d

15c Permission, obligation, & clarification

Permission

can I? **kann ich?**
could I? **könnte ich?**
OK? **geht das?**
may I? **darf ich?**
might I? **dürfte ich?**
will you allow me to **erlauben Sie mir zu** +inf?
would it be possible? **wäre es möglich?**
Why of course! **ja natürlich!**
sure! **ja klar!**
OK! **okay!, in Ordnung!**
yes, that's OK! **ja, das geht!**
allowed **erlaubt/gestattet**
I allow you to.... **ich erlaube Ihnen zu** +inf
it doesn't bother me, if you … **es stört mich nicht, wenn Sie …**
carry on! **machen Sie ruhig weiter!**
of course you can … **Sie dürfen selbstverständlich …**
you can if you want **du kannst, wenn du willst**
as far as I'm concerned, you can … **meinetwegen können Sie …**
do you mind if …? **stört es Sie wenn …?**
yes, if you must **ja, wenn es sein muss**
do you object? **haben Sie was dagegen?**
permission **die Erlaubnis(se)**
as you wish **wie Sie wollen**
you are not allowed to **du darfst nicht**
no, you can't … **nein, du kannst/darfst nicht …**
certainly not! **durchaus nicht!**
certainly not **auf keinen Fall, keinesfalls**
it is just not done! **das tut man nicht!**
forbidden **untersagt, verboten**

smoking forbidden **Rauchverbot**
impossible! **ausgeschlossen!**
no, certainly not **nein, keineswegs**
not at all **gar/überhaupt nicht**
it's not possible **es geht leider nicht**
of course not! **überhaupt nicht!**
out of the question! **es kommt nicht in Frage!**
please don't! **bitte nicht!**
I'd rather you didn't! **lieber nicht!**
I have no right to … **ich habe kein Recht zu** +inf
I'm sorry! **tut mir leid!**
under no circumstances **auf keinen Fall**

Obligation

it's compulsory **es ist Vorschrift/obligatorisch**
I have got to **ich muss unbedingt/auf jeden Fall**
you've got to! **das muss sein!**
I have to **ich muss**
do I have to? **muss ich?**
you don't have to **du musst nicht**
I have a lot to do **ich habe viel zu tun**
I intend to … **ich habe vor zu** +inf
I intend to **ich habe die Absicht**
I must **ich muss**
you must pay a fee **es ist gebührenpflichtig**
it is not necessary **es ist nicht nötig**
not necessarily **nicht unbedingt**
you do not need to **du brauchst nicht zu** +inf
you needn't do it **du kannst es ruhig lassen**
I am obliged to **ich bin verpflichtet zu** +inf

I am not supposed to   **ich soll nicht**
I want to   **ich will**
what is to be done?   **was ist zu tun?**

Clarifying

and so on, etc.   **und so weiter, usw.**
I ask   **ich frage**
may I ask a question?   **dürfte ich
   eine Frage stellen?**
example   **das Beispiel(e)**
for example   **zum Beispiel,
   beispielsweise**
I explain   **ich erkläre**
I hear   **ich höre**
can you still hear me?   **hören Sie
   mich noch?**
are you still there?   **sind Sie noch
   da?**
I didn't hear   **ich habe nicht gehört**
I forget   **ich vergesse**
in other words   **mit anderen
   Worten, anders gesagt**
I know   **ich weiß**
I don't know how you say ...   **ich
   weiß nicht, wie man sagt ...**
loud   **laut**
louder   **lauter**
not so loud!   **nicht so laut!**
I mean   **ich meine**
it means   **es bedeutet**
what does it mean?   **was heißt das?**
what do you mean   **was meinen Sie?**
what do you mean by that?   **was
   meinen Sie damit?**

I pronounce   **ich spreche aus***
how do you pronounce it?   **wie
   spricht man das aus?**
I have a question   **ich habe eine
   Frage**
quick(ly)   **schnell**
not so quick   **nicht so schnell**
quiet please!   **Ruhe bitte!**
quietly!   **leise!**
I repeat   **ich wiederhole**
could you repeat that?   **könnten
   Sie das wiederholen?**
I say   **ich sage**
how do you say that in German?
   wie sagt man das auf Deutsch?
what would you say?   **was würden
   Sie sagen?**
what did you say?   **was haben Sie
   gesagt?**
slow   **langsam**
slower   **langsamer**
sorry   **Entschuldigung!**
I translate into German   **ich
   übersetze ins Deutsche**
I understand   **ich verstehe**
can you understand me?   **können
   Sie mich verstehen?**
what is it in English?   **wie/was
   heißt das auf Englisch?**
what do you call it in German?   **wie
   nennt man das auf Deutsch?**
what was that?   **wie war das? was
   war das gleich?**

Excuse me, could you say that a
little louder? I didn't hear you.

– May I interrupt you for a
moment?
– Certainly.
– Would you please repeat that
last point? I didn't understand it.

**Entschuldigung, könnten Sie
das ein bisschen lauter sagen?
Ich habe Sie nicht gehört.**
**– Darf ich Sie mal
unterbrechen?**
– Selbstverständlich.
**– Würden Sie bitte den letzten
Punkt wiederholen? Ich habe
ihn nicht verstanden.**

COMMUNICATING WITH OTHERS

15d Interjections, apologizing, & farewells

Surprise

at last! **endlich!**
amazed **erstaunt**
Fancy that! **Na, so was!**
funny **komisch!**
funny he never told me! **komisch, dass er mir nicht Bescheid sagte!**
God! **O Gott!**
God be praised! **Gott sei Dank!**
Good God! **meine Güte!**
goodness **um Himmels willen**
I surprise **ich überrasche**
impossible **unmöglich**
that's incredible! **das ist ja unglaublich!**
possible **möglich**
that can't be possible! **das ist doch nicht möglich!**
really? **(also) wirklich?**
so what? **na, und?**
surely **doch**
surely you know **du weißt doch ...**
surprised **überrascht**
surprising **überraschend**
what a surprise! **das ist aber eine Überraschung!**
I think **ich denke**
I would never have thought that **das hätte ich nicht gedacht**
true **wahr**

that can't be true! **das darf doch nicht wahr sein!**
is that true? **ist das wahr? stimmt das?**
Well I never! **Na, so was!**
what! **was!**
luck **das Glück**
what luck (that)! **ein Glück (dass)!**
wow! **Mensch!**

Hesitating

aha **aha, ach so**
as it were **sozusagen**
but ... **aber ...**
by the way **nebenbei**
definitely? **bestimmt? sicher?**
is that so? **ist das so?**
I don't know **ich weiß nicht**
you know **wissen Sie**
maybe **es kann sein**
moreover **übrigens**
oh! **ach!**
one minute please **eine Minute, einen Moment bitte**
one moment! **(einen) Moment mal**
or? **oder? gell?**
or not? **oder nicht?**
pardon **bitte? Verzeihung?**
I beg your pardon **bitte?**
perhaps **vielleicht**

– I just don't know what to do.

It can't be true! I have to go to a meeting shortly and my husband took the car!

– You've got time on Friday, don't you?
– I don't know. Just a moment, let me check my calendar.

– **Ich weiß einfach nicht, was ich machen soll.**

Das darf doch nicht wahr sein! Ich muss gleich zu einer Besprechung, und mein Mann hat das Auto genommen!

– **Du hast doch am Freitag Zeit, oder nicht?**
– **Ich weiß nicht. Einen Moment mal, lass mich mal in meinem Kalender nachsehen.**

please go on **mach weiter**
really? **wirklich? tatsächlich?**
something like that **so etwas**
I suppose **ich vermute**
supposedly **vermutlich, wohl**
that is, i.e. **das heißt, d.h.**
that is to say **das heißt**
what next? **was nun?**
what shall I do now? **was mache ich jetzt?**
well … **na, nun …**
well OK! **na gut!**
well then … **also**
what now? **was jetzt/nun?**
why? **warum**
why not? **warum nicht?**
yes, but … **(ja) schon aber, schon gut aber …**

Agreeing

I agree **das finde ich auch**
agreed! **einverstanden!, abgemacht!**
both … and **sowohl … als auch**
certain **sicher**
certainly! **bestimmt!, allerdings!, eben!**
definitely **bestimmt, gewiss**
exactly! **genau!**
firstly **erstens**
in short **kurz (gesagt)**
I know **ich weiß**
no! **nein!**
not only … but also **nicht nur … sondern auch**
obviously! **selbstverständlich!**
that's obvious **das ist klar**
of course! **freilich!**
it occurs to me **es fällt mir ein***
right! **richtig!**
is that right? **ist das richtig?**
isn't that so/right? **nicht wahr?**
secondly **zweitens**
something else **was anderes**
I tell **ich erzähle**
tell us **erzählen Sie mal**
I think so too! **das glaub ich auch!**

do you think so? **finden/glauben/ meinen Sie?**
true **wahr**
that's true! **das stimmt!**
is that true? **ist das wahr?**
I want **ich will**
as you want **wie Sie wollen/meinen**
if you want **wenn Sie Lust haben**
well, that's that **so, das wär's**
yes! **ja!**

Apologizing

I apologize (for) **ich entschuldige mich (für +acc)**
apology **die Entschuldigung(en)**
excuse me **entschuldigen Sie**
sorry! **Entschuldigung!, Verzeihung!**
I'm sorry **das tut mir leid!**
I am so sorry! **Entschuldigen Sie bitte!**
it doesn't matter! **das macht nichts!**
that's OK! **schon gut!**

Farewells

Goodbye! **Auf Wiedersehen!**
Goodbye! *(telephone)* **Auf Wiederhören!**
Bye! **Tschüs!**
See you soon! **Bis bald!**
See you tomorrow! **Bis morgen!**
greetings to the family! **viele Grüße an die Familie!**
greet Manfred from me! **grüß Manfred von mir!**
all the best! **alles Gute!, mach's gut!**
best wishes to your wife! **einen schönen Gruß an Ihre Frau!**
have fun! **viel Spaß!**
have a good time! **viel Vergnügen!**
have a good journey! **gute Reise!**
have a safe journey! **komm gut nach Hause!**
have a good holiday/vacation! **schöne Ferien!**
same to you! **danke gleichfalls!**

COMMUNICATING WITH OTHERS

15e Post/Mail & telephone

Post/Mail

abroad **im/ins Ausland**
addressee **der Adressat(en)** *(wk)* **[-in]**
answer **die Antwort(en)**
any news? **irgendwelche Nachricht(en)?**
by air **per Luftpost**
airmail **die Luftpost**
collection/pickup **die Leerung(en)**
I correspond **ich korrespondiere**
correspondent **der Korrespondent(en)** *(wk)* **[-in]**
counter **der Schalter(-)**
customs declaration **die Zollerklärung(en)**
express delivery **die Eilzustellung**
franking-machine/postage meter **die Frankiermaschine(n)**
freepost **Gebühr bezahlt Empfänger**
I get/receive **ich bekomme**
I hand in **ich reiche ein***
letter **der Brief(e)**
letter rate **die Briefgebühr(en)**
mailbox **der Briefkasten(-̈e)**
I finish *(letter)* **ich beende**
news **die Neuigkeit(en), die Nachricht(en)**
I note down **ich schreibe auf, ich notiere**

package **das Päckchen(-)**
parcel **das Paket(e)**
parcel rate **die Paketgebühr(en)**
pen pal **der Brieffreund(e) [-in]**
post/mail **die Post**
post office **das Postamt(-̈er)**
poste restante **postlagernd**
postage **das Porto**
postman/mail carrier **der Briefträger(-) [-in]**
I receive **ich erhalte**
recorded delivery **per Einschreiben**
registered mail **die eingeschriebene Post**
reply **die Antwort(en)**
sealed **versiegelt**
I send **ich schicke**
I send (greetings) **ich bestelle (Grüße)**
sender **der Absender(-)**
stamp **die Briefmarke(n)**
I write **ich schreibe**
zip code **die Postleitzahl(en)**

Telephoning

I call **ich rufe an**
I connect **ich verbinde**
I dial **ich wähle**
I fax **ich faxe**
I hang up **ich lege auf***
I hold **ich warte**

Jan corresponds a lot with clients abroad.	**Jan korrespondiert viel mit Kunden im Ausland.**
When does the mail arrive?	**Wann trifft die Post ein?**
I am writing on behalf of my father, concerning …	**Ich schreibe im Namen meines Vaters bezüglich …**
I look forward to hearing from you.	**Ich hoffe bald von Ihnen zu hören.**

I pick up **ich hebe ab***
I press **ich drücke**
I put ... through (to) **ich stelle zu**
+dat **... durch***
I speak to ... **ich spreche mit** +dat
I telephone/phone **ich telefoniere**

Telephone & telecommunications

answering machine **der Anrufbeantworter**
booth **die Telefonzelle(n)**
button **der Knopf(-e)**
push the button **auf den Knopf drücken!**
call-box **die Telefonzelle(n)**
communication **die Kommunikation(en)**
conversation **das Gespräch(e)**
I dial **ich wähle**
E-mail **E-mail**
engaged/busy *(phone)* **besetzt**
I am ex-directory/not listed **ich stehe nicht im Telefonbuch**
extension **der Anschluss(-e)**
fax **das Fax-Gerät(e), das Fax**
fax modem **das Fax-Modem**
information highway **die Datenautobahn**
line **die Telefonverbindung(en)**
link **der Anschluss(-e)**

local call **das Ortsgespräch(e)**
long-distance call **das Ferngespräch(e)**
nought/zero/0 **Null**
number **die Nummer(n)**
operator **die Zentrale(n)**
optical fibre/fiber **das Glasfaserkabel(-)**
order **in Betrieb**
out of order **außer Betrieb**
receiver **der Hörer(-)**
reverse charge call/collect call **das R-Gespräch(e)**
satellite **der Satellit(en)** *(wk)*
slot **der Schlitz(e)**
telecommunications **die Telekommunikation(en)**
telephone **das Telefon(e)**
car phone **das Autotelefon(e)**
cellular/mobile phone **das Handy(s)**
telephone directory **das Telefonbuch(-er)**
telephone kiosk **die Telefonzelle**
teletext **der Videotext**
I transmit **ich übertrage**
wrong number **falsch verbunden**

Can I dial direct?	**Kann ich direkt durchwählen?**
– Who's speaking?	**– Wer ist am Apparat?**
– This is John Smith (speaking).	**– Hier spricht John Smith.**
Could you put me through to Mr. Müller?	**Können sie mich mit Herrn Müller verbinden?**
– Please hold! Are you still there?	**–Bitte bleiben Sie am Apparat.**
I'm afraid Mr. Müller's not in.	**Sind sie noch dran? Herr Müller ist leider nicht da.**
– I will call back later.	**–Ich werde später zurückrufen.**
Good-bye!	**Auf Wiederhören.**

➤ COMPUTERS 15f

COMMUNICATING WITH OTHERS

15f Computers

Computer applications

adventure game **das Abenteuerspiel(e)**
application **die Anwendung(en)**
artificial intelligence **die künstliche Intelligenz**
barcode **der Bar-Code(s)**
barcode reader **der Scanner**
barcoded **mit Bar-Code**
calculator **der Rechner(-)**
computer control **die Computerkontrolle(n)**
computer science/studies **die Informatik**
computerized **computerisiert**
desktop publishing/DTP **das DTP-Programm(e)**
game **das Spiel(e)**
grammar checker **der Grammatiküberprüfer**
information **die Information(en)**
information technology **die Informationstechnologie**
internet **das Internet**

simulation **die Simulation(en)**
simulator **der Simulator(en)** *(wk)*
spell-check **die Rechtschreibkontrolle(n)**
synthesizer **der Synthesizer(-)**
thesaurus **das Synonymwörterbuch(⁻er)**
word processor **das Textverarbeitungsgerät(e)**
word processing **die Textverarbeitung**

Word processing & operating

I abort **ich breche ab***
I access **ich rufe auf***
I append **ich hänge an***
I back-up **ich sichere**
I block *(text)* **ich markiere**
I boot up **ich boote**
I browse **ich browse**
I cancel *(command)* **ich deaktiviere**
I click on **ich klicke an***
I communicate **ich kommuniziere**
I copy **ich kopiere**
I count **ich zähle**

It's all done by computer.

In a spreadsheet you can fill the cells with text, figures or formulas.

You must analyze the problem and decide what formulas to use.

Das geht alles per Computer.

In einer Tabellenkalkulation kann man die Zellen mit Text, Zahlen oder Formeln füllen.
Sie müssen die Aufgabe analysieren und entscheiden, welche Formeln Sie einsetzen müssen.

– This disk is corrupted. It has wiped out my file!
– Have you checked for a virus?

– Diese Diskette ist defekt. Sie hat meine Datei gelöscht!
– Haben Sie auf Viren überprüft?

I create **ich erstelle**
I cut and paste **ich schneide aus
    und füge ein***
I debug **ich beseitige den Fehler**
I delete **ich lösche**
I download **ich lade**
I drag **ich ziehe**
I embolden **ich formatiere in
    Fettschrift**
I enter (text) **ich gebe (Text) ein***
I erase **ich lösche**
I exit (the program) **ich beende
    (das Programm)**
I export **ich exportiere**
I file **ich lege an***
I format **ich formatiere**
I handle *(text)* **ich verarbeite**
I import **ich importiere**
I insert **ich füge ein***
I install **ich installiere**
I key in **ich gebe ein***
I list **ich liste auf***
I log off **ich beende das Progamm**
I log on/off **ich logge ein/aus***
I merge **ich schließe zusammen***
I move *(a file)* **ich verschiebe
    (eine Datei)**

I move **ich verschiebe**
I network **ich vernetze**
I open (a file) **ich öffne (eine
    Datei)**
I paste **ich füge ein***
I print **ich drucke**
I print out **ich drucke aus***
I (word) process **ich verarbeite**
I program **ich programmiere**
I read **ich lese**
I receive **ich empfange**
I record **ich nehme auf***
I remove **ich streiche**
I replace **ich ersetze**
I retrieve **ich rufe ab*/auf*** .
I run **ich lade, ich lasse laufen***
I save **ich speichere**
I search **ich suche**
I send **ich (ver)sende**
I shift **ich speichere**
I simulate **ich simuliere**
I sort **ich sortiere**
I store **ich speichere, ich lege an***
I switch on/off **ich schalte ein/aus***
I underline **ich unterstreiche**
I update **ich aktualisiere**

The data is in memory.	**Die Daten befinden sich im Arbeitsspeicher.**
Copy the files onto a CD.	**Kopieren Sie die Dateien auf eine CD.**
Make a backup copy.	**Machen Sie eine Sicherheitskopie.**
Which operating system do you use?	**Welches Betriebssystem verwenden Sie?**
How easy is this spreadsheet to use?	**Wie einfach ist es, diese Bildschirmtabelle zu benutzen?**
I don't like the software package with this PC.	**Ich mag die Software auf diesem PC nicht.**

16 | Leisure & sport

16a Leisure

activity **die Aktivität(en)**
I am free **ich habe Zeit**
archery **das Bogenschießen**
bar **die Bar(s)**
I begin **ich beginne**
book **das Buch("-er)**
boring **langweilig**
camera **der Fotoapparat(e), die Kamera(s)**
card **die (Spiel)karte(n)**
card game **das Kartenspiel(e)**
card table **der Spieltisch(e)**
casino **das Kasino(s)**
chess **das Schach, das Schachspiel(e)**
cinema **das Kino(s)**
closed **geschlossen**
club **der Klub(s)**
I collect **ich sammle**
coin **die Münze(n)**
crosswords **das Kreuzworträtsel(-)**
collection **die Sammlung(en)**
collectors fair **die Sammlerausstellung(en)**
discotheque **die Diskothek(en)**

I draw (etch) **ich zeichne**
holiday/vacation **die Ferien** (pl)
interest **das Interesse(n)**
energy **die Energie(n)**
enthusiasm **die Begeisterung**
enthusiastic **begeistert**
entrance **der Eingang("-e)**
entry fee **der Eintritt(e)**
excitement **die Aufregung(en), die Erregung(en)**
exciting **aufregend, erregend**
excursion **der Ausflug("-e)**
excursionist **der Ausflügler(-) [-in]**
exit **der Ausgang("-e)**
fair **die Ausstellung(en), die Messe(n)**
fascinating **faszinierend**
finished **beendet, zu Ende**
I fish **ich angle**
free time **die freie Zeit, die Freizeit**
fun **der Spaß("-e)**
I gamble **ich spiele um Geld**
I go out **ich gehe aus***
guide **der Reiseführer(-) [-in]**
guided tour **die Reisetour(en)**

Do you do a lot of sport?
I like going for long walks.

Treibst du viel Sport?
Ich wandere gern.

Sometimes I go fishing, which can be highly recommended for stressed executives!

Manchmal gehe ich fischen, was sehr empfehlenswert für gestresste Manager ist.

I can meet you at the swimming pool or, if you prefer, at the gym.

Wir können uns an der Schwimmhalle oder, wenn du willst, an der Turnhalle treffen.

hobby **das Hobby(s)**
energetic **energisch**
interesting **interessant**
it is over **es ist vorbei**
I join **ich trete in** +acc **ein*, ich schließe mich (jdm.) an***
leisure **die Freizeit**
line **die Schlange(n)**
I get in line **ich stelle mich an***
I listen to **ich höre** +dat **zu***
I look **ich sehe, ich blicke**
market **der Markt(-e)**
    antiques market **der Antiquitätenmarkt(-e)**
    flea market **der Flohmarkt(-e)**
I meet **ich treffe**
meeting place **der Treffpunkt(e)**
member **das Mitglied(er)**
membership **die Mitgliedschaft(en)**
nightclub **der Nachtklub(s)**
open **offen, auf**
organization **die Organisation(en)**
I organize **ich organisiere**
photograph **die Fotografie(n), die Aufnahmen(n)**
picnic **das Picknick(s)**
place **der Ort(e)**
I play **ich spiele**
pleasure **das Vergnügen(-), die Freude(n)**
politics **die Politik**
I prefer **ich bevorzuge, ich ziehe**

vor*
private **privat**
public **öffentlich**
line **die Schlange(n)**
I queue **ich stehe an***
I read **ich lese**
season **die Jahreszeit(en)**
secluded **abgelegen, ruhig**
I sew **ich nähe**
slide/chute **die Rutsche(n)**
I slide **ich rutsche**
sold out **ausverkauft**
spectator **der Zuschauer(-) [-in]**
I start (doing) **ich beginne, zu** +inf
I stop (doing) **ich höre auf*, zu** +inf
I stroll **ich schlendere, ich spaziere**
subscription **das Abonnement(s)**
I take photos **ich fotografiere**
television **der Fernseher(-)**
ticket **die Eintrittskarte(n)**
time **die Zeit(en)**
theatre **das Theater(-)**
tour **die Tour(en)**
vacation **die Ferien, der Urlaub**
I visit **ich besuche**
visit **der Besuch(e)**
I walk **ich gehe spazieren***
I watch **ich schaue** +dat **zu*, ich sehe** +dat **zu***
youth club **der Jugendklub(s)**
zoo **der Zoo(s)**

– What do you like doing on a rainy day?
– Perhaps playing cards, but not with my brother: he cheats!

– **Was machst du gern, wenn es regnet?**
– **Vielleicht Karten spielen, aber nicht mit meinem Bruder: er mogelt!**

– Are there any special rates for students?
– Yes, but only on Friday nights.

– **Gibt es besondere Studentenermäßigungen?**
– **Ja, aber nur Freitag abends.**

➤ LEISURE WEAR, LEISURE EQUIPMENT 16c; PHOTOGRAPHY App.16a

16b Sporting activity

aerobics **das Aerobic**
against **gegen** +acc
athlete **der Athlet(en)** *(wk)* **[-in],
der Sportler(-) [-in]**
athletic **sportlich**
I attack **ich greife an***
bathtowel **das Badetuch(¨-er)**
I defend **ich verteidige**
I bet **ich wette**
boat **das Boot(e)**
I box **ich boxe**
boxer **der Boxer(-)**
I bowl **ich bowle, ich gehe
bowlen**
captain **der Kapitän(e)**
I catch **ich fange**
champion **der Meister(-) [-in]**
championship **die
Meisterschaft(en)**
changing/locker room **der
Umkleideraum(¨-e)**
I climb **ich klettere**
climber **der Bergsteiger(-) [-in]**
club **der Klub(s)**
coach **der Trainer(-) [-in]**
crew **die Mannschaft(en)**
cup *(tournament)* **der Pokal(e)**
cycle **das Fahrrad(¨-er)**
I cycle **ich fahre Rad**
defeat **die Niederlage(n)**
I dive **ich tauche**
I do (sport) **ich treibe (Sport)**
I draw **ich spiele unentschieden**
it was a draw **es war
unentschieden**
effort **die Anstrengung(en)**
I make an effort **ich strenge
mich an***
endurance **die Ausdauer**
equipment **die Ausstattung(en)**
I exercize **ich bewege mich**
exercize **die Bewegung(en)**
I fall **ich falle, ich stürze**
fall **der Sturz(¨-e)**
field **das Feld(er)**

finals **das Finale(s), das
Endspiel(e)**
fit **fit**
fitness **die Fitness** *(no pl)*
game **das Spiel(e)**
I get fit **ich trimme mich**
goal **das Tor(e)**
ground **der Boden**
gym(nasium) **die Turnhalle(n)**
I hit **ich schlage, ich treffe**
hit **der Schlag(¨-e), der Treffer(-)**
horse race **das Pferderennen(-)**
I ice-skate **ich laufe Schlittschuh**
ice rink **die Eisbahn(en)**
injury **die Verletzung(en)**
instructor **der Lehrer(-) [-in]**
I jog **ich jogge**
jogger **der Jogger(-) [-in]**
I jump **ich springe**
jump **der Sprung(¨-e)**
lawn **der Rasen(-)**
league **die Liga(s)**
league leader **der
Tabellenführer(-)**
locker room **der
Umkleideraum(¨-e)**
I lose **ich verliere**
marathon **der Marathon(s)**
match **das Spiel(e)**
medal **die Medaille(n)**
    bronze/gold/silver **Bronze-/
Gold-/Silber-**
muscle **der Muskel(n)**
Olympic Games (Winter) **die
Olympischen (Winter)spiele**
I pass (ball) **ich spiele jdm. (den
Ball) zu***
pedal **das Pedal(e)**
I pedal **ich strample, ich trete**
physical **körperlich**
I pitch **ich werfe**
pitcher **der Werfer(-)**
pitch/field **das Spielfeld(er)**
I play **ich spiele**
player **der Spieler**

point der Moment(e), der Zeitpunkt(e)
professional **professionell**
I race **ich renne (um die Wette)**
race **das Wettrennen(-)**
referee **der Schiedsrichter(-) [-in]**
rest **die Pause(n)**
result **das Ergebnis(se)**
I ride **ich reite, ich fahre**
riding **das Reiten**
riding school **die Reitschule(n)**
I row **ich rudere**
I run **ich renne, ich laufe**
run **der Lauf(-̈e)**
runner **der Läufer(-) [-in]**
sailing school **die Segelschule(n)**
I sail **ich segle**
I save *(goal)* **ich halte**
I score (a goal) **ich schieße (ein Tor)**
score **das Spielergebnis(se), die Punktzahl(en), der Spielstand(-̈e)**
I ski **ich laufe Ski**
I shoot *(ball, puck)* **ich schieße**
show **die Show(s)**
skier **der Skiläufer(-) [-in]**
ski lift **der Skilift(e)**
sponsor **der Sponsor(en)**
sponsorship **die Förderung**
sport **der Sport (Sportarten)**

sports field/pitch **der Sportplatz(-̈e)**
sprint **der Sprint(s)**
stadium **das Stadion (-ien)**
stamina **das Durchhaltevermögen**
strength **die Kraft(-̈e)**
supporter **der Anhänger(-) [-in]**
I swim **ich schwimme**
team **die Mannschaft(en)**
team sport **das Mannschaftsspiel(e)**
I throw **ich werfe**
timing **das Timing**
tournament **das Turnier(e)**
track **die Rennbahn(en), die Piste(n)**
I train **ich trainiere**
trainer **der Trainer(-) [-in]**
training **das Training**
triumph **der Sieg(e)**
trophy **die Trophäe(n)**
I am unfit **ich bin nicht fit**
victory **der Sieg(e)**
I win **ich gewinne**
weight training **das Krafttraining**
workout **das Training**
world championship **die Weltmeisterschaft(en)**
world cup *(soccer)* **die Fußballweltmeisterschaft(en)**

The victory was a remarkable achievement for the national team, which played extremely well.

Der Sieg war eine bemerkenswerte Leistung der Nationalmannschaft, die besonders gut gespielt hat.

The team has been training in very trying weather conditions. Each athlete was ready to give his best.

Die Mannschaft hat unter äußerst schwierigen Wetterverhältnissen trainiert. Jeder Spieler war bereit, das Beste zu geben.

Unfortunately, a member of the team was seriously injured during the last race.

Unglücklicherweise hat sich ein Mitglied der Mannschaft während des letzten Rennens ernsthaft verletzt.

➤ SPORTING EQUIPMENT 16c

LEISURE & SPORT

16c Sports & equipment

Sports

athletics **die Leichtathletik**
badminton **das Badminton, der Federball**
baseball **der Baseball**
basketball **der Basketball**
billiards **das Billard**
bowling **das Bowling**
boxing **das Boxen**
car racing **das Autorennen, der Rennsport**
climbing **das Bergsteigen, das Klettern**
  free climbing **das Freeclimbing**
  rock climbing **das Felsenklettern**
cricket **das Cricket**
cycling **das Radfahren**
decathlon **der Zehnkampf(-̈e)**
diving **das Tauchen**
deep-sea diving **das Tiefseetauchen**
football(*American*) **der Football**
handball **der Handball**
hockey **das Hockey**
horse racing **das Pferderennen**
horse riding **der Reitsport**
ice hockey **das Eishockeyspiel(e)**

ice skating **das Schlittschuhlaufen**
jogging **das Joggen**
paragliding **das Gleitschirmfliegen**
pentathlon **der Fünfkampf(-̈e)**
polo **das Polo**
pool **das Poolbillard**
racing **das Rennen, der Wettlauf(-̈e)**
roller skating **das Rollschuhlaufen**
rugby **das Rugbyspiel(e)**
sailing **das Segeln**
skiing **das Skilaufen**
  cross-country skiing **der Langlauf**
  downhill skiing **der Abfahrtslauf**
soccer **der Fußball**
swimming **das Schwimmen**
table tennis **das Tischtennis**
tennis **das Tennis**
volleyball **der Volleyball**
water polo **der Wasserball**
weightlifting **das Gewichtheben**

– Did you watch the match?
– No, I had to leave before the end. Who won?

– We lost three to one. I still cannot understand how our team could lose so disastrously after a brilliant season.

– **Hast du das Spiel gesehen?**
– **Nein, ich musste vor dem Ende gehen. Wer hat gewonnen?**

– **Wir haben drei zu eins verloren. Ich kann immer noch nicht verstehen, wie unsere Mannschaft nach einer sehr guten Saison so verheerend verlieren konnte.**

Leisure wear & sports clothes

anorak **der Anorak(s)**
bathing suit **der Badeanzug(ӱe)**
boots **die Stiefel(-)**
cycling shorts **die Radlerhose(n)**
dancing shoes **der Tanzschuh(e)**
gardening gloves **der Gartenhandschuh(e)**
leotard **der Gymnastikanzug(ӱe)**
parka **der Parka(s)**
swimsuit **der Badeanzug(ӱe)**
swimming trunks **die Badehose(n)**
rugby shirt **das Rugbyshirt(s)**
track suit **der Trainingsanzug(ӱe)**
trainers athletic shoes **der Turnschuh(e)**
walking boot **der Wanderschuh(e)**
waterproof jacket **die Wetterjacke(n)**
Wellington boot **der Gummistiefel(-)**
wet suit **der Kälteschutzanzug(ӱe)**

Leisure & sports equipment

arrow **der Pfeil(e)**
ball **der Ball(ӱe)**
bat **der Schläger(-)**
binoculars **das Fernglas(ӱer)**
boxing gloves **der Boxhandschuh(e)**
bow **der Bogen(-)**
camera **die Kamera(s)**

crash helmet **der Schutzhelm(e)**
exercise bike **der Heimtrainer(-)**
equipment **die Ausrüstung(en)**
fishing rod **die Angelrute(n)**
headphone **der Kopfhörer(-)**
hi-fi **die Hi-Fi-Anlage**
knapsack **der Rucksack(ӱe)**
knitting needles **die Stricknadel(n)**
javelin **der Speer(e)**
mountain bike **das Mountainbike(s)**
net **das Netz(e)**
oar **das Ruder(-)**
puck **die Scheibe(n), der Puck(s)**
racket **der Schläger(-)**
rifle **das Gewehr(e)**
roller skate **der Rollschuh(e)**
rowing machine **das Motorboot(e)**
rowing boat **das Ruderboot(e)**
rucksack **der Rucksack(ӱe)**
sailing-boat **das Segelboot(e)**
sewing kit **das Nähzeug**
skate **der Schlittschuh(e)**
skis **der Ski(er)**
ski boot **der Skistiefel(-)**
ski pole **der Skistock(ӱe)**
stick *(hockey)* **der Hockeyschläger(-)**
sports bag **die Sporttasche(n)**
surf board **das Surfbrett(er)**
weight **das Gewicht(e)**
yacht **die Yacht(en)**

All the sports commentators agreed that it was particularly unfortunate when the referee insisted on the penalty kick.

Alle Sportreporter waren sich einig, dass es besonderes Pech war, als der Schiedsrichter auf dem Strafstoß bestand.

– Do you develop your own photos?
– I would like to, but I do not have a dark room.

– Entwickelst du deine Fotos selbst?
– Ich würde es gern, aber ich habe keine Dunkelkammer.

➤ PHOTOGRAPHY App.16a; GARDENING 8c   **133**

The arts

17a Appreciation & criticism

abstract **abstrakt**
abstruse **schwer verständlich**
action **die Handlung(en)**
aesthete **der Ästhet(en)** *(wk)*
aesthetics **die Ästhetik**
I analyze **ich analysiere**
I appreciate **ich schätze**
appreciation **das Verständnis(se)**
art **die Kunst(¨e)**
artist **der Künstler(-) [-in]**
artistic **künstlerisch**
atmosphere **die Atmosphäre(n)**
atmospheric **atmosphärisch**
author **der Verfasser(-) [-in]**
award **der Preis(e)**
avant-garde **die Avantgarde**
believable **glaubhaft**
character **der Charakter(e)**
characterization **die Charakterisierung(en)**
characteristic **charakteristisch**
climax **der Höhepunkt(e)**
I close **ich schließe**
comic **der Komiker(-) [-in]**
  comic *(adj)* **lustig, komisch**
commentary **der Kommentar(e)**
conflict **der Konflikt(e)**
contemporary **zeitgenössisch, modern**
contrast **der Kontrast(e)**
it creates **es schafft**
creative **kreativ**
creativity **die Kreativität** *(no pl)*
credible **glaubwürdig**
critic **der Kritiker(-) [-in]**
criticism **die Kritik(en)**
cultivated **gebildet**
culture **die Kultur(en)**
it deals with **es handelt von** +dat
it describes **es beschreibt**

it develops **es entwickelt (sich)**
development **die Entwicklung(en)**
device **der Kunstgriff(e)**
dialog **der Dialog(e)**
disturbing **störend**
empathy **das Einfühlungsvermögen**
ending **der Schluss(¨e)**
endless **endlos**
it ends **es endet**
entertaining **amüsant**
entertainment **die Unterhaltung**
epic **die Epik**
  epic *(adj)* **episch**
event **das Ereignis(se)**
eventful **ereignisreich**
example **das Beispiel(e)**
excited **aufgeregt**
exciting **aufregend, spannend**
I explain **ich erläutere**
explanation **die Erläuterung(en)**
it explores **es untersucht**
it expresses **es drückt aus***
extravagant **überschwänglich**
fake **die Fälschung(en)**
  fake *(adj)* **gefälscht**
fantastic **phantastisch**
fantasy **die Phantasie(n)**
farcical **possenhaft**
figure **die Figur(en)**
funny **komisch**
genre **das Genre(s)**
image **das Bild(er)**
imaginary **frei erfunden**
imagination **die Phantasie(n)**
inspiration **die Inspiration(en)**
inspired by **inspiriert durch** +acc
intense **intensiv**
intensity **die Intensität**
interpretation **die Deutung(en)**

interpreter **der Interpret(en)** *(wk)* **[-in]**
interpretation **die Interpretation(en)**
invention **die Erfindung(en)**
inventive **erfinderisch**
inventiveness **die schöpferische Kraft(¨e)**
ironic **ironisch**
irony **die Ironie(n)**
issue **die Frage(n)**
long-winded **umständlich**
lyrical **lyrisch**
modern **modern**
mood **die Stimmung(en)**
moral **die Moral, die Ethik**
  moral *(adj)* **moralisch**
morality **die Sittlichkeit(en)**
moving **ergreifend**
mystery **das Geheimnis(se)**
mysterious **geheimnisvoll**
mystical **mystisch**
mysticism **die Mystik(en)**
nature **die Natur**
obscure **unklar, undeutlich**
obscene **obszön**
obscenity **die Obszönität(en)**
opinion **die Meinung(en)**
optimism **der Optimismus**
optimistic **optimistisch**
parody **die Parodie(n)**
passion **die Leidenschaft(en)**
passionate **leidenschaftlich**
pessimism **der Pessimismus**
pessimistic **pessimistisch**
poetic **poetisch**
it portrays **es zeigt, es schildert**
portrayal **die Schilderung(en)**

precious **gekünstelt, affektiert**
protagonist **der Protagonist(en), der Held(en)** *(wk)*
I read **ich lese**
reader **der Leser(-) [-in]**
readership **die Leserschaft**
realistic **realistisch**
reference **die Erwähnung(en), die Anspielung(en)**
I reflect **ich denke nach***
it reflects **es widerspiegelt**
reflection **die Reflektion(en)**
relationship **die Beziehung(en)**
it represents **es stellt dar***
representation **die Darstellung(en)**
review **die Kritik(en)**
romantic **romantisch**
sad **traurig**
satire **die Satire(n)**
it satirizes **es verspottet**
satirical **satirisch**
style **der Stil(e)**
  in the style of **im Stil des/der**
stylish **stilvoll**
subject **das Thema (-en)**
Surrealism **der Surrealismus**
technique **die Technik(en)**
tension **die Spannung(en)**
theme **das Thema (-en)**
tone **der Ton(¨e)**
tragedy **die Tragödie(n)**
tragic **tragisch**
true **wahr**
vivid **lebhaft**
vividly **anschaulich**
viewpoint **der Gesichtspunkt(e)**
witty **witzig, geistreich**
work of art **das Kunstwerk(e)**

The predominant theme of painting of the period was the landscape.
The painters tried to represent moral values symbolically.

Das vorrangige Motiv der Malerei dieser Zeit war die Landschaft.
Die Maler versuchten Moralwerte symbolisch zu veranschaulichen.

THE ARTS

antique **die Antiquität(en)**
  antique *(adj)* **antik**
antiquity **das Altertum, die Antike**
architect **der Architekt(en)** *(wk)*
  [-in]
art **die Kunst(-̈e)**
artifact **das Artefakt(e)**
artist **der Künstler(-)**
art student **der Kunststudent(en)**
  (wk) **[-in]**
I auction **ich versteigere**
auction sale **die Auktion(en)**
auctioneer **der Auktionator(en)**
balance **das Gleichgewicht(e)**
beam **der Balken(-)**
bronze **die Bronze(n)**
brush **der Pinsel(-)**
I build **ich baue**
building **das Gebäude(-)**
bust **die Büste(n)**
caricature **die Karikatur(en)**
I carve **ich schnitze, ich haue**
I cast **ich gieße**
ceramics **die Keramik(en)**
charcoal **die Holzkohle(n)**
chisel **der Meißel(-)**
clay **der Ton**
collage **die Collage(n)**
decorated **dekoriert**
decoration **die Verzierung(en)**
I design **ich entwerfe**
design **der Entwurf(-̈e), das**
  Design(s)
dimension **die Dimension(en)**
I draw **ich zeichne**
drawing **die Zeichnung(en)**
drawing board **das Reißbrett(er)**
easel **die Staffelei(en)**
elevation **der Aufriss(e)**
enamel **die Emaille(n)**
I engrave **ich graviere ein***
engraving **der (Kupfer-/**
  Stahl)stich(e)
I etch **ich ätze**

etching **der Kupferstich(e)**
exhibition **die Ausstellung(en)**
figure **die Form(en), Figur(en)**
figurine **die Figurine(n)**
fine arts **die schönen Künste** *(pl)*
form **die Gestalt(en)**
freehand **Freihand-**
fresco **die Freskomalerei(en)**
frieze **das Fries(-)**
gouache **die Gouache**
graphic arts **die Grafik(en)**
holography **die Holographie(n)**
interior **das Innere, die**
  Innengestaltung
intricate **kompliziert, fein**
iron **das Eisen**
landscape *(painting)* **das**
  Landschaftsbild(er)
landscape architect **der**
  Landschaftsarchitekt(en) *(wk)*
landscape painter **der**
  Landschaftsmaler(-)
large-scale **in großem Maßstab**
late works **die späten Arbeiten**
light **das Licht**
  light *(adj)* **leuchtend, hell**
lithograph(y) **die Lithographie(n)**
luminosity **die Helligkeit**
luminous **leuchtend**
masterpiece **das Meisterwerk(e)**
metal **das Metall(e)**
miniature **die Miniatur(en)**
model **das Modell(e)**
mosaic **das Mosaik(e)**
museum **das Museum (-en)**
oil painting **das Ölgemälde(-)**
ornate **geschmückt**
I paint **ich male**
paint **die Farbe(n)**
painting **das Gemälde(-)**
pastel **das Pastell(e)**
pattern **das Muster(-)**
portrait **das Porträt(s)**

potter   der Töpfer(-) [-in]
pottery   die Töpferware(n)
reproduction   die
   Reproduktion(en)
restoration   die Restaurierung(en)
I restore   **ich restauriere**
restored   **restauriert**
restorer   der Restaurierer(-) [-in]
roughcast   der Rauputz
school   die Schule(n)
I sculpt   **ich bildhauere**
sculptor   der Bildhauer(-) [-in]
sculpture   die Skulptur(en)
seascape   das Seestück(e)
shadow   der Schatten(-)
shape   die Form(en)
I shape   **ich forme, ich gestalte**
sketch   die Skizze(n)
I sketch   **ich skizziere**
stained glass   **das farbige Glas,
   die Glasmalerei**

statuary   die Plastik(en)
statue   die Statue(n)
still life   **das Stillleben**
studio   **das Studio(s)**
symbolic   **symbolisch**
tapestry   der Wandbehang(¨e)
town planning   die
   Stadtplanung(en)
translucent   **lichtdurchlässig**
transparent   **durchsichtig**
visual arts   die bildenden Künste
   (pl)
watercolor   das Aquarell(e)
weathering   die Verwitterung(en)
wood   **das Holz**
wood-carving   die
   Holzschnitzerei(en)
woodcut   der Holzschnitt(e)

Historical periods

Alemannic   **alemannisch**
Charlemagne   **Karl der Große**
Enlightenment   die Aufklärung
First World War   **der Erste
   Weltkrieg**
Frankish   **fränkisch**
Hitler period   die Hitlerzeit, das
   Dritte Reich
Holy Roman Empire   **das Heilige
   Römische Reich**
Hundred Years War   **der
   Hundertjährige Krieg**
Middle Ages   das Mittelalter
migration of peoples   die
   Völkerwanderung
Reformation   die Reformation
Roman age   die Römerzeit
Roman Empire   das Römische
   Reich

Second World War   **der Zweite
   Weltkrieg**
Thirty Years War   der
   Dreißigjährige Krieg
Weimar Republic   die Weimarer
   Republik

Bronze Age   die Bronzezeit
Iron Age   **die Eisenzeit**
Neolithic Age   die Jungsteinzeit
Palaeolithic Age   die Altsteinzeit
prehistoric   **vorgeschichtlich**
prehistory   die Vorgeschichte
Stone Age   die Steinzeit

the 20th Century   das
   zwanzigste (20.) Jahrhundert
in the 13th Century   **im
   dreizehnten Jahrhundert**

THE ARTS

17c Literature

autograph **die Originalhandschrift(en)**
book **das Buch(¨-er)**
bookshop/store **der Buchladen(¨-e)**
bookseller **der Buchhändler(-) [-in]**
character **die Figur(en), die Gestalt(en)**
comic **lustig**
it concerns **es handelt (sich) um** +acc
dialog **der Dialog(e)**
fictional **frei erfunden**
hardback **eine gebundene Ausgabe(n)**
I imagine **ich stelle mir vor***
imagination **die Einbildungskraft(¨-e)**
inspiration **die Inspiration(en)**
inspired by **inspiriert durch**
it introduces **es führt ein***
introduction **die Einleitung(en)**
I leaf through **ich blättere durch***
librarian **der Bibliothekar(e) [-in]**
library **die Bibliothek(en)**
 public library **die öffentliche Bibliothek(en)**
 reference library **die Präsenzbibliothek(en)**

library ticket **der Leserausweis(e)**
literal(ly) **wörtlich**
main character **die Hauptfigur(en)**
myth **der Mythos (-en)**
mythology **die Mythologie(n)**
it narrates **es erzählt**
narrative **die Erzählung(en)**
narrator **der Erzähler(-) [-in]**
note **die Anmerkung(en)**
page **die Seite(n)**
paperback **das Taschenbuch(¨-er)**
poem **das Gedicht(e)**
poetic **poetisch**
poetry **die Poesie, die Dichtkunst**
quotation **das Zitat(e)**
I quote **ich zitiere**
I read **ich lese**
I recount **ich erzähle**
review **die Rezension(en), die Kritik(en)**
rhyme **der Reim(e)**
secondary character **die Nebenfigur(en)**
it is set in **es spielt in** +dat
subtitle **der Untertitel(-)**
table **der Tabelle(n)**
text **der Text(e)**
title **der Titel(-)**
verse **der Strophe(n)**

Buddenbrooks is the great epic novel of the early 20th Century.

After the war, the "Gruppe 47" played an important role. Poetry blossomed again, above all in East Germany.

Günter Grass shows intense political involvement and an inexhaustible imagination.

Buddenbrooks ist der große Bildungsroman des frühen zwanzigsten Jahrhunderts.

Nach dem Krieg spielte die "Gruppe 47" eine wichtige Rolle. Die Lyrik blühte wieder auf, vor allem in der DDR.

Günter Grass zeigt großes politisches Engagement und eine unerschöpfliche Phantasie.

Types of books

adventure story **die Abenteuergeschichte(n)**

atlas **der Atlas(se/Atlanten)**

(auto)biography **die (Auto)biographie(n)**

children's literature **die Kinderliteratur**

comic novel **die humoristische Erzählung(en)**

cookbook **das Kochbuch(¨er)**

crime novel **der Kriminalroman(e), der Krimi(s)**

dictionary **das Wörterbuch(¨er)**
 bilingual **zweisprachiges**
 monolingual **einsprachiges**

diary **das Tagebuch(¨er)**

encyclopedia **die Enzyklopädie(n)**

epic poem **das Epos (-en), das epische Gedicht(e)**

epic poetry **die Epik**

essay **der Aufsatz(¨e)**

fable **die Fabel(n)**

fairy tale **das Märchen(-)**

feminist literature **die Frauenliteratur**

fiction **die Belletristik**

Greek tragedy **die griechische Tragödie(n)**

horror story **die Horrorgeschichte(n)**

letters **die Literatur(en)**

light reading **die Unterhaltungslektüre(n)**

manual **das Handbuch(¨er)**

memoirs **die Memoiren** *(pl)*

mystery play **das Mysterienspiel(e)**

novel **der Roman(e)**

novella **die Novelle(n)**

non-fiction **das Sachbuch(¨er)**

parody **die Parodie(n)**

picaresque novel **der Schelmenroman(e)**

poetry **die Dichtkunst**

reference book **das Nachschlagewerk(e)**

satire **die Satire(n)**

science fiction story **die Science-Fiction-Erzählung(en)**

short story **die Kurzgeschichte(n)**

spy story **die Spionagegeschichte(n)**

teenage fiction **die Jugendliteratur**

travel book **der Reisebericht(e)**

war novel **der Kriegsroman(e)**

Heinrich Böll received the Nobel prize for literature. A central theme of his novels is Roman Catholicism. He describes the troubles and worrries of the "little people."

Heinrich Böll erhielt den Nobelpreis für Literatur. Ein zentrales Thema seiner Romane ist das katholische Christentum. Er schildert die Nöte und Sorgen der "kleinen Leute".

Baroque richness, precision of description and autobiographical details are typical of the period.

Barocke Fülle, Genauigkeit der Darstellung und autobiographische Details kennzeichnen diese Periode.

THE ARTS

17d Music & dance

accompaniment **die Begleitung**
accompanist **der Begleiter(-) [-in]**
I accompany **ich begleite**
acoustics **die Akustik**
agent **der Agent(en)** *(wk)*
album **das Album (-en)**
alto **der Alt(e), die Altstimme(n)**
amplifier **der Verstärker(-)**
audience **das Publikum**
audition **das Vorspielen(-)**
I audition **ich spiele/singe vor***
auditorium **das Auditorium (-ien)**
ballet **das Ballett**
baton **der Taktstock(-̈e)**
brass band **die Blaskapelle(n)**
canned music **die
   Musikberieselung**
cassette tape **die Kassette(n)**
cassette deck **das
   Kassettendeck(s)**
chamber music **die Kammermusik**
chart **die Hitliste(n)**
choir **der Chor(-̈e)**
choral society **der
   Gesangverein(e)**
choreography **die
   Choreographie(n)**
chorus **der Refrain(s)**
classical music **die klassische
   Musik**
compact disc/disk **die
Compactdisc(s)**

competition **der Wettbewerb(e)**
I compose **ich komponiere**
composer **der Komponist(en)**
composition **die Komposition(en)**
concert **das Konzert(e)**
concert hall **die Konzertsaal
   (-säle)**
dance **der Tanz(-̈e)**
I dance **ich tanze**
dancer **der Tänzer(-) [-in]**
dance music **die Tanzmusik**
discotheque **die Diskothek(en)**
disc jockey **der Discjockey(s)**
ensemble **das Ensemble(s)**
folk music **die Volksmusik**
folksong **das Volkslied(er), der
   Folksong(s)**
gig **das Konzert(e)**
group **die Gruppe(n)**
harmony **die Harmonie(n)**
harmonic **harmonisch**
hit *(song)* **der Hit(s)**
hit parade **die Hitparade(n)**
I hum **ich summe**
instrument **das Instrument(e)**
instrument maker **der
   Instrumentenbauer**
I interpret **ich interpretiere**
interpretation **die
   Interpretation(en)**
jazz **der Jazz**
juke box **die Musikbox(en)**

Phillip always sings out of tune.
His sister Natalie, on the other
Hand, has perfect pitch.

**Phillip singt immer falsch.
Seine Schwester Natalie
hingegen hat das absolute
Gehör.**

You must tune your violin. It is flat.

**Du musst die Violine stimmen.
Sie ist zu tief.**

My parents love going to concerts.
Last week they went to a recital at
the city theater.

**Meine Eltern gehen sehr gern
ins Konzert. Letzte Woche sind
sie zu einem Liederabend im
Stadttheater gegangen.**

lesson **der Musikunterricht** *(no pl)*
librettist **der Librettist(en)** *(wk)*
I listen to **ich höre** +dat **zu***
microphone **das Mikrofon(e)**
music **die Musik**
musically **musikalisch**
musician **der Musiker(-) [-in]**
musicologist **der Musikwissenschaftler(-) [-in]**
note **die Note(n)**
orchestra **das Orchester(-)**
orchestration **die Orchesterbearbeitung(en)**
part **die Stimme(n)**
I perform **ich führe vor/auf**
performance **die Aufführung(en)**
performer **der Künstler(-) [-in]**
piano tuner **der Klavierstimmer(-) [-in]**
piece **das Stück(e)**
I play **ich spiele**
player **der Spieler(-) [-in]**
popular music/pop **die Popmusik**
I practice **ich übe**
promotional video **das Werbevideo(s)**
recital **das Konzert(e), der Liederabend(e)**
record **die Schallplatte(n)**
I record **ich nehme auf***
recording **die Aufnahme(n)**

recording studio **das Aufnahmestudio(s)**
I rehearse **ich probe**
rehearsal **die Probe**
rhythm **der Rhythmus (-en)**
rhythmic **rhythmisch**
rock music **die Rockmusik**
show **die Show**
I sing **ich singe**
singer **der Sänger(-) [-in]**
solo **das Solo(s)**
soloist **der Solist(en)** *(wk)* **[-in]**
song **das Lied(er)**
song writer **der Liedermacher(-) [-in]**
string **die Saite(n)**
string orchestra **das Streichorchester(-)**
tour **die Tournee(n)**
on tour **auf Tournee**
tune **der Klang**
I sing in tune **ich singe richtig**
out of tune **falsch, verstimmt**
I tune **ich stimme**
tuning fork **die Stimmgabel(n)**
voice **die Stimme(n)**
I whistle **ich pfeife**
wind band **die Blaskapelle(n)**
wind instrument **das Blasinstrument(e)**

– We play a lot of music at home.
– Do you play an instrument?

– **Wir musizieren viel zu Hause.**
– **Spielst du ein Instrument?**

– Yes, I've been playing the piano since I was little.

– **Ja, ich spiele schon seit meiner Kindheit Klavier.**

During the summer, you can often hear street musicians in many European cities.

Während des Sommers kann man in vielen europäischen Städten oft Straßenmusikanten hören.

THE ARTS

17e Theater & film/Theater & the movies

act   der Akt(e)
I act   ich spiele
acting school   die
   Schauspielschule(n)
actor   der Schauspieler(-) [-in]
I applaud   ich klatsche Beifall
applause   der Beifall
audience   die Zuschauer(-)
auditorium   der Zuschauerraum(ːe)
I book   ich buche
box   die Loge(n)
box office   die (Theater)kasse(n)
cabaret   das Kabarett(s)
camera   die Kamera(s)
camera crew   das Kamerateam(s)
cameraman   der Kameramann(ːer)
cartoon   der Trickfilm(e)
choreographer   der
   Choreograph(en) (wk) [-in]
cinema/movies   das Kino(s)
cinema/movie buff   der Kinofan(s)
circle/gallery   der Rang(ːe)
circus   der Zirkus(se)
I clap   ich klatsche Beifall
cloakroom   die Garderobe(n)
comedian   der Komiker(-) [-in]
contract   der Vertrag(ːe)
critic   der Kritiker(-) [-in]
curtain   der Vorhang(ːe)
I design   ich entwerfe
I direct   ich führe Regie
director   der Regisseur(e)

distribution system   das
   Vertriebssystem(e)
drama   das Drama (-en)
dress rehearsal   die
   Generalprobe(n)
dubbed   synchronisiert
dubbing   die Synchronisation
I enter   ich trete auf*
exciting   spannend
I exit   ich gehe ab*
expectation   die Erwartung(en)
farce   der Schwank(ːe), die
   Farce(n)
film/movie   der Film(e)
I film   ich filme, ich verfilme
film/movie maker   der
   Filmemacher(-)
filmstar/movie star   der Filmstar(s)
film/movie producer   der
   Filmproduzent(en) (wk)
first night   die Uraufführung(en)
floor show   die Vorstellung(en)
flop   der Reinfall(ːe)
intermission/interval   die Pause(n)
lights   die Beleuchtung(en)
limelights   das Rampenlicht(er)
lobby   das Foyer(s)
location work   die
   Außenaufnahmen (pl)
I make a film/movie   ich drehe
   einen Film
masterpiece   das Meisterwerk(e)

The play begins at eight p.m.

**Das Theater beginnt um acht
Uhr abends.**

Have you seen the latest
production of Faust? The principal
actors are excellent. Its been
playing to full houses for weeks
already.

**Hast du die neueste Faust-
Inszenierung gesehen? Die
Hauptdarsteller sind vortrefflich.
Das Stück läuft schon seit
Wochen vor ausverkauftem
Haus.**

matinée **die Matinee(s)**
melodrama **das Melodrama (-en)**
mime **die Pantomime(n)**
movie **der Film(e)**
music hall **das Varieté(s)**
off-stage **hinter den Kulissen**
one-act play **der Einakter(-)**
opening night **die Eröffnungsvorstellung(en)**
ovation **der Beifallssturm(¨e)**
performance **die Aufführung(en)**
photography **die Aufnahmen** *(pl)*
play **das (Theater)stück(e)**
I play **ich spiele**
playwright **der Dramatiker(-) [-in]**
premiere **die Premiere(n)**
I produce **ich produziere, ich inszeniere**
producer **der Regisseur(e)**
production **die Inszenierung(en)**
projector **der Projektor(en)**
public **die Öffenlichkeit, die Zuschauer** *(pl)*
retrospective **der Rückblick**
retrospective *(adj)* **rückblickend**
review **die Rezension(en)**
role **die Rolle(n)**
row **die Reihe(n)**
scene **die Szene(n)**
scenery **das Bühnenbild(er)**
screen **die Leinwand(¨e)**
screen test **die Probeaufnahmen** *(pl)*

screening **die Vorführung(en)**
I shoot *(a film/movie)* **ich drehe, ich filme**
script **das Drehbuch(¨er)**
scriptwriter **der Drehbuchautor(en)**
seat **der Sitzplatz(¨e)**
sequel **die Folge(n)**
sequence **die Reihenfolge(n)**
I show *(film/movie)* **ich führe auf*, ich bringe**
it is shown at **es wird im ... gezeigt/gegeben**
sold out **ausverkauft**
sound track **der Ton, die Filmmusik**
special effects **die Spezialeffekte** *(pl)*
stage **die Bühne(n)**
stage directions **die Bühnenanweisungen** *(pl)*
stage designer **der Bühnenbildner(-) [-in]**
stage effects **die Bühneneffekte** *(pl)*
stage-fright **das Lampenfieber**
stalls **das Parkett**
stunt person **der Stuntman**
it takes place in **es spielt in**
trailer/preview **die Vorschau**
understudy **die zweite Besetzung**
usherette **die Platzanweiserin(nen)**
walk-on part **die Statistenrolle(n)**
I zoom **ich zoome**

An exciting film was shown on TV last evening. It was set in Vienna. The time and place of the action are Berlin in the 20s.

The latest book by John Grisham is being adapted to the screen. Despite their experience, many actors still suffer from stage fright every time they get on stage.

Ein spannender Film wurde gestern Abend im Fernsehen gezeigt. Er spielte in Wien. Ort und Zeit der Handlung sind Berlin in den 20er Jahren.

Das neueste Buch von John Grisham wird verfilmt. Trotz ihrer Erfahrung leiden viele Schauspieler immer noch unter Lampenfieber, wenn sie auf die Bühne treten.

➤ APPRECIATION & CRITICISM 17a

18 The media

18a General terms

admission **der Eintritt(e), der Einlass**
I analyze **ich analysiere**
analysis **die Analyse(n)**
I appeal to **ich appelliere an** +acc
I argue **ich argumentiere**
argument **das Argument(e)**
attitude **die Einstellung(en), die Weltanschauung(en)**
biased **voreingenommen**
campaign **die Aktion(en)**
censorship **die Zensur**
 press censorship **die Pressezensur**
cogent **überzeugend**
comment **der Kommentar(e)**
conspiracy **die Verschwörung(en)**
criticism **die Kritik(en)**
cultural **kulturell**
culture **die Kultur(en)**
cultured **kultiviert**
current events **die aktuellen Ereignisse** (pl)
declaration **die Erklärung(en)**

I declare **ich erkläre**
detailed **detailliert**
it discriminates **es diskriminiert**
disaster **die Katastrophe(n)**
disinformation **die Fehlinformation(en)**
educational **Bildungs-**
I entertain **ich unterhalte**
ethical **ethisch**
event **das Ereignis(se)**
example **das Beispiel(e)**
expectation **die Erwartung(en)**
I exploit **ich beute aus***
fallacious **trügerisch**
fallacy **der Irrtum(¨er)**
freedom **die Freiheit(en)**
 freedom of the press **die Pressefreiheit**
full/detailed **voll**
gullible **leichtgläubig**
hidden **versteckt**
homophobic **homophobisch**
ignorance **die Unwissenheit**

During the recent elections it was difficult to find an example of unbiased reporting.

Während der letzten Wahlen war es schwierig, ein Beispiel unbeeinflusster Berichterstattung zu finden.

In recent years many war correspondents have lost their lives while reporting from the front or have been taken hostage.

In den letzten Jahren wurden viele Kriegskorrespondenten bei der Berichterstattung getötet oder als Geiseln genommen.

I am a freelance journalist.

Ich bin ein freischaffender Journalist.

I ignore **ich sehe über** +acc **hinweg***
influential **einflussreich**
information **die Information(en)**
informative **informativ**
interview **das Interview(s)**
I intrude **ich störe**
intrusion **die Zudringlichkeit(en)**
intrusive **zudringlich**
issue *(problem)* **das Problem(e)**
journalese **der Pressejargon**
I keep up with (news) **ich bleibe auf dem Laufenden**
libel **die Verleumdung(en)**
libellous **verleumderisch**
local **Orts-, Regional-**
material **der Stoff(e)**
I meddle **ich mische mich ein***
medium **das Medium (-ien)**
media **die Medien** *(pl)*
news **die Nachrichten** *(pl)*
news agency **die Nachrichtenagentur(en)**
news item **die Neuigkeit(en)**
partisan **parteiisch**
persuasion **die Überzeugung(en)**
persuasive **überzeugend**
prejudice **das Vorurteil(e)**
political **politisch**
politician **der Politiker(-) [-in]**
politics **die Politik** *(no pl)*

policy **die Politik** *(no pl)*
press **die Presse**
privacy **das Privatleben**
problem **das Problem(e)**
I report **ich berichte**
reportage **der Bericht(e)**
reporter **der Reporter(-) [-in]**
review **die Kritik(en)**
I review **ich bespreche**
it comes under review **es wird geprüft**
scoop **der Knüller(-)**
sensational **sensationell**
sensationalism **die Sensationsgier**
sexism **der Sexismus**
sexist **der Sexist(en)** *(wk)*
shrewd **klug, scharf**
summary **der Überblick(e)**
  summary *(adj)* **kurzgefasst**
it takes place **es findet statt***
trust **das Vertrauen**
I trust **ich glaube** +dat
trustworthy **glaubwürdig**
truth **die Wahrheit(en)**
truthful **ehrlich**
unbiased **unparteiisch**
untrustworthy **unzuverlässig**
up to date **aktuell**
weekly **wöchentlich**

Although British newspapers have correspondents in all the European capitals, they do not always report/cover current events.

Obwohl die britische Presse in allen europäischen Hauptstädten Berichterstatter hat, berichten diese nicht immer über aktuelle Ereignisse.

Media barons dominate the press in many western countries.

Die Medienbarone beherrschen die Presse in vielen westlichen Ländern.

18b The press

article   **der Artikel(-)**
back page   **die Rückseite(n)**
barons   **der Pressezar(en)** *(wk)*
broadsheet flyer   **das Flugblatt(-̈er)**
cartoon   **der Cartoon(s), der Zeichentrickfilm(e)**
chief editor   **der Chefredakteur(e)**
circulation   **die Auflage(n)**
color supplement   **das Magazin(e), die Beilage(n)**
column (of print)   **die Spalte(n)**
column *(article)*   **die Kolumne(n)**
comic   **das Comic-Heft(e)**
correspondent   **der Korrespondent(en)** *(wk)* **[-in]**
   foreign correspondent   **der Auslandskorrespondent**
   sports correspondent   **der Sportkorrespondent**
   war correspondent   **der Kriegskorrespondent**
daily newspaper   **die Tageszeitung(en)**
I edit   **ich gebe heraus***
edition   **die Ausgabe(n)**
editor   **der Redakteur(-) [-in]**

glossy magazine   **das Hochglanzmagazin(e)**
gutter press   **die Boulevardpresse**
headline   **die Schlagzeile(n)**
heading   **die Überschrift(en)**
illustration   **die Illustration(en)**
I publish   **ich veröffentliche**
it is published   **es ist erschienen**
journalist   **der Journalist(en)** *(wk)* **[-in]**
layout   **das Layout(s)**
local paper   **die Lokalzeitung(en)**
magazine   **die Illustrierte(n)**
monthly   **die Monatsschrift(en)**
national newspaper   **die nationale Zeitung(en)**
newsagent   **der Zeitungshändler(-)**
newspaper   **die Zeitung(en)**
news stand   **der Zeitungskiosk(e)**
page   **die Seite(n)**
pamphlet   **die Broschüre**
periodical   **die Zeitschrift(en)**
power   **die Macht(-̈e)**
powerful   **einflussreich**

The constitution guarantees the right of freedom of expression and the freedom of the press.

Das Grundgesetz garantiert das Recht der freien Meinungsäußerung und die Pressefreiheit.

Die Frankfurter Allgemeine, die Süddeutsche Zeitung and *Die Welt* are the best known newspapers in the country. They are national newspapers.

***Die Frankfurter Allgemeine, Die Süddeutsche Zeitung* und *Die Welt* sind die bekanntesten Zeitungen im Land. Sie sind überregionale Zeitungen.**

Die *Bild Zeitung* is the most widely read newspaper in Germany.

Die *Bild Zeitung* ist die meist-gelesene Zeitung in Deutschland.

press agency **die Presseagentur(en)**
press conference **die Pressekonferenz(en)**
I print **ich drucke**
I publish **ich veröffentliche**
publisher **der Verleger(-) [-in]**
publishing company **der Verlag(e)**
quality press **die Qualitätspresse**

reader **der Leser(-) [-in]**
special issue **die Sonderausgabe(n)**
I subscribe to **ich abonniere**
subscription **das Abonnement(s)**
tabloid **die Boulevardzeitung(en)**
type(face) **die Schriftart(en)**
weekly **die Wochenzeitung(en)**

Newspaper sections & features

announcements **Anzeigen**
arts **Feuilleton**
crossword puzzles **Kreuzwort-rätsel**
economy **Wirtschaft**
editorial **Kommentar**
entertainment **Kulturangebot**
finance **Finanzen, Börse**
food and drink **Essen und Trinken**
front page **die erste Seite**
editorials **Leitartikel**
gossip column **Klatschspalte**
home news **Landesspiegel, Meldungen aus dem Inland**

horoscope **Horoskop**
international news **internationale Nachrichten**
leaders **Leitartikel**
obituaries **Todesanzeigen**
politcs **Politik**
problem page **Problemseite**
property **Immobilien**
small ads **Kleinanzeigen, Inserate**
sports page **Sport**
travel **Reisen**
women's page **Frauen**

Der Spiegel is an influential news magazine.

Der Spiegel ist ein einfluss-reiches Nachrichtenmagazin.

Many local newspapers are disappearing as a result of mergers.

Viele Lokalzeitungen sind infolge Fusionen verschwunden.

Many people think that diversity and independence will be lost.

Viele Leute meinen, dass Vielfalt und Unabhängigeit verloren gehen.

The gutter press has a surprisingly high readership.

Die Klatschpresse hat eine überraschend hohe Leserzahl.

Uncle Richard always reads the obituaries and the sports page.

Onkel Richard liest immer die Todesanzeigen und die Sportseite.

▶ PUBLISHING 17c; ADVERTISING 18d

THE MEDIA

18c Television & radio

aerial/antenna **die Antenne(n)**
anchor **der**
    Nachrichtensprecher(-) [in]
announcer **der Ansager(-) [in]**
audience **die Zuhörer/-schauer**
    (pl)
I broadcast **ich sende**
broadcasting station **die**
    Sendestation(en)
cable TV **das Kabelfernsehen**
    by cable **über Kabel**
cameraman **der Kameramann(¨er)**
    [-frau]
I change channel **ich schalte um***
channel **der Kanal(¨e), das**
    Programm(e)
commercial **die Fernsehwerbung**
couch potato **der Dauerglotzer(-)**
    [-in]
dubbed **synchronisiert**
earphone **der Kopfhörer(-)**
episode **die Fortsetzung(en)**
goggle box **die Glotze(n)**
interactive **interaktiv**
light entertainment **die**
    Unterhaltungssendung(en)

listener **der Zuhörer(-) [-in]**
live broadcast **die**
    Liveübertragung(en)
live coverage/commentary **die**
    Liveberichterstattung(en)
loudspeaker **der Lautsprecher(-)**
microphone **das Mikrofon(e)**
news flash **die Kurzmeldung(en)**
newsreader/caster **der**
    Nachrichtensprecher(-) [-in]
production studio **das**
    Aufnahmestudio(s)
program(me) **die Sendung(en)**
radio **das Radio(s), der Hörfunk**
    on radio **im Radio**
I receive **ich empfange**
I record **ich nehme auf***
recording **die Aufnahme(n)**
remote control **die**
    Fernbedienung(en)
I repeat **ich wiederhole**
repeat **die Wiederholung(en)**
satellite **der Satellit(en)** *(wk)*
satellite dish **die**
    Satellitenschüssel(n)

– What! You're still glued to the TV? You've been sitting there all evening. I'm afraid you're becoming a real couch potato.

– I'm just going to record this film then I'll join you. Do we have a blank videocassette somewhere?

Was the Pavarotti concert broadcast live?

– Was! Du klebst immer noch vor dem Fernseher? Du sitzt schon den ganzen Abend da. Ich fürchte du wirst ein echter Stubenhocker.

– Ich möchte nur diesen Film aufnehmen, danach mache ich bei euch mit. Haben wir irgendwo eine leere Videokassette?

Wurde das Pavarotti-Konzert live übertragen?

satellite TV **das Satellitenfernsehen**
screen **der Bildschirm(e)**
I show **ich zeige**
signal **das Signal(e)**
station **der Sender(-)**
subtitles **der Untertitel(-)**
I switch off **ich schalte ab***
I switch on **ich schalte an***
teletext **der Bildschirmtext(e)**
television/TV **das Fernsehen**
  on TV **im Fernsehen**
television set **das Fernsehgerät(e), der Fernseher(-)**
television studio **das Fernsehstudio(s)**
I transmit **ich übertrage, ich sende**
video clip **der Videoclip(s)**
videogame **das Videospiel(e)**
video library **die Videothek(en)**
video recorder **der Videorecorder(-)**
video recording **die Videoaufnahme(n)**
viewer **der Zuschauer(-) [-in]**
I watch **ich schaue zu***, **ich sehe mir an***

TV and radio programs

cartoon **der Zeichentrickfilm(e), der Cartoon(s)**

children program(me) **das Kinderprogramm(e)**
comedy **die Komödie(n)**
current affairs program(me) **die Tagesschau**
drama **das Drama (-en)**
documentary **der Dokumentarfilm(e)**
education program(me) **das Bildungsprogramm(e)**
feature film/movie **der Spielfilm(e)**
light entertainment **die leichte Unterhaltung** *(no pl)*
newscast **die Nachrichtensendung(en)**
quiz program(me) **das Quizprogramm(e), die Quizsendungen** *(pl)*
radio play **das Hörspiel(e)**
regional news **die Regionalnachrichten** *(pl)*
soap **die Fernsehserie(n)**
science program(me) **die Wissenschaftssendung(en)**
school broadcasting **die Schulsendung(en)**
sports program(me) **die Sportsendung(en)**
TV film/movie **der Fernsehfilm(e)**
weather report **der Wetterbericht(e)**

Public broadcasting companies

ARD Arbeitsgemeinschaft der öffentlich-rechtlichen Rundfunkanstalten Deutschlands
ORF der Österreichische Rundfunk

SRG die Schweizerische Radio- und Fernsehgesellschaft
ZDF Zweites Deutsches Fernsehen
Deutsche Welle
Deutschlandfunk *(radio)*

➤ FILM/MOVIE GENRES App.17e

THE MEDIA

18d Advertising

I advertise **ich werbe für** +acc
advertisement **die Anzeige(n), die Reklame(n)**
advertising **die Werbung(en)**
advertising column **die Litfaßsäule(n)**
advertising industry **die Werbeindustrie**
appeal **der Reiz(e)**
it appeals to **es spricht jdn. an***
billboard **das Werbeplakat(e)**
brand **die Marke(n)**
brand awareness **das Markenbewußtsein**
brochure **die Broschüre(n)**
campaign **die Kampagne(n)**
it catches the eye **es ist auffallend**
commercial **der Werbespot(s)**
commercial *(adj)* **kommerziell**
commercial break **die Werbepause(n)**
competition *(rival)* **die Konkurrenz** *(no pl)*
competition *(game)* **das Preisausschreiben(-)**
consumer **der Verbraucher(-)**
consumer society **die Verbrauchergesellschaft(en)**
copywriter **der Werbetexter(-)**
I covet **ich begehre**
it creates a need **es schafft den Bedarf**
demand **die Nachfrage**
direct/junk mail **die Postwurfsendung(en)**
disposable income **das verfügbare Einkommen**
distributor **der Händler(-) [-in]**
ethical **ethisch**
good(s) **die Ware(n)**
hidden persuasion **die versteckte Beeinflussung**
image **das Image(s)**
launch **die Einführung**
lifestyle **der Lebensstil(e)**
I manipulate **ich manipuliere**
market **der Markt(¨e)**
model **das Modell(e)**
I motivate **ich motiviere**
need **das Bedürfnis(se), der Mangel(¨)**
persuasion **die Überredung**

It's important that our advertising campaign is targeted to young women with a high income.

Es ist wichtig, dass sich unsere Werbekampagne an junge Frauen mit hohem Einkommen richtet.

It pays to advertise!

Werbung zahlt sich aus!

The buildings are covered by ugly advertising billboards.

Die Gebäude sind mit hässlichen Werbeplakaten bedeckt.

Until recently most TV spots portrayed women in exclusively traditional roles.

Bis vor kurzem zeigten die meisten Fernsehspots Frauen in ausschließlich traditionellen Rollen.

poster **das Poster(-)**
product **das Produkt(e)**
I promote **ich fördere, ich werbe
    für** +acc
promotion (of) **das Werbung (für)**
publicity **die Werbung(en)**
I publicize **ich mache Werbung
    für** +acc
purchasing power **die Kaufkraft**
radio advertisement **die
    Radiowerbung(en)**
slogan **der Slogan(s), der
    Werbespruch(-̈e)**
status symbol **das
    Statussymbol(e)**
stunt **der Gag(s)**
I target **ich ziele auf** +acc **ab***
target group **die Zielgruppe(n)**
I tempt **ich locke an***
trademark **der Handelsname(n)**
trend **der Trend(s)**
truthful **wahrhaft**
TV advertisement **die
    Fernsehwerbung(en)**
unethical **sittenwidrig**

Small ads

accommodation **Häusermarkt**
appointments
    Stellenangebote
births **Geburten**
courses and conferences
    Kurse und Konferenzen
deaths **Todesanzeigen**
exchange **Wechselkurs**
exhibitions **Ausstellungen**
for sale **zum Verkauf**
health **Gesundheit**
holidays **Ferien**
lonely hearts
    Kontaktanzeigen
marriages **Heiratsanzeigen**
personal services
    Persönliches
property **Immobilien** (*pl*)
travel **Reisen**
wanted **Kaufgesuche,
    gesucht**

A Mercedes is still considered a status symbol.

Ein Mercedes wird immer noch als Statussymbol angesehen.

Coca Cola is a world renowned trademark.

Coca Cola ist ein weltbekannter Markenname.

We absolutely have to hire a new ad-writer.

Wir müssen unbedingt einen neuen Werbetexter einstellen.

Do you think that TV advertisements are more effective than advertisements in newspapers?

Denkst du, dass Fernsehwerbung effektiver ist als Zeitungsanzeigen?

➤ THE PRESS 18b; TELEVISION & RADIO 18c

TRAVEL

19a General terms

accident **der Unfall(-̈e)**
adult **der/die Erwachsene** *(adj/n)*
announcement **die Ansage(n)**
 special announcement **die Sondermeldung(en)**
arrival **die Ankunft(-̈e)**
I arrive at **ich komme in ... an**
assistance **die Hilfe** *(no pl)*
automatic **automatisch**
available **erhältlich**
bag **die Tasche(n), der Beutel(-)**
baggage **das Gepäck** *(no pl)*
bar **die Bar(s)**
I book **ich buche**
booking office **der Fahrkartenschalter(-)**
business trip **die Geschäftsreise(n)**
I buy a ticket **ich kaufe/löse eine Fahrkarte**
he calls/stops at **er hält in** +dat
I cancel *(trip)* **ich sage ab***
 I cancel *(ticket)* **ich entwerte**
I carry **ich trage**
I catch **ich erwische, ich erreiche**
I check *(tickets)* **ich überprüfe, ich kontrolliere**
child **das Kind(er)**
class **die Klasse(n)**
coin **die Münze(n)**
I confirm **ich bestätige**
connection **die Verbindung(en)**
I cross **ich überquere**
delay **die Verspätung(en)**
delayed **verspätet, verzögert**
he is delayed **er hat Verspätung**
I depart **ich fahre ab***
departure **die Abfahrt(en)**
destination **das Reiseziel(e)**
direct **direkt**

direction **die Richtung(en)**
disabled **behindert**
distance **die Entfernung(en)**
document **das Dokument(e)**
early **früh**
emergency **der Notfall(-̈e)**
emergency call **der Notruf(e)**
I enquire about **ich erkundige mich nach** +dat
enquiry **die Erkundigung(en)**
en route **auf dem Weg**
entrance **der Eingang(-̈e)**
exit **der Ausgang(-̈e)**
extra charge **der Zuschlag(-̈e)**
fare **der Fahrpreis(e)**
fast **schnell**
I fill in a form **ich fülle ein Formular aus***
free *(not occupied)* **frei**
I go away **ich verreise**
information **die Information(en), die Auskunft**
information office **das Informationsbüro(s)**
insurance **die Versicherung(en)**
help **die Hilfe**
helpful **hilfsbereit**
holdall/travel bag **die Reisetasche(n)**
late **(zu) spät**
I leave **ich fahre ab***
I leave *(person/object)* **ich verlasse**
luggage/baggage office **die Gepäckaufbewahrung(en)**
lost **verloren**
lost & found office **das Fundbüro(s)**
loudspeaker **der Lautsprecher(-)**
luggage/baggage **das Gepäck** (no pl)
message **die Nachricht(en)**
I miss *(train)* **ich verpasse**

money **das Geld(er)**
nonsmoker **Nichtraucher(-)**
notice **die Anzeige(n), die Mitteilung(en)**
nuisance **das Ärgernis(se)**
occupied **besetzt**
on board **an Bord**
on time **pünktlich**
I pack **ich packe**
passenger **der Passagier(e)**
porter (hotel) **der Portier(s)**
reduced fare **zu ermäßigtem Preis**
reduction **die Ermäßigung(en)**
reservation **die Reservierung(en)**
I reserve **ich reserviere**
I return **ich komme zurück***
return **die Rückkehr**
round-trip ticket **die Rückfahrkarte(n)**
round-trip **die Rundreise(n)**
safe **sicher**
safety **die Sicherheit(en)**
seat **der (Sitz)platz(-e)**
seatbelt **der Sicherheitsgurt(e)**
I set/take off **ich mache mich auf den Weg**
slow **langsam**
I slow down **ich fahre langsamer**
small change **das Wechselgeld**
smoking **das Rauchen**
speed **die Geschwindigkeit(en)**

I speed up **ich fahre schneller**
staff **das Personal**
I start from **ich fahre von ... ab***
stop **der Halt, die Haltestelle(n)**
I stop **ich halte**
suitcase **der Koffer(-)**
I take (bus, train) **ich nehme**
ticket **die Fahrkarte(n)**
ticket desk **der Fahrkartenschalter(-)**
timetable **der Fahrplan(-e)**
to **nach, Richtung**
toilet/restroom **die Toilette(n)**
I travel **ich reise**
travel **die Reise(n)**
  document **das Reisedokument(e)**
  office **das Reisebüro(s)**
  pass **der Reisepass(-e)**
  sickness **die Reisenkrankheit**
traveller **der/die Reisende(n)** (adj/n)
tunnel **der Tunnel(s/-)**
unexpected **unerwartet**
I unpack **ich packe aus***
valid **gültig**
visitor **der Besucher(-) [-in]**
warning **die Warnung(en)**
way in/entrance **der Eingang(-e)**
way out/exit **der Ausgang(-e)**
on weekdays **an Wochentagen**
weekend **das Wochenende(n)**
welcome **der Empfang(-e)**
welcoming **freundlich**

---

by air **mit dem Flugzeug**
by car **mit dem Auto**
by ferry **mit der Fähre**
on foot **zu Fuß**

on horseback **mit dem Pferd**
by sea **auf dem Seeweg**
by train **mit dem Zug, mit der Bahn**

I usually fly, but today I am taking the train.

Meistens fliege ich, aber heute nehme ich den Zug.

Are you walking or driving to the movies?

Fährst du oder gehst du zu Fuß zum Kino?

➤ HOLIDAYS/VACATION 20a; DIRECTIONS 2b; MOVEMENT 2c

19b Going abroad & travel by boat

Going abroad

Channel Tunnel **der Kanaltunnel(s/-)**

I cross the English Channel **ich überquere den Ärmelkanal**

currency **die Währung(en)**

currency exchange office **die Wechselstube(n)**

customs **der Zoll(¨e)**

customs control **die Zollkontrolle(n)**

customs officer **der Zollbeamte(n)** *(wk)*

customs regulation **die Zollbestimmung(en)**

declaration **die Zollerklärung(en)**

I declare **ich verzolle**

duty **der Einfuhrzoll(¨e)**

duty-free goods **die zollfreie Ware(n)**

duty-free shop **der Dutyfreeshop**

exchange rate **der Wechselkurs(e)**

foreign currency **die Devisen** *(pl)*

frontier/border **die Grenze(n)**

I go through customs **ich gehe durch den Zoll**

I go through passport control **ich gehe durch die Passkontrolle**

immigration office **die Einwanderungsbehörde(n)**

immigration rules **die Einwanderungsgesetze** *(pl)*

passport **der Pass(¨e)**

I pay duty on **ich zahle Zoll auf** +acc

smuggler **der Schmuggler(-)**

smuggling **das Schmuggeln**

visa **das Visum (-en/-a)**

Travel by boat

bridge **die Brücke(n)**

cabin **die Kabine(n)**

calm **still**

captain **der Kapitän(e)**

car ferry **die Autofähre(n)**

Channel **der (Ärmel)kanal**

choppy **bewegt**

coast **die Küste(n)**

crew **die Besatzung(en)**

crossing **die Überfahrt(en)**

cruise **die Kreuzfahrt(en)**

deck **das Deck(s)**

  below deck **unter Deck**

  lower deck **das Unterdeck**

  on deck **an Deck**

  upper deck **das Oberdeck**

deck chair **der Liegestuhl(¨e)**

I disembark **ich gehe von Bord**

disembarkation **die Landung(en)**

dock **die Landungsbrücke(n)**

I embark (for) **ich schiffe mich (nach +dat) ein***

The passport and customs formalities have been taken care of.	**Die Pass- und Zollformalitäten sind erledigt.**
What is the fastest way to Zürich?	**Wie kommt man am schnellsten nach Zürich?**
My final destination is Milan.	**Mein Reiseziel ist Mailand.**

embarkation card **die Bordkarte(n)**
I go on board **ich gehe an Bord**
harbor **der Hafen(⁻)**
heavy *(sea)* **schwer**
lifejacket **die Schwimmweste(n)**
lifeboat **das Rettungsboot(e)**
lounge **der Salon(s)**
luggage **das Gepäck**
ocean **der Ozean(e), das Meer(e)**
officer **der Offizier(e)**
offshore **vor der Küste**
on board **an Bord**
overboard **über Bord**
port **der Hafen(⁻)**
purser **der Zahlmeister(-)**
quay **der Kai(s)**
reclining seat **der Liegesitz(e)**
sea **die See**
seasickness **die Seekrankheit(en)**
seaman **der Seemann (-leute)**
shipping forecast **der Seewetterbericht(e)**
shipyard **die Werft(en)**
smooth **ruhig**
storm **der Sturm(⁻e)**
stormy **stürmisch**
tide **die Gezeiten** *(pl)*
　high tide **die Flut**
　low tide **die Ebbe**

waves **die Wellen**
wind **der Wind(e)**
windy **windig**

Ships & boats

aircraft carrier **der Flugzeugträger(-)**
canoe **das Kanu(s)**
cargo boat **das Transportschiff(e)**
dinghy *(rubber)* **das Schlauchboot(e)**
ferry **die Fähre(n)**
hovercraft **das Luftkissenboot(e)**
hydrofoil **das Tragflächenboot(e)**
life boat **das Rettungsboot(e)**
merchant ship **das Handelsschiff(e)**
motorboat **das Motorboot(e)**
ocean liner **der Überseedampfer(-)**
oil tanker **der Öltanker(-)**
rowing boat **das Ruderboot(e)**
sailing boat **das Segelboot(e)**
ship **das Schiff(e)**
speed boat **das Rennboot(e)**
submarine **das U-Boot(e)**
towboat **der Schlepper(-)**
warship **das Kriegsschiff(e)**
yacht **die Yacht(en)**

Can we meet on deck?	**Können wir uns an Deck treffen?**
In stormy weather the ship pitches a lot.	**Bei stürmischem Wetter schaukelt das Schiff sehr.**
I felt very sick on the crossing.	**Bei der Überfahrt war mir sehr übel.**
The boat docked at 10:00 p.m.	**Das Boot legte um 22.00 Uhr an.**

COUNTRIES App.20a; CURRENCIES 9a

19c Travel by road

I accelerate **ich gebe Gas**
access **der Zugang(ᵉe)**
alley **die Gasse(n), der Durchgang(ᵉe)**
I allow **ich erlaube**
avenue **die Allee(n)**
I back up/reverse **ich setze zurück***
bend/curve **die Kurve(n)**
bike/bicycle **das Fahrrad(ᵉer)**
black ice **das Glatteis**
bottleneck **der Engpass(ᵉe)**
breathalyzer test **die Alkoholkontrolle(n)**
I break down **ich habe eine Panne**
breakdown **die Panne(n)**
breakdown service **der Pannendienst(e)**
bridge **die Brücke(n)**
broken **kaputt**
built-up/residential area **das Wohngebiet(e)**
bump **die Beule(n), der Stoß(ᵉe)**
bus **der Bus(se)**
bus fare **der Busfahrpreis(e)**
bus stop **die Bushaltestelle(n)**
bypass **die Umgehungsstraße(n)**
car **das Auto(s)**
car rental **der Autoverleih**
car part **das Ersatzteil(e)**
carwash **die Autowaschanlage(n)**
caravan/camping trailer **der Wohnwagen(-)**
careful **vorsichtig**
caution **die Vorsicht** *(no pl)*
caution *(legal)* **die Warnung(en)**
central reservation/median **der Mittelstreifen(-)**
I change gear **ich schalte**
chauffeur **der Chauffeur(e)**
I check **ich (über)prüfe**
closed *(road)* **gesperrt**
I collide with **ich stoße mit** +dat **zusammen***

collision **der Zusammenstoß(ᵉe)**
company car **der Firmenwagen(-)**
conductor *(bus)* **der Schaffner(-) [-in]**
corner **die Ecke(n), die Kurve(n)**
I cross **ich überquere**
crossing **die Übergang(ᵉe)**
crossroad **die Kreuzung(en)**
cul-de-sac **die Sackgasse(n)**
dangerous **gefährlich**
detour **der Umweg(e)**
diesel **der Diesel, das Dieselöl**
I do 30 km **ich fahre 30**
I drive **ich fahre**
drive **die Fahrt(en)**
driver **der Fahrer(-) [-in]**
driving **Fahr-**
    instructor **der Fahrlehrer(-)**
    lesson **die Fahrstunde(n)**
    licence/driver's license **der Führerschein(e)**
    school **die Fahrschule(n)**
    test **die Fahrprüfung(en)**
drunken driving **betrunken am Steuer**
emergency stop **die Vollbremsung(en)**
engine trouble **der Motorschaden (ᵉen)**
entrance/exit **die Ein-/Ausfahrt(en)**
eyewitness **der Augenzeuge(n)** *(wk)*
I fasten my seatbelt **ich schnalle mich an***
fatality **das Todesopfer(-)**
I fill up **ich tanke**
I find my way **ich finde mich zurecht***
I fix **ich repariere**
forbidden **verboten**
for hire/rent **zu vermieten**
garage **die Garage(n), die Werkstatt(ᵉen)**
gas station **die Tankstelle(n)**
gasoline **das Benzin**
    premium **das Superbenzin**

regular **das Normalbenzin**
gear **der Gang(-̈e)**
  in gear **der Gang ist eingelegt**
  in first gear **im ersten Gang**
  in neutral **im Leerlauf**
  in reverse **im Rückwärtsgang**
I get in the car **ich steige ein***
I get in lane **ich ordne mich ein***
I get out **ich steige aus***
I give way/yield **ich lasse (jdm.)
  die Vorfahrt**
green card *(insurance)* **die grüne
  Versicherungskarte**
I have it repaired **ich lasse es
  reparieren**
highway **die Landstraße(n)/die
  Autobahn**
highway code **die
  Straßenverkehrsordnung**
highway police **die
  Autobahnpolizei**
I hire/rent **ich miete**
hired/rented car **der Mietwagen(-)**
I hitchhike **ich trampe, ich fahre
  per Anhalter**
hitchhiker **der Tramper(-) [-]**
I honk **ich hupe**
inside lane **die Innenspur(en)**
insurance **die Versicherung(en)**
insurance policy **die
  Versicherungspolice(n)**
I am insured **ich bin versichert**
intersection **die Kreuzung(en)**
international driving licence **der
  internationale Führerschein(e)**
jack **der Wagenheber(-)**
it is jammed **es klemmt**
junction **die Kreuzung(en)**
key **der Schlüssel(-)**
keyring **der Schlüsselring(e)**
kilometer **der Kilometer(-)**
lane **die Fahrspur(en)**
lay-by/rest stop **der Rastplatz(-̈e)**
lead-free **bleifrei**
learner driver **der Fahrschüler(-)**
level/railroad crossing **der
  Bahnübergang(-̈e)**

limit **die (Geschwindigkeits)-
  begrenzung(en)**
line of cars **die Autoschlange(n)**
liter **der Liter(-)**
logbook/vehicle registration **der
  Kraftfahrzeugschein(e)**
main **Haupt-**
main street **die Hauptstraße(n)**
I make a statement **ich mache
  eine Aussage**
make of car **die Automarke(n)**
MOT/vehicle validation/inspection
  der TÜV
maximum speed **die
  Höchstgeschwindigkeit(en)**
mechanic **der Mechaniker(-) [-in]**
mechanic *(adj)* **mechanisch**
motel **das Motel(s)**
motor caravan/trailer **das
  Wohnmobil(e)**
motor/car show **die
  Automobilausstellung(en)**
motorway/expressway **die
  Autobahn(en)**
  entry **die Auffahrt(en)**
  exit **die Ausfahrt(en)**
  hard shoulder **die
    Standspur(en)**
  junction **die Kreuzung(en)**
  police **die (Autobahn)polizei**
  services **die Raststätte(en)**
  toll **die Autobahngebühr(en)**
one-way **Einbahn-**
one-way street **die
  Einbahnstraße(n)**
outside lane **die Überholspur(en)**
I overtake/pass **ich überhole**
overtaking/passing **das Überholen**
I park **ich parke**
parking **das Parken**
parking ban **das Parkverbot(e)**
parking deck **die Hochgarage(n)**
  underground parking **die
    Tiefgaragen(n)**
parking lot **der Parkplatz(-̈e)**

TRAVEL

parking meter **die Parkuhr(en)**
parking ticket **der Strafzettel(-)**
I pass **ich fahre vorbei***
passenger **der Passagier(e)**
pedestrian **der Fußgänger(-) [-in]**
pedestrian crossing **der Fußgängerübergang(¨e)**
pedestrian zone **die Fußgängerzone(n)**
picnic area **der Picknickplatz(¨e)**
police **die Polizei**
policeman **der Polizist(en)** *(wk)* **[-in]**
police station **das Polizeirevier(e)**
private car **der eigene Wagen(-)**
private property **das Privateigentum**
public transport **das öffentliche Verkehrsmittel(-)**
puncture/flat **der platte Reifen(-)**
I put on my seat belt **ich schnalle mich an***
ramp **die Auffahrt(en)**
registration papers **die Autopapiere** *(pl)*

rental charge **der Mietpreis(e)**
repair **die Reparatur(en)**
I repair **ich repariere**
I reverse **ich fahre zurück***
(in) reverse **im Rückwärtsgang**
right of way **die Vorfahrt**
ring road/bypass **die Umgehungsstraße(n)**
road **die Straße(n)**
  accident **der Unfall(¨e)**
  block **die (Straßen)sperrung(en)**
  hog **der Verkehrsrowdy(s)**
  map **die Straßenkarte(n)**
  sign **das Straßenschild(er)**
  signals/traffic light **die Ampel(n)**
  side **der Straßenrand(¨er)**
  works **der Straßenbau**
roundabout/circle **der Kreisverkehr**
route **die Route(n)**
I run over **ich überfahre**
rush hour **der Berufsverkehr**
secondhand car **der Gebrauchtwagen(-)**

If you don't put money into the parking meter immediately, you'll get a parking ticket.

Wenn du nicht sofort Geld in die Parkuhr steckst, kriegst du einen Strafzettel.

Fill her up!

Bitte voll tanken!

When the engine starts, step on the clutch, put the car into first gear and step on the gas pedal.

Wenn der Motor anspringt, treten Sie die Kupplung, dann legen Sie den ersten Gang ein und geben Gas.

In heavy traffic you have to go slowly.

Im dichten Straßenverkehr muss man langsam fahren.

Keep to the right!

Rechts halten!

This morning I almost hit a man at a pedestrian crossing.

Heute Morgen habe ich fast einen Mann an einem Fußgängerüberweg überfahren.

service **die Inspektion(en)**
I set off **ich mache mich auf den Weg**
side street **die Nebenstraße(n)**
signpost **der Wegweiser(-), das Schild(er)**
I skid **ich rutsche aus***
slippery **glatt**
slow **langsam**
I slow down **ich fahre langsamer**
speed **die Geschwindigkeit(en)**
I speed up **ich fahre schneller**
speed limit **die Geschwindigkeits-begrenzung(en)**
spot traffic fine **die Geldstrafe(n)**
I start (engine) **ich lasse an***
street **die Straße(n)**
I switch off **ich schalte ab***
taxi/cab **das Taxi(s)**
taxi driver **der Taxifahrer(-)**
taxi rank/stand **der Taxistand(̈e)**
I test **ich prüfe**
tool **das Werkzeug(e)**
I tow away **ich schleppe ab***
town plan/map **der Stadtplan(̈e)**
town traffic **der Stadtverkehr**
traffic **der Verkehr**
traffic jam **der Stau(s)**

traffic light **die Ampel(n)**
traffic offence **das Verkehrsdelikt(e)**
traffic news **die Verkehrsmeldung(en)**
traffic police **die Verkehrspolizei**
traffic-free zone **die verkehrsfreie Zone(n)**
truck **der Lastwagen(-)**
truck driver **der LKW-Fahrer(-) [-in]**
I turn **ich biege**
I turn left **ich biege nach links ein***
I turn right **ich biege nach rechts ein***
I turn off at **ich biege ab***
I turn off (engine) **ich schalte ... ab***
underground garage **die Tiefgarage(n)**
underground passage **die Unterführung(en)**
unleaded/(gasoline) **bleifrei**
U-turn **das Wenden** (no pl)
vehicle **das Fahrzeug(e)**
I wait **ich warte**
warning **die Warnung(en)**
warning triangle **das Warndreieck(e)**

We must take a detour because of the road construction.

Wir müssen wegen der Baustelle einen Umweg fahren.

Can you please tell me where the next police station is?

Können Sie mir bitte sagen, wo das nächste Polizeirevier ist?

Be careful around the next turn. It's always very slippery when it rains.

Sei bei der nächsten Kurve vorsichtig. Die ist bei Regen immer sehr glatt.

When you come to visit us, take the Autobahn in the direction of Hannover and get off at the exit Gütersloh-Verl.

Wenn du uns besuchen kommst, nimm die Autobahn in Richtung Hannover und fahr an der Ausfahrt Gütersloh-Verl ab.

The rental price for the car is 350 euros per week.

Der Mietpreis für den Wagen beträgt 350 Euro pro Woche.

➤ PARTS OF THE CAR, ROAD SIGNS App.19c; DIRECTIONS 2b

19d Travel by air

aeroplane/airplane **das Flugzeug(e)**
airline **die Fluglinie(n)**
airline desk **der Flugschalter(-)**
air travel **der Flugverkehr**
airport **der Flughafen(-)**
I am airsick **mir wird schlecht beim Fliegen**
baggage **das Gepäck**
baggage reclaim **die Gepäckausgabe**
body search **die Leibeskontrolle(n)**
I board a plane **ich gehe an Bord eines Flugzeugs**
boarding card **die Bordkarte(n)**
business class **die Businessklasse(n)**
by air **per Flugzeug**
cabin **die Kabine(n)**
cancelled **gestrichen**
carousel **das Gepäckband(-er)**
charter flight **der Charterflug(-e)**
I check in **ich checke ein***
check-in operations **das Einchecken**

control tower **der Kontrollturm(-e)**
co-pilot **der Copilot(en)** *(wk)* **[-in]**
crew **die Besatzung(en)**
direct flight **der Direktflug(-e)**
domestic flights **der Inlandflug(-e)**
during landing **während der Landung**
during take-off **während des Starts**
during the flight **während des Fluges**
duty-free goods **die zollfreie Ware(n)**
economy class **die Touristenklasse(n)**
emergency exit **der Notausgang(-e)**
emergency landing **die Notlandung(en)**
excess baggage **das Übergewicht**
flight **der Flug(-e)**
flight attendant **der Flugbegleiter(-) [-in]**
I fly **ich fliege**
I fly at a height of **ich fliege in einer Höhe von**

We are about to land in Zürich.	**Wir befinden uns im Anflug auf Zürich.**
Please fasten your safety belt and stop smoking.	**Wir bitten Sie, sich jetzt anzuschnallen und das Rauchen einzustellen.**
Rosie and Tony are flying on the early flight to Mallorca.	**Rosie und Tony fliegen mit der Frühmaschine nach Mallorca.**
Your ticket is waiting at the Lufthansa desk, Mr. Richter.	**Ihr Ticket liegt am Lufthansa-Schalter bereit, Herr Richter.**
When you go downtown, you can park in the underground garage at Hertie's.	**Wenn du in die Stadt fährst, kannst du bei Hertie in der Tiefgarage parken.**
Can I change my reservation?	**Kann ich umbuchen?**

flying **das Fliegen**
fuselage **der Flugzeugrumpf(ẅe)**
gate **der Ausgang(ẅe)**
instructions **die Gebrauchsanweisung(en)**
hand luggage **das Handgepäck**
headphone **der Kopfhörer**
highjacker **der Luftpirat(en)** *(wk)*
immigrant **der Immigrant(en)** *(wk)* **[-in]**
immigration **die Einwanderung**
immigration rules **die Einwanderungsgesetze**
information desk **die Information**
I land **ich lande**
landing **die Landung(en)**
landing lights **die Landebeleuchtung**
no-smoking sign **das Rauchen-Verboten-Schild**
nonstop **Non-stop-**
on board **an Bord**
parachute **der Fallschirm(e)**
passenger **der Passagier(e)**
passengers lounge **die Wartehalle(n)**

passport control **die Passkontrolle(n)**
pilot **der Pilot(en)** *(wk)*
plane **die Maschine(n)**
refreshments **die Erfrischungen** *(pl)*
runway **die Start- und Landebahn(en)**
safety jacket **die Rettungsweste(n)**
security measures **die Sicherheitsmaßnahmen** *(pl)*
security staff **das Sicherheitspersonal**
I take off **ich starte, ich fliege ab***
takeoff **der Abflug(ẅe)**
terminal **das Terminal(s)**
tray **das Tablett(s/e)**
turbulence **die Turbulenzen** *(pl)*
view **die Aussicht(en)**
window **das Fenster(-)**
window seat **der Fensterplatz(ẅe)**

There was a problem in the baggage hall. The flight to London has been delayed by half an hour.

Es gab ein Problem bei der Gepäckaufgabe. Der Flug nach London hat eine halbe Stunde Verspätung.

There are still some seats available on the plane.

In der Maschine sind noch Plätze frei.

Passengers continuing to Rome please go to gate 18.

Passagiere im Weiterflug nach Rom bitte zu Ausgang 18 gehen.

I need a wheelchair for a disabled passenger.

Ich brauche einen Rollstuhl für einen behinderten Passagier.

Frankfurt Airport is called the gateway to the world.

Man nennt den Frankfurter Flughafen das Tor zur Welt.

19e Travel by rail

buffet **das Büfett(s)**
buffet car/dining car **der Speisewagen(-)**
coach **der Waggon(s)**
compartment **das Abteil(e)**
connection **der Anschluss(¨e)**
direct train **der durchgehende Zug(¨e)**
express train **der Schnellzug(¨e)**
fare **der Fahrpreis(e)**
first class **erster Klasse**
inspector **der Kontrolleur(e)**
Intercity train **der Intercity, der IC-Zug**
level crossing **der Bahnübergang(¨e)**
luggage/baggage rack **die Gepäckablage(n)**
nonrefundable **keine Rückzahlung**
occupied **besetzt**
on time **pünktlich**

platform **der Bahnsteig(e), das Gleis(e)**
porter **der Gepäckträger(-)**
I punch *(ticket)* **ich entwerte**
railway/railroad **die Eisenbahn(en)**
station **der Bahnhof(¨e)**
track **das Gleis(e)**
reduction **die Ermäßigung(en)**
reservation **die Reservierung(en)**
reserved **reserviert**
return/round trip ticket **die Rückfahrkarte(n)**
second class **zweiter Klasse**
single/one-way ticket **die einfache Fahrkarte(n)**
sleeper **der Schlafwagen(-)**
(non) smoking compartment **das (Nicht)raucherabteil(e)**
stop **die Haltestelle(n)**

Have you checked the timetable?	**Hast du im Fahrplan nachgesehen?**
– When is the first train to Cologne? – At four p.m. from platform 3.	**– Wann fährt der erste Zug nach Köln? – Um sechzehn Uhr von Gleis 3.**
The train from Vienna arrived punctually.	**Der Zug aus Wien ist pünktlich angekommen.**
Have you got your ticket?	**Haben Sie Ihren Fahrschein?**
Paul travelled without a ticket.	**Paul ist schwarzgefahren.**
Don't forget to pay the supplement for the Inter-City train.	**Vergessen Sie nicht, den Zuschlag für den Intercityzug zu bezahlen.**
Where do I change?	**Wo muss ich umsteigen?**

I stop **ich halte**
suitcase **der Koffer(-)**
supplement **der Zuschlag(-̈e)**
taxi rank/stand **der Taxistand(-̈e)**
ticket **die Fahrkarte(n)**
 collector **der Schaffner(-)**
 office **der Fahrkartenschalter(-)**
timetable **der Fahrplan(-̈e)**
 change **die Fahrplanänderung(en)**
 summer timetable **der Sommerfahrplan(-̈e)**
 winter timetable **der Winterfahrplan(-̈e)**
toilets **die Toilette(n)**
track **das Gleis(e)**
traveller **der/die Reisende** *(wk)*

train **der Zug(-̈e)**
 Intercity train **der Intercity-Zug(-̈e)**
 local train **die S-Bahn(en)**
 night train **der Nachtzug(-̈e)**
trolley **der Kofferkuli(s)**
waiting-room **der Wartesaal (-säle)**
wagon-lits **der Schlafwagen(-)**
warning **die Warnung(en)**
window **das Fenster(-)**
window seat **der Fensterplatz(-̈e)**

– Is there a connection to Basle? – Yes, but only runs on Sundays and holidays.

– **Gibt es eine Verbindung nach Basel? – Ja, aber nur an Sonn- und Feiertagen.**

This is a no-smoking compartment.

Dies ist ein Nichtraucherabteil.

German Railways is the largest transport business in Germany.

Die Deutsche Bahn (DB) ist das größte Transportunternehmen in Deutschland.

There is a lot of commuter traffic, above all in large built up areas.

Es gibt einen starken Pendlerverkehr, vor allem in den großen Ballungsgebieten.

On Sundays and holidays ...

An Sonn- und Feiertagen ...

On weekdays ...

An Werktagen ...

163

Holidays/Vacation

20a General terms

abroad   **im/ins Ausland**
accommodation   **die Unterkunft(¨e)**
alone   **allein**
amenities   **die Möglichkeiten** *(pl)*
area   **das Gebiet(e)**
arrival   **die Ankunft(¨e)**
it is available   **er steht zur Verfügung**
beach   **der Strand(¨e)**
camera   **die Kamera(s), der Fotoapparat(e)**
clean   **sauber**
climate   **das Klima(s)**
closed   **geschlossen**
clothes   **die Kleidung**
cold   **kalt**
comfortable   **bequem**
congested   **überfüllt**
cost   **die Kosten** *(pl)*
country   **das Land(¨er)**
   in the country   **auf dem Land(e)**
countryside   **die Landschaft(en)**
departure   **die Abfahrt(en)**
dirty   **schmutzig**
disorganized *(untidy)*   **unordentlich**
I am disorganized   **ich bin schlecht organisiert**
exchange *(money)*   **die Wechselstube(n)**
folding chair   **der Klappstuhl(¨e)**
folding table   **der Klapptisch(e)**
food   **das Essen**
free   **frei, kostenlos**
full   **voll**
I get tan   **ich werde braun**
I go away   **ich verreise**
group   **die Gruppe(n)**
group travel   **die Gruppenreise(n)**
guide   **der Reiseführer(-) [-in]**
guided tour   **die Reisetour(s)**

guided walk   **die Führung(en)**
holidays/vacation   **die Ferien** *(pl)*, **der Urlaub** *(no pl)*
I go on holiday/vacation   **ich fahre in Urlaub**
holiday/vacation dates   **die Ferientermine** *(pl)*
land   **das Land(¨er)**
landscape   **die Landschaft(en)**
journey   **die Reise(n)**
map   **die Landkarte(n)**
mild *(climate)*   **mild**
money   **das Geld(er)**
in the mountains   **im Gebirge**
no vacancy *(hotel)*   **ausgebucht**
open   **offen, geöffnet**
it is open   **es ist offen**
organization   **die Organisation(en)**
I organize   **ich organisiere**
organized   **organisiert**
I pack   **ich packe ein***
I plan   **ich plane**
portable   **tragbar**
postcard   **die Ansichtskarte(n)**
rucksack/knapsack   **der Rucksack(¨e)**
sea   **das Meer(e), die See(n)**
seaside resort   **der Badeort(e)**
shade   **der Schatten(-)**
I shop   **ich kaufe ein***
show   **die Vorstellung(en)**
sight   **die Sehenswürdigkeit(en)**
I spend *(time)*   **ich verbringe (Zeit)**
stay   **der Aufenthalt(e)**
I stay   **ich wohne**
sun   **die Sonne(n)**
I sunbathe   **ich liege in der Sonne**
tour   **die Tour(en), die Fahrt(en)**
tourism   **der Tourismus**
tourist   **der Tourist(en)** *(wk)*

tourist menu **das Touristenmenü(s)**
tourist office **das Verkehrsamt(¨er)**
town **die Stadt(¨e)**
town plan **der Stadtplan(¨e)**
travel **das Reisen**
I travel **ich reise**
travel adaptor **der Adapter(-)**
trip **der Ausflug(¨e)**
uncomfortable **unbequem**
I understand **ich verstehe**
I unpack **ich packe aus***
visit **der Besuch(e)**
I visit **ich besuche**
visiting hours **die Besuchszeit(en)**
visitor **der Besucher(-)**
welcome **der Empfang(¨e)**
I welcome **ich begrüße**
worth seeing **sehenswert**

Holidays/Vacation activities

beach holiday/vacation **der Urlaub am Meer**
boating **das Bootfahren(-)**
camping **das Zelten**
canoeing **das Kanufahren**
coach holiday/vacation bus tour **die Busreise(n)**

cruise **die Kreuzfahrt(en)**
cycling **das Radfahren**
exchange (school) **der Austausch(e)**
fishing **das Angeln, das Fischen**
fruit picking **das Obstpflücken**
hunting **die Jagd** *(no pl)*
I go hunting **ich gehe auf die Jagd**
mountain climbing **das Bergsteigen**
package holiday/tour **die Pauschalreise(n)**
rock climbing **das Klettern**
safari **die Safari(s)**
sailing **das Segeln**
shopping **das Einkaufen**
sightseeing **die Besichtigungstour(en)**
skiing **das Skilaufen**
study holiday **die Informationstour(en)**
sunbathing **das Sonnenbaden**
trekking **das Trekking**
volunteer work **ehrenamtlich arbeiten**
walking/hiking tour **das Wandern**
wine tasting **die Weinprobe(n)**

– When are you on vacation? Do you have your holiday/vacation dates already?
– We are going on vacation in July.

– I hope you had a restful vacation.
– Yes, we spent it on a farm. We did a lot of walking and cycling.

– **Wann hast du Urlaub? Hast du schon deine Ferientermine?**

– **Wir fahren im Juli in Urlaub.**

– **Hoffentlich haben Sie einen erholsamen Urlaub gehabt.**
– **Ja, wir haben ihn auf einem Bauernhof verbracht. Wir sind viel gewandert und Rad gefahren.**

➤ COUNTRIES App.20a; HOBBIES 16a; ON THE BEACH App.20a

20b Accommodation & hotel

Accommodation

accommodation **die Unterkunft(ˉe)**
apartment **die Wohnung(en)**
bed and breakfast **die Übernachtung mit Frühstück** "Bed & Breakfast" **"Fremdenzimmer"**
campsite **der Campingplatz(ˉe)**
caravan/trailer **der Wohnwagen(-)**
guest **der Gast(ˉe)**
farm **der Bauernhof(ˉe)**
full board **die Vollpension**
half board **die Halbpension**
holiday flat/vacation apartment **die Ferienwohnung(en)**
home exchange **der Haustausch(e)**
hotel **das Hotel(s)**
mobile home **das Wohnmobil(e)**
inn **das Wirtshaus(ˉer)**
self-catering/service **mit Selbstverpflegung**
villa **die Villa(s)**
youth hostel **die Jugendherberge(n)**

Booking & payment

I afford **ich leiste mir**
all included **(alles mit) inbegriffen, inklusiv**
bill **die Rechnung(en)**
I book **ich buche**
cash *(money)* **das (Bar)geld**
I cash **ich löse ein***
cheap **billig, preiswert**
check **der Scheck(s)**
cost **der Preis(e)**
credit **der Kredit(e)**
credit card **die Kreditkarte(n)**
exclusive **exklusiv**
expensive **teuer**
extra charge **zusätzliche Kosten** *(pl)*
I fill in **ich fülle aus***
form **das Formular(e)**

free **kostenlos, frei**
I pay **ich bezahle**
payment **die Bezahlung(en)**
by cheque/check **mit Scheck**
with cash **in bar**
price **der Preis(e)**
price list **die Preisliste(n)**
receipt **die Quittung(en)**
reduction **der Ermäßigung(en)**
refund **die Rückvergütung(en)**
reservation **die Reservierung(en)**
I reserve **ich reserviere**
I sign **ich unterschreibe**
signature **die Unterschrift(en)**
traveller's check **der Reisescheck(s)**
VAT/sales tax **die Mehrwertsteuer, MwSt.**

In the hotel

amenities **die Einrichtungen** *(pl)*
balcony **der Balkon(s)**
ball **der Ball(ˉe)**
bank card **die Bankkarte(n)**
basement **das Kellergeschoss(e)**
bath **das Bad(ˉer)**
bed **das Bett(en)**
double bed **das Doppelbett(en)**
single bed **das Einzelbett(en)**
twin beds **mit zwei Betten**
bedding **das Bettzeug** *(no pl)*
bedspread **der Überwurf(ˉe)**
billiard room **der Billardraum(ˉe)**
breakfast **das Frühstück(e)**
English breakfast **das englische Frühstück**
broken **kaputt**
it is broken **es ist zerbrochen**
business conference **die Geschäftskonferenz(en)**
button **der Knopf(ˉe)**
call **der Anruf(e)**
I call **ich rufe an***
I check in **ich melde mich an***
I check out **ich fahre/reise ab***

coathanger **der Kleiderbügel(-)**
comfortable **bequem**
I complain (about) **ich beschwere mich (über** +acc)
complaint **die Beschwerde(n)**
conference **die Konferenz(en)**
conference facilities **die Konferenzeinrichtungen** *(pl)*
damage **der Schaden(-̈)**
dining room **der Speiseraum(-̈e)**
dry cleaning **die Reinigung**
early morning call **der Weckruf(e)**
en-suite bathroom **mit Bad**
evening meal **das Abendessen(-)**
extravagant **luxuriös**
facilities **die Einrichtungen** *(pl)*
fax **das Fax(e)**
it is on fire **es brennt!**
fire alarm **der Feueralarm**
fire exit **der Notausgang(-̈e)**
fire extinguisher **der Feuerlöscher(-)**
first floor **die erste Etage**
ground floor **das Erdgeschoss(e)**
guest **der Gast(-̈e)**
hairdresser **der Friseur(e)**
hairdryer **der Fön®(s)**
heating **die Heizung(en)**
key **der Schlüssel(-)**
laundry **die Wäsche** *(no pl)*
laundry bag **der Wäschebeutel(-)**

laundry service **der Wäscheservice**
elevator **der Fahrstuhl(-̈e), der Aufzug(-̈e)**
night porter **der Nachtportier(s)**
noisy **laut**
nuisance **das Ärgernis(se)**
parking space **der Parkplatz(-̈e)**
pleasant **angenehm, freundlich**
plug **der Stecker(-)**
porter **der Portier(s)**
private **privat**
privacy **die Ruhe**
proof of identity **der Ausweis(e)**
quality **die Qualität(en)**
quiet **still, ruhig**
reception **die Rezeption(en)**
receptionist **der Empfangschef/dame**
room **das Zimmer(-)**
double room **das Doppelzimmer**
room service **der Zimmerservice**
service **die Bedienung**
stay **der Aufenthalt(e)**
I stay **ich wohne**
suitcase **der Koffer(-)**
terrace **die Terrasse(n)**
view **die Aussicht(en)**

Our hotel room was large and sunny. And from our balcony, we had a great view of the mountains.

Unser Hotelzimmer war groß und sonnig. Und von unserem Balkon aus hatten wir einen wunderbaren Ausblick auf die Berge.

The children spent a lot of time in the swimming pool.

Die Kinder verbrachten viel Zeit im Swimmingpool.

You can pay the bill by credit card if you'd like.

Sie können die Rechnung gern mit Kreditkarte bezahlen.

We have a large parking lot for our guests behind the hotel.

Wir haben einen großen Parkplatz für unsere Gäste hinter dem Hotel.

➤ ROOMS 8a; FURNISHINGS 8c; EATING OUT 10a

20c Camping & self-service

At the campsite

air bed **die Luftmatratze(n)**
ant **die Ameise(n)**
barbeque **der Grill(s), das Grillfest(e)**
battery **die Batterie(n)**
I camp **ich zelte**
camp bed **das Campingbett(en)**
camper **der Camper(-)**
camping **das Zelten**
camping equipment/gear **die Campingausrüstung(en)**
camping gas **das Campinggas**
campsite **der Zeltplatz(¨e)**
caravan/trailer **der Wohnwagen(-)**
connected **mit elektrischem Anschluss**
cooking facilities **die Kochmöglichkeiten** (pl)
dark **dunkel**
disconnected **ohne elektrischen Anschluss**
drinking water **das Trinkwasser**
dry **trocken**
dustbin/trash can **der Mülleimer(-)**

extension lead/cord **das Verlängerungskabel(-)**
forbidden **verboten**
fun **der Spaß** (no pl)
gas cooker **der Gaskocher(-)**
gas cylinder **die Gasflasche(n)**
ground sheet **der Zeltboden(¨)**
we make friends **wir freunden uns an***
medicine box **der Arzneikasten(¨)**
mosquito **die Stechmücke**
mosquito bite **der Mückenstich(e)**
mosquito net **das Moskitonetz(e)**
pan **der Kochtopf(¨e)**
peg **der Pflock(¨e)**
pillow **das Kissen(-)**
I pitch/put up (tent) **ich stelle auf***
potty **das Töpfchen(-)**
private **privat**
proprietor **der Eigentümer(-) [-in]**
registration **die Anmeldung(en)**
reservation **die Reservierung(en)**
services **der Strom- und Wasseranschluss(¨e)**
shadow **der Schatten(-)**
sheet **das Bettlaken(-)**
site **der Platz(¨e)**

Last week we went camping. We pitched our tent in the shade near the lake. Unfortunately, there were many bugs, because it was damp. I didn't sleep well, because the ground was hard and I only had a sleeping bag. Next time I'm taking an air bed along.

Letzte Woche haben wir gezeltet. Wir haben das Zelt im Schatten dicht am See aufgeschlagen. Leider gab es dort viel Ungeziefer, weil es feucht war. Ich habe nicht gut geschlafen, weil der Boden hart war und ich nur einen Schlafsack hatte. Das nächste Mal nehme ich eine Luftmatratze mit.

sleeping bag **der Schlafsack(-̈e)**
space **der Platz(-̈e)**
I take down (tent) **ich baue (das Zelt) ab***
tent **das Zelt(e)**
tin/can opener **der Dosenöffner(-)**
toilet **die Toilette(n)**
flashlight **die Taschenlampe(n)**
uncomfortable **unbequem, ungemütlich**
vehicle **das Fahrzeug(e)**
washing facilities **die Waschgelegenheiten** *(pl)*
water filter **der Wasserfilter(-)**

Self-catering/service

agency **die Agentur(en)**
agreement **der Vertrag(-̈e)**
amenity **die Annehmlichkeit(en)**
apartment **die Wohnung(en)**
clean **sauber**
I clean **ich mache sauber***
I cook **ich koche**
damaged **defekt**
damages **der Schadensersatz** *(no pl)*
electricity **die Elektrizität**

equipment **die Ausstattung(en)**
facilities **die Einrichtungen** *(pl)*
farm **der Bauernhof(-̈e)**
furniture **die Möbel** *(pl)*
ironing board **das Bügelbrett(er)**
landlord **der Wirt(e) [-in]**
maid **das Dienstmädchen(-)**
meter **der Zähler(-)**
owner **der Besitzer(-) [-in]**
rent **die Miete(n)**
I rent **ich miete**
I rent out **ich vermiete**
repair **die Reparatur(en)**
I repair **ich repariere**
I return *(give back)* **ich gebe wieder***
ruined **zerstört**
self-service **die Selbstbedienung**
set of keys **der Schlüsselbund(-̈e)**
I share **ich teile**
shutters **die Fensterläden** *(pl)*, **die Rollläden** *(pl)*
smelly **übel riechend**
spare key **der Ersatzschlüssel(-)**
well **der Brunnen(-)**
well kept **gut gepflegt**

Klaus and Ursula rented a vacation cottage this summer.

Klaus und Ursula haben diesen Sommer ein Ferienhaus gemietet.

It was really worthwhile.

Es hat sich wirklich gelohnt.

The cottage had two double bedrooms, one with bunk beds, a modern kitchen and a bathroom with shower.

Das Haus hatte zwei Doppelzimmer, ein Zimmer mit Etagenbetten, eine modern eingerichtete Küche und ein Bad mit Dusche.

It was in a quiet location. The advertisement said there was a view, and that was really true.

Die Lage war ruhig. In der Anzeige hieß es, dass man eine gute Aussicht hatte, und das stimmte wirklich.

➤ FURNISHINGS 8c; COOKING UTENSILS App. 10d

21 Language

21a General terms

accuracy **die Genauigkeit**
accurate **genau sein**
I adapt **ich passe mich an***
I adopt **ich übernehme**
advanced **fortgeschritten**
aptitude **die Begabung**
artificial language **die künstliche Sprache(n)**
it is based on **es basiert auf** +dat
bilingual **zweisprachig**
bilingualism **die Zweisprachigkeit**
branch **der Zweig(e)**
classical language **die klassische Sprache(n)**
it derives from **es stammt aus** +dat
development **die Entwicklung(en)**
difficult **schwer**
easy **leicht**
error **der Fehler(-)**
foreign language **die Fremdsprache(n)**
I forget **ich vergesse**
grammar **die Grammatik(en)**
grammatical **grammatisch**

I improve **ich verbessere (mich)**
influence **der Einfluss(¨e)**
isolation **die Isoliertheit**
known **bekannt**
language **die Sprache(n)**
    language course **der Sprachkurs(e)**
    language family **die Sprachfamilie(n)**
    language school **die Sprachschule(n)**
    language skill **die (Sprach)fertigkeit(en)**
I learn **ich lerne**
learning **das Lernen**
level **das Sprachniveau(s)**
linguistics **die Sprachwissenschaft(en)**
link **die Verbindung(en)**
living **lebendig**
loan-word **das Lehnwort(¨er)**
major language **die Weltsprache(n)**
it means **das bedeutet**
I mime **ich ahme nach***

– You speak such good German, Mr. Brown. Did you learn it in school?

– No, but my mother is German, and she always spoke German to me at home.

I am not very good at languages, but my sister is a good linguist.

– **Sie sprechen sehr gut Deutsch, Herr Brown. Haben Sie es in der Schule gelernt?**

– **Nein, aber meine Mutter ist Deutsche, und sie hat zu Hause immer mit mir Deutsch gesprochen.**

Ich bin nicht sehr gut in Sprachen, aber meine Schwester ist sehr sprachbegabt.

minor language **die kleinere Sprache(n)**

mistake **der Fehler(-)**

monolingual **einsprachig**

mother tongue **die Muttersprache(n)**

mutation/change **der Wandel** *(no pl)*

name **der Name(n)** (gen **des Namens**) *(wk)*

nation **das Volk(-̈er)**

national **national**

native **Mutter-, Heimat-**

natural **natürlich**

official **offiziell**

offshoot **der Zweig(e)**

origin **die Herkunft(-̈e)**

phenomenon **die Erscheinung(en)**

I practise/practice **ich übe**

preserved **erhalten**

question **die Frage(n)**

register **das Verzeichnis (-sse), das Register(-)**

separate **einzeln**

sign language **die Zeichensprache(n)**

survival **das Überleben**

it survives **es überlebt**

I translate **ich übersetze, ich übertrage**

translation **die Übersetzung(en)**

I understand **ich verstehe**

unknown **unbekannt**

widely used **weit verbreitet**

witticism **die witzige Bemerkung(en)**

Words & vocabulary

antonym **das Antonym(e)**

colloquial **umgangssprachlich**

consonant **der Konsonant(en)**

dictionary **das Wörterbuch(-̈er)**

expression **der Ausdruck(-̈e)**

idiom **die Redewendung(en)**

idiomatic **idiomatisch**

jargon **der Jargon(s)**

lexicographer **der Lexikograph(en)** *(wk)* [-in]

lexicon **das Lexikon(s/-a)**

phrase **die Phrase(n)**

phrase book **der Sprachführer(-)**

sentence **der Satz(-̈e)**

slang **der Slang** *(no pl)*

syllable **die Silbe(n)**

synonym **das Synonym(e)**

vocabulary **der Wortschatz(-̈e)**

vowel **der Vokal(e)**

word *(individual)* **das Wort(-̈er)**

word *(in text)* **das Wort(e)**

word game **das Wortspiel(e)**

Claudia and her boyfriend always talk French.

Claudia und ihr Freund unterhalten sich immer auf Französisch.

I practice my Spanish with a native speaker.

Ich übe mein Spanisch mit einem Muttersprachler.

Writing Urdu is a problem for me as the alphabet is quite different. They use the Arabic script.

Es ist für mich ein Problem, Urdu zu schreiben, da das Alphabet ganz anders ist. Man verwendet die arabische Schrift.

LANGUAGE

21b Using language

Speaking & listening

accent **der Akzent(e)**
  regional accent **die regionale Aussprache(n)**
I am articulate **ich spreche klar aus***
I articulate **ich artikuliere**
clear **klar, deutlich**
colloquial language **die Umgangssprache**
I communicate **ich kommuniziere, ich teile jdm. mit*** +dat
conversation **das Gespräch(e)**
I converse (with) **ich unterhalte mich (mit** +dat)
dialect **der Dialekt(e)**
diction **die Ausdrucksweise(n)**
I express (myself) **ich drücke (mich) aus***
fluent(ly) **fließend**
I interpret **ich dolmetsche**
interpreter **der Dolmetscher(-) [-in]**
intonation **die Betonung(en)**
lisp **das Lispeln**
I lisp **ich lisp(e)le**
I listen to **ich höre jdm. zu*** +dat
listening **das Hören**
listening skills **das Hörverständnis(se)**

I mispronounce **ich spreche falsch aus***
mispronunciation **die falsche Aussprache**
oral **mündlich**
I pronounce **ich spreche aus***
pronunciation **die Aussprache(n)**
rhythm **der Rhythmus (-en)**
I say **ich sage**
sound **der Laut(e)**
I sound **ich klinge**
I speak **ich spreche, ich rede**
speaking **das Sprechen**
speaking skills **die Sprechfähigkeit(en)**
speech **die Sprache(n), die Rede(n)**
I give a speech **ich halte eine Rede**
speed **die Schnelligkeit(en)**
spoken **gesprochen**
spoken language **die gesprochene Sprache**
stress **die Betonung(en)**
stressed (un-) **(un)betont**
I stutter/stammer **ich stottere**
I talk **ich spreche, ich rede**
I tell **ich sage, ich erzähle**
unpronounceable **unaussprechbar**
verbal(ly) **verbal**

When you travel in a foreign country, it's very useful to take along a phrase book. | **Wenn man ins Ausland reist, ist es sehr nützlich einen Sprachführer mitzunehmen.**
How do you pronounce that? | **Wie spricht man das aus?**
How do you spell that? | **Wie schreibt man das?**
Could you please translate that into English? | **Könnten Sie das bitte ins Englische übersetzen?**

Writing & reading

accent mark **das Akzentzeichen(-)**
alphabet **das Alphabet(e)**
alphabetically **alphabetisch**
in bold **fett**
Braille **die Blindenschrift**
character **das Schriftzeichen**
code **der Kode**
I correct **ich korrigiere**
I correspond with **ich korrespondiere mit +dat**
correspondence **die Korrespondenz**
I decypher **ich entziffere**
I draft **ich entwerfe**
graphic **graphisch**
handwriting **die Handschrift**
illiterate **der Analphabet(en)** *(wk)* **[-in]**
italic **der Kursivdruck**
in italics **kursiv gedruckt**
letter *(alphabet)* **der Buchstabe(n)** *(wk)*
he is literate **er kann lesen und schreiben**
literature **die Literatur(en)**
note **die Anmerkung(en)**
paragraph **der Absatz(ᵉe)**
philology **die Sprachwissenschaft(en)**
philologist **der Sprachwissenschaftler(-) [-in]**

pictogram(me) **das Piktogramm(e), die Bilddarstellung(en)**
I print **ich drucke**
I read **ich lese**
reading **das Lesen, die Lektüre**
reading matter **die Lektüre(n), der Lesestoff**
reading skills **das Leseverständnis(se)**
I re-write **ich schreibe neu, ich schreibe um***
scribble **das Gekritzel**
I scribble **ich kritz(e)le**
sign **das Zeichen(-)**
I sign **ich unterschreibe**
signature **die Unterschrift(en)**
I spell **ich buchstabiere**
spelling **die Rechtschreibung**
text **der Text(e)**
I transcribe **ich schreibe ab*/nieder***
transcription **die Abschrift(en), die Umschrift(en)**
umlaut **der Umlaut(e)**
I underline **ich unterstreiche**
I write **ich schreibe**
writing **das Schreiben**
writing skills **die Schreibfähigkeit(en)**
written language **die Schriftsprache(n)**

What is the right spelling?	**Was ist die richtige Schreibweise?**
Don't worry about spelling mistakes.	**Mach dir keine Sorgen wegen der Schreibfehler.**
The stem is modified by an umlaut.	**Der Stamm wird umgelautet.**
The verb goes to the end.	**Das Verb steht am Ende.**
That is colloquial German.	**Das ist Umgangssprache.**

22 Education

22a General terms

absent **abwesend**
achievement **die Leistung(en)**
admission **die Einschulung**
    I am admitted to school **ich werde eingeschult**
after school activity **die Arbeitsgemeinschaft(en)**
age group **die Altersstufe(n)**
aptitude **die Fertigkeit(en), das Talent(e)**
I analyze **ich analysiere**
answer **die Antwort(en)**
I answer **ich antworte**
    I answer (someone) **ich antworte (jdm.)**
    I answer (a question) **ich antworte auf (eine Frage)**
I ask (a question) **ich stelle (eine Frage)**
    I ask (someone) **ich frage (jdn.)**
I attend (a school) **ich besuche (eine Schule)**
career **die Berufslaufbahn(en)**
career advice **die Berufsberatung(en)**
career advisor **der Berufsberater(-)**
caretaker **der Hausmeister(-)**
I catch up **ich hole nach***
chapter **das Kapitel(-)**
I cheat **ich mogele, ich betrüge**
class **die Klasse(n)**
class representative **der Klassensprecher(-)**
class teacher **der Klassenlehrer(-)**
class trip **die Klassenfahrt(en)**
club **der Klub(s), der Verein(e)**
I complete **ich vollende**

comprehension **das Verständnis(se)**
compulsory schooling **die Schulpflicht**
computer **der Computer(-)**
concept **das Konzept(e)**
I copy (out) **ich schreibe ... ab***
copy **die Kopie(n)**
course **der Kurs(e), das Seminar(e)**
deputy head **der/die stellvertretende Schulleiter(-) [in]**
detention **das Nachsitzen**
    I am in detention **ich sitze nach***
difficult **schwierig**
discuss **besprechen**
easy **leicht**
education **die Bildung, die Erziehung**
educational system **das Bildungssystem(e)**
I encourage **ich fördere**
essay **der Aufsatz(¨e)**
example **das Beispiel(e)**
excellent **ausgezeichnet, vortrefflich**
favorite **der Liebling(e), Lieblings-**
favorite subject **das Lieblingsfach(¨er)**
I forget **ich vergesse**
governing body **der Schulausschuss(¨e)**
grade **die Klasse(n)**
holidays/vacation **die Ferien** *(pl)*
principal **der Schulleiter(-)[-in]**
homework **die Hausaufgabe(n)**
instruction **der Unterricht**
interesting **interessant**
I learn **ich lerne**

I leave **ich verlasse**
lesson **die Stunde(n)**
    lesson *(chapter)* **die Lektion(en)**
    lessons **der Unterricht**
I listen **ich höre** +dat **zu***
local education authority **die Schulbehörde(n)**
I look at **ich sehe ... an***
I misunderstand **ich missverstehe**
modular **aus Elementen zusammengesetzt**
module **die Einheit(en), das Element(e)**
oral **mündlich**
outdoor **im Freien**
parents' evening **der Elternabend(e)**
I play truant **ich schwänze die Schule**
principal **der Direktor(en) [-in]**
project **das Projekt(e), die Projektarbeit(en)**
punctual **pünktlich**
I punctuate **ich setze die Satzzeichen**
punctuation mark **das Satzzeichen(-)**
I punish **ich bestrafe**
punishment **die Strafe(n)**
pupil **der Schüler(-)[-in]**
qualification **die Qualifikation(en)**
I qualify **ich qualifiziere**
question **die Frage(n)**
I question **ich befrage (jdn.)**
I read **ich lese**
reading **das Lesen**
I repeat a year **ich wiederhole das Jahr**
report **das Zeugnis(se)**
research **die Forschung(en)**
I research **ich forsche**
resources centre/center **die Mediathek(en)**
scheme of work **der Lehrplan(-̈e)**

school book **das Schulbuch(-̈er)**
school friend **der Klassenkamerad(en)**
set **die Leistungsgruppe(n)**
    setted *(by ability)* **differenziert nach Leistung**
skill **die Fertigkeit(en)**
special achievement course **die Leistungsgruppe(n)**
specialist teacher **der Fachlehrer(-)**
spelling **die Rechtschreibung, die Orthographie**
I stay down/fail **ich bleibe sitzen**
strict **streng**
I study **ich studiere, ich lerne**
sum **die Rechenaufgabe(n)**
I summarize **ich fasse zusammen***
I swot **ich büffele, ich pauke**
task **die Aufgabe(n)**
I teach **ich lehre, unterrichte**
teacher **der Lehrer(-) [-in]**
teaching **der Unterricht**
teaching staff/falculty **das Lehrerkollegium (-ien)**
term/semester **das Semester(-)**
I train **ich lasse mich ausbilden**
training **die Ausbildung(en)**
I translate **ich übersetze**
translation **die Übersetzung(en)**
tutor **der Privatlehrer(-) [-in]**
I understand **ich verstehe**
understanding **das Verständnis(se)**
unit (of work) **die Einheit(en)**
I work **ich arbeite**
    I work at ... **ich arbeite an** +dat
work experience **das Betriebspraktikum (-a)**
I write **ich schreibe**
written work **die schriftliche Arbeit(en)**

EDUCATION

22b School

blackboard **die Tafel(n)**
blackout **das Blackout**
book **das Buch(¨er)**
break **die Pause(n)**
briefcase **die Mappe(n)**
cassette *(audio/video)* **die Kassette(n)**
cassette recorder **der Kassettenrecorder(-)**
classroom **das Klassenzimmer(-)**
computer **der Computer(-)**
desk **das Pult(e)**
gym(nasium) **die Turnhalle(n)**
headphone **der Kopfhörer(-)**
interactive TV **das interaktive Fernsehen**
laboratory **das Laboratorium (-ien)**
language laboratory **das Sprachlabor(s)**
library **die Bibliothek(en)**
lunch hour **die Mittagspause(n)**
note **die Anmerkung(en)**
office **das Büro(s)**
playground **der Schulhof(¨e)**
radio **das Radio(s)**
rubber/eraser **der Radiergummi(s)**
ruler **das Lineal(e)**
slide **das Dia(s)**

satellite TV **das Satellitenfernsehen**
school hall **der Saal(Säle), die Halle(n)**
schoolbag/satchel/bookbag **die Schultasche(n)**
sports field **der Sportplatz(¨e)**
sports hall **die Sporthalle(n)**
staffroom **das Lehrerzimmer(-)**
timetable **der Stundenplan(¨e)**
video **das Video(s)**
video player **das Videogerät(e)**
video camera **die Videokamera(s)**
video cassette **die Videokassette(n)**
video recorder **der Videorecorder(-)**
workshop **die Werkstatt(¨en)**

Type of school

boarding school **das Internat(e)**
comprehensive school **die Gesamtschule(n)**
further education **die Weiterbildung**
high school **das Gymnasium(-en)**
infant school **die Vorschule(n)**
nursery school **der Kindergarten(¨)**
playgroup **die Spielgruppe(n)**
primary school **die Grundschule(n)**
school **die Schule(n)**
school type **die Schulform(en)**

– At what age do children start school in Germany?

– They have to go to school when they are six. Our son already goes to kindergarten and is looking forward to school.

I would like to go to college to study math.

– **In welchem Alter kommen die Kinder in Deutschland in die Schule?**
– **Mit sechs werden sie schulpflichtig. Unser Sohn geht schon in den Kindergarten und freut sich auf die Schule.**

Ich möchte gern auf die Hochschule gehen, um Mathematik zu studieren.

of school age **schulpflichtig**
secondary **Sekundar-**
secondary school/junior high school
die Sekundarschule(n)
secondary modern school/senior
high school **die Hauptschule(n)**
sixth form/senior year **die
Oberstufe(n)**
special school **die Sonderschule(n)**
technical school **die Realschule(n)**

Classroom commands

Answer the question! **Beantworte
die Frage!**
Be careful! **Vorsicht!, Pass auf!**
Be quiet! **Ruhe!**
Be quick! **Macht schnell!**
Bring me your work! **Bring' mir
deine Aufgabe!**
Clean the blackboard! **Mach' die
Tafel sauber!**
Close the door! **Mach die Tür bitte
zu!**
Come here! **Komm' mal her!**
Come in! **Herein!**
Copy these sentences! **Schreibt
diese Sätze ab!**

Do your homework! **Macht eure
Hausaufgaben!**
Don't talk/chatter! **Bitte nicht reden!**
Go out! **Geht hinaus!**
Learn the vocabulary! **Lern' die
Vokabeln!**
Listen carefully! **Hör gut zu!**
Make less noise! **Mach nicht so
viel Krach!**
Make notes! **Macht euch Notizen!**
Open the window! **Mach' das
Fenster auf!**
Pay attention! **Passt gut auf!**
Put on the headphones! **Setzt die
Kopfhörer auf!**
Read the text! **Lies' den Text (vor)!**
Show me your book! **Zeig' mir dein
Heft!**
Sit down! **Setzt euch!**
Stand up! **Aufstehen!**
Work in pairs/groups! **Arbeitet mit
einem Partner/ in Gruppen!**
Write an essay! **Jetzt schreiben wir
einen Aufsatz!**
Write it down! **Schreibt es auf!**
Write out in rough! **Macht einen
Entwurf!**

Our daughter goes to elementary
school. She reads to her teacher
every day and can read well now.

– Have you moved up a class every
year?
– No, last year I had to stay back a
year.

**Unsere Tochter geht in die
Grundschule. Jeden Tag liest
sie ihrer Lehrerin vor und kann
jetzt gut lesen.**

**– Bist du jedes Jahr versetzt
worden?**
**– Nein, letztes Jahr bin ich
sitzen geblieben.**

EDUCATION

22c School subjects & examinations

School subjects

arithmetic **das Rechnen**
art **die Kunst, das Zeichnen**
biology **die Biologie**
business studies **die Wirtschaftslehre**
chemistry **die Chemie**
CDT/crafts, design and technology **das Werken**
compulsory subject **das Pflichtfach(-̈er)**
computer studies **die Informatik**
design technology **die Technologie**
elective/option(al subject) **das Wahlfach(-̈er)**

English **Englisch**
foreign language **die Fremdsprache(n)**
French **Französisch**
geography **die Erdkunde, die Geographie**
German **Deutsch**
Greek **Griechisch**
gymnastics **das Turnen**
history **die Geschichte**
home economics **die Hauswirtschaft**
Italian **Italienisch**
Latin **Latein**

Examinations in Germany

das Abitur A-level exam
der Abiturient(en) [-] A-level candidate
die mittlere Reife 16+ examination
die Abschlussprüfung(en) school-leaving exam/finals **der Hauptschulabschluss(-̈e)** school-leaving certificate
der Realschulabschluss(-̈e) school-leaving certificate

Marks

1 sehr gut very good
2 gut good
3 befriedigend satisfactory
4 ausreichend pass
5 mangelhaft poor
6 ungenügend unsatisfactory

– Is your son now at the university?

– Yes, and he likes it a lot.

– My daughter is also studying. She'll graduate next year.

– **Ist Ihr Sohn jetzt an der Universität?**

– **Ja, und es gefällt ihm sehr gut.**

– **Meine Tochter studiert auch. Sie macht nächstes Jahr ihren Abschluss.**

main subject **der Leistungskurs(e)**
mathematics **die Mathematik**
metalwork **die Metallarbeit**
music **die Musik**
philosophy **die Philosophie**
physical education **der Sport**
physics **die Physik**
religious education **die Religion**
science **die Naturwissenschaft(en)**
sex education **die Sexualerziehung**
social studies **die
    Gemeinschaftskunde**
sociology **die Sozialkunde**
Spanish **Spanisch**
sport **der Sport**
    type of sport **die Sportart(en)**
subject **das Fach(ˉ-er)**
subsidiary subject **das
    Nebenfach(ˉ-er)**
technical drawing **das technische
    Zeichnen**
textiles **Textiles Werken**
woodwork **die Holzarbeit(en)**

Examinations

I assess **ich bewerte, ich benote**
assessment **die Bewertung(en)**
certificate **das Zertifikat(e)**
degree **das Diplom(e)**
diploma **das Diplom(e)**
dissertation **die Dissertation(en)**

distinction **die Auszeichnung(en)**
doctorate **das Doktorat(e)**
examination **die Prüfung(en), das
    Examen(-)**
external **extern**
final **Abschluss-**
grade **die Zensur(en), die Note(n)**
I grade **ich benote, ich zensiere**
graduate engineer **der
    Diplomingenieur(-)**
listening comprehension **das
    Hörverständnis(se)**
mark **die Note(n)**
mark system **das Notensystem(e)**
masters **die Magisterarbeit(en)**
merit **die Auszeichnung(en)**
oral **mündlich**
point **der Punkt(e)**
post-graduate course **der
    Anschlusskurs(e)**
reading comprehension **das
    Leseverständnis(se)**
I pass (an exam) **ich lege (ein
    Examen) ab***
I test **ich teste, ich prüfe**
test **der Test(s)**
thesis **die Doktorarbeit(en)**
trainee **der Azubi(s)/
    Auszubildende(n)** *(adj/n)*
written test **die schriftliche
    Prüfung(en)**

My favorite subject is physical education.	**Mein Lieblingsfach ist Sport.**
Since Robert was an exchange student in the USA, he speaks fluent English.	**Seitdem Robert Austauschschüler in den USA war, spricht er fließend Englisch.**
After school I do sports, and I am on the soccer team in our town.	**Nach der Schule mache ich Sport, und ich bin Mitglied der Fußballmannschaft unserer Stadt.**

➤ SCHOOL 22b; USING LANGUAGE 21b

EDUCATION

22d Further & higher education

adult **der/die Erwachsene(n)** *(adj/n)*
adult *(adj)* **erwachsen**
adult education **die Erwachsenenbildung**
alumnus **der ehemalige Schüler(-)**
apprentice **der Lehrling(e)**
apprenticeship **die Lehre(n)**
chair **der Lehrstuhl (⁼e)**
college **die Hochschule(n)**
   college of FE **die berufsbildende Schule(n)**
   college of HE **die Fachhochschule(n)**
continuing education **der zweite Bildungsweg**
course of study **das Studium (-ien)**
diploma **das Diplom(e)**
dual system **das duale System**
faculty **das Seminar(e), die Fakultät(en)**
hall of residence/residence hall **das Wohnheim(e)**
in-service training **die Weiterbildung**
lecture **das Referat(e), die Vorlesung(en)**
lecture hall **der Hörsaal (-säle)**
lecturer **der Referent(en)** *(wk)* **[-in]**
masters degree **der Magisterabschluss(⁼e)**
part-time FE **die Berufschule(n)**

part-time education **die Teilzeitschule(n)**
polytechnic **die technische Hochschule(n)**
practical **das Praktikum (-a)**
principal **der Direktor(en) [-in]**
professor/college professor **der Professor(en) [-in]**
quota (for university entry) **der Numerus clausus**
research **die Forschung(en)**
retraining **die Umschulung**
I retrain **ich lasse mich umschulen**
scholarship **das Stipendium (-ien)**
seminar **das Seminar(e)**
sorority/fraternity **die Studentenverbindung(en)**
student **der Student(en)[-in]**wk
student grant **das Bafög (Bundesausbildungsförderungsgesetz), die Studienbeihilfe**
student association **die Studentenvereinigung(en)**
teacher training college **die pädagogische Hochschule(n)**
technical college **die technische Hochschule(n)**

The technical colleges now belong to the university sector.

Die Fachhochschulen gehören jetzt zum Universitätsbereich.

Admission to the technical colleges is possible without the *Abitur*. The length of course is four years (eight semesters).

Der Zugang zu den Fachhochschulen ist auch ohne Abitur möglich. Die Studiendauer beträgt vier Jahre (acht Semester).

Financial support is of the greatest importance.

Die finanzielle Förderung ist von größter Bedeutung.

university/college **die Universität(en)**
university entrance qualification **die Hochschulreife**

Subjects

accountancy/accounting **die Buchführung**
architecture **die Architektur**
business management **die Betriebswirtschaftslehre**
catering **das Gaststättengewerbe**
classics **die Altphilologie**
civil engineering **der Hoch- und Tiefbau**
construction **das Bauwesen**
education **die Pädagogik**
electronics **die Elektronik**
electrical engineering **die Elektrotechnik**
economics **die Volkswirtschaftslehre**
engineering **das Ingenieurwesen**

environmental sciences **die Umweltkunde**
foreign languages **die Fremdsprachen** *(pl)*
history of art **die Kunstgeschichte**
hotel management **das Hotelwesen**
law **die Rechtswissenschaft, Jura**
leisure and tourism **(die) Freizeit und (der)Tourismus**
literature **die Literatur**
mechanical engineering **der Maschinenbau**
medicine **die Medizin**
pharmacy **die Pharmarzie**
nuclear science **die Kernwissenschaft**
office skills **das Bürowesen**
philosophy **die Philosophie**
psychology **die Psychologie**
sociology **die Soziologie**
theology **die Theologie**

Many students get a state grant.

Viele Studenten erhalten staatliche Beihilfe.

Many students apply for places to study but they cannot all be admitted.

Viele Studenten bewerben sich um einen Studienplatz, aber sie können nicht alle zugelassen werden.

There is now an entrance restriction. Admission depends on marks in the *Abitur*.
Particularly high marks are required for medicine.

Es gibt jetzt den Numerus clausus. Die Zulassung hängt von den Noten im Abitur ab. Für Medizin braucht man besonders gute Zensuren.

Our results are always outstanding.

Unsere Prüfungsergebnisse sind immer hervorragend.

➤ LANGUAGES App.21a; SCIENTIFIC DISCIPLINES App.23a

Science: the changing world

23a Science & biology

Scientific method

academic paper **die theoretische/ akademische Arbeit(en)**
I analyze **ich analysiere**
authentic **authentisch**
I challenge **ich stelle in Frage**
I check **ich prüfe**
classification **die Klassifizierung(en), die Einteilung(en)**
I classify **ich klassifiziere, ich ordne**
I conduct *(an experiment)* **ich führe durch*, ich leite**
control **die Kontrolle(n)**
I control **ich kontrolliere**
dial **die Skala (-en)**
experiment **das Experiment(e), der Versuch(e)**
I experiment **ich experimentiere**
flask **der Kolben(-)**
gauge **das Messgerät(e)**
hypothesis **die Hypothese(n)**
I identify **ich identifiziere**
invention **die Erfindung(en)**

I investigate **ich untersuche**
laboratory **das Laboratorium (-ien)**
material **das Material(ien)**
I measure **ich messe**
measurement **die Messung(en), das Maß(e)**
(electron) microscope **das (Elektronen)mikroskop(e)**
I observe **ich beobachte**
observation **die Beobachtung(en)**
origin **der Ursprung(¨e)**
pipette **die Pipette(n)**
research **die Forschung(en)**
I research **ich (er)forsche**
result **das Resultat(e)**
scientific **wissenschaftlich**
I solve (a problem) **ich löse (ein Problem)**
I sort **ich sortiere**
test **die Probe(n)**
I test **ich teste, ich prüfe**
test tube **das Reagenzglas(¨er)**
theory **die Theorie(n)**
I transfer **ich übertrage**

Research on human embryo tissue is likely to remain highly controversial.

Die Forschung am menschlichen Embryogewebe wird wohl sehr umstritten bleiben.

The researcher took a sample, mounted it on a slide and put it under the microscope for examination. All the results from the experiments support her hypothesis.

Die Forscherin nahm eine Probe, gab sie auf einen Objektträger und legte sie zum Untersuchen unter das Mikroskop. Alle Untersuchungsergebnisse stützen ihre Hypothese.

Life sciences

bacteria   **das Bakterium(en)**
botanical   **botanisch**
I breathe   **ich atme**
cell   **die Zelle(n)**
chlorophyll   **das Chlorophyll**
it circulates   **es zirkuliert, es fließt**
decay   **der Verfall**
it decays   **es verfault**
decline   **der Nieder-/Rückgang(-̈e)**
it declines   **es geht zurück***
it excretes   **es scheidet aus***
excretion   **die Ausscheidung(en)**
it feeds (on)   **es frisst, es ernährt
    sich (von +dat)**
food chain   **die Nahrungskette(n)**
gene   **das Gen(e)**
gene bank   **die Gen-Bank(en)**
genetic   **genetisch**
genetics   **die Genetik**
genetic disorder   **die genetische
    Krankheit(en)**
it grows   **es wächst**
growth   **das Wachstum**
habitat   **der Lebensraum(-̈e)**
I inherit   **ich erbe**
mammal   **das Säugetier(e)**
membrane   **die Membran(en)**
it mutates   **es verändert sich, es
    mutiert**
nucleus   **der Nukleus (Nuklei)**
organic   **organisch**
organism   **der Organismus (-en)**
photosynthesis   **die
    Photosynthese(n)**
population   **die Menge(n), die
    Bevölkerung**
process   **der Prozess(e)**
it reproduces   **es reproduziert sich**
respiration   **die Atmung(en)**
sample   **die Probe(n)**
sensitivity   **die Empfindlichkeit(en)**
slide   **der Objektträger(-)**
survival   **das Überleben**
it survives   **es überlebt**
virus   **das Virus (-en)**

Medical science & research

ante-natal tests (on foetus)   **die
    Schwangerschaftsunter-
    suchung(en)**
cosmetic surgery   **die
    Schönheitsoperation(en)**
DNA   **die DNS**
donor   **der Blutspender(-) [-in]**
embryo   **der Embryo(s)**
embryo research   **die
    Embryonenforschung**
ethical consideration   **ethische
    Erwägungen** (pl)
ethics of human reproduction   **die
    Ethik** (pl) **der menschlichen
    Fortpflanzung**
experiment on animals   **der
    Tierversuch(e)**
hereditary illness   **die
    Erbkrankheit(en)**
IVF (in vitro fertilization)   **die
    In-vitro-Befruchtung**
I justify   **ich rechtfertige**
microorganism   **der
    Mikroorganismus (-en)**
organ transplant   **die
    Organtransplantation(en)**
pacemaker   **der
    (Herz)schrittmacher(-)**
I permit   **ich erlaube jdm.**
plastic surgery   **die plastische
    Chirurgie**
psychology   **die Psychologie**
recipient   **der Empfänger(-) [-in]**
I reject (an organ)   **ich stoße (ein
    Organ) ab***
risk   **das Risiko (-en)**
I risk   **ich riskiere**
survival rate   **die Überlebensrate**
test-tube baby   **das Retortenbaby
    (-s)**
transplant   **das Transplantat(e)**
X-ray   **die Röntgenstrahlung(en)**
I X-ray   **ich röntge**

➤ MEDICAL TREATMENT 11c; THE ANIMAL WORLD 24b

23b Physical sciences

Chemistry

acid **die Säure(n)**
air **die Luft(¨e)**
alkali **das Alkali**
alkaline **basisch**
alkaline solution **die Lauge(n)**
boiling point **der Siedepunkt(e)**
Bunsen burner **der Bunsenbrenner(-)**
I calculate **ich berechne, ich kalkuliere**
chemical **chemisch**
compound **die Verbindung(en)**
composition **die Zusammensetzung(en)**
it dissolves **es löst sich (auf)***
it dissolves in water **es ist wasserlöslich**
element **das Element(e)**
emulsion **die Emulsion(en)**
equation **die Gleichung(en)**
gas **das Gas(e)**
inorganic **anorganisch**
insoluble **unlöslich**
liquid **die Flüssigkeit(en)**
liquid *(adj)* **flüssig**
Litmus paper **das Lackmuspapier**
matter **die Materie, der Stoff(e)**
metal **das Metall(e)**
natural gas **das Erdgas(e)**
opaque **undurchsichtig**
periodic table **das Periodensystem**
physical **physikalisch**
pure **rein**
it reacts **es reagiert**
reaction **die Reaktion(en)**
salt **das Salz(e)**
solid **der Festkörper(-)**
solid *(adj)* **fest**
soluble **löslich**
solution **die Lösung(en)**
stable **fest, stabil**
substance **die Substanz(en)**
transparent **durchsichtig**

Physics & mechanics

it accelerates **es beschleunigt**
acceleration **die Beschleunigung(en)**
acoustic(s) **die Akustik**
analysis **die Analyse(n)**
artificial **künstlich**
automatic **automatisch**
ball bearing **das Kugellager(-)**
conservation **die Erhaltung**
density **die Dichte(n)**
distance **die Distanz(en)**
energy **die Energie**
engine **der Motor(en)**
it expands **es dehnt sich aus***
fiber **die Faser(n)**
force **die Kraft(¨e), die Stärke(n)**
it freezes **es gefriert**
formula **die Formel(n)**
freezing point **der Gefrierpunkt(e)**
friction **die Reibung(en), die Friktion**
gear **das Getriebe**
gravity **die Schwerkraft(¨e)**
 center of gravity **der Schwerpunkt(-)**
 law of gravity **das Gravitationsgesetz**
I heat **ich erhitze**
heat **die Hitze, die Wärme**
heat loss **der Wärmeverlust(e)**
laser **der Laser(-)**
laser beam **der Laserstrahl(en)**
light **das Licht(er)**
light beam **der Lichtstrahl(en)**
lubricant **das Schmiermittel(-)**
machinery **der Mechanismus (-en), die Maschinerie(en)**
magnetism **der Magnetismus**
magneto **der Magnetzünder(-)**
mass **die Masse(n)**
mechanics **der Maschinenbau**
mechanical **mechanisch**
mechanism **der Mechanismus (-en)**
mechanics **die Mechanik**

metallurgy **die Metallurgie**
microscope **das Mikroskop(e)**
microwave **die Mikrowelle(n)**
mineral **das Mineral(e)**
missile **das Geschoss(e), die Rakete(n)**
model **das Modell(e)**
motion **die Bewegung(en)**
I operate *(machinery)* **ich bediene**
optics **die Optik**
pressure **der Druck(¨-e)**
property **die Eigenschaft(en)**
proportional **proportional**
ray **der (Licht)strahl(en)**
reflection **die Reflexion(en)**
refraction **die Brechung(en)**
relativity **die Relativität**
relativity theory **die Relativitätstheorie**
resistance **der Widerstand(¨-e)**
resistant **widerstandsfähig**
robot **der Roboter(-)**
sound **der Schall(¨-e)**
speed **die Geschwindigkeit(en)**
structure **die Struktur(en)**
synthetic **synthetisch, künstlich**
temperature **die Temperatur(en)**
theory **die Theorie(n)**
transmission **die Übertragung(en)**
I transmit **ich übertrage**
vapor **der Dampf(¨-e)**
it vibrates **es vibriert**
vibration **die Vibration(en)**
wave **die Welle(n)**
long wave **die Langwelle(n)**
medium/short wave **die Kurzwelle(n)**
wavelength **die Wellenlänge(n)**

Electricity

alternating current **der Wechselstrom**
battery **die Batterie(n)**
charge **die Ladung(en)**
I charge the battery **ich lade die Batterie auf***
circuit **der Stromkreis(e)**
current **der Strom(¨-e), die Strömung(en)**
direct current **der Gleichstrom**
electrical **elektrisch**
electricity **die Elektrizität**
electrode **die Elektrode(n)**
electron **das Elektron(en)**
electronic **elektronisch**
electronics **die Elektronik**
positive **positiv**
negative **negativ**
voltage **die Spannung(en)**

Nuclear physics

atom **das Atom(e)**
atomic **atomar, Atom-**
fission **die Spaltung(en)**
fusion **die Verschmelzung(en)**
molecular **molekular**
molecule **das Molekül(e)**
neutron **das Neutron(en)**
nuclear **Nuklear-, Kern-**
nuclear energy **die Nuklearenergie**
nuclear reactor **der Kernreaktor(en)**
nucleus **der Nukleus, der Kern(e)**
particle **das Partikel(-)**
proton **das Proton(en)**
quantum theory **die Quantentheorie(n)**
radiation **die (Aus)strahlung(en)**

Water has a boiling point of 100 degrees centigrade.

Der Siedepunkt des Wassers liegt bei 100 Grad Celsius.

What is the wattage of this appliance?

Wie viel Watt hat dieses Gerät?

SCIENCE: THE CHANGING WORLD

23c The earth & space

Energy & fuels

coal   die Kohle(n)

concentration   die Konzentration(en)

coolant   das Kühlmittel(-)

energy   die Energie(n)

energy conservation   die Energiesparmaßnahmen (pl)

energy consumption   der Energieverbrauch

energy crisis   die Energiekrise(n)

energy needs   der Energiebedarf

energy source   die Energiequelle(n)

energy waste   die Energieverschwendung

fossil fuel   der fossile Brennstoff(e)

fuel   der Treibstoff

fuel consumption   der Kraftstoffverbrauch

it generates   es erzeugt

geothermal energy   die geothermische Energie

global warming   die globale Erwärmung

greenhouse effect   der Treibhauseffekt

hole in the ozone layer   das Ozonloch(-̈er)

hydroelectric dam   der hydro-elektrische Damm(-̈e)

hydroelectric power   die Wasserkraft

insulation   die Isolation

natural gas   das Erdgas(e)

nuclear energy   die Atomenergie, die Kernkraft

nuclear power station   das Kernkraftwerk(e)

oil   das Öl(e)

oil production   die Ölförderung

oil-producing country   das Ölförderland(-̈er)

ozone layer   die Ozonschicht

petroleum   das Petroleum, das Erdöl(e)

propellant (rocket fuel)   der Raketentreibstoff(e)

raw materials   der Rohstoff(e)

solar cell   die Solarzelle(n)

solar energy   die Solarenergie

thermal energy   die Wärmeenergie

wave power   die Wellenkraft

tidal power station   das Gezeitenkraftwerk

wind energy/power   die Windenergie

Geology

carbon-dating   die Kohlenstoffdatierung

I excavate   ich grabe aus*

geologist   der Geologe(n) (wk)

gemstone   der Edelstein(e)

layer   die Schicht(en)

loam   der Lehm

mine   das Bergwerk(e)

I mine (for)   ich grabe (nach +dat)

ore   das Erz(e)

quarry   der Steinbruch(-̈e)

sand   der Sand(e)

sediment   das Sediment(e), die Ablagerung(en)

soil   das Erdreich

stalactite   der Stalaktit(en) (wk)

stalagmite   der Stalagmit(en) (wk)

Space

asteroid   der Asteroid(en)

eclipse   die Finsternis(se)

it eclipses   es verfinstert

galactic   galaktisch

galaxy   das Sternsystem(e)

light year   das Lichtjahr(e)

meteorite   der Meteorit(en) (wk)

moon   der Mond(e)

full moon   der Vollmond

new moon   der Neumond

orbit **der Orbit(s), die Planetenbahn(en)**

planet **der Planet(en)**

shooting-star **die Sternschnuppe(n)**

solar system **das Sonnensystem(e)**

solstice **die Sonnenwende(n)**

space **der Raum, das Weltall**

star **der Stern(e)**

sun **die Sonne(n)**

sunspot **der Sonnenfleck(en)**

the heavens **der Himmel(-)**

universe **das Universum (-en), das Weltall**

Space research & travel

antenna **die Antenne(n)**

astrologer **der Astrolog(en)** *(wk)*

astronomer **der Astronom(en)** *(wk)*

astronaut **der Astronaut(en)** *(wk)*

big-bang theory **die Urknalltheorie**

cosmonaut **der Kosmonaut(en)** *(wk)*

dish antenna **die Parabolantenne(n)**

gravitational pull **die Anziehungskraft**

launch **der Raketenabschuss(¨e)**

launch pad **die Abschussrampe(n)**

space module **die Raumkapsel(n)**

moon-buggy **das Mondfahrzeug(e)**

moon-landing **die Mondlandung(en)**

observatory **das Observatorium (-ien)**

planetarium **das Planetarium (-ien)**

it re-enters **es tritt wieder ein***

relativity **die Relativität**

rocket **die Rakete(n)**

rocket fuel **der Raketenkraftstoff(e)**

satellite **der Satellit(en)** *(wk)*

communications **der Kommunikationssatellit(en)**

spy **der Spionagesatellit(en)**

weather **der Wettersatellit(en)**

sky lab **das Observatorium (-ien)**

space **der Weltraum**

space flight **der Weltraumflug(¨e)**

space probe **die Weltraumsonde(n)**

space shuttle **die Raumfähre(n)**

space walk **der Weltraumspaziergang(¨e)**

spacecraft **das Raumschiff(e)**

spacesuit **der Raumanzug(¨e)**

stratosphere **die Stratosphäre**

telescope **das Teleskop(e)**

time-warp **die Zeitschleife**

touchdown **die Landung(en), das Aufsetzen**

zodiac **der Tierkreis(e)**

By studying the light received from stars many millions of light years away, scientists hope to discover the origins of the universe.

Durch die Untersuchung des Lichtes, welches von Sternen empfangen wird, die viele Lichtjahre entfernt sind, hoffen Wissenschaftler, den Ursprung des Universums zu entdecken/ergründen.

The earth orbits the sun.

Die Erde umkreist die Sonne.

24 The environment: the natural world

24a Geography

area das Gebiet(e), die Gegend(en)
bottom der Fuß(-̈e), der Grund(-̈e)
clean sauber
continent der Kontinent(e)
country das Land(-̈er), das Gelände(-)
in the country auf dem Land(e)
countryside die Landschaft(en)
dangerous gefährlich
deep tief
dirty schmutzig
earth tremor die Erderschütterung(en)
earthquake das Erdbeben(-)
equator der Äquator
equatorial äquatorial
eruption der Ausbruch(-̈e)
it erupts es bricht aus* (brechen)
flat flach, glatt
it floods es läuft über* (laufen), es überschwemmt
it flows es fließt

friendly freundlich, angenehm
geographical geographisch
geography die Geographie
gradient/climb die Steigung(en)
hemisphere die Hemisphäre(n), die Halbkugel(n)
high hoch
incline das Gefälle(-)
it is situated es ist gelegen, es liegt
land das Land(-̈er)
land (property/real estate) der Grund und Boden
it is located es ist gelegen, es liegt
location die Lage(n)
map die Karte(n)
national park der Nationalpark(s)
nature die Natur
nature conservancy der Naturschutz
nature trail der Naturlehrpfad(e)
peaceful ruhig, friedlich, still
pleasant angenehm

Germany extends from the mountains of the Alps to the North and Baltic Seas. There are no natural frontiers to the west and east.

Deutschland reicht vom Hochgebirge der Alpen bis zur Nord- und Ostsee. Es gibt keine natürliche Abgrenzung nach Westen und Osten.

The Zugspitze is the highest mountain in the Bavarian Alps.

Die Zugspitze ist der höchste Berg in den Bayerischen Alpen.

In the central mountain area one finds plateaux, hills, volcanic mountains and valleys.

In der Mittelgebirgszone findet man Hochflächen, Berglandschaften, vulkanische Formen und Tallandschaften.

pole **der Pol(e)**
province **die Provinz(en)**
region **die Region(en), das Gebiet(e)**
regional **regional**
sand **der Sand(e)**
scenery **die Landschaft(en)**
by the seaside **am Meer**
slope **der Abhang(-̈e)**
steep **steil**
tall **hoch**
territory **das Gebiet(e)**
top **die Spitze(n), der Gipfel(-)**
the tropics **die Tropen** *(pl)*
unfriendly **unfreundlich**
water **das Wasser(-)**
   fresh water **das Süßwasser**
   salt water **das Salzwasser**
zenith **der Zenit** *(no pl)*
zone **die Zone(n)**

Manmade features

aqueduct **das Aquädukt(e)**
bridge **die Brücke(n)**
canal **der Kanal(-̈e)**
capital (city) **die Hauptstadt(-̈e)**

city **die Großstadt(-̈e)**
country road **die Landstraße(n)**
dam **der Damm(-̈e), der Stausee(n)**
embankment **die Böschung(en)**
factory **die Fabrik(en), das Werk(e)**
farm **der Bauernhof(-̈e), das Gut(-̈er)**
farmland **der Acker(-̈), das Ackerland**
field **das Feld(er)**
hamlet **das kleine Dorf(-̈er)**
harbor **der Hafen(-̈)**
industry **die Industrie(n)**
marina **der Yachthafen(-̈)**
oasis **die Oase(n)**
reclaimed land **das gewonnene Land**
reservoir **das Reservoir(s), der Speicher(-)**
town **die Stadt(-̈e)**
track **der Feldweg(e)**
village **das Dorf(-̈er)**
well **der Brunnen(-)**

The surface of the North German plain was formed by the glaciers of the ice ages.	**Die Oberfläche des Norddeutschen Tieflandes wurde von den Gletschern der Eiszeiten geformt.**
The North Sea has very high and low tides. Many islands and low islands rise out of the shallow coastal waters.	**Die Nordsee hat ausgeprägte Gezeiten (Ebbe - Flut). Vor der Küste erheben sich aus dem Wattenmeer viele Inseln und Halligen.**
The bog was drained by ditches and reclaimed.	**Das Moor wurde durch Kanäle entwässert und urbar gemacht.**

24b The animal world

Animals

animal **das Tier(e)**
it barks **es bellt**
it bites **es beißt**
it bounds **es springt**
it breeds **es vermehrt sich**
burrow **der (Kaninchen)bau(e)**
cage **der Käfig(e)**
carnivore **der Fleischfresser(-)**
cat **die Katze(n)**
it crawls **es kriecht**
den **die Höhle(n), das Versteck(e)**
dog **der Hund(e)**
I feed **ich füttere**
it feeds **es frisst** *(fressen)*
food **das Futter**
gerbil **die Wüstenspringmaus(:-e)**
goldfish **der Goldfisch(e)**
guinea pig **das Meerschweinchen(-)**
habitat **der Lebensraum(:-e)**
hamster **der Hamster(-)**
herbivore **der Pflanzenfresser(-)**
it hibernates **es hält Winterschlaf**
it howls **es heult**
hut/hutch **der Stall(:-e)**
I keep a cat **ich halte eine Katze**
kitten **das Kätzchen(-)**
lair **das Lager(-), die Höhle(n)**
it leaps **es springt**
litter **der Wurf(:-e)**
mammal **das Säugetier(e)**
it meows **es miaut**
omnivore **der Allesfresser(-)**
pack **das Rudel(-)**
pet **das Haustier(e)**
predator **das Raubtier(e)**
prey **die Beute, das Beutetier(e)**
puppy **das Hündchen(-)**
rabbit **das Kaninchen(-)**
rabies **die Tollwut**
reptile **das Reptil(ien)**
it roars **es brüllt**

safari park **der Safaripark(s)**
snail **die Schnecke(n)**
it squeaks **es piept, es quiekt**
I stroke **ich streich(e)le**
tortoise **die Schildkröte(n)**
I walk *(the dog)* **ich führe ... aus***
wildlife park **das Wildreservat(e), das Wildschutzgebiet(e)**
zoo **der Zoo(s), der Tiergarten(:-)**

Birds

claw **die Klaue(n)**
it crows **es kräht**
it flies **es fliegt**
flock **die Schar(en), der Schwarm(:-e)**
it hovers **es schwebt, es steht**
it migrates **es zieht nach Süden**
migratory bird **der Zugvogel(:-)**
nest **das Nest(er)**
it nests **es nistet**
it pecks at **es pickt**
it sings **es singt**

Sealife/Waterlife

alligator **der Alligator(en)**
anemone **die Seeanemone(n)**
angling **das Angeln**
coral **die Koralle(n)**
crab **der Krebs(e)**
crocodile **das Krokodil(e)**
dolphin **der Delphin(e)**
fish **der Fisch(e)**
I fish **ich fische**
harpoon **die Harpune(n)**
hook **der Haken(-)**
marine **Meeres-, See-**
mollusc **die Molluske(n)**
net **das Netz(e)**
octopus **der Tintenfisch(e), der Krake(n)** *(wk)*
plankton **das Plankton** *(no pl)*
rod **die Rute(n)**
seal **der Seehund(e)**

shark **der Hai(e)**
shoal **der Schwarm("e)**
shrimp **die Krabbe(n)**
starfish **der Seestern(e)**
it swims **es schwimmt**
turtle **die Wasserschildkröte(n)**
whale **der Wal(e)**
whaling **der Walfang** *(no pl)*

Insects

ant **die Ameise(n)**
bee **die Biene(n)**
  queen bee **die**
  Bienenkönigin(nen)
  worker bee **die**
  Arbeiterbiene(n)
bedbug **die Wanze(n)**
beetle **der Käfer(-)**
bug **das Insekt(en)** *(wk)*, **der**
  Käfer(-)
butterfly **der Schmetterling(e)**
it buzzes **es summt**
caterpiller **die Raupe(n)**
cocoon **der Kokon(s)**
cockroach **die Kakerlake(n)**
cricket **die Grille(n)**
dragonfly **die Libelle(n)**

flea **der Floh("e)**
fly **die Fliege(n)**
hive **der Bienenkorb("e)**
insect **das Insekt(en)**
invertebrate **wirbellos**
ladybird/lady bug **der**
  Marienkäfer(-)
larva **die Larve(n)**
locust **die Heuschrecke(n)**
it metamorphoses **es verwandelt**
  sich
mosquito **die Stechmücke(n), der**
  Moskito(s)
moth **die Motte(n)**
scorpion **der Skorpion(e)**
silkworm **die Seidenraupe(n)**
slug **die Nacktschnecke(n)**
spider **die Spinne(n)**
it spins (a web) **es spinnt (ein**
  Netz)
it stings **es sticht**
termite **die Termite(n)**
tick **die Zecke(n)**
web **das Spinnennetz(e)**
wasp **die Wespe(n)**
worm **der Wurm("er)**

The small low islands are important as a resting and migration
area for northern birds of passage.

Die Halligen sind wichtig als
Rast- und Durchzugszone für
nordische Zugvögel.

The state recognizes the value of
the area for flora and fauna.

Der Wert des Gebietes für die
Pflanzen- und Tierwelt ist
staatlich anerkannt.

Many animals are threatened with
extinction.

Viele Tiere sind vom Aussterben
bedroht.

They are scattered, rare or
endangered.

Sie sind zerstreut, selten oder
gefährdet.

Seals get caught in the remains of
nets.

Seehunde verfangen sich in
Netzresten.

➤ BIRDS App.24b; FISH & SEA FOOD 10b, POULTRY 10c

24c Farming & gardening

Farm animals

bull **der Bulle(n)** *(wk)*
cattle **das Vieh** *(no pl)*, **die Rinder** *(pl)*
chicken **das Huhn(-̈er)**
cock **der Hahn(-̈e)**
cow **die Kuh(-̈e)**
it crows **es kräht**
dairy *(adj)* **Milch-**
duck **die Ente(n)**
it eats **es frisst** *(fressen)*
feed **das Futter** *(no pl)*
it feeds **es frisst** *(fressen)*
foal **das Fohlen(-)**
fodder **das Futter**
food **die Nahrung**
it gallops **es galoppiert**
goat **die Ziege(n)**
goose **die Gans(-̈e)**
it grazes **es grast, es weidet**
I groom **ich striegle, ich putze**
it grunts **es grunzt**
horse **das Pferd(e)**
horseshoe **das Hufeisen(-)**
it kicks **es tritt** *(treten)*
kid **das Zicklein(-)**
I milk **ich melke**
it moos **es muht**
it neighs **es wiehert**
ox **der Ochse(n)**
pasture **die Weide(n)**
it pecks **es pickt**

pig **das Schwein(e)**
pony **das Pony(s)**
poultry **das Geflügel** *(no pl)*
produce **das Produkt(e)**
it quacks **es quakt**
I ride (a horse) **ich reite (ein Pferd)**
rooster **der Hahn(-̈e), das Hähnchen(-)**
I shear **ich schere**
sheep **das Schaf(e)**
sheep dog **der Schäferhund(e)**
I slaughter **ich schlachte**
stallion **der Zuchthengst(e)**
it trots **es trabt**

On the farm

agricultural **landwirtschaftlich**
agriculture **die Landwirtschaft**
arable land **das Ackerland** *(no pl)*
barn **die Scheune(n)**
combine harvester **der Mähdrescher(-)**
crop **die Ernte(n)**
dairy **die Molkerei(en)**
farm **der Bauernhof(-̈e)**
farmhouse **das Bauernhaus(-̈er)**
farm labourer/laborer **der Landarbeiter(-)**
farmyard **der Hof(-̈e)**
fence **der Zaun(-̈e)**
harvest **die Ernte(n)**

The most important grain crops in Germany are wheat and rye. Besides grain, fruit, vegetables and wine are cultivated.

Die wichtigsten Getreidearten in Deutschland sind Weizen und Roggen. Neben Getreide werden Obst, Gemüse und Wein angebaut.

The common agricultural policy has as its aim to increase agricultural productivity and to stabilize the markets.

Die gemeinsame Agrarpolitik hat als Ziel, die Produktivität der Landwirtschaft zu steigern und die Märkte zu stabilisieren.

I harvest **ich ernte**
hay **das Heu**
haystack **der Heuschober(-)**
irrigate **ich bewässere**
milk churn **die Milchkanne(n)**
milking machine **die Melkmaschine(n)**
orchard **der Obstgarten(⁻)**
pen **der Pferch(e), die Hürde(n)**
pigsty **der Schweinestall(⁻e)**
silage **die Silage** *(no pl)*
slaughterhouse **der Schlachthof(⁻e)**
stable **der Stall(⁻e)**
stud farm **das Gestüt(e)**
tractor **der Traktor(en)**

Agriculture & gardening

acorn **die Eichel(n)**
allotment **der Schrebergarten(⁻)**
barley **die Gerste**
it blooms **es blüht**
bloom **die Blüte(n)**
bouquet **der Strauß(⁻e)**
bud **die Knospe(n)**
bulb **die Zwiebel(n), die Knolle(n)**
bush **der Busch(⁻e), der Strauch(⁻e)**
compost **der Kompost(e)**
corn **das Getreide(-), das Korn(⁻er)**
corn *(U.S.)* **der Mais**
I cultivate **ich kultiviere**
I dig **ich grabe**
flower **die Blume(n), die Blüte(n)**
it flowers **es blüht**
flower bed **das Blumenbeet(e)**
flower pot **der Blumentopf(⁻e)**
foliage **das Laub, die Blätter**
forestry **die Forstwirtschaft**
garden/yard *(U.S.)* **der Garten(⁻)**
I garden/work in the yard **ich arbeite im Garten**
gardening **die Gartenarbeit(en)**
I gather **ich ernte, ich sammle**
grain **das Getreide(-), das Korn(⁻er)**
grass **das Gras(⁻er)**
I grow **ich ziehe, ich baue ... an***

it grows **es wächst** *(wachsen)*
hedge **die Hecke(n), der Zaun(⁻e)**
horticulture **der Gartenbau**
house plant **die Zimmerpflanze(n)**
lawn **der Rasen(-)**
leaf **das Blatt(⁻er)**
maize **der Mais**
market gardening **der Gemüsebau**
I mow **ich mähe**
oats **der Hafer**
petal **das Blütenblatt(⁻er)**
I pick **ich pflücke**
I plant **ich pflanze**
plant **die Pflanze(n)**
pollen **der Pollen(-)**
I reap **ich schneide, ich mähe**
ripe **reif**
it ripens **es reift**
rockery **der Steingarten(⁻)**
root **die Wurzel(n)**
rotten **faul, morsch, verdorben**
rye **der Roggen**
sap **der Saft(⁻e)**
seed **der Samen(-)**
species **die Art(en)**
stem **der Stiel(e), der Stamm(⁻e)**
thorn **der Dorn(en)/der Dornenbusch(⁻e)**
I trim *(hedge)* **ich stutze**
I transplant **ich verpflanze, ich pflanze ... um***
tree **der Baum(⁻e)**
tuber **die Knolle(n)**
undergrowth **das Unterholz(⁻er), das Gebüsch, das Gestrüpp**
vegetable(s) **das Gemüse** *(no pl)*
vegetable garden **der Gemüsegarten(⁻)**
vegetation **die Vegetation(en)**
vine **die Weinrebe(n)**
vineyard **der Weinberg(e)**
I water **ich bewässere, ich gieße**
weed **das Unkraut(⁻er)**
I weed **ich jäte**
wheat **der Weizen**
it wilts **es welkt**
wine cultivation **der Wein(an)bau**

➤ FLOWERS & WEEDS, TREES App.24c; TOOLS App.8b

THE ENVIRONMENT: THE NATURAL WORLD

24d Weather

anticyclone **das Hochdruckgebiet(e)**
avalanche **die Lawine(n)**
average temperature **die Durchschnittstemperatur(en)**
bad weather **das Schlechtwetter**
bright **heiter**
bright period **die Aufheiterung(en)**
centigrade **das Grad Celsius**
changeable **veränderlich**
clear skies **der klare Himmel**
climate **das Klima(te/s)**
climatic **klimatisch**
cloud **die Wolke(n)**
clouded over **bewölkt**
cloudless **wolkenlos**
cloudy **wolkig**
cold **kalt**
it is cold **es ist kalt**
cold front **die Kaltfront(en)**
it is cool **es ist kühl/frisch**
cyclone **das Tiefdruckgebiet(e)**
damp **feucht**
day temperature **die Tagestemperatur(en)**
degree **das Grad(e)**
   above zero **über null**
   below zero **unter null**
depression **das Tiefdruckgebiet(e)**
drizzle **der Nieselregen(-), der Sprühregen(-)**
drought **die Dürre**
dry **trocken**
dull **trüb, grau, verhangen**
earth tremor **die Erschütterung(en)**
earthquake **das Erdbeben(-)**
it's fine **es ist schön**
flash/lightning **der Blitz(e)**
fog **der Nebel(-)**
it is foggy **es ist nebelig**
it's freezing **es ist eisig, es friert**
freezing fog **der gefrierende Nebel**
frost **der Frost(̈e)**
frosty **frostig**
gale **der Sturm(̈e)**
gale warning **die Sturmwarnung(en)**
it's hailing **es hagelt**
hailstone **das Hagelkorn(̈er)**
   soft hail **die Graupel(n)**
heat **die Hitze**
heatwave **die Hitzewelle(n)**
high pressure **der Hochdruck**
highest temperature **die Höchsttemperatur(en)**
it's hot **es ist heiß/warm**

The forecast is for strong winds and icy polar air. Thick snow caused 90-kilometer-long traffic jams.

Die Vorhersage meldet starken Wind und eisige Polarluft. Dicker Schnee verursachte Staus von 90 Kilometern Länge.

Further outlook: bright to start with, then overcast with thunder showers. Highest temperatures around nine degrees.

Weitere Aussichten: anfangs aufgeheitert, sonst stark bewölkt mit gewittrigen Schauern. Die Höchstwerte liegen um neun Grad.

A stormy low pressure trough is moving east.

Der Ausläufer eines Sturmtiefs zieht nach Osten.

hurricane **der Orkan(e)**
ice **das Eis**
Indian summer **der Altweibersommer**
low pressure **der Tiefdruck**
lowest temperature **die Tiefsttemperatur(en)**
mild **mild**
mist **der Dunst**
misty **dunstig**
meteorology **die Wetterkunde**
monsoon **der Monsun(e)**
moon **der Mond(e)**
overcast **bedeckt**
it pours **es gießt in Strömen**
rain **der Regen(-)**
it's raining **es regnet**
rainy **regnerisch**
shade **der Schatten(-)**
it shines **es scheint**
shower **der Schauer(-)**
snow **der Schnee**
snowball **der Schneeball(¨e)**
snowdrift **die Schneewehe(n)**
snowfall **der Schneefall(¨e)**
snowflake **die Schneeflocke(n)**
snowman **der Schneemann(¨er)**
snow conditions **die Schneeverhältnisse** *(pl)*
it's snowing **es schneit**
snowstorm **der Schneesturm(¨e)**

storm **der Sturm(¨e)**
stormy **stürmisch**
sultry **schwül**
sun/sunshine **der Sonnenschein**
sunny **sonnig**
thunder **der Donner(-)**
it's thunder and lightning **es blitzt und donnert**
thunderbolt **der Blitzeinschlag(¨e)**
thunderstorm **das Gewitter(-)**
torrent **der Sturzbach(¨e), die Flut(en)**
torrential **sintflutartig**
tropical **tropisch**
trough **der Ausläufer(-)**
typhoon **der Taifun(e)**
warm **warm**
warm front **die Warmfront(en)**
weather **das Wetter**
weather conditions **die Witterungsbedingungen**
weather forecast **die Wettervorhersage(n)**
weather report **der Wetterbericht(e)**
wet **nass**
wind **der Wind(e)**
windy **windig**
wonderful **wunderschön, wunderbar**

What foul weather! In this weather we stay home.

Was für ein Mistwetter! Bei diesem Wetter bleiben wir zu Hause.

Germany belongs to the temperate zone with rainfall at all seasons. The average temperature in summer is 17-21° centigrade.

Deutschland gehört zur gemäßigten Zone, mit Niederschlägen zu allen Jahreszeiten. Die durchschnittlichen Sommertemperaturen liegen bei 17° bis 20°C.

THE ENVIRONMENT: THE NATURAL WORLD

24e Pollution

balance of nature **das Gleichgewicht der Natur**

it becomes extinct **es stirbt aus* (sterben)**

conservation **der Umweltschutz**

conservationist **der Umweltschützer(-)**

I conserve **ich konserviere, ich erhalte**

I consume **ich verbrauche**

consumption **der Verbrauch** *(no pl)*

corrosion **die Korrosion**

I damage **ich beschädige**

damaging **schädlich**

danger (to) **die Gefahr** (+acc)

I destroy **ich zerstöre**

disaster **das Unglück(e)**

disposable **Einweg-, Wegwerf-**

disposal **die Beseitigung(en)**

I dispose of **ich beseitige**

I do without **ich komme ohne aus***

ecology **die Ökologie**

ecosystem **das Ökosystem(e)**

environment **die Umwelt**

environmentally friendly **umweltfreundlich**

harmful substance **der Schadstoff(e)**

I improve **ich verbessere**

I insulate **ich isoliere**

litter/garbage **die Abfälle** *(pl)*, **der Müll** *(no pl)*

natural resources **die Bodenschätze** *(pl)*

nuclear reprocessing plant **die Atom(müll)wiederaufberei-tungsanlage(n)**

nuclear waste **der Atommüll**

ozone **das Ozon**

poison **das Gift(e)**

I poison **ich vergifte**

pollutant **der Schadstoff(e)**

I pollute **ich verschmutze**

pollution **die (Umwelt)verschmutzung**

I predict **ich sage voraus***

I protect **ich beschütze**

recyclable **wiederverwertbar**

I recycle **ich verwerte wieder***

recycled paper **das Recyclingpapier**

recycling skip/bin **der Recyclingcontainer(-)**

refuse **der Müll** *(no pl)*

residue **der Rückstand(-e), der Rest(e)**

it runs out **es geht aus***, **es wird verbraucht**

scrap metal **der Schrott**

solar power **der Solarstrom**

I throw away **ich werfe weg***

waste *(domestic)* **der Abfall(-e), der Müll**

waste disposal **die Abfallbeseitigung(en)**

Chemical solvents can cause headaches and allergies.
Chemische Lösungsmittel können Kopfschmerzen und Allergien verursachen.

Artificial fertilizers and insecticides poison the soil and groundwater.
Kunstdünger und Schädlingsbekämpfungsmittel verseuchen Boden und Grundwasser.

Young people are committed to environmental causes.
Junge Leute engagieren sich für den Umwelt- und Naturschutz.

waste disposal unit **der Müllschlucker**

waste product **das Abfallprodukt(e)**

wind power **die Windenergie**

On the earth

artificial fertilizer **der Künstdünger(-)**

biodegradable **biologisch abbaubar**

deforestation **die Abholzung(en)**

destruction of forests **die Zerstörung der Wälder**

nature reserve **das Naturschutzgebiet(e)**

nitrate **das Nitrat(e)**

pesticide **das Pestizid(e)**

radioactive **radioaktiv**

rain forest **der Regenwald(¨er)**

rubbish/garbage dump **die Abfalldeponie(n)**

soil erosion **die Bodenerosion**

weedkiller **das Unkrautvertilgungsmittel(-)**

In the atmosphere

acid rain **der saure Regen**

aerosol **das Treibgas**

aerosol can **die Spraydose(n)**

air pollution **die Luftverschmutzung(en)**

catalytic convertor **der Katalysator(en)** *(wk)*

CFCs **der FCKW**

emission (of gas) **die Emission(en), das Ausströmen**

it emits **es gibt ab*, es strahlt aus***

exhaust pipe **das Auspuffrohr(e)**

hole in the ozone layer **das Ozonloch(¨er)**

incinerator **der Verbrennungsofen(¨)**

lead-free/unleaded petrol/gasoline **das bleifreie Benzin**

skin cancer **der Hautkrebs**

I spray **ich spritze**

waste gases **die Abgase** *(pl)*

In rivers & seas

drainage **die Kanalisation, die Entwässerung**

drought **die Dürre(n)**

effluent/sewage **das Abwasser(¨)**

flooding **die Überschwemmung(en)**

ground water **das Grundwasser**

oil slick **der Ölteppich(e)**

phosphate **das Phosphat(e)**

sewage **das Abwasser(¨)**

sewage treatment **die Abwasserbehandlung(en)**

water consumption **der Wasserverbrauch**

water level **der Wasserstand**

water pollution **die Wasserverschmutzung**

water supply *(to town)* **die Wasserversorgung**

The development of harmful ozone must be prevented.

Die Entwicklung des schädlichen Ozons muss bekämpft werden.

People talk a lot about ecological farming, alternative energy sources and recycling.

Man spricht viel von ökologischem Landbau, alternativen Energien und Recycling.

Glass is recycled.

Glas wird wiederverwertet.

➤ NUCLEAR PHYSICS 23b

25 Government & politics

25a Political life

I abolish **ich schaffe ab***
act (of parliament) **das Gesetz(e)**
administration **die Verwaltung(en)**
I appoint **ich berufe, ich ernenne**
appointment **die Berufung(en)**
asylum-seeker **der Asylbewerber(-)**
it becomes law **es wird (zum) Gesetz**
bill **der Gesetzentwurf(-̈e)**
I bring down *(government)* **ich bringe zu Fall**
citizen **der Bürger(-) [-in]**
civil disobedience **der zivile Ungehorsam, die Unruhe(n)**
civil servant **der/die Beamte** *(adj/n)* **[-in]**
civil war **der Bürgerkrieg(e)**
coalition **die Koalition(en)**
it comes into effect **es tritt in Kraft**
common **gemeinsam**
constitution **das Grundgesetz(e), die Verfassung(en)**
cooperation **die Kooperation(en)**
corruption **die Korruption(en)**
county **der Bezirk(e), der Kreis(e)**
coup **der Staatsstreich(e)**
crisis **die Krise(n)**
debate **die Debatte(n)**
decree **der Erlass(e)**
delegate **der/die Delegierte** *(adj/n)*
I demonstrate **ich demonstriere**
demonstration **die Demonstration(en)**
I discuss **ich diskutiere, ich bespreche**
discussion **die Diskussion(en)**
I dismiss **ich entlasse**
I dissolve **ich löse auf***
district **der Kreis(e), der Bezirk(e)**

I draw up *(a bill)* **ich setze auf*, ich entwerfe**
duty **die Pflicht(en)**
I emigrate **ich emigriere**
equality **die Gleichheit(en)**
executive **die Exekutive**
executive *(government)* **exekutiv**
foreign policy **die Auslandspolitik** *(no pl)*
I form a pact with **ich schließe einen Pakt mit jdm.**
freedom **die Freiheit(en)**
freedom of speech **die Redefreiheit(en)**
federal state **das Bundesland(-̈er)**
I govern **ich regiere**
government **die Regierung(en)**
human right **das Menschenrecht(-)**
I introduce *(a bill)* **ich bringe ein***
judiciary **die Gerichtsbehörden** *(pl)*
law **das Gesetz(e)**
I lead **ich leite, ich führe**
legislation **die Gesetzgebung(en)**
legislature **die Legislative**
liberty **die Freiheit(en)**
local affairs/politics **die Kommunalpolitik**
local government **die Kreis-/ Stadtverwaltung(en)**
long-term **langfristig**
majority **die Mehrheit(en)**
meeting **dis Sitzung(en)**
middle-class **der Mittelstand** *(no pl)*
middle-class *(person)* **der Vertreter der Mittelschicht**
ministry/department **das Ministerium (-ien)**

minority   die **Minderheit(en)**

moderate   **der/die Gemäßigte**
(adj/n)
   moderate (adj)   **mäßig**

nation   die **Nation(en), das**
Volk(-er)

national   **national**

national flag   die
Nationalflagge(en)

I nationalize   **ich verstaatliche**

I oppose   **ich bekämpfe**

opposition   die **Opposition(en)**

I organize   **ich organisiere**

I overthrow   **ich stürze**

pact   der **Pakt(e)**

I pass (a bill)   **ich verabschiede**
(ein Gesetz)

policy   die **Politik**

political   **politisch**

political group   die **Fraktion(en)**

politician   der **Politiker(-) [-in]**

politics   die **Politik**

power   die **Macht(-e)**

I privatize   **ich privatisiere**

I protest   **ich protestiere**

public   die **Öffentlichkeit**
   public (adj)   **öffentlich**

public good   **das öffentliche**
Interesse, das Gemeinwohl

public opinion   die **öffentliche**
Meinung(en)

I ratify   **ich bestätige/ratifiziere**

reactionary   **reaktionär**

I reform   **ich reformiere**

reform   die **Reform(en)**

I reject   **ich lehne ab***

I repeal (an act)   **ich hebe auf***

I represent   **ich vertrete**

I repress   **ich unterdrücke**

I resign   **ich trete zurück***

responsible   **verantwortlich**

responsiblity   die
Verantwortlichkeit(en)

reunification   die **Wiederver-**
einigung(en), die Wende (fam)

I rule   **ich herrsche**

sanction   die **Sanktion(en)**

seat   der **Sitz(e)**

solidarity   die **Solidarität**

speech   die **Rede(n)**

state   der **Staat(en)**

statesman   der **Staatsmann(-er)**

I support   **ich unterstütze**

I take power   **ich ergreife die**
Macht

term of office   die **Wahlperiode(n)**

I throw out a bill   **ich lehne ein**
Gesetz ab*

unconstitutional
verfassungswidrig

unilateral   **einseitig**

unity   die **Einheit**

veto   das **Veto(s)**

I veto   **ich lege ein Veto ein***

working class   die
Arbeiterklasse(n)

working-class (person)   der
Arbeiter(-) [-in]

The wall between east and west
was opened in 1989. The
totalitarian communist regime was
removed.

Die Mauer zwischen Ost und
West wurde 1989 geöffnet. Das
totalitäre, kommunistische
Regime wurde beseitigt.

German unity was completed in
1990, when the first free elections
for the whole of Germany took
place.

Die deutsche Einheit wurde 1990
vollendet, als die erste freie
gesamtdeutsche Wahl stattfand.

➤   WAR 27a; SOCIAL ISSUES 12; THE ECONOMY 14e

25b Elections & political ideology

Elections

ballot **die Abstimmung(en)**
ballot box **die Wahlurne(n)**
ballot paper **der Wahlzettel(-)**
by-election **die Nachwahl(en)**
campaign **der Wahlkampf(⁻e)**
candidate **der Kandidat(en)** *(wk)*
constituency **der Wahlkreis(e)**
I count **ich zähle**
I elect **ich wähle**
election **die Wahl(en)**
electorate **die Wähler** *(pl)*
enfranchised **wahlberechtigt**
entitled to vote **wahlberechtigt**
floating voter **der Wechselwähler(-)**
general election **allgemeine Wahlen**
I go to the polls **ich gehe zur Abstimmung/Wahl**
I hold an election **ich halte eine Wahl ab***
opinion poll **die Meinungsumfrage(n)**
poll **die Abstimmung(en)**
I recount **ich zähle nach***
referendum **das Referendum (-en)**
right to vote **das Wahlrecht(e)**
I stand for election **ich stelle mich zur Wahl**
suffrage **das Stimmrecht(e)**
swing **der Meinungsumschwung(⁻e)**
term of office **die Regierungszeit(en)**
universal suffrage **das allgemeine Wahlrecht**
vote **die Stimme(n)**
I vote (for X) **ich stimme (für X)**
voter **der Wähler(-) [-in]**

Political ideology

anarchist **der Anarchist(en)** *(wk)* **[-in]**
anarchy **die Anarchie(n)**
anti-Semitic **antisemistisch**
anti-Semitism **der Antisemitismus**
aristocracy **die Aristokratie**
aristocrat **der Aristokrat(en)** *(wk)* **[-in]**
aristocratic **aristokratisch**
capitalism **der Kapitalismus**
capitalist **der Kapitalist(en)** *(wk)*
center **die Mitte**
communism **der Kommunismus**
communist **der Kommunist(en)** *(wk)* **[-in]**

The members of parliament are elected for four years. The 5% clause means that a party must get 5% of votes before it gets a seat in parliament.

Die Mitglieder des Bundestages werden auf vier Jahre gewählt. Die "Fünf-Prozent-Klausel" bedeutet, dass eine Partei fünf Prozent der Stimmen bekommen muss, bevor sie einen Sitz im Parlament bekommt.

– How do you vote? – I have always voted Christian-Democrat.

– Was wählst du? – Ich wähle seit jeher die Christdemokraten.

Since reunification we can freely visit the West.

Seit der Wende können wir den Westen uneingeschränkt besuchen.

conservatism **der Konservatismus**
conservative **konservativ**
democracy **die Demokratie(n)**
democrat **der Demokrat(en)** *(wk)* **[-in]**
democratic **demokratisch**
duke **der Herzog(-̈e) [-in]**
empire **das Reich(e)**
emperor/empress **der Kaiser(-) [-in]**
extremist **der Extremist(en)** *(wk)* **[-in]**
far left **linksradikal/-extrem**
far right **rechtsradikal/-extrem**
fascism **der Faschismus**
fascist **der Faschist(en) [-in]**
I gain independence **ich erlange die Unabhängigkeit**
ideology **die Ideologie(n)**
imperialism **der Imperialismus**
imperialist **der Imperialist(en)** *(wk)*
independence **die Unabhängigkeit**
independent **unabhängig**
king **der König(e)**
left **links**
left wing **der linke Flügel**
liberal **liberal**
liberalism **der Liberalismus**
Liberals **die Liberalen** *(pl)*

marxism **der Marxismus**
marxist **der Marxist(en)** *(wk)*
monarchy **die Monarchie(n)**
nationalism **der Nationalismus**
nationalist **der Nationalist(en)** *(wk)*
Nazi **der Nazi(s)**
patriotic **patriotisch**
patriotism **der Patriotismus**
prince **der Prinz(en)** *(wk)*
princess **die Prinzessin(nen)**
queen **die Königin(nen)**
radicalism **der Radikalismus**
radical **radikal**
republic **die Republik(en)**
republican **der Republikaner(-) [-in]**
republican *(adj)* **republikanisch**
republicanism **der Republikanismus**
revolutionary **revolutionär**
right **rechts**
right wing **der rechte Flügel**
royal **königlich**
royalist **königstreu**
socialism **der Sozialismus**
Socialist **der Sozialist(en)**
socialist *(adj)* **sozialistisch**

Young Germans are not very interested in politics. Those who belong to the Green Party or to the extreme left parties are politically active.

Deutsche Jugendliche sind politisch nicht stark engagiert. Anhänger der Grünen oder der linksextremen Parteien sind politisch aktiv.

The chancellor is elected by Parliament. In the 12th Parliament the CDU/CSU/FDP coalition was in power.

Der Bundeskanzler wird vom Bundestag gewählt. Im 12. Deutschen Bundestag war die CDU-CSU-FDP-Koalition an der Macht.

26 Crime & justice

26a Crime

accomplice **der Komplize(n)** *(wk)* **[-in]**

alias **der Deckname(n)** *(wk)*

armed **bewaffnet**

arson **die Brandstiftung**

assault **der Überfall(-̈e)**

assault and battery **die Körperverletzung**

attack **das Attentat(e)**

battered baby **das misshandelte Baby**

bomb attack **der Bombenanschlag(-̈e)**

fire bomb attack **der Brandanschlag(-̈e)**

bribery **die Bestechung**

burglar **der Einbrecher(-) [-in]**

burglary **der Einbruch(-̈e)**

I burgle/burglarize **ich breche ein***

car theft **der Autodiebstahl(-̈e)**

child abuse **die Kindesmisshandlung**

I come to blows **ich schlage mich (mit** +dat)

I commit **ich begehe**

crime **das Verbrechen(-)**

crime rate **die Kriminalitätsrate(n)**

crime wave **die Verbrechenswelle(n)**

criminal **der Verbrecher(-) [-in]**

I deceive **ich täusche**

delinquency **die Kriminalität**

drug abuse **der Drogenmissbrauch**

drug addict **der/die Drogenabhängige** *(adj/n)*

drug baron **der Drogenbaron(e)**

drug dealer **der Drogenhändler(-)**

drug pusher **der Dealer(-)**

drugs **die Drogen**

drug-trafficking **der Drogenhandel**

I embezzle **ich unterschlage**

embezzlement **die Unterschlagung(en)**

espionage **die Spionage**

extortion **die Erpressung(en)**

I fight **ich streite, ich kämpfe**

fight **der Streit(e), der Kampf(-̈e)**

firearm **die Schusswaffe(n)**

I forge **ich fälsche**

forged **gefälscht**

forgery **die Fälschung(en)**

fraud **der Betrug(-̈e)**

gang **die Bande(n)**

gang warfare **der Bandenkrieg(e)**

grievous bodily harm (GBH) **die schwere Körperverletzung(en)**

gun **die Schusswaffe(n)**

Carlos was captured in the Sudan. He was the internationally most wanted terrorist.

He had many aliases and he was on the run. He confessed to one bomb attack.

Carlos wurde im Sudan festgenommen. Er war der international meistgesuchte Terrorist.

Er trug viele Decknamen und war auf der Flucht. Er bekannte sich zu einem Bombenanschlag.

---

handbag snatching **der Taschendiebstahl(⁻e)**
handcuffs **die Handschellen** *(pl)*
Help! **Hilfe!**
I hi-jack **ich entführe**
hi-jacker **der Entführer(-)**
hold-up **die Überfall(⁻e)**
hooker **die Nutte(n)**
hostage **die Geisel(n)**
illegal **illegal**
I importune/harass **ich belästige**
I injure/wound **ich verletze**
I kidnap **ich entführe, ich kidnappe**
kidnapper **der Entführer(-), der Kidnapper(-)**
kidnapping **die Entführung, das Kidnapping**
I kill **ich töte, ich ermorde**
killer **der Mörder(-) [-in]**
knife **das Messer(-)**
I knife **ich ersteche**
knifing **die Messerstecherei(en)**
legal **legal**
living off immoral earnings **die Zuhälterei**
mafia **die Mafia**
I mug **ich raube ... aus*, ich überfalle**
mugger **der Straßenräuber(-)**
mugging **der Straßenraub** *(no pl)*
murder **der Mord(e)**
I murder **ich ermorde**
murderer **der Mörder(-)**
I offend **ich werde straffällig**

pickpocket **der Taschendieb(e)**
pickpocketing **der Taschendiebstahl(⁻e)**
pimp **der Zuhälter(-)**
pimping **die Zuhälterei**
poison **das Gift(e)**
I poison **ich vergifte**
I procure **ich beschaffe**
prostitute **der/die Prostituierte** *(adj/n)*
prostitution **die Prostitution**
I rape **ich vergewaltige**
rape **die Vergewaltigung(en)**
receiver **der Hehler(-) [-in]**
reprisals **die Vergeltung(en)**
I shoot at **ich schieße** (auf + acc)
shop-lifting **der Ladendiebstahl(⁻e)**
slander **die Verleumdung(en)**
I smuggle **ich schmuggle**
spy **der Spion(e) [-in]**
I steal **ich stehle**
stolen goods **das Diebesgut**
tax evasion **die Steuerhinterziehung(en)**
terrorist **der Terrorist(en)** *(wk)*
torture **die Folter(n)**
I torture **ich foltere**
theft **der Diebstahl(⁻e)**
thief **der Dieb(e)**
traffic offence/violation **der Verkehrsverstoß (⁻e)**
I traffick **ich schiebe**
underworld **die Unterwelt(en)**
vandalism **der Vandalismus**
victim **das Opfer(-)**

Plutonium smugglers demand millions of dollars.	**Plutonium-Schmuggler verlangen Millionen von Dollar.**
They were caught red-handed.	**Sie wurden auf frischer Tat ertappt.**
We went to the police.	**Wir sind zur Polizei gegangen.**

➤ WEAPONS 27b; ADDICTION & VIOLENCE 12d

26b Trial

accusation **die Anklage(n)**
I accuse **ich klage ... an***
accused person **der/die Angeklagte** *(adj/n)*
I acquit **ich spreche jdn. frei***
appeal **der Einspruch(¨e)**
I appeal **ich erhebe Einspruch**
I appear in court **ich erscheine vor Gericht**
case **der Fall(¨e)**
compensation **die Entschädigung(en)**
confession **das Geständnis(se)**
I confess **ich gestehe**
I convince **ich überzeuge**
costs **die Kosten** *(pl)*
counsel for the defense **der Verteidiger(-) [-in]**
court **das Gericht(e)**
court of appeal **das Berufungsgericht(e)**
courtroom **der Gerichtssaal (-säle)**
I cross-question **ich verhöre**
I debate **ich debattiere**
defence/defense **die Verteidigung**
I defend (myself) **ich verteidige (mich)**
defendant **der/die Angeklagte** *(adj/n)*
diminished responsibility/insanity **verminderte Zurechnungsfähigkeit**
I disagree **ich stimme nicht überein***

I discuss **ich diskutiere**
dock **die Anklagebank(¨e)**
I enquire/examine **ich untersuche**
evidence **die Aussage(n), der Beweis(e)**
examining magistrate **der Untersuchungsrichter(-)**
extenuating circumstances **mildernde Umstände** *(pl)*
I extradite **ich liefere aus***
eyewitness **der Augenzeuge(n)** *(wk)* **[-in]**
I find guilty **ich befinde für schuldig, ich spreche jdn. schuldig**
I give evidence **ich bezeuge**
I give evidence **ich sage für jdn. aus***
guilt **die Schuld**
guilty **schuldig**
high court of appeal **die höchste Berufungsinstanz(en)**
I impeach **ich klage an***
impeachment **die Anfechtung(en), die Anklage(n)**
indictment **die Anklageschrift(en)**
innocence **die Unschuld**
innocent **unschuldig**
judge **der Richter(-) [-in]**
juror **der/die Geschworene** *(adj/n)*
jury **die Geschworenen** *(pl)*
jury box **die Geschworenenbank(¨e)**
justice **die Gerechtigkeit**
lawsuit **der Prozess(e)**

What's the case for the prosecution? **Worauf stützt sich die Anklage?**

We haven't enough evidence. **Wir haben nicht genug Beweise.**

The police search was without result. **Die Polizeifahndung blieb ohne Erfolg.**

lawyer **der Rechtsanwalt(ː̈e)**
leniency **die Nachsichtigkeit(en)**
life imprisonment **die lebenslängliche Haft** *(no pl)*
litigation **der Prozess(e)**
magistrate/Justice of Peace **der (Friedens)richter(-) [-in]**
magistrate's court/court **das Gericht(e)**
mercy **die Gnade**
minor offence **das leichte Vergehen(-)**
miscarriage of justice **das Fehlurteil(e)**
motive **das Motiv(e)**
not guilty **nicht schuldig**
oath **der Eid(e), der Schwur(ː̈e)**
offence **die Straftat(en), das Vergehen(-)**
on remand/in detention **in Untersuchungshaft**
I pass judgement **ich fälle das Urteil**
perjury **der Meineid** *(no pl)*
plea **das Plädoyer(s)**
plea bargaining **die Verhandlung(en)**
I plead guilty/not guilty **ich bekenne mich schuldig/ unschuldig**
premeditation **der Vorsatz**
I prosecute **ich verfolge**
prosecution **die strafrechtliche Verfolgung**
public prosecutor **der Staatsanwalt(ː̈e)**
district attorney **der Bezirksstaatsanwalt(ː̈e)**

public prosecutor's office **die Staatsanwaltskanzlei**
I question **ich befrage**
I interrogate **ich verhöre**
retrial **die Wiederaufnahme des Verfahrens**
I rescue **ich rette**
I reward **ich belohne**
speech for the defence/defense **die Verteidigung**
I stand accused **ich bin angeklagt**
I stand bail (for someone) **ich bürge (für jdn.)**
statement **die Aussage(n)**
I sue/I take to court **ich verklage, ich bringe vor Gericht**
I sue for divorce **ich reiche die Scheidung ein***
summons **die Vorladung(en)**
I suspect **ich verdächtige**
suspect **der/die Verdächtige** *(adj/n)*
Supreme Court **der Oberste Gerichtshof**
sustained! **stattgegeben!**
I swear **ich schwöre**
I take legal proceedings **ich bringe vor Gericht**
I take prisoner **ich nehme gefangen**
trial **das Verfahren(-)**
unanimous **einstimmig**
verdict **das Urteil(e)**
I witness **ich bezeuge**
witness **der Zeuge(n)** *(wk)* **[-in]**
witness box **der Zeugenstand**
writ **der Haftbefehl(e)**

– They've caught her. She pleaded guilty.
– What was the verdict?
– She went to prison. She got life.

– Sie wurde erwischt/gefasst. Sie hat sich schuldig bekannt.
– Wie lautete das Urteil?
– Sie kam ins Gefängnis. Sie hat lebenslänglich bekommen.

26c Punishment & crime prevention

Punishment

confinement **die Haft**
  in solitary confinement **die Einzelhaft**
I convict **ich erkläre jdn. für schuldig**
convict **der Sträfling(e)**
death penalty **die Todesstrafe(n)**
I deport **ich weise aus***
I escape **ich fliehe aus** +dat, **ich entkomme** +dat
fine **die Geldstrafe(n)**
I fine **ich belege mit einer Geldstrafe**
he was fined **er musste eine Strafe bezahlen**
I free **ich spreche frei***
hard labour/labor **die Zwangsarbeit**
I imprison **ich inhaftiere**
jail sentence **die Gefängnisstrafe(n)**
prison **das Gefängnis(se)**
prisoner **der/die Gefangene** *(adj/n)*
I punish **ich bestrafe**
punishment **die Bestrafung(en), die Strafe(n)**
I release on bail **ich lasse jdn. gegen Kaution frei***
I reprieve **ich begnadige**
I sentence to death **ich verurteile zum Tode**
I serve a sentence **ich sitze eine Strafe ab***

sentence **die Strafe(n)**
severity **die Strenge**
suspended sentence **(zur Bewährung) ausgesetztes Urteil**

Crime prevention

alarm **der Alarm(e), die Sicherung(en)**
  burglar alarm **die Alarmanlage(n)**
  car alarm **die Autosicherung(en)**
autopsy **die Autopsie(n)**
arrest **die Verhaftung(en)**
I arrest **ich verhafte, ich stelle**
baton **der Knüppel(-)**
(hearing) in camera **hinter verschlossenen Türen**
I break the law **ich breche das Gesetz**
I catch **ich ertappe, ich fange**
chief of police **der Polizeichef(s)**
civil law **das Zivilrecht**
clue **die Spur(en)**
crime prevention **die Verbrechensverhütung**
criminal law **das Strafgesetz(e)**
I have a criminal record **ich bin vorbestraft**
customs **der Zoll** *(no pl)*
customs officer **der Zollbeamte(n)** *(adj/n)* **[-in]**
deportation **die Abschiebung(en)**

The accused has no previous convictions. He was given a fine.

Der Angeklagte ist nicht vorbestraft. Er wurde zu einer Geldstrafe verurteilt.

His friend is on probation.

Sein Freund steht unter Bewährungsaufsicht.

Rainer has been inside.

Rainer hat gesessen.

detective der Detektiv(e) [-in]
drugs raid die Drogenrazzia (-ien)
drugs squad die Drogenfahndungsbehörde(n)
enquiry die Untersuchung(en), die Nachforschung(en)
error der Fehler(-)
escape die Flucht(en)
I escape (from) ich flüchte (vor +dat)
examination/interrogation das Verhör(e)
I examine ich verhöre
extradition die Auslieferung(en)
fingerprint der Fingerabdruck(-̈e)
fugitive der Flüchtling(e)
guard dog der Wachhund(e)
handcuff die Handschelle(n)
I handcuff ich lege die Handschellen an*
identikit/photofit picture das Phantombild(er)
I inform the police ich verständige die Polizei
informer der Informant (wk) [-in]
interview die Befragung(en)
I interview ich befrage
I investigate ich untersuche
investigation die Ermittlungen (pl)
investigator der Ermittler
private investigator der Privatdetektiv(e)
key der Schlüssel(-)
law das Gesetz(e)

law and order die öffentliche Ordnung
lock das Schloss(-̈er)
I lock ich schließe ab*
padlock das Vorhängeschloss (-̈er)
plain-clothes police der Polizist (wk) in Zivil
police die Polizei
police headquarters das Polizeipräsidium(-en)
police informer der Polizei-spitzel(-)
police station das Polizeirevier(e)
policeman der Polizist(en) (wk)
policewoman die Polizistin(nen)
I question ich vernehme
ransom das Lösegeld(er)
reward die Belohnung(en)
riot police das Überfallkommando(s)
search die Fahndung(en)
secret service der Geheimdienst(e)
security die Sicherheit
security firm der Sicherheitsdienst(e)
speed trap die Radarfalle(n)
station das Revier(e)
traffic police die Verkehrspolizei
traffic warden die Politesse(n)
truncheon der Polizeiknüppel(-)
warrant der Haftbefehl(e)
search warrant der Durchsuchungsbefehl(e)

He was declared guilty and given a suspended sentence of two years. **Er wurde schuldig gesprochen und zu zwei Jahren Gefängnis mit Bewährung verurteilt.**

The witness is under police protection. **Der Zeuge steht unter Polizeischutz.**

There's a reward for the finder. **Es gibt einen Finderlohn.**

War & peace

27a War

I abduct **ich entführe**
aggression **die Aggression(en)**
air force **die Luftwaffe(n)**
airlift **die Luftbrücke(n)**
air raid **der Luftangriff(e)**
air-raid shelter **der Luftschutzbunker(-)**
air-raid warning **der Fliegeralarm(e)**
ambush **der Hinterhalt(e)**
antiaircraft **die Flugabwehr**
army **die Armee(n), das Heer(e)**
I assassinate **ich ermorde**
assault **der Angriff(e)**
atomic **Atom-**
I attack **ich greife an***
attack **der Angriff(e)**
barracks **die Kaserne(n)**
battle **die Schlacht(en)**
battlefield **das Schlachtfeld(er)**
blast **die Explosion(en)**
I blockade **ich blockiere**
blockade **die Blockade(n)**
I blow up **ich sprenge**
brave **mutig**
war breaks out **der Krieg bricht aus***
I call up **ich berufe ein***
camp **das Lager(-)**
campaign **der Feldzug(¨e)**
I capture **ich nehme gefangen**
cause **die Ursache(n)**
I claim responsibility for **ich erkläre mich verantwortlich für**
I commit **ich begehe**
conflict **der Konflikt(e)**
confrontation **die Konfrontation(en)**
conquest **die Eroberung(en)**
I contaminate **ich verseuche**

conventional (weapon) **konventionell (Waffen)**
court-marshal **das Kriegsgericht(e)**
cowardly **feige**
the plane crashes **das Flugzeug stürzt ab***
I crush (opposition) **ich vernichte (den Gegner)**
I declare (war) **ich erkläre (den Krieg)**
defeat **die Niederlage(n)**
I defeat **ich schlage**
defence/defense **die Verteidigung(en)**
I defend **ich verteidige**
I destroy **ich zerstöre**
I detain **ich verhafte**
I detect **ich entdecke**
devastating **verheerend**
enemy **der Feind(e)**
espionage **die Spionage(n)**
ethnic cleansing **die ethnische Säuberung(en)**
I evacuate **ich evakuiere**
evacuation **die Evakuierung(en)**
I fight a battle **ich führe einen Kampf**
I fight off **ich wehre ab***
I flee (from) **ich fliehe (vor** +dat)
front **die Front(en)**
guerrilla warfare **der Guerrillakrieg(e)**
harmful **schädlich**
headquarters **das Hauptquartier(e)**
hostilities **die Feindseligkeiten** *(pl)*
I interrogate **ich verhöre**
interrogation **das Verhör(e)**
I intervene **ich schreite ein***
intervention **das Eingreifen**

intimidation **die Einschüchterung(en)**
I invade **ich überfalle**
invasion **die Invasion(en)**
I issue an ultimatum **ich stelle ein Ultimatum**
manoeuvres/maneuvers **das Manöver(-)**
massacre **das Massaker(-)**
missing in action **vermisst**
military service **der Kriegsdienst(e)**
mobilization **die Mobilmachung(en)**
I mobilize **ich mobilisiere**
morale **die Moral**
multilateral **multilateral**
navy **die Kriegsmarine(n)**
nuclear **Kern-**
occupation **die Besetzung(en)**
I occupy **ich besetze**
offensive **die Offensive(n)**
I patrol **ich patrouilliere**
peace **der Frieden**
propaganda **die Propaganda**
I protect (from) **ich schütze (vor +dat)**
I provoke **ich provoziere**
it rages **es tobt**
raid **der Angriff(e)**
reinforcements **die Verstärkung(en)**
reprisals **die Repressalie(n)**
I resist **ich leiste Widerstand**
resistance **der Widerstand(¨e)**

retreat **der Rückzug(¨e)**
review **die Parade(n)**
I revolt **ich rebelliere**
revolution **die Revolution(en)**
riot **der Aufruhr(e)**
rubble **die Trümmer** *(pl)*
security check **die Sicherheitskontrolle(n)**
shelter **die Sicherheit**
siege **die Belagerung(en)**
skirmish **das Gefecht(e)**
I spy **ich spioniere**
I start a war **ich fange einen Krieg an***
strategy **die Strategie(n)**
strike power **die Schlagkraft(¨e)**
the vessel submerges/surfaces **das Schiff taucht unter*/auf***
survival **das Überleben**
tactics **die Taktik** *(no pl)*
terrorist attack **der Terroranschlag(¨e)**
I threaten **ich drohe** +dat
trench **der Schützengraben(¨)**
underground **die Untergrundbewegung(en)**
victory **der Sieg(e)**
war-mongering **die Kriegshetze**
I win **ich gewinne**
wound **die Wunde(n)**
I wound **ich verwunde, ich verletze**

The event which has most marked the twentieth century is the Second World War. Hitler invaded Poland on September 1, 1939.

Two days later, Britain and France declared war on Germany.

Der 2. Weltkrieg war das einschneidendste Ereignis des 20. Jahrhunderts. Hitler überfiel Polen am 1. September 1939.

Zwei Tage später erklärten Großbritannien und Frankreich Deutschland den Krieg.

WAR & PEACE

27b Military personnel & weaponry

Military personnel

aggressor **der Aggressor(en)**
ally **der/die Verbündete** *(adj/n)*
Allies **die Alliierten** *(pl)*
archer **der Bogenschütze(n)** *(wk)*
assassin **der Mörder(-) [-in]**
casualty *(dead)* **das Opfer(-)**
cavalry **die Kavallerie(n)**
civilian **der Zivilist(en)** *(wk)*
commandos **die Kommandos** *(pl)*
conscientious objector **der
    Kriegsdienstverweigerer(-)**
conscript **der/die Wehrpflichtige**
    (adj/n)
convoy **der Konvoi(s)**
deserter **der Deserteur(e)**
division **die Division(en)**
foot soldier **der Infanterist(en)** *(wk)*
general **der General(ᵋe)**
guard **die Wache(n)**
guerrilla **der Guerrilla(s), der
    Freischärler(-)**
hostage **die Geisel(n)**
infantry **die Infanterie(n)**
intelligence officer **der
    Nachrichtenoffizier(e)**
marine(s) **die Marine(n)**
NCO **der Unteroffizier(e)**
orderly **der Sanitäter(-)**
parachutist **der
    Fallschirmspringer(-) [-in]**
prisoner of war **der/die
    Kriegsgefangene** *(adj/n)*
rank **der Rang(ᵋe)**
rebel **der Rebell(en)** *(wk)*
recruit **der Rekrut(e)** *(wk)*
regiment **das Regiment(e)**
seaman/sailor **der Seemann
    (-leute)**
Secretary of War **der
    Kriegsminister(-)**
secret agent **der Geheimagent(en)**
    (wk)
sentry **der Wachposten(-)**

sniper **der Scharfschütze(n)** *(wk)*
soldier **der Soldat(en)** *(wk)*
spy **der Spion(e) [-in]**
squadron **das Schwadron(e)**
staff **das Personal, der Stab(ᵋe)**
terrorist **der Terrorist(en)** *(wk)*
traitor **der Verräter(-) [-in]**
troop **die Truppe(n)**
victor **der Sieger(-)**
War Minister **der Kriegs-
    minister(-)**

Weaponry

I aim (at) **ich ziele (auf** +acc)
aircraft carrier **der
    Flugzeugträger(-)**
ammunition **die Munition(en)**
armaments **die Ausrüstung(en)**
armored car **der Panzerwagen(-)**
arms **die Waffen** *(pl)*
arms trade **der Waffenhandel**
arms race **das Wettrüsten**
artillery **die Artillerie(n)**
bacteriological **bakteriologisch**
barbed wire **der Stacheldraht(ᵋe)**
bayonet **das Bajonett(e)**
aerial bombing **der Luftangriff(e)**
I bomb(ard) **ich bombardiere**
bomb **die Bombe(n)**
bomb alert **der Bombenalarm(e)**
bombardment **die
    Bombardierung(en)**
bomber *(aircraft)* **der Bomber(-)**
bullet **die Kugel(n)**
car bomb **die Autobombe(n)**
chemical warfare **die chemische
    Kriegsführung**
chemical weapon **die chemische
    Waffe(n)**
crossbow **die (Stand)armbrust(ᵋe)**
destroyer *(ship)* **der Zerstörer(-)**
I execute **ich richte hin***
I explode a bomb **ich bringe eine
    Bombe zur Explosion**

explosive **der Sprengstoff(e)**
   explosive *(adj)* **explosiv**
fallout **der Fall-out** *(no pl)*
fighter plane **das Jagdflugzeug(e)**
I fire (at) **ich feure (auf** +acc)**, ich verschieße**
frigate **die Fregatte(n)**
gas **das Gas(e)**
gas attack **der Gasangriff(e)**
gun **die Schusswaffe(n)**
hand-grenade **die Handgranate(n)**
H-bomb **die Wasserstoffbombe(n)**
I hit **ich treffe**
jet *(plane)* **der Jet(s)**
I kill **ich töte, ich bringe ums Leben**
knife **das Messer(-)**
laser **der Laser(-)**
letter bomb **die Briefbombe(n)**
machine gun **das Maschinengewehr(e)**
minefield **das Minenfeld(er)**
mine sweeper **das Minensuchboot(e)**
missile **die Rakete(n)**
missile launcher **der Raketenwerfer(-)**
mortar **der Minenwerfer(-)**
neutron bomb **die Neutronenbombe(n)**
nuclear warfare **der Atomkrieg(e)**
nuclear warhead **der Nuklearsprengkopf(-̈e)**
pistol **die Pistole(n)**

poison gas **das Giftgas(e)**
radar **der Radar** *(no pl)*
radar screen **der Radarschirm(e)**
radiation **die Strahlung(en)**
radiation sickness **die Strahlenkrankheit(en)**
radioactive **radioaktiv**
revolver **der Revolver(-)**
rifle **das Gewehr(e)**
rocket **die Rakete(n)**
rocket attack **der Raketenangriff(e)**
I sabotage **ich sabotiere**
shell **die Granate(n)**
I shoot at **ich beschieße**
I shoot dead **ich erschieße**
shotgun **die Schrotflinte(n)**
shrapnel **das Schrapnell** *(no pl)*
I sink the ship **ich versenke das Schiff**
the ship sinks **das Schiff sinkt**
I stockpile **ich lege Vorräte an***
submachine gun **die Maschinenpistole(n)**
submarine **das U-Boot(e)**
tank **der Panzer(-)**
target **das Ziel(e)**
I test **ich prüfe, ich teste**
torpedo **der Torpedo(s)**
torpedo attack **der Torpedoangriff(e)**
I torpedo **ich torpediere**
warship **das Kriegsschiff(e)**
weapon **die Waffe(n)**

War is waged on the civil population.

Der Krieg wird gegen die Zivilbevölkerung geführt.

Conventional weapons do not deter.

Konventionelle Waffen schrecken nicht ab.

Six people were wounded when a shell landed in the old town.

Sechs Leute wurden verwundet, als eine Granate in die Altstadt einschlug.

WAR & PEACE

27c Peace & international relations

Peace

I ban **ich verbiete**
cease-fire **der Waffenstillstand(ᐟe)**
control **die Kontrolle(n)**
I demobilize **ich demobilisiere**
deterrent **das Abschreckungsmittel(-)**
I diminish tension **ich entspanne die Lage**
disarmament **die Abrüstung(en)**
exchanges of information **der Informationsaustausch(e)**
Federal Armed Forces service **der Bundeswehrdienst**
free **frei**
I free **ich befreie**
freedom **die Freiheit(en)**
human rights **die Menschenrechte** (pl)
I make peace **ich schließe den Frieden**
I mediate **ich vermittle**
I negotiate **ich verhandle**
negotiation **die Verhandlung(en)**
neutral **neutral**
neutrality **die Neutralität**
pacifist **der Pazifist(en)** (wk)
pacifism **der Pazifismus**
peace plan **der Friedensplan(ᐟe)**

peace protester **der Friedensdemonstrant(en)** (wk)
peace talks **die Friedensverhandlung(en)**
peace-keeping force **die Friedenstruppen** (pl)
I ratify (treaty) **ich ratifiziere**
surrender **die Kapitulation(en)**
I surrender **ich kapituliere**
test ban **der Teststopp(s)**
treaty **der Vertrag(ᐟe), das Abkommen(-)**
uncommitted **nicht verpflichtet/ungebunden**
victory **der Sieg(e)**

International relations

aid **die (Entwicklungs)hilfe**
ambassador **der Botschafter(-) [-in]**
arms limitation **die Rüstungsbegrenzung**
attaché **der Attaché(s)**
citizen **der Staatsbürger(-) [-in]**
citizenship **die Staatsbürgerschaft**
consul **der Konsul(n) [-in]**
consulate **das Konsulat(e)**
developing country **das Entwicklungsland(ᐟer)**

We are looking for a compromise.

Wir suchen nach einem Kompromiss.

The conditions in the ultimatum must be respected.

Die Bedingungen des Ultimatums müssen beachtet werden.

The areas which had been annexed had to be given back.

Die Gebiete, die erobert worden waren, mussten zurückgegeben werden.

The use of UN forces is demanded.

Man verlangt den Einsatz der UN-Truppen.

diplomacy **die Diplomatie**
diplomat **der Diplomat(en)** *(wk)*
diplomatic immunity **die Immunität**
embassy **die Botschaft(en)**
emergency aid **die Nothilfe**
envoy **der/die Gesandte** *(adj/n)*
famine **die Hungersnot(-̈e)**
foreign affairs **die Außenpolitik**
foreign aid **die Auslandshilfe**
foreigner **der Ausländer(-) [-in]**
I join *(organization)* **ich trete** +dat
  bei*
national security **die**
  Staatssicherheit
non-aligned **blockfrei**
overseas **in Übersee**
relief organization **die**
  Hilfsorganisation(en)
relief supplies **die Hilfsgüter** *(pl)*
I represent **ich vertrete**
sanctions **die Sanktion(en)**
summit meeting **die**
  Gipfelkonferenz(en)
Third World **die Dritte Welt**

Trade

agricultural policy **die Agrarpolitik**
balance of payments **die**
  Zahlungsbilanz(en)

balance of trade **die**
  Handelsbilanz(en)
Common market **die EU, der**
  Binnenmarkt(-̈e)
currency **die Währung(en)**
customs **der Einfuhrzoll(-̈e)**
customs union **die Zollunion(en)**
exchange rate **der Wechselkurs(e)**
exports **die Ausfuhr** *(no pl)*
floating currency **die freigegebene**
  Währung(en)
it floats **es schwebt, es variiert**
foreign exchange **die Devisen** *(pl)*
foreign investment **die**
  ausländischen Investition(en)
free-trade zone **die Freie**
  Handelszone(n)
gap between rich and poor **der**
  Unterschied(e) zwischen Arm
  und Reich
GNP (gross national product) **das**
  Bruttosozialprodukt
import control **die Importkontrolle(n)**
import **die Einfuhr** *(no pl)*
tariff barriers **die Zollschranken**
  (pl)
tariff **der (Zoll)tarif(e)**
trade gap (negative) **die (negative)**
  Handelsspanne(n)

An intervention by NATO could
bring peace closer or extend the
war.

**Eine Intervention der Nato
könnte den Frieden näher
bringen oder den Krieg
verlängern.**

There is no foreign exchange to
pay for German goods.

**Die Devisen fehlen, um
deutsche Lieferungen zu
bezahlen.**

Trade with the East is to be
encouraged.

**Der Osthandel soll gefördert
werden.**

GATT (General Agreement on
Tariffs and Trade)

**das Allgemeine Zoll- und
Handelsabkommen**

INTERNATIONAL ORGANIZATIONS 27c; THE ECONOMY 14e

C
SUBJECT INDEX

Subject index

3b Clocks & watches*

alarm clock **der Wecker(-)**
clock **die Uhr(en)**
cuckoo clock **die Kuckucksuhr(en)**
dial **das Zifferblatt(-er)**
digital watch **die Digitaluhr(en)**
egg-timer **die Sanduhr(en)**
grandfather clock **die Standuhr(en)**
hand (of a clock) **der Zeiger(-)**
   hour hand **der kleine Zeiger(-)**
   minute hand **der Minutenzeiger(-)**
   second hand **der Sekundenzeiger(-)**
hourglass **die Sanduhr(en)**
pendulum **der Pendel(-)**
stopwatch **die Stoppuhr(en)**
sundial **die Sonnenuhr(en)**
timer (on cooker) **der Zeitmesser(-)**
watch **die Armbanduhr(en)**
   watch strap **das Uhrarmband(-er)**
I wind up **ich ziehe ... auf***

4d Mathematical & geometrical terms

acute **spitz**
algebra **die Algebra**
algebraic **algebraisch**
Arabic numerals **arabische Ziffern** *(pl)*
arithmetic **das Rechnen**
arithmetical **Rechen-**
average **der Durchschnitt(e)**
   average *(adj)* **durchschnittlich**
axis **die Achse(n)**
calculus **die Infinitesimalrechnung**
circumference **der Umfang(-e)**
complex **komplex**
constant **die Konstante(n)**
cube **die dritte Potenz**
cube root **die Kubikwurzel(n)**
cubed **hoch drei**
cubic **Kubik-**
decimal **die Dezimalzahl(en)**
   decimal *(adj)* **dezimal**

decimal point **das Komma(s)**
equality **die Gleichheit**
factor **der Faktor(en)**
I factorize **ich zerlege in Faktoren**
fraction **der Bruch(-e)**
function **die Funktion(en)**
geometry **die Geometrie**
geometry set **das Reißzeug(e)**
geometrical **geometrisch**
imaginary number **die imaginäre Zahl(en)**
integer **die ganze Zahl(en)**
irrational **irrational**
logarithm **der Logarithmus**
mean **der Mittelwert(e)**
median **der Zentralwert(e)**
multiple **das Vielfache**
natural **natürlich**
nine is to three as ... **neun verhält sich zu drei wie ...**
numerical **numerisch**
obtuse **stumpf**
prime number **die Primzahl(en)**
probability **die Wahrscheinlichkeit(en)**
product **das Produkt(e)**
quotient **der Quotient(en)**
I raise to a power **ich erhebe in die zweite Potenz**
   2 to the power of 2 **2 hoch 2**
   to the *n*th power **die n-te Potenz**
radius **der Halbmesser(-)**
ratio **das Verhältnis(se)**
rational **rational**
real **reell**
reciprocal **der reziproke Wert(e)**
Roman numeral **die römische Ziffer(n)**
set **die Reihe(n), die Menge(n)**
square **die Quadratzahl(en)**
   the square of 2 **die zweite Potenz zu zwei**
square root **die Quadratwurzel(n)**
symmetry **die Symmetrie(n)**
symmetrical (a-) **(a)symmetrisch**
table *(multiplication)* **das Einmaleins**

* Appendices are numbered by most relevant Vocabulary.

tangent **die Tangente(n)**
trigonometry **die Trigonometrie**
variable **die Variable(n)**
vector **der Vektor(en)**

5b Parts of the body

---

ankle **der Knöchel(-), das Fußgelenk(e)**
appendix **der Blinddarm(¨e)**
arm **der Arm(e)**
artery **die Arterie(n)**
back **der Rücken(-)**
backbone **das Rückgrat(e)**
bladder **die Blase(n)**
blood **das Blut** *(no pl)*
blood pressure **der Blutdruck(¨e)**
body **der Körper(-)**
bone **der Knochen(-)**
bowel **der Darm(¨e)**
brain **das Gehirn(e)**
breast **die Brust(¨e)**
buttocks **das Gesäß(e)**
cheek **die Backe(n), die Wange(n)**
chest **der Brustkorb(¨e)**
chin **das Kinn(e)**
ear **das Ohr(en)**
elbow **der Ellbogen(¨/)**
eye **das Auge(n)**
eyeball **der Augapfel(¨)**
eyebrow **die Augenbraue(n)**
eyelash **die Augenwimper(n)**
eyelid **das Augenlid(er)**
face **das Gesicht(er)**
finger **der Finger(-)**
fingernail **der Fingernagel(¨)**
foot **der Fuß(¨e)**
forehead **die Stirn(en)**
genitalia **die Genitalien** *(pl)*
gland **die Drüse(n)**
hair **das Haar(e)**
hand **die Hand(¨e)**
head **der Kopf(¨e)**
heart **das Herz(en)**
hip **die Hüfte(n)**
hormone **das Hormon(e)**
index finger **der Zeigefinger(-)**
jaw **der Kiefer(-)**
kidney **die Niere(n)**

knee **das Knie(-)**
knuckle **der (Finger)knöchel(-)**
leg **das Bein(e)**
lip **die Lippe(n)**
liver **die Leber(n)**
lung **die Lunge(n)**
mouth **der Mund(¨er)**
muscle **der Muskel(n)**
nape of neck **der Nacken(-)**
neck **der Hals(¨e)**
nerve **der Nerv(en)**
nervous system **das Nervensystem(e)**
nose **die Nase(n)**
nostril **das Nasenloch(¨er)**
organ **das Organ(e)**
penis **der Penis(se/Penes)**
rib **die Rippe(n)**
shoulder **die Schulter(n)**
skin **die Haut(¨e)**
stomach **der Magen(/ ¨)**
thigh **der Schenkel(-)**
throat **der Hals(¨e)**
thumb **der Daumen(-)**
toe **die Zehe(n)**
tongue **die Zunge(n)**
tonsil **die Mandel(n)**
tooth **der Zahn(¨e)**
vagina **die Scheide(n)**
vein **die Vene(n)**
waist **die Taille(n)**
womb **die Gebärmutter(¨)**
wrist **das Handgelenk(e)**

6a Human characteristics*

---

absentminded(ness) **zerstreut, die
    Zerstreutheit**
active **aktiv**
adaptable **anpassungsfähig**
adaptability **die Anpassungsfähigkeit**
affectionate **liebevoll**
aggression **die Aggression**
aggressive **aggressiv**
ambition **der Ehrgeiz, die
    Ambition(en)**
ambitious **ehrgeizig**
amusing **amüsant, lustig**
anxious **ängstlich**

---

* German negative forms are indicated where possible by **(in)** or **(un)**.　　**217**

6a Human characteristics (cont.)

anxiety   **die Ängstlichkeit**
arrogance   **die Arroganz**
arrogant   **arrogant**
artistic   **künstlerisch**
attractive   **attraktiv**
boring   **langweilig**
brave   **mutig, tapfer**
careless(ness)   **unvorsichtig, die Unvorsichtigkeit**
caution   **die Vorsichtigkeit**
cautious   **vorsichtig**
charm   **der Charme** *(no pl)*
cheek   **die Unverschämtheit(en)**
cheeky   **frech**
cold   **kalt**
comic   **lustig**
confidence   **das Selbstvertrauen**
conscientious   **gewissenhaft**
courage   **der Mut**
courteous   **höflich**
courtesy   **die Höflichkeit**
cowardly   **feig, feige**
creative (-ity)   **kreativ, die Kreativität**
critical   **kritisch**
cruel(ty)   **grausam, die Grausamkeit**
cultured   **gebildet**
cunning   **schlau, die Schlauheit**
curious   **neugierig**
curiosity   **die Neugierde**
decisive (in-)   **(un)entschlossen**
demanding   **anspruchsvoll**
dependent (in-)   **(un)abhängig**
dependence (in-)   **die (Un)abhängigkeit**
diligence   **der Fleiß**
distrust   **das Misstrauen**
distrustful   **misstrauisch**
eccentric   **exzentrisch**
energetic   **energisch**
energy   **die Energie**
envy (-ious)   **der Neid, neidisch**
extroverted   **extravertiert**
extroversion   **die Extravertiertheit**
faithful (un-)   **(un)treu**
faithfulness   **die Treue**
friendliness (un-)   **die (Un)freundlichkeit**
frivolous   **leichtsinnig**

generocity   **die Großzügigkeit**
gentle   **sanft(mütig)**
gentleness   **die Sanftmut**
greed(y)   **die Habgier, habgierig**
honesty (dis-)   **die (Un)ehrlichkeit**
honor   **die Ehre**
humane (in-)   **(in)human**
humble   **bescheiden**
hypocritical   **heuchlerisch**
idealistic   **idealistisch**
imagination   **die Phantasie(n)**
imaginative   **phantasievoll**
independent   **selbstständig**
individualistic   **individuell**
innocence   **die Unschuld**
inquisitive   **neugierig**
introverted   **introvertiert**
introvertion   **die Introvertiertheit**
ironic   **ironisch**
liberal   **liberal**
likeable   **sympathisch**
lonely (-iness)   **einsam, die Einsamkeit**
loveable   **liebenswürdig**
mad(ness)   **verrückt, die Verrücktheit**
malicious(ness)   **boshaft, die Boshaftigkeit**
mature (im-)   **(un)reif**
mean/stingy   **knauserig**
modest(y)   **bescheiden, die Bescheidenheit**
mood   **die Laune(n)**
moody   **launenhaft**
naive(ty)   **naiv, die Naivität**
natural   **natürlich**
nervousness   **die Ängstlichkeit**
niceness   **die Freundlichkeit**
obedience (dis-)   **der (Un)gehorsam**
obedient (dis-)   **(un)gehorsam**
open(ness)   **offen, die Offenheit**
original   **originell**
originality   **die Originalität**
patience (im-)   **die (Un)geduld**
politeness (im-)   **die (Un)höflichkeit**
possessive   **gebieterisch**
prejudiced (un-)   **(un)voreingenommen gegen** +acc
pride   **der Stolz**

proud **stolz**
rebellious **rebellisch**
reserve **die Zurückhaltung**
reserved **zurückhaltend**
respectable **angesehen, anständig**
responsible (ir-) **(un)zuverlässig**
rudeness **die Unhöflichkeit(en)**
sad(ness) **traurig, die Traurigkeit**
sarcasm **der Sarkasmus (-en)**
sarcastic **sarkastisch**
scorn **der Spott**
scornful **spöttisch**
self-confident **selbstbewusst**
self-confidence **das Selbstbewusstsein**
selfish **selbstsüchtig**
selfishness **der Egoismus**
self-sufficient **selbstständig**
self-sufficiency **die Selbstständigkeit**
sensible (not) **(un)vernünftig**
sensitive (in-) **(un)empfindlich**
sensitivity (in-) **die (Un)empfindlichkeit**
shyness **die Schüchternheit**
silent **schweigsam**
silly **dumm, doof, albern**
sincere **aufrichtig**
sincerity **die Aufrichtigkeit**
skill/skillfulness **die Geschicktheit, die Fertigkeit(en)**
sociability (un-) **die (Un)geselligkeit**
strange(ness) **eigenartig, fremd, die Fremdheit, Eigenartigkeit**
strict(ness) **streng, die Strenge**
stubborn(ness) **eigensinnig, die Eigensinnigkeit**
sweet **süß, lieb**
sympathetic (un-) **sympathisch, (un)verständnisvoll**
talkative **gesprächig**
thoughtful **rücksichtsvoll**
thoughtless **rücksichtslos**
tidy (un-) **(un)ordentlich**
tolerance (in-) **die (In)toleranz**
tolerant (in-) **(in)tolerant**
traditional **traditionell**
trust **das Vertrauen**
unselfish(ness) **selbstlos, die Selbstlosigkeit**

vain **eitel, eingebildet**
vanity **die Eitelkeit(en)**
violent (-ence) **brutal, die Brutalität**
virtuous **tugendhaft**
warm **warm, warmherzig**
well-adjusted **ausgeglichen**
well-behaved **wohlerzogen**
wisdom **die Klugheit**
wise **klug, weise**

7a Relatives

distant relative **der/die entfernte Verwandte** *(adj/n)*
distantly related **entfernt miteinander verwandt**
godchild **das Patenkind(er)**
goddaughter **die Patentochter(¨)**
godfather **der Pate(n)** *(wk)*
godson **der Patensohn(¨e)**
great-aunt **die Großtante(n)**
great grandchild **der Urenkel(-) [-in]**
great-grandfather **der Urgroßvater(¨)**
great-grandmother **die Urgroßmutter(¨)**
great-nephew **der Großneffe(n)** *(wk)*
great-niece **die Großnichte(n)**
great-uncle **der Großonkel(-)**

8b Tools

axe/ax **die Axt(¨e)**
bit **der Bohreinsatz(¨e)**
blade **die Klinge(n)**
bolt **der Bolzen(-)**
bucket **der Eimer(-)**
chisel **der Meißel(-), der Beitel(-)**
crowbar **das Brecheisen** *(no pl)*
drill **der Bohrer(-)**
file **die Feile(n)**
garden glove **der Gartenhandschuh(e)**
garden shears **die Heckenschere(n)**
hammer **der Hammer(¨)**
hedge clippers **die Heckenschere(n)**
hoe **die Hacke(n)**
hose **der Schlauch(¨e)**
ladder **die Leiter(n)**
lawn mower **der Rasenmäher(-)**
mallet **der Holzhammer(¨)**
nail **der Nagel(¨)**

nut die (Schrauben)mutter(n)
paint die Farbe(n), der Lack(e)
paint brush der Pinsel(-)
pickaxe/ax die Spitzhacke(n)
plane der Hobel(-)
pliers die (Kombi)zange(n)
rake die Harke(n)
roller die Walze(n)
    roller *(for paint)* die Rolle(n)
sandpaper das Schmirgelpapier *(no pl)*
saw die Säge(n)
screw die Schraube(n)
screwdriver der Schraubenzieher(-)
shovel die Schaufel(n), die Schippe(n)
spade der Spaten(-)
spanner/wrench *(adjustable)* der
   Schraubenschlüssel(-)
spirit level die Wasserwaage(n)
step-ladder die Stufenleiter(n)
tool das Werkzeug(e)
    gardening tool das (Garten)gerät(e)
toolbox der Werkzeugkasten(-)
trowel die Kelle(n)
varnish der Lack(e)
vice/vise der Schraubstock(-e) ·

9a Shops, stores, & services

antique shop/store der
   Antiquitätenladen(-)
art shop/store die Kunsthandlung
baker's/bakery die Bäckerei(en)
bank die Bank(en)
betting shop/bookmaker's das
   Wettbüro(s)
bookshop/store die Buchhandlung
boutique die Boutique(n)
butcher's die Metzgerei(en), die
   Fleischerei(en)
cakeshop/store die Konditorei(en)
car accessory/spares shop/store der
   Laden für Autozubehör
chemist's/drugstore die Apotheke(n),
   die Drogerie(n)
clothes shop/store das
   Kleidergeschäft(e)
cobbler's/shoemaker der
   Schuhmacher(-), der Sattler(-)

cosmetics shop/store der
   Kosmetikladen(-)
covered market der überdachte
   Markt(-e)
dairy die Molkerei(en)
delicatessen der Delikatessenladen(-)
department store das Warenhaus(-er)
drugstore die Drogerie(n)
dry-cleaners die chemische
   Reinigung(en)
electrical shop/store der Elektroladen(-)
fishmonger's der Fischladen(-)
fishstall der Fischstand(-e)
florist's das Blumengeschäft(e)
furniture shop/store das
   Möbelgeschäft(e)
garden center das Gartencenter(-), die
   Gärtnerei(en)
greengrocer's der Obst- und
   Gemüseladen(-)
grocer's der Lebensmittelladen(-)
hairdresser's der Friseur(salon)
hardware shop/store der
   Eisenwarenladen(-)
health-food shop/store das
   Reformhaus(-er)
hypermarket der Verbrauchermarkt(-e)
indoor market der überdachte Markt
jeweller/jeweler der Juwelier(e)
jeweller's/jewelry store das
   Schmuckwarengeschäft(e)
kiosk der Kiosk(e)
launderette der Waschsalon(s)
lottery kiosk die Lottoannahmestelle
market der Markt(-e)
menswear shop/store das Geschäft für
   Männerbekleidung
music shop/store das Musikgeschäft
newsagent's/newsstand der
   Zeitungshändler/-stand(-e)
newspaper kiosk der Zeitungskiosk(e)
open-air/outdoor market der Markt(-e)
optician's der Optiker(-) [-in]
petshop/pet store die Tierhandlung(en)
pharmacy die Apotheke(n)
photographic shop/store der
   Fotoladen(-)

post-office **die Post** (no pl), **das Postamt(¨-er)**
pottery shop/store **das Töpferwarengeschäft(e)**
shoe repair shop/store **die Schusterei(en)**
shoeshop/store **das Schuhgeschäft(e)**
shop/store **das Geschäft(e), der Laden(¨)**
shopping arcade **die Einkaufspassage(n)**
shopping center/mall **das Einkaufszentrum (-en)**
souvenir shop/store **der Souvenirladen(¨)**
sports shop/store **das Sportgeschäft(e)**
stationer's/stationery store **das Schreibwarengeschäft(e)**
store **das Warenhaus(¨-er)**
superstore **das Kaufhaus(¨-er)**
supermarket **der Supermarkt(¨-e)**
sweetshop/candy store **der Süßwarenladen(¨)**
take-out food shop/store **der Schnellimbiss**
tobacconist's/tobacco store **der Tabakwarenladen(¨)**
toyshop/store **das Spielwarengeschäft(e)**
travel agent's/store **das Reisebüro(s)**
vendor **der Verkäufer(-) [-in]**
vending machine **der Automat(en)**
video-shop/store **der Videoladen(¨)**

9a Currencies

euro **der Euro(-)**
pound sterling **das Pfund(-)**
rouble **der Rubel(-)**
Swiss franc **der Schweizer Franken(-)**
yen **der Yen(s)**

9c Jeweler/Jewelry

bangle **der Armreif(e)**
chain bracelet **das Gliederarmband(¨-er)**
brooch **die Brosche(n)**
carat **das Karat(e)**
chain **die Kette(n)**
charm **das Amulett(e)**
crown **die Krone(n)**
crown jewels **die Kronjuwelen** (pl)
cuff links **die Manschettenknöpfe** (pl)
earring **der Ohrring(e)**
engagement ring **der Verlobungsring(e)**
eternity ring **der Erinnerungsring(e)**
jewel **das Juwel(en), der Edelstein(e)**
jewel box **das Schmuckkästchen(-)**
jewelery/jewelry **der Schmuck** (no pl)
medal **die Medaille(n)**
medallion **das Medaillon(s)**
necklace **die Halskette(n)**
pendant **der Anhänger(-)**
precious stone/gem **der Edelstein(e)**
real **echt**
ring **der Ring(e)**
semi-precious stone **der Halbedelstein(e)**
signet ring **der Siegelring(e)**
tiara **das Diadem(e)**
tie pin **die Krawattennadel(n)**
wedding ring **der Ehering(e)**

9c Precious stones & metals

agate **der Achat(e)**
amber **der Bernstein** (no pl)
amethyst **der Amethyst(e)**
chrome **das Chrom** (no pl)
copper **das Kupfer** (no pl)
coral **die Koralle(n)**
crystal **das Kristall** (no pl)
diamond **der Diamant(en)**
emerald **der Smaragd(e)**
gold **das Gold** (no pl)
gold plate **vergoldet**
ivory **das Elfenbein(e)**
jade **der/die Jade** (no pl)
mother of pearl **das Perlmutt** (no pl)
onyx **der Onyx(e)**

mother of pearl **das Perlmutt** *(no pl)*
onyx **der Onyx(e)**
pearl **die Perle(n)**
pewter **das Zinn** *(no pl)*
platinum **das Platin** *(no pl)*
quartz **der Quarz(e)**
ruby **der Rubin(e)**
sapphire **der Saphir(e)**
silver plate **versilbert**
silver **das Silber** *(no pl)*
topaz **der Topas(e)**
turquoise **der Türkis(e)**

10c Herbs & spices

aniseed **der Anis(e)**
basil **das Basilikum** *(no pl)*
bay leaf **das Lorbeerblatt(-er)**
caraway **der Kümmel** *(no pl)*
chives **der Schnittlauch** *(no pl)*
cinnamon **der Zimt(e)**
clove **die Nelke(n)**
dill **der Dill(e)**
garlic **der Knoblauch** *(no pl)*
ginger **der Ingwer** *(no pl)*
horseradish **der Meerrettich(e), der Kren** *(no pl)*
juniper **der Wacholder** *(no pl)*
marjoram **der Majoran(e)**
mint **die Minze(n)**
mixed herbs **die Kräuter** *(pl)*
nutmeg **die Muskatnuss(-e)**
oregano **der Origano** *(no pl)*
parsley **die Petersilie** *(no pl)*
pepper **der Pfeffer(-)**
rosemary **der Rosmarin** *(no pl)*
saffron **der Safran(e)**
sage **der Salbei** *(no pl)*
tarragon **der Estragon** *(no pl)*
thyme **der Thymian(e)**

10d Cooking utensils

alumin(i)um foil **die Aluminiumfolie(n)**
baking tray **das Kuchenblech(e)**
cake tin **die Springform(en)**
carving knife **das Tranchiermesser(-)**
colander **das Sieb(e)**
food processor **die Küchenmaschine(n)**

fork **die Gabel(n)**
frying pan/fry-pan **die Bratpfanne(n)**
grater **die Reibe(n)**
greaseproof/wax paper **das Pergamentpapier** *(no pl)*
grill **der Grill(s)**
kettle **der Kessel(-)**
knife **das Messer(-)**
lid **der Deckel(-)**
pot **der Topf(-e)**
rolling pin **das Nudelholz(-er)**
saucepan/casserole dish **der Kochtopf(-e)**
scales **die Waage(n)**
sieve **das Sieb(e)**
skewer **der Spieß(e)**
spatula **der Teigschaber(-)**
spoon **der Löffel(-)**
tablespoon(ful) **der Esslöffel (voll)**
teaspoon(ful) **der Teelöffel (voll)**
tenderizer **der Fleischklopfer(-)**
tin/can-opener **der Büchsenöffner(-)**

11c Illnesses & diseases

AIDS **AIDS**
angina **die Angina**
appendicitis **die Blinddarmentzündung(en)**
arthritis **die Arthritis**
asthma **das Asthma**
bronchitis **die Bronchitis**
bubonic plague **die Beulenpest**
cancer **der Krebs**
chickenpox **die Windpocken** *(pl)*
cholera **die Cholera**
colic **die Kolik**
cold **die Erkältung(en), der Schnupfen(-)**
constipation **die Verstopfung(en)**
dermatitis **die Hautentzündung(en)**
diabetes **die Diabetes, die Zuckerkrankheit**
diarrhea **der Durchfall**
diphtheria **die Diphtherie(n)**
eczema **das Ekzem(e), der Hautausschlag(-e)**

epilepsy **die Epilepsie(n)**
fever **das Fieber(-)**
fit **der epileptische Anfall(-̈e)**
flu **die Grippe(n)**
food-poisoning **die Lebensmittelvergiftung(en)**
gall-stone **der Gallenstein(e)**
German measles **die Röteln** *(pl)*
gingivitis **die Zahnfleischentzündung(en)**
gonorrhoea **der Tripper**
haemorrrhoid **die Hämorrhoide(n)**
heart attack **der Herzanfall(-̈e)**
hepatitis **die Hepatitis**
hernia **der Bruch(-̈e)**
HIV-positive **HIV-positiv, HIV-infiziert**
incontinence **die Inkontinenz**
influenza **die Grippe(n)**
jaundice **die Gelbsucht**
leukaemia **die Leukämie**
malaria **die Malaria**
measles **die Masern** *(pl)*
meningitis **die Hirnhautentzündung(en)**
mumps **der Mumps** *(no pl)*
pile **die Hämorrhoide(n)**
pneumonia **die Lungenentzündung(en)**
polio **die Kinderlähmung**
rabies **die Tollwut**
salmonella **die Salmonellen** *(pl)*
scabies **die Krätze**
seasickness **die Seekrankheit(en)**
sickness **die Übelkeit**
smallpox **die Pocken** *(pl)*
stroke **der Schlaganfall(-̈e)**
syphilis **die Syphilis**
temperature **das Fieber**
tetanus **der Tetanus, der Wundstarrkrampf**
thrombosis **die Thrombose(n)**
tonsillitis **die Mandelentzündung(en)**
tuberculosis **die Tuberkulose(n)**
ulcer **das Geschwür(e)**
urinary infection **die Harnwegsinfektion(en)**
venereal disease **die Geschlechtskrankheit(en)**
whooping cough **der Keuchhusten**
yellow fever **das Gelbfieber**

13b Holidays & religious festivals

All Saints (Nov 1) **Allerheiligen**
All Souls (Nov 2) **Allerseelen**
Ascension Day **der Himmelfahrtstag(e)**
Ash Wednesday **der Aschermittwoch(e)**
Assumption Day (Aug 15) **Mariä Himmelfahrt**
Candlemas **Mariä Lichtmess**
Christmas **Weihnachten**
Christmas Day **der erste Weihnachtstag**
Christmas Eve **der Heiligabend(e)**
Corpus Christi **Fronleichnam**
Easter **das Osterfest(e)**
Easter Monday **der Ostermontag(e)**
Easter Sunday **der Ostersonntag(e)**
Good Friday **der Karfreitag(e)**
Labour/Labor Day **der Tag der Arbeit**
Lent **die Fastenzeit(en)**
New Year's Day **der Neujahrstag(e)**
New Year's Eve **Silvester**
Palm Sunday **der Palmsonntag(e)**
Passover **das Passah**
Ramadan **der Ramadan**
Sabbath **der Sabbat**
Shrove Tuesday **der Faschingsdienstag(e)**
Whitsun **das Pfingstfest(e)**

14b Jobs & professions

The arts

actor/actress **der Schauspieler(-) [-in]**
announcer **der Ansager(-) [-in]**
architect **der Architekt(en)** *(wk)* **[-in]**
artist **der Künstler(-) [-in]**
book-seller **der Buchhändler(-) [-in]**
cameraman **der Kameramann(-̈er) [-frau]**
editor **der Herausgeber(-) [-in]**
film/movie director **der Filmdirektor(en) (wk) [-in]**
film/movie star **der Filmstar(s)**

journalist der Journalist(en) *(wk)* [-in]
musician der Musiker(-) [-in]
painter *(artist)* der Maler(-) [-in]
photographer der Photograph(en) [-in]
poet der Dichter(-) [-in]
printer der Drucker(-) [-in]
producer *(theatre/theater)* der
    Regisseur(e) [-in]
publisher der Verleger(-) [-in]
reporter der Reporter(-) [-in]
sculptor der Bildhauer(-) [-in]
singer der Sänger(-) [-in]
TV announcer der Fernsehansager(-)
    [-in]
writer der Schriftsteller(-) [-in]

Education & research

headteacher/principal der Direktor(en)
    (wk) [-in], der Schulleiter(-) [-in]
lecturer der Dozent(en) *(wk)* [-in]
primary teacher der
    Grundschullehrer(-) [-in]
researcher der Forscher(-) [-in]
scientist der Wissenschaftler(-) [-in]
secondary teacher der Gymnasial/
    Realschullehrer(-) [-in]
student der Schüler(-), der
    Student(en) *(wk)* [-in]
technician der Techniker(-) [-in]

Food & retail

baker der Bäcker(-) [-in]
brewer der Brauer(-)
butcher der Fleischer(-) [-in], der
    Metzger(-) [-in], der Schlachter
    (-)[-in]
buyer der Käufer(-) [-in]
caterer *(supplying meals)* der
    Lieferant(en) *(wk)*
chemist/druggist der Apotheker(-) [-in],
    der Drogist(en) *(wk)* [-in]
cook der Koch(¨e) [¨in]
farmer der Bauer(n), die Bäuerin(nen)
fisherman der Fischer(-)
fishmonger der Fischhändler(-) [-in]
florist der Florist(en) *(wk)* [-in]
greengrocer der Obst- und

Gemüsehändler(-) [-in]
grocer der Lebensmittelhändler(-)
    [-in]
jeweller/jeweler der Juwelier(e)
pharmacist der Apotheker(-)[-in]
representative der Vertreter(-) [-in]
shop assistant der Verkäufer(-) [-in]
shopkeeper/storekeeper der
    Ladenbesitzer(-) [-in]
tobacconist der Tabakhändler(-) [-in]
waiter der Kellner(-) [-in]
wine-grower der Weinbauer(n)
    [-bäuerin(nen)]

Government service

civil-servant der Beamte *(adj/n)*, die
    Beamtin(nen)
clerk der Angestellte(n) *(adj/n)*
customs officer der Zollbeamte(n)
    (adj/n)
fireman der Feuerwehrmann(¨er)
judge der Richter(-) [-in]
member of Parliament/senator der/die
    Abgeordnete *(adj/n)*, der
    Senator(en) [-in]
minister der Minister(-) [-in]
officer der Offizier(e)
policeman/woman der Polizist(en) *(wk)*
    [-in]
politician der Politiker(-) [-in]
sailor der Matrose(n) *(wk)*
secret agent der Geheimagent(en)
    (wk) [-in]
serviceman der Soldat(en) *(wk)*
soldier der Soldat(en) *(wk)*

Health care

dentist der Zahnarzt(¨e) [¨in]
doctor (Dr) der Arzt(¨e) [¨in]
midwife die Hebamme(n)
nurse die Krankenschwester(n)
optician der Optiker(-) [-in]
psychiatrist der Psychiater(-) [-in]
psychologist der Psychologe(n) *(wk)*
    [-in]
surgeon der Chirurg(en) *(wk)* [-in]
vet der Tierarzt(¨e) [¨in]

Manufacturing & construction

bricklayer **der Maurer(-)**
builder **der Bauunternehmer(-)**
carpenter **der Zimmermann**
  (-leute)
engineer **der Ingenieur(e) [-in]**
foreman **der Vorarbeiter(-) [-in]**
glazier **der Glaser(-)**
industrialist **der/die Industrielle** *(adj/n)*
laborer **der Arbeiter(-) [-in]**
manufacturer **der Hersteller(-) [-in]**
mechanic **der Mechaniker(-) [-in]**
metalworker **der Metallarbeiter(-) [-in]**
miner **der Bergarbeiter(-) [-in]**
plasterer **der Gipser(-) [-in]**
stonemason **der Steinmetz(en)** *(wk)*

Services

accountant **der Buchhalter(-) [-in]**
actuary/sales agent **der Vertreter(-)**
  [-in]
agent **der Agent(en)** *(wk)* **[-in]**
bank manager **der Bankmanager(-)**
  [-in]
businessman **der Geschäftsmann**
  (-leute)
businesswoman **die Geschäftsfrau(en)**
careers adviser **der Berufsberater(-)**
  [-in]
caretaker **der Hausmeister(-) [-in]**
cleaner **die Putzfrau(en)**
computer programmer **der**
  Computerprogrammierer(-) [-in]
counsellor **der Berater(-) [-in]**
drautsman/draftsman **der technische**
  Zeichner(-) [-in]
dustman/garbageman **der**
  Müllmann(ẍer/-leute)
electrician **der Elektriker(-) [-in]**
estate/real estate agent **der**
  Grundstücksmakler(-) [-in]
furniture remover **der Spediteur(e)**
gardener **der Gärtner(-) [-in]**
gasman **der Gasmann(ẍer)**
guide **der (Stadt-/Reise)führer(-) [-in]**
hairdresser **der Friseur(e) [-euse]**
insurance agent/broker **der**

Versicherungsvertreter(-) [-in]
interpreter **der Dolmetscher(-) [-in]**
lawyer **der Anwalt(ẍe) [ẍin]**
librarian **der Bibliothekar(e) [-in]**
office worker **der Büroarbeiter(-) [-in]**
painter & decorator **der Anstreicher(-)**
  [-in]
plumber **der Klempner(-) [-in]**
postman **der Briefträger(-) [-in]**
priest **der Priester(-) [-in]**
receptionist **der Empfangschef(s)**
  [-dame(n)]
social worker **der Sozialarbeiter(-) [-in]**
solicitor **der Rechtsanwalt(ẍe) [ẍin]**
stockbroker **der Börsenmakler(-) [-in]**
surveyor **der Landvermesser(-) [-in]**
tax inspector **der Steuerbeamte** *(adj/n)*
  [-beamtin]
trade-unionist **der Gewerkschafter(-)**
  [-in]
translator **der Übersetzer(-) [-in]**
travel agent **der Reisebürokaufmann**
  (-kaufleute)
typist **die Schreibkraft(ẍe)**
undertaker **der Leichenbestatter(-)**
  [-in]

Transport

bus driver **der Busfahrer(-) [-in]**
driver **der Fahrer(-) [-in]**
driving instructor **der Fahrlehrer(-) [-in]**
flight attendant **der Flugbegleiter(-) [-in]**
lorry/truck driver **der LKW-Fahrer(-)**
  [-in]
pilot **der Pilot(en)** *(wk)* **[-in]**
taxi driver **der Taxifahrer(-) [-in]**
ticket inspector **der**
  Fahrkartenkontrolleur(e)

14b Places of work

blast furnace **der Hochofen(ẍ)**
branch office **die Zweigstelle(n)**
brewery **die Brauerei(en)**
business park **der Industriepark(s)**
construction site **die Baustelle(n)**
distillery **die Schnapsbrennerei(en)**
factory **die Fabrik(en)**

farm **der Bauernhof(-̈e)**
foundry **die Gießerei(en)**
head office **die Hauptgeschäftsstelle(n)**
hospital **das Krankenhaus(-̈er)**
mill **die Mühle(n)**
　paper mill **die Papierfabrik(en)**
　rolling mill **das Walzwerk(e)**
　sawmill **die Sägemühle(n)**
　spinning mill **die Spinnerei(en)**
　steel mill **das Stahlwerk(e)**
　weaving mill **die Weberei(en)**
mine **das Bergwerk(e)**
office **das Büro(s)**
plant **die Fabrik(en)**
shop/store **der Laden(-̈e), das Kaufhaus(-̈er)**
steelworks/steel plant **das Stahlwerk(e)**
theme park **der Freizeitpark(s)**
vineyard/winery **der Weinberg(e)**
warehouse **das Lagerhaus(-̈er)**
workshop **die Werkstatt(-̈en), die Werkstätte(n)**

14b Company personnel & departments

accounts department **die Buchhaltung(en)**
apprentice **der Lehrling(e)**
assistant **der Assistent(en)** *(wk)* **[-in]**
associate **der Kollege(n)** *(wk)*, **die Kollegin(nen)**
board of directors **der Vorstand(-̈e)**
boss **der Chef(s) [-in]**
colleague **der Kollege(n)** *(wk)*
department **die Abteilung(en)**
director **der Direktor(en) [-in]**
division **die Abteilung(en)**
employee **der/die Angestellte** *(adj/n)*
employer **der Arbeitgeber(-) [-in]**
executive **der Manager(-) [-in]**
foreman **der Vorarbeiter(-) [-in]**
labourer/laborer **der Arbeiter(-) [-in]**
line manager **der/die Vorgesetzte** *(adj/n)*
management **das Management(s)**
manager/ess **der Manager(-) [-in]**

managing director/CEO **der Geschäftsführer(-) [-in]**
marketing department **die Marketingabteilung(en)**
personal assistant **der persönliche Assistent(en)** *(wk)* **[-in]**
president **der Präsident(en)** *(wk)*
production department **die Produktionsabteilung(en)**
sales department **die Verkaufsabteilung(en)**
secretary **der Sekretär(e) [-in]**
specialist **der Spezialist(en)** *(wk)* **[-in]**
staff/personnel **das Personal**
team **das Team(s)**
trainee **der Praktikant(en)** *(wk)* **[-in]**
vice president **der Vizepräsident(en)** *(wk)* **[-in]**

15e Letter writing formulae

Dear Mr. & Mrs. ... **Sehr geehrter Herr ..., sehr geehrte Frau ...**
Dear Hans **Lieber Hans**
Dear Anja **Liebe Anja**
Dear Anja and Hans **Liebe Anja, lieber Hans**
Dear Sir or Madam **Sehr geehrte Damen und Herren**
Dear colleague **Lieber Kollege, liebe Kollegin**
My dear friends **Liebe Freunde**
I am pleased **ich bin erfreut**
I enclose **ich füge bei***
All the best **Alles Gute**
Greetings from **Grüße aus/von**
Love from **Viele liebe Grüße von** +dat, **alles Liebe**
With best wishes **mit den besten Wünschen**
With kind regards **mit freundlichen Grüßen**
With greetings from **Herzliche Grüße von deinem ...,**

Yours sincerely **mit freundlichen Grüßen**

15f Computer hardware

adaptor **der Adapter(-)**
battery **die Batterie(n)**
brightness **die Helligkeit**
CD-ROM **die CD-ROM**
central processing unit **das CPU**
charger **das Ladegerät(e)**
chip **der Chip(s)**
compatibility **die Kompatibilität**
compatible **kompatibel**
computer **der Computer(-)**
computer system **das Computersystem(e)**
cursor **der Cursor(s)**
disc/disk drive **das Laufwerk(e)**
disc/disk **die Festplatte(n)**
diskette **die Diskette(n)**
display **die Anzeige(n)**
dot matrix **der Nadeldrucker(-)**
drive **das Laufwerk(e)**
floppy disc/disk **die Diskette(n)**
floppy drive **das Diskettenlaufwerk(e)**
function key **die Funktionstaste(n)**
hard copy **der Ausdruck(⁻e)**
hard disc/disk **die Festplatte(n)**
hardware **die Hardware**
IBM-compatible **IBM-kompatibel**
incompatible **inkompatibel**
ink cartridge **die Patrone(n)**
inkjet **der Tintenstrahldrucker(-)**
input **die Eingabe(n)**
integrated circuit **die integrierte Schaltung(en)**
interface **die Schnittstelle(n)**
keyboard **die Tastatur(en)**
laptop **der Laptop(s)**
laser printer **der Laserdrucker(-)**
liquid crystal display **die Flüssigkristallanzeige(n)**
low/high density **niedrige/hohe Dichte(n)**
mainframe computer **der Großrechner(-)**
microprocessor **der Mikroprozessor(en)** *(wk)*

mini computer **der Minicomputer(-)**
memory **der Arbeitsspeicher(-), die Speicherkapazität(en)**
modem **das Modem(s)**
mouse **die Maus(⁻e)**
network **das Netz(werk)(e)**
note book **das Notebook(s)**
on line **online**
package **das Paket(e)**
personal computer/PC **der Personalcomputer(-), der PC(s)**
plug-in drive **das externe Diskettenlaufwerk(e)**
port **der Anschluss(⁻e), die Schnittstelle(n)**
printer **der Drucker(-)**
processor **der Prozessor(en), der Rechner(-)**
RAM **das RAM, der Arbeitsspeicher(-)**
screen **der Bildschirm(e)**
server **der Server(-)**
socket/port **der Anschluss(⁻e)**
storage **die Speicherung(en)**
terminal **das Terminal(s)**
toner **der Toner(-)**
VDU **das Bildschirmgerät(e)**
viewdata system **der Bildschirmtext**
visual display unit **das Datensichtgerät(e)**

15f Computer software

algebraic **algebraisch**
algorithm **der Algorithmus (-en)**

227

application die Anwendung(en)
bug der Programmierfehler(-)
byte das Byte(s)
coding das Kodieren
command der Befehl(e)
computer aided design (CAD) das rechnergestützte Konstruieren
computer aided learning (CAL) das computergestützte Lernen
computer language die Computersprache(n)
copy die Kopie(n)
data die Daten *(pl)*
data capture das Datenerfassen
databank die Datenbank(en)
data processing die Datenverarbeitung(en)
database das Datenbankprogramm(e)
default option der Default(s), die Voreinstellung(en)
directory das Verzeichnis(se)
double clicking das Doppelklicken
escape die Escapetaste
field das Feld(er)
file die Datei(en)
flow chart das Flussdiagramm(e)
format das Format(e)
function die Funktion(en)
grahical graphisch, Grafik-
graphical application das Grafikprogamm(e)
graphics die Graphiken *(pl)*
help die Hilfe(n)
help menu das Hilfsprogramm(e)
language die Sprache(n)
logic circuit die logische Schaltung(en)
macro der Makro(s)
memory der Arbeitsspeicher(-)
menu das Menü(s)
operating system das Betriebssystem(e)
output die Ausgabe(n)
password das Passwort(¨-er)
program(me) das Programm(e)
programmable programmierbar
programmer der Programmierer(-) [-in]

programming das Programmieren
pull-down menu das Hilfefenster(-)
reference archive das Nachschlagearchiv(e)
return die Eingabetaste(n)
software die Software
software package das Softwarepaket(e)
space bar die Leertaste(n)
spreadsheet das Spreadsheet(s), das Tabellenkalkulationsprogramm(e)
statistics package das Statistikpaket(e)
virus der Virus (-en)

16a Hobbies

angling das Angeln
birdwatching das Vögelbeobachten
archeology die Archäologie
ballroom dancing die Gesellschaftstänze *(pl)*
carpentry das Tischlern
chess das Schach
collecting antiques Antiquitäten sammeln
collecting stamps Briefmarken sammeln
dancing das Tanzen
DIY/do it yourself das Basteln
fishing das Fischen, das Angeln
gardening die Gartenarbeit
gambling das Glücksspiel(e)
going to the cinema/movies ins Kino gehen
listening to music Musik hören
knitting das Stricken
photography das Fotografieren
reading das Lesen
sewing das Nähen
spinning das Spinnen
walking das Spazierengehen, das Wandern
watching television das Fernsehen

16c Photography

automatic automatisch
camera die Kamera(s)

camera case **die Fototasche(n)**
I develop **ich entwickle**
developing/processing **die Entwicklung**
I enlarge **ich vergrößere**
exposure counter **der Zähler(-)**
film **der Film(e)**
　　black and white film **der Schwarzweißfilm(e)**
　　colour/color film **der Farbfilm(e)**
filter **das/der Filter(-)**
flash **der Blitz(e)**
flash attachment **das Blitzlicht(er)**
home movie **das Heimkino(s)**
I focus the camera **ich stelle ein***
　　in focus **scharf (eingestellt)**
　　out of focus **unscharf**
it is jammed **es klemmt**
lens **das Objektiv(e)**
　　telephoto lens **das Teleobjektiv(e)**
　　wide-angle lens **das Weitwinkelobjektiv(e)**
lens cap **die Schutzkappe(n)**
light **das Licht, die Beleuchtung**
　　daylight **das Tageslicht**
light meter **der Belichtungsmesser(-)**
movie camera **die Filmkamera(s)**
negative **das Negativ(e)**
over-exposed **überbelichtet**
over-exposure **die Überbelichtung**
picture **das Bild(er)**
photogenic **fotogen**
photo(graph) **das Foto(s), die Fotografie(n)**
　　holiday/vacation photo **die Aufnahme(n)**
　　passport photo **das Passfoto(s)**
photograph album **das Fotoalbum(s/-en)**
shutter **der Verschluss(¨e)**
slide **das Dia(s), das Diapositiv(e)**
snap **der Schnappschuss(¨e)**
I take (photos) **ich nehme auf***
video camera **die Videokamera(s)**
video cassette **die Videokassette(n)**
I wind on **ich spule weiter***

17a Artistic styles & periods

Art Nouveau **der Jugendstil**
Baroque **der Barock**
baroque **barock**
Bauhaus **das Bauhaus**
Byzantine **byzantinisch**
Celtic **keltisch**
classical **klassisch**
classical artist/writer **der Klassiker(-)**
Classical period **die Klassik**
Cubism **der Kubismus**
Dada **der Dadaismus**
Expressionism **der Expressionismus**
expressionist **der Expressionist(en)** *(wk)*
expressionistic **expressionistisch**
Flemish **flämisch**
Germanic **germanisch**
Gothic art **die Gotik**
Gothic **gotisch**
Greek **griechisch**
Impressionism **der Impressionismus**
Impressionist **der Impressionist(en)** *(wk)*
Impressionist **impressionistisch**
Naturalism **der Naturalismus**
naturalistic **naturalistisch**
Neo-classical **der Klassizismus**
Neo-gothic **die Neugotik**
New Objectivity **die Neue Sachlichkeit**
Norman **normannisch**
pop art **die Pop-Art**
Realism **der Realismus**
realist **der Realist(en)** *(wk)*
realistic **realistisch**
Renaissance **die Renaissance**
Rococo **das Rokoko**
Roman **römisch**
Romanesque **romanisch**
Romantic age **die Romantik**
Romantic **der Romantiker(-)**
romantic **romantisch**
Storm and Stress **der Sturm und Drang**
Surrealism **der Surrealismus**
Surrealist **der Surrealist(en)** *(wk)*
surrealistic **surrealistisch**
Venetian **venezianisch**

SUBJECT INDEX

17b Architectural features

aisle **das Seitenschiff(e)**
arch **der Bogen(-)**
bas relief **das Basrelief(s)**
battlement **die Zinnen** *(pl)*
buttress **der Strebepfeiler**
capital **das Kapitell(e)**
choir **der Chor(e/-e)**
colonnade **der Säulengang(-e)**
column **die Säule(n)**
  corinthian **korinthisch**
  doric **dorisch**
  ionic **ionisch**
crossing **die Vierung(en)**
crypt **die Krypta (-en)**
cupola **die Kuppel(n)**
drawbridge **die Zugbrücke(n)**
eave **der Dachvorsprung(-e)**
façade **die Fassade(n)**
gable **der Giebel(-)**
gargoyle **der Wasserspeier(-)**
gothic arch **der Spitzbogen(-)**
half-timbered **das Holzfachwerk**
half-timbered house **das Fachwerkhaus(-er)**
headstone **der Grabstein(e)**
nave **das Schiff(e)**
overhanging **vorstehend**
pagoda **die Pagode(n)**
pilaster **der Halbpfeiler(-)**
porch **die Vorhalle(n)**
portico **der Portikus (-en)**
relief **das Relief(s)**
roof **das Dach(-er)**
sacristy **die Sakristei(en)**
spire/steeple **der Kirchturm(-e)**
stucco **der Stuck**
transept **das Querschiff(e)**
triumphal arch **der Triumphbogen(-)**
vault **das Gewölbe(-)**
vaulted **gewölbt**

17c Publishing

abridged version **die gekürzte Ausgabe(n)**
acknowledgments to **mein/unser Dank gilt** +dat
appendix **der Anhang(-e)**
author **der Autor(en) [-in], der Verfasser(-) [-in]**
best seller **der Bestseller(-)**
bibliography **die Bibliographie(n)**
book fair **die Buchmesse(n)**
catalogue/catalog **der Katalog(e)**
chapter **das Kapitel(-)**
contents **der Inhalt(e)**
  table of contents **das Inhaltsverzeichnis(se)**
contract **der Vertrag(-e)**
copy **das Exemplar(e)**
copyright **das Copyright**
cover *(of book)* **der Buchumschlag(-e)**
deadline **der Redaktionsschluss(-e)**
dedicated to **gewidmet** + dat.
edition **die Ausgabe(n)**
  first edition **die Erstausgabe(n)**
  latest edition **die neueste Ausgabe**
editor **der Redakteur(e), der Herausgeber(-)**
  desk editor **der Lektor(en) [-in]**
  general editor **der Chefredakteur(e) [-in]**
footnotes **die Fußnote(n)**
illustrations **die Illustration(en)**
manuscript **das Manuskript(e)**
out of print **vergriffen**
paperback **das Taschenbuch(-er)**
preface **das Vorwort(e)**
I print **ich drucke**
proofreading **das Korrekturlesen**
publication date **das Erscheinungsdatum (-en)**
I publish **ich bringe heraus*, ich veröffentliche**
just published **neu erschienen**
publisher **der Verleger(-)**
publishing **das Verlagswesen(-)**
publishing house **das Verlagshaus(-er)**
translation **die Übersetzung(en), die Übertragung(en)**
version **die Fassung(en)**
with a forward by **mit einem Vorwort von** +dat

17d Musicians & instruments

accompanist **der Begleiter(-) [-in]**
accordion **das Akkordeon(s)**
alto **der Alt(e), die Altstimme(n)**
bagpipe **der Dudelsack(-e)**
band leader **der Kapellmeister(-)**
baritone **der Bariton**
bass (singer) **der Bassist(en)**
bassoon **das Fagott(e)**
bells **die Glocke(n)**
castanets **die Kastagnette(n)**
cellist **der Cellist(en) [-in]**
cello **das Cello(s/-i)**
cembalo **das Cembalo(s)**
chorister **der Chorknabe(n)** *(wk)*
clarinet **die Klarinette(n)**
classical guitar **die klassische Gitarre(n)**
clavicord **das Klavichord(e)**
conductor **der Dirigent(en)** *(wk)* **[-in]**
contralto **der Alt(e), die Altstimme(n)**
cymbal **das Becken(-)**
double bass **der Kontrabass(-e)**
drum **das Schlagzeug(e)**
flautist **der Flötist(en)** *(wk)* **[-in]**
flute **die Querflöte(n)**
French horn **das Waldhorn(-er)**
grand piano **der Flügel(-)**
guitar **die Gitarre(n)** *(wk)* **[-in]**
guitarist **der Gitarrist(en)**
harmonium **das Harmonium (-ien)**
harp **die Harfe(n)**
harpist **der Harfenspieler(-) [-in]**
harpsichord **das Cembalo(s)**
horn **das Horn(-er)**
hurdy-gurdy **der Leierkasten(-)**
jews' harp **die Maultrommel(n)**
lyre **die Leier(n)**
mandolin **die Mandoline(n)**
mezzo-soprano **der Mezzosopran(e)**
mouth-organ **die Mundharmonika(s)**
oboe **die Oboe(n)**
orchestra leader **der Konzertmeister(-) [-in]**
orchestra player **das Orchestermitglied(er)**
organ **die Orgel(n)**

organist **der Organist(en) [-in]**
percussion **das Schlagzeug** *(no pl)*
percussionist **der Schlagzeuger(-) [-in]**
pianist *(professional)* **der Pianist(en) [-in]**
piano **das Klavier(e)**
pipe **die Flöte(n)**
recorder **die Blockflöte(n)**
saxophone **das Saxophon(e)**
soprano **der Sopran(e)**
spinet **das Spinett(e)**
squeeze-box **die Ziehharmonika(s)**
street musician(s) **der Straßenmusikant(en)** *(wk)* **[-in]**
synthesizer **der Synthesizer(-)**
tenor **der Tenor(-e)**
timpani **die Timpani** *(pl)*, **die Kesselpauken**
triangle **der/das Triangel(-)**
trombone **die Posaune(n)**
trumpet **die Trompete(n)**
tuba **die Tuba(s)**
viol **die Viola (-en)**
viola **die Bratsche(n)**
viola player **der Bratschenspieler(-) [-in]**
violin **die Violine(n)**
violinist **der Violinist(en)** *(wk)* **[-in]**
violoncello **das Violoncello (-i)**
vocalist **der Sänger(-) [-in]**
xylophone **das Xylophon(e)**

17d Musical forms

aria **die Arie(n)**
ballad **die Ballade(n)**
cantata **die Kantate(n)**
chamber music **die Kammermusik** *(no pl)*
choral music **die Chormusik** *(no pl)*
chorale **der Choral(-e)**
concerto **das Konzert(e), das Concerto (-i)**
    piano concerto **das Klavierkonzert(e)**
duet **das Duett(e)**
fugue **die Fuge(n)**
madrigal **das Madrigal(e)**

march **die Marschmusik, der Marsch(-̈e)**

music drama **das Musikdrama (-en)**

musical *(comedy)* **das Musical(s)**

nocturne **das Nocturne(s)**

octet **das Oktett(e)**

opera **die Oper(n)**

operetta **die Operette(n)**

oratorio **das Oratorium (-ia/-ien)**

overture **die Ouvertüre(n)**

prelude **das Präludium (-ia/-ien)**

quartet **das Quartett(e)**

quintet **das Quintett(e)**

recitative **das Rezitativ(e)**

requiem Mass **die Totenmesse(n)**

rondo **das Rondo(s)**

sacred music **die geistliche Musik**

septet **das Septett(e)**

serenade **die Serenade(n)**

sextet **das Sextett(e)**

sonata **die Sonate(n)**

song-cycle **der Liederzyklus (-en)**

string quartet **das Streichquartett(e)**

suite **die Suite(n)**

symphonietta **die Sinfonietta (-en)**

symphony **die Symphonie(n)**

trio **das Trio(s)**

    piano trio **das Klaviertrio(s)**

17d Musical terms

accompaniment **die Begleitung(en)**

arpeggio **das Arpeggio(s)**

bar **der Takt(e)**

beat **der Schlag(-̈e)**

bow **der Bogen(-̈)**

bowing **die Bogenführung**

cadence **die Kadenz(en)**

chord **der Akkord(e)**

clef **der Notenschlüssel(-)**

    bass **der F-Schlüssel**

    treble **der Violinschlüssel**

conductor **der Dirigent(en)** *(wk)* **[-in]**

I conduct **ich dirigiere**

discord **die Disharmonie(n)**

first violin **die erste Geige(n)**

harmony **die Harmonie(n)**

improvisation **die Improvisation(en)**

key **der Notenschlüssel(-), die Tonart(en)**

    major **das Dur** *(no pl)*

    minor **das Moll** *(no pl)*

note **der Ton(-̈e), die Note(n)**

    breve **die ganze Note(n)**

    minim/half note **die Halbe(n)**

    crotchet/quarter note **das Viertel(-)**

    quaver/eighth note **das Achtel(-)**

    semibreve **die ganze Taktnote(n)**

    semiquaver/sixteenth note **das Sechzehntel(-)**

    semitone **der Halbton(-̈e)**

    tone **der Ton(-̈e)**

mute **der Dämpfer(-)**

reed **das Rohrblattinstrument(e)**

scale **die Tonleiter(n)**

score **die Partitur(en)**

sheet *(of music)* **das Notenblatt(-̈er)**

triplet **die Triole(n)**

Notes & keys

C, C sharp, C flat **das C, Cis, Ces**

D, D sharp, D flat **das D, Dis, Des**

E, E sharp, E flat **das E, Eis, Es**

F, F sharp, F flat **das F, Fis, Fes**

G, G sharp, G flat **das G, Gis, Ges**

A, A sharp, A flat **das A, Ais, As**

B, B sharp **das H, His**

B flat **B**

B-minor **H-Moll**

B flat minor **B-Moll**

C double sharp, etc. **Cisis, usw.**

C double flat, etc. **Ceses, usw.**

B double flat, etc. **Bes, usw.**

flat sign **das B**

sharp sign **das Kreuz(e)**

natural sign **das Auflösungszeichen(-)**

17e Film/Movie genres

adventure **der Abenteuerfilm(e)**

animation **der Trickfilm(e)**

black and white **schwarz-weiß**

black comedy **der schwarze (Galgen)humor**

B-movie **der B-Film(e)**

cartoons **der Trickfilm(e)**

comedy die Komödie(n)
documentary der Dokumentarfilm(e)
feature film/movie der Spielfilm(e)
horror der Horrorfilm(e)
low-budget der Film mit kleinem
  Budget
sci-fi **Science-Fiction**
short film/movie der Kurzfilm(e)
silent film/movie der Stummfilm(e)
tear-jerker der Schmachtfetzen(-)
thriller der Thriller(-), der Krimi(s)
video-clip der Videoclip(s)
war film/movie der Kriegsfilm(e)
western der Western(-)

19c Parts of the car

alternator die Lichtmaschine(n)
automatic gear die Getriebeautomatik
back wheel das Hinterrad(-er)
battery die Batterie(n)
bodywork die Karosserie(n)
bonnet/hood die Motorhaube(n)
boot/trunk der Kofferraum(-e)
brake die Bremse(n)
bumper die Stoßstange(n)
carburettor der Vergaser(-)
catalytic converter der Katalysator(-)
choke der Choke(s)
clutch die Kupplung(en)
dashboard das Armaturenbrett(er)
door die Tür(en)
  front door die Vordertür(en)
  passenger door die
    Beifahrertür(en)
engine/motor der Motor(en)
exhaust der Auspuff
front seat der Vordersitz(e)
front wheel das Vorderrad(-er)
gearbox das Getriebe(-)
headlight der Scheinwerfer(-)
horn die Hupe(n)
hood die Haube(n)
indicator der Blinker(-)
license plate das Nummernschild(er)
lights die Beleuchtung(en)
passenger seat der Beifahrersitz(e)
pedal das Pedal(e)

accelerator das Gaspedal(e)
brake das Bremspedal(e)
clutch das Kupplungspedal(e)
plug die Zündkerze(n)
rearview mirror der Rückspiegel(-)
registration number das amtliche
  Kennzeichen(-)
roof das Dach(-er)
roof rack der Dachgepäckträger(-)
safety belt der Sicherheitsgurt(e)
spare **Ersatz-**
  spare part das Ersatzteil(e)
  spare wheel das Ersatzrad(-er)
speedometer der Tachometer(-)
starter der Anlasser(-)
steering wheel das Steuer(rad)(-er)
tank der Tank(s)
tire der Reifen(-)
  back tire der Hinterreifen(-)
  front tire der Vorderreifen(-)
  spare tire der Ersatzreifen(-)
tire pressure der Reifendruck(-e)
wheel das Rad(-er)
windscreen/windshield die
  Windschutzscheibe(n)
windscreen/windshield wiper der
  Scheibenwischer(-)

19c Road signs

Danger! **Gefahr!, Vorsicht!**
Diversion/Detour **Umleitung**
End of diversion **Ende der Umleitung**
Entry **Einfahrt**
Exit **Ausfahrt**
Expressway entrance die
  Autobahnauffahrt(en)
Expressway junction das
  Autobahnkreuz
Free parking **Parken gebührenfrei**
Keep clear **Halteverbot, Ausfahrt
  freihalten**

Maximum speed die
  Höchstgeschwindigkeit(en)
Men at work!/Road Construction
  Achtung, Baustelle!
No entry **Kein Zugang, Keine Zufahrt**

No parking **Parken verboten, Parkverbot**
No passing **Überholverbot**
One way **Einbahnstraße**
Pedestrians crossing **der Fußgängerübergang**
Pedestrian zone **die Fußgängerzone**
Residents only **Anlieger frei**
Road closed **Straße gesperrt**
Roadworks **Straßenbau**
Stop **Halt!, Stop!**
Toll **gebührenpflichtige Straße**

20a Tourist sights

abbey **die Abtei(en)**
amusement park **der Vergnügungspark(s)**
amphitheater **das Amphitheater(-)**
aquarium **das Aquarium (-ien)**
art gallery **die Kunstgalerie(n)**
battle field **das Schlachtfeld(er)**
battlements **die Zinnen** *(pl)*
boulevard **der Boulevard(s)**
casino **das (Spiel)kasino(s)**
castle **das Schloss (⁻er)**
catacombs **die Katakomben** *(pl)*
cathedral **die Kathedrale(n), der Dom(e)**
cave **die Höhle(n)**
cemetery **der Friedhof(⁻e)**
circus **der Zirkus(se)**
city **der Stadt(⁻e)**
city wall **die Stadtmauer(n)**
chapel **die Kapelle(n)**
church **die Kirche(n)**
concert hall **die Konzerthalle(n)**
convent **das Kloster(⁻)**
exhibition **die Ausstellung(en)**
fortress **die Festung(en)**
fountain **der (Spring)brunnen(-)**
gardens **der Botanische Garten(⁻)**
harbor **der Hafen(⁻)**
library **die Bibliothek(en)**
mansion **das Herrenhaus(⁻er)**
market **der Markt(⁻e)**
monastery **das Kloster(⁻)**
monument **das Denkmal(⁻er)**

museum **das Museum (Museen)**
opera house **das Opernhaus(⁻er)**
palace **der Palast(⁻e), das Schloss (⁻er)**
parliament building **das Parlamentsgebäude(-)**
pier **die Landungsbrücke(n)**
planetarium **das Planetarium (-ien)**
ruin **die Ruine(n)**
shopping area **das Geschäftsviertel(-)**
square **der Platz(⁻e)**
stadium **das Stadion (-ien)**
statue **die Statue(n)**
temple **der Tempel(-)**
theater **das Theater(-)**
tomb **das Grab(⁻er)**
tower **der Turm(⁻e)**
town centre/downtown **die Stadtmitte(n)**
town hall **das Rathaus(⁻er)**
university **die Universität(en)**
wall **die Mauer(-)**
zoo **der Zoo(s)**

20a On the beach

bathing hut/cabana **die Badekabine(n)**
beach **der Strand(⁻e)**
beach ball **der Wasserball(⁻e)**
bucket and spade/pail and shovel **der Eimer(-) und die Schaufel(-)**
deck-chair **der Liegestuhl(⁻e)**
I dive **ich springe, ich tauche**
diver **der Taucher(-) [-in]**
sand **der Sand** *(no pl)*
  grain of sand **das Sandkorn(⁻er)**
sandcastle **die Sandburg(en)**
sandy beach **der Sandstrand(⁻e)**
scuba diving **das Sporttauchen**
sea **das Meer(e)**
sea shore **der Strand(⁻e)**
snorkel **das Schnorchel(-)**
I go snorkelling **ich gehe schnorcheln**
suntan lotion **das Sonnenöl(e)**
sunshade **der Sonnenschirm(e)**
I surf **ich surfe**
surfboard **das Surfbrett(er)**
surfboarder **der Surfer(-) [-in], der Wellenreiter(-) [-in]**

surfing **das Surfen, das Surfing**
I swim **ich schwimme**
water skiing **das Wasserskilaufen**
windbreak **der Windschutz** *(no pl)*
windsurfing/sailboarding **das Windsurfen**
I go windsurfing **ich gehe windsurfen**

20a Countries/Regions –adjectives–inhabitants

All countries are neuter unless otherwise shown. Where an article is shown, it should always be used with the name of the country.

The adjective is normally used as a neuter noun to form the language, e.g. **Englisch** (sometimes **das Englische**). When used as an adjective it always starts with a lower case letter, e,g, **englisch**.

The inhabitants are shown in the masculine singular. They fall into the following groups:
– those ending in **-r** have no plural ending, and form the feminine by adding **-in(nen)**;
– those ending in **-e** are weak masculine nouns with an **-n** ending in every case except the nominative; the feminine is formed by dropping the **-e** and adding **-in(nen)**.
Note **der Franzose** fem. **die Französin**; **der Schwabe** fem. **die Schwäbin**.
– **der Deutsche** (**ein Deutscher**, fem. **die/eine Deutsche**) is an adjectival noun.

Africa **Afrika, afrikanisch, Afrikaner**
Alsace **Elsass, elsässisch, Elsässer**
America **Amerika, amerikanisch, Amerikaner**
Arabia **Arabien, arabisch, Araber**
Argentina **Argentinien, argentinisch, Argentinier**
Asia **Asien, asiatisch, Asiat(en)** *(wk)*
Australia **Australien, australisch, der Australier**
Austria **Österreich, österreichisch, der Österreicher**
Bavaria **Bayern, bayrisch, Bayer**
Belgium **Belgien, belgisch, Belgier**
Bosnia **Bosnien, bosnisch, Bosnier**

Brazil **Brasilien, brasilianisch, Brasilianer**
Bulgaria **Bulgarien, bulgarisch, Bulgare**
Canada **Kanada, kanadisch, Kanadier**
China **China, chinesisch, Chinese**
Czech Republic **die Tschechische Republik, tschechisch, Tscheche**
Denmark **Dänemark, dänisch, Däne**
Egypt **Ägypten, ägyptisch, Ägypter**
England **England, englisch, Engländer**
Europe **Europa, europäisch, Europäer**
Finland **Finnland, finnisch, Finne**
France **Frankreich, französisch, Franzose**
Germany **Deutschland, deutsch, Deutsche** *(adj/n)*
Great Britain **Großbritannien, britisch, Brite**
Greece **Griechenland, griechisch, Grieche**
Holland **Holland, holländisch, Holländer**
Hungary **Ungarn, ungarisch, Ungar**
Iceland **Island, isländisch, Isländer**
India **Indien, indisch, Inder**
Iran **der Iran, iranisch, Iraner**
Iraq **Irak, irakisch, Iraker**
Ireland **Irland, irisch, Ire**
Israel **Israel, israelisch, hebräisch, Israeli(s)**
Italy **Italien, italienisch, Italiener**
Japan **Japan, japanisch, Japaner**
Lebanon **der Libanon, libanesisch, Libanese**
Lorraine **Lothringen, lothringisch, Lothringer**
Luxemburg **Luxemburg, luxemburgisch, Luxemburger**
Morocco **Marokko, marokkanisch, Marokkaner**
Netherlands **die Niederlande, niederländisch, Niederländer**
New Zealand **Neuseeland, neuseeländisch, Neuseeländer**
Northern Ireland **Nordirland,**

nordirisch, Nordire

Norway **Norwegen, norwegisch, Norweger**

Pakistan **Pakistan, pakistanisch, Pakistaner**

Palestine **Palästina, palästinensisch, Palästinenser**

Poland **Polen, polnisch, Pole**

Portugal **Portugal, portugiesisch, Portugiese**

Romania **Rumänien, rumänisch, Rumäne**

Russia **Russland, russisch, Russe**

Saudi Arabia **Saudi-Arabien, saudi-arabisch, Saudi(s)**

Scandinavia **Skandinavien, skandinavisch, Skandinavier**

Scotland **Schottland, schottisch, Schotte**

Slovakia **die Slowakei, slowakisch, Slowake**

South Africa **Südafrika, südafrikanisch, Südafrikaner**

South America **Südamerika, südamerikanisch, Südamerikaner**

Spain **Spanien, spanisch, Spanier**

Sudan **der Sudan, sudanesisch, Sudanese**

Swabia **Schwaben, schwäbisch, Schwabe**

Sweden **Schweden, schwedisch, Schwede**

Switzerland **die Schweiz, schweizerisch, Schweizer**

Turkey **die Türkei, türkisch, Türke**

Wales **Wales, walisisch, Waliser**

The East German states **die neuen Bundesländer**

European Union **die Europäische Union**

The Far East **der Ferne Osten**

The Near East **der Nahe Osten**

United Kingdom **das Vereinigte Königreich**

United States **die Vereinigten Staaten, die USA** *(pl)*

Former countries

Czechoslovakia **die Tschechoslowakei**

East Germany **die DDR (Deutsche Demokratische Republik)**

Jugoslavia **Jugoslawien**

West Germany **die BRD (die Bundesrepublik Deutschland)**

Soviet Union **die Sowjetunion**

Soviet *(adj)* **sowjetisch**

USSR **die UdSSR** *(pl)*

20a Some towns

The adjectives are formed in most cases by adding **-er**. The capital letter is retained, e.g. **der Kölner Dom**.

Note: **Basler, hannoverisch, mailändisch, Münchner, römisch.**

The inhabitant ends in **-er**, fem. **-erin**. Note: **Hannoveraner, Mailänder, Münchner, Römer.**

Aix -la-Chapelle **Aachen**

Antwerp **Antwerpen**

Athens **Athen**

Basle **Basel**

Belgrade **Belgrad**

Bruges **Brügge**

Brussels **Brüssel**

Cairo **Kairo**

Cologne **Köln**

Dunkirk **Dünkirchen**

Edinburgh **Edinburg**

Geneva **Genf**

the Hague **Den Haag**

Hanover **Hannover**

Liege **Lüttich**

Lisbon **Lissabon**

Milan **Mailand**

Moscow **Moskau**

Mulhouse **Mülhausen**

Munich **München**

Naples **Neapel**

Nice **Nizza**

Nuremberg **Nürnberg**

Prague **Prag**

Rome **Rom**

Strasbourg **Straßburg**

Venice **Venedig**
Vienna **Wien**
Warsaw **Warschau**
Zurich **Zürich**

20a Rivers, lakes, mountains

Alps **die Alpen**
Antarctic **die Antarktis**
Antarctic Circle **der südliche Polarkreis**
Antartic Ocean **das Südpolarmeer**
Arctic **die Arktis**
Arctic Circle **der nördliche Polarkreis**
Arctic Ocean **das Nordpolarmeer**
Atlantic **der Atlantik**
Baltic **die Ostsee**
Caspian Sea **das Kaspische Meer**
Danube **die Donau**
Dead Sea **das Tote Meer**
Everest **der Mount Everest**
Himalayas **der Himalaja**
Lake Constance **der Bodensee**
Mediterranean **das Mittelmeer**
Moselle **die Mosel**
North Pole **der Nordpol**
North See **die Nordsee**
Pacific **der Pazifik, der Stille Ozean**
Pyrenees **die Pyrenäen**
Red Sea **das Rote Meer**
Rhine **der Rhein**
South Pole **der Südpol**
Thames **die Themse**
Vesuvius **der Vesuv**
Volga **die Wolga**

21a Languages*

Afrikaans **Afrikaans**
Basque **Baskisch**
Celtic *(adj)* **keltisch**
Flemish **Flämisch**
Gaelic **Gälisch**
Germanic *(adj)* **germanisch**
Hindi **Hindi**
Indo-European *(adj)* **indoeuropäisch**
Indo-Germanic *(adj)* **indogermanisch**
Latin **Latein, Lateinische**
Low German **Plattdeutsch**

Romance *(adj)* **romanisch**
Slavonic *(adj)* **slawisch**
Swiss German **Schweizerdeutsch**
Urdu **Urdu**

21b Grammar

accusative **der Akkusativ**
  accusative *(adj)* **Akkusativ-**
adjective **das Adjektiv(e)**
adverb **das Adverb(ien)**
agreement **die Übereinstimmung(en)**
  it agrees with **es stimmt mit** +dat **überein***
article **der Artikel(-)**
case **der Fall(-e)**
case ending **die Endung(en)**
clause **der Satz(-e)**
comparative **der Komparativ**
conjunction **die Konjunktion(en)**
dative **der Dativ**
declension **die Deklination(en)**
definite **bestimmt**
demonstrative **Demonstrativ-**
direct object **das direkte Objekt(e)**
exception **die Ausnahme(n)**
feminine **weiblich**
gender **das Geschlecht(er)**
genitive **der Genitiv**
indefinite **unbestimmt**
indirect object **das indirekte Objekt(e)**
interrogative **der Interrogativ**
masculine **männlich**
negative **negativ**
neuter **sächlich**
nominative **der Nominativ**
noun **das Substantiv(e), das Nomen(-)**
object **das Objekt(e)**
phrase **die Phrase(n)**
plural **der Plural, die Mehrzahl**
possessive **Possessiv-**
prefix **die Vorsilbe(n)**
preposition **die Präposition(en)**
pronoun **das Pronomen (-a)**
  interrogative **das Interrogativpronomen**
  personal **das Personalpronomen**
  relative **das Relativpronomen**

---

* For other languages ➤App.20a Countries/Regions-adjectives-inhabitants

reflexive **die reflexive Form(en)**
rule **die Regel(n)**
sequence (of words) **die Wortfolge(n)**
singular **die Einzahl, der Singular**
suffix **die Nachsilbe(n)**
superlative **der Superlativ(e)**
subject **das Subjekt(e)**
syntax **die Syntax**
word order **die Wortstellung(en)**

Verbs

active voice **das Aktiv**
auxiliary **das Hilfsverb(en)**
compound **zusammengesetzt**
conditional **der Konditional**
formation **die Bildung(en)**
future **das Futur**
gerund **das Gerundium**
imperative **der Imperativ**
imperfect **das Imperfekt**
impersonal **unpersönlich**
infinitive **der Infinitiv**
intransitive **intransitiv**
irregular **unregelmäßig**
passive voice **das Passiv**
participle **das Partizip**
  past participle **das Partizip
  Perfekt**
past **die Vergangenheit**
  past *(adj)* **vergangen**
perfect **das Perfekt**
person **die Person(en)**
  first person singular **erste Person
  Singular**
present **das Präsens**
reflexive **das Reflexiv**
  reflexive *(adj)* **reflexiv**
regular **regelmäßig**
sequence (of verbs) **die Zeitenfolge(n)**
simple **einfach**
stem **der Stamm(¨e)**
strong **stark**
subjunctive **der Konjunktiv**
system **das System(e)**
tense **die Zeitform(en)**
transitive **transitiv**
use **der Gebrauch**

verb **das Verb(en)**
weak **schwach**

21b Punctuation

apostrophe **der Apostroph(e)**
asterisk **das Sternchen(-)**
bracket **die Klammer(n)**
colon **der Doppelpunkt(e)**
comma **das Komma(s)**
dash **der Bindestrich(e)**
decimal point **das Komma(s)**
exclamation mark **das
  Ausrufezeichen(-)**
full stop/period **der Punkt(e)**
quotation mark **das
  Anführungszeichen(-)**
parentheses **die Klammer(n)**
question mark **das Fragezeichen(-)**
semicolon **das Semikolon(s), der
  Strichpunkt(e)**

22b The class in Germany

die Grundstufe(n) primary phase
die erste Klasse Class 1 (age 6/7)
die zweite Klasse Class 2 (age 7/8)
die dritte Klasse Class 3 (age 8/9)
die vierte Klasse Class 4 (age 9/10)
die Orientierungsstufe(n) transition
  phase
die fünfte Klasse Class 5 (age 10/11)
die sechste Klasse Class 6 (age 11/12)
die Sekundarstufe(n) secondary phase
die siebte Klasse Class 7 (age 12/13)
die achte Klasse Class 8 (age 13/14)
die neunte Klasse Class 9 (age 14/15)
die zehnte Klasse Class 10 (age 15/16)
die Oberstufe(n) sixth form/final years
in der Oberstufe in the sixth form/final
  years

die elfte Klasse Class 11 (age 16/17)
die zwölfte Klasse Class 12 (age 17/18)
die dreizehnte Klasse Class 13 (age
  18/19)

22b Stationery

adhesive tape **das Klebeband(¨-er)**
ball-point **der Kugelschreiber(-)**
biro **der Kuli(s)**
boardrubber/eraser **der Schwamm(¨-e)**
card index **die Kartei(en)**
chalk **die Kreide(n)**
clip board **das Klemmbrett(er)**
compasses **der Zirkel(-)**
correction fluid **die
    Korrekturflüssigkeit(en)**
diary/datebook **der Terminkalender(-)**
drawing pin **die Reißzwecke(n)**
envelope **der Briefumschlag(¨-e)**
exercise book **das Heft(e)**
felt-tip **der Filzstift(e)**
fiber/fiber-tip **der Faserschreiber(-)**
file **die Akte(n)**
filing cabinet **der Aktenschrank(¨-e)**
fountain pen **der Füllfederhalter(-)**
glue **der Klebstoff(e)**
highlighter **der Textmarker(-)**
hole punch **der Locher(-)**
ink **die Tinte(n)**
ink refill **die Nachfüllpatrone(n)**
in-tray/out-tray **die Ablage für
    Eingänge/Ausgänge**
label **das Etikett(e)**
marker **der Stift(e), der Marker(-)**
note book **das Notizbuch(¨-er)**
note paper **das Briefpapier(e)**
OHP **der Overheadprojector**
paper **das Papier(e)**
paper clip **die Büroklammer(n)**
paper cutter **die Schneidemaschine**
pen **der Stift(e)**
pencil **der Bleistift(e)**
photocopier **der Kopierer(-)**
pocket calculator **der Taschenrechner(-)**
protractor **der Winkelmesser(-)**
ring binder **der Ringordner(-)**
rubber band/elastic band **das
    Gummiband(¨-er)**
rubber/eraser **der Radiergummi(s)**
ruler **das Lineal(e)**
scissors **die Schere(n)**
screen **der Bildschirm(e)**

set square **das Zeichendreieck(e)**
sheet of paper **das Blatt(¨-er)**
shredder **der Reißwolf(¨-e)**
stamp **der Stempel(-)**
stapler **die Heftmaschine(n)**
staple remover **der
    Heftklammerentferner(-)**
textbook **das Lehrbuch(¨-er)**
transparency **die Folie(n)**
wastepaper basket **der Abfalleimer(-),
    der Papierkorb(¨-e)**
whiteboard **die Weißwandtafel(n)**

23a Scientific disciplines

applied sciences **die angewandten
    Wissenschaft(en)**
anthropology **die Anthropologie(n)**
astronomy **die Astronomie**
biochemistry **die Biochemie**
biology **die Biologie**
botany **die Botanik**
chemistry **die Chemie**
geology **die Geologie**
medicine **die Medizin**
microbiology **die Mikrobiologie**
physics **die Physik**
physical sciences **die
    Naturwissenschaft(en)**
physiology **die Physiologie**
psychology **die Psychologie**
social sciences **die
    Sozialwissenschaft(en)**
technology **die Technologie(n)**
zoology **die Zoologie**

23b Chemical elements

aluminium/aluminum **das Aluminium**
arsenic **das Arsen**
calcium **das Kalzium**
carbon **der Kohlenstoff**

chlorine **das Chlor**
copper **das Kupfer**
gold **das Gold**
hydrogen **der Wasserstoff**
iodine **das Jod**
iron **das Eisen**
lead **das Blei**
magnesium **das Magnesium**
mercury **das Quecksilber**
nitrogen **der Stickstoff**
oxygen **der Sauerstoff**
phosphorus **der Phosphor**
platinum **das Platin**
plutonium **das Plutonium**
potassium **das Kalium**
silver **das Silber**
sodium **das Natrium**
sulphur **der Schwefel**
uranium **das Uran**
zinc **das Zink**

23b Minerals, compounds & alloys

acetic acid **die Essigsäure(n)**
alloy **die Metalllegierung(en)**
ammonia **das Ammoniak**
asbestos **der Asbest**
bauxite **der Bauxit**
brass **das Messing**
carbon dioxide **das Kohlendioxid(e)**
carbon monoxide **das Kohlenmonoxid(e)**
chalk **die Kreide(n)**
chalky **kalkhaltig**
clay **der Lehm**
copper oxide **das Kupferoxid(e)**
diamond **der Diamant(en)** *(wk)*
granite **der Granit(e)**
graphite **der Graphit(e)**
hydrochloric acid **die Salzsäure(n)**
iron oxide **das Eisenoxid(e)**
lead oxide **das Bleioxid(e)**
lime **der Kalk(e)**
limestone **der Kalkstein(e)**
loam **der Lehm**
marble **der Marmor**
nickel **der Nickel**
nitric acid **die Salpetersäure(n)**

it oxidizes **es oxydiert**
ore **das Erz(e)**
ozone **das Ozon**
propane **das Propan**
quartz **der Quarz(e)**
sand **der Sand**
sandstone **der Sandstein(e)**
silica **die Kieselerde**
silver nitrate **das Silbernitrat(e)**
slate **der Schiefer**
sodium bicarbonate **das Natron**
sodium carbonate **das Natriumkarbonat(e)**
sodium chloride **das Natriumchlorid(e)**
sulphuric acid **die Schwefelsäure(n)**
tin **das Zinn**

23c The zodiac

Aries **der Widder(-)**
Taurus **der Stier(e)**
Gemini **die Zwillinge** (pl)
Cancer **der Krebs(e)**
Leo **der Löwe(n)**
Virgo **die Jungfrau(en)**
Libra **die Waage(n)**
Scorpio **der Skorpion(e)**
Sagittarius **der Schütze(n)**
Capricorn **der Steinbock(-̈e)**
Aquarius **der Wassermann(-̈er)**
Pisces **die Fische** *(pl)*

23c Planets & stars

Earth **die Erde**
Venus **die Venus**
Mercury **der Merkur**
Pluto **der Pluto**
Mars **der Mars**
Jupiter **der Jupiter**
Saturn **der Saturn**
Uranus **der Uranus**
Neptune **der Neptun**
Pole star **der Polarstern**
Halley's comet **der Halleysche Komet**
Southern cross **das Kreuz des Südens**
Great Bear **der Große Bär** *(wk)*

24a Geographical features

archipelago **der Archipel(e)**
bank *(river)* **das Ufer(-)**
bay **die Bucht(en)**
beach **der Strand(ˉe)**
canyon **der Cañon(s)**
cliff **die Klippe(n)**
coast(line) **die Küste(n)**
creek **der Bach(ˉe)**
current **die Strömung(en), der Strom**
delta **das Delta(s)**
desert **die Wüste(n)**
escarpment **der Steilhang(ˉe), die Böschung(en)**
estuary **die Mündung(en)**
fjord **der Fjord(e)**
foothills **die Gebirgsausläufer** *(pl)*
forest **der Wald(ˉer)**
  coniferous forest **der Nadelwald(ˉer)**
  deciduous forest **der Laubwald(ˉer)**
geyser **der Geysir(e)**
heath **die Heide**
hill **der Hügel(-), der Berg(e)**
island **die Insel(n), die Hallig(en)**
jungle **der Dschungel(-), der Urwald(ˉer)**
lake **der See(n)**
marsh **der Sumpf(ˉe)**
meadow **die Wiese(n)**
moor **das Hochmoor(e)**
mountain **der Berg(e)**
  mountains **das Gebirge(-)**
mountain range **die Bergkette(n), die Gebirgskette(n)**
mudflat **das Watt**
ocean **der Ozean(e), das Meer(e)**
ocean floor **der Meeresboden(ˉ)**
peak **der Gipfel(-), die Bergspitze(n)**
peninsula **die Halbinsel(n)**
plateau **das Plateau(s), die Hochebene(n)**
reef **das Riff(e)**
ridge **der Rücken**
river **der Fluss(ˉe)**
  river *(major)* **der Strom(ˉe)**
riverbed **das Flussbett(en)**

sea **die See(n), das Meer(e)**
  shallow sea **das Wattenmeer**
by the seaside **am Meer**
shore **das Ufer(-), der Strand(ˉe)**
spring **die Quelle(n)**
steppe **die Steppe(n)**
stream **der Bach(ˉe), die Strömung(en)**
tundra **die Tundra (-en)**
valley **das Tal(ˉer)**
volcano **der Vulkan(e)**
waterfall **der Wasserfall(ˉe)**
woods **der Wald(ˉer)**
woodland **das Waldland(ˉer)**

24b Wild animals

badger **der Dachs(e)**
bear **der Bär(en)** *(wk)*
beaver **der Biber(-)**
bison/buffalo **der Büffel(-)**
coyote **der Kojote(n)** *(wk)*
deer **der Hirsch(e)**
elephant **der Elefant(en)** *(wk)*
elk **der Elch(e)**
fox **der Fuchs(ˉe)**
frog **der Frosch(ˉe)**
grizzly bear **der Grizzlybär(en)** *(wk)*
hare **der Hase(n)**
hedgehog **der Igel(-)**
lion **der Löwe(n)** *(wk)*
lizard **die Eidechse(n)**
mole **der Maulwurf(ˉe)**
monkey **der Affe(n)** *(wk)*
moose **der Elch(e)**
mouse **die Maus(ˉe)**
otter **der Otter(-)**
rat **die Ratte(n)**
reindeer **das Ren(e)**
snake **die Schlange(n)**
tiger **der Tiger(-)**
toad **die Kröte(n)**
whale **der Wal(e)**
wildcat **die Wildkatze(n)**
wolf **der Wolf(ˉe)**

24b Birds

albatross   der Albatros(se)
blackbird   die Amsel(n)
bluetit/chickadee   die Blaumeise(n)
budgerigar   der Wellensittich(e)
buzzard   der Bussard(e)
chaffinch   der Buchfink(en)
crow   die Krähe(n)
dove   die Taube(n)
eagle   der Adler(-)
 golden eagle   der Steinadler(-)
emu   der Emu(s)
hawk/falcon   der Falke(n) *(wk)*, der Habicht(e)
heron   der Reiher(-)
hummingbird   der Kolibri(s)
kingfisher   der Eisvogel(⁻)
magpie   die Elster(n)
ostrich   der Strauß(e)
owl   die Eule(n)
parrot   der Papagei(en)
peacock   der Pfau(e)
pelican   der Pelikan(e)
penguin   der Pinguin(e)
robin   das Rotkehlchen(-)
seagull   die Möwe(n)
sparrow   der Sperling(e), der Spatz(en)
starling   der Star(e)
swallow   die Schwalbe(n)
swan   der Schwan(⁻e)
swift   der Mauersegler(-)
thrush   die Drossel(n)
woodpecker   der Specht(e)
wren   der Zaunkönig(e)

24b Animal body parts

beak   der Schnabel(⁻)
claw   die Kralle(n)
comb   der Kamm(⁻e)
feather   die Feder(n)
fin   die Flosse(n)
fleece   das Schaffell(e)
fur   der Pelz(e)
gills   die Kieme(n)
hide   das Fell(e)
hoof   der Huf(e)

mane   die Mähne(n)
paw   die Pfote(n), die Tatze(n)
pelt   der Pelz(e), das Fell(e)
scale   die Schuppe(n)
shell   die Schale(n)
tail   der Schwanz(⁻e)
trunk   der Rüssel(-)
tusk   der Stoßzahn(⁻e)
udder   das Euter(-)
wing   der Flügel(-)

24c Trees

apple tree   der Apfelbaum(⁻e)
ash   die Esche(n)
beech   die Buche(n)
cherry tree   der Kirschbaum(⁻e)
chestnut   der Kastanienbaum(⁻e)
cypress   die Zypresse(n)
eucalyptus   der Eukalyptusbaum(⁻e)
fig tree   der Feigenbaum(⁻e)
fir tree   die Tanne(n), die Fichte(n)
fruit tree   der Obstbaum(⁻e)
holly   die Stechpalme(n)
maple   der Ahornbaum(⁻e)
oak   die Eiche(n)
olive tree   der Olivenbaum(⁻e)
palm   die Palme(n)
peach tree   der Pfirsichbaum(⁻e)
pear tree   der Birnbaum(⁻e)
pine   die Kiefer(n)
plum tree   der Pflaumenbaum(⁻e)
poplar   die Pappel(n)
rhododendron   der Rhododendron (-en)
walnut tree   der Walnußbaum(⁻e)
willow   die Weide(n)
yew   die Eibe(n)

24c Flowers & weeds

azalea   die Azalee(n)
cactus   der Kaktus (-een)
carnation   die Nelke(n)
chrysanthemum   die Chrysantheme(n)
clover   der Klee
crocus   der Krokus(se)
daffodil   die Osterglocke(n)
dahlia   die Dahlie(n)

daisy **das Gänseblümchen(-)**
dandelion **der Löwenzahn(-̈e)**
foxglove **der Fingerhut(-̈e)**
fern **der Farn(e), das Farnkraut(-̈er)**
geranium **die Geranie(n)**
hydrangea **die Hortensie(n)**
lily **die Seerose(n), die Lilie(n)**
lily of the valley **das Maiglöckchen(-)**
nettle (stinging) **die Nessel(n), die**
Brennnessel(n)
orchid **die Orchidee(n)**
pansy **das Stiefmütterchen(-)**
poppy **der Mohn**
primrose **die Erdschlüsselblume(n)**
rose **die Rose(n)**
snowdrop **das Schneeglöckchen(-)**
sunflower **die Sonnenblume(n)**
thistle **die Distel(n)**
tulip **die Tulpe(n)**
violet **das Veilchen(-)**

25b Political institutions

assembly **die Versammlung(en)**
association **der Verein(e), der**
Verband(-̈e)
cabinet **das Kabinett(e)**
shadow cabinet *(UK)* **das**
Schattenkabinett
confederation **der Bund(-̈e)**
congress **der Kongress(e)**
council **der (Stadt)rat(-̈e)**
federal council **der Bundesrat(-̈e)**
federal government **der Bundestag(e)**
federation **der Staatenbund(-̈e)**
House of Representatives **das**
Repräsentantenhaus
local authority **die Behörde(n)**
Lower Chamber/House **das**
Unterhaus(-̈er)
parliament *(UK)* **das Parlament(e)**
party **die Partei(en), die Fraktion(en)**
Senate **der Senat(e)**
state parliament **der Landtag(e)**
town council **der Stadtrat(-̈e)**
town hall **das Rathaus(-̈er)**
Upper House/Chamber **das**
Oberhaus(-̈er)

25b Representatives & politicians

Chancellor **der Kanzler(-) [-in]**
federal chancellor **der**
Bundeskanzler(-)
congressman/woman **der/die**
Kongressabgeordnete
Foreign Minister/Secretary of State **der**
Außenminister(-) [-in]
head of state **das Staatsoberhaupt(-̈er)**
leader **der Fraktionschef(s) [-in]**
leader of the party/party leader **der/die**
Parteivorsitzende *(adj/n)*
mayor **der Bürgermeister(-) [-in]**
member of parliament **der/die**
Abgeordnete *(adj/n)*
minister **der Minister(-) [-in]**
Home Secretary/Minister of the Interior
der Innenminister(-) [-in]
politician **der Politiker(-) [-in]**
President **der Präsident(en)** *(wk)* **[-in]**
federal president **der**
Bundespräsident(en) *(wk)* **[-in]**
Prime Minister **der Premierminister(-)**
[-in]
representative **der/die Abgeordnete**
(adj/n)
senator **der Senator(en)**
Speaker **der (Regierungs)sprecher(-)**
[-in], der/die Vorsitzende *(adj/n)*

German political parties

CDU/Christlich-Demokratische Union
Christian Democratic Union
CSU/Christlich-Soziale Union
Christian-Social Union
FDP/Freie Demokratische Partei Free
Democratic party
die Grünen/Bündnis 90 Green parties
KPD/Kommunistische Partei
Deutschlands Communist Party
PDS/Partei des Demokratischen
Sozialismus Democratic Socialism
Party
SPD/Sozialdemokratische Partei
Deutschlands Social Democratic
Party

SUBJECT INDEX

27b Military ranks

admiral **der Admiral(e/-̈e)**
air marshal **der Marschall(-̈e) der Luftstreitkräfte**
brigadier **der Brigadegeneral(e)**
captain **der Hauptmann(-̈er) (-leute)**
commodore **der Flotillenadmiral(e/-̈e)**
corporal **der Obergefreite** *(adj/n)*
field marshal **der Feldmarschall(-̈e)**
general **der General(e)**
lieutenant **der Leutnant(s)**
major **der Major(e)**
private **der einfache Soldat(en)** *(wk)*
rear-admiral **der Konteradmiral(e/-̈e)**
sergeant **der Feldwebel(-)**
sergeant-major **der Oberfeldwebel(-)**

27c International organizations

Council of Europe **der Europarat**
Council of Ministers **der Ministerrat**
EU/European Union **die Europäische Union, EU**

NATO/North Atlantic Treaty Organization **die Nato**
OECD/Organization for Economic Cooperation and Development **die OECD**
Security Council **der Sicherheitsrat**
United Nations **die Vereinten Nationen, die UN**
WHO/World Health Organization **die Weltgesundheitsorganisation, die WHO**
World Bank **die Weltbank**

D
VOCABULARY INDEX

Vocabulary index

References are to Vocabulary Topics

A

abroad, going 19b
accidents 11a
accommodation 8a, 12c, 20b
actions 8d
addiction 12d
advertising 18d
aeroplane/airplane 19d
age 5a, 7c
agreeing 15d
agriculture 24c
animals 24b, App.24b, 24c
appearance, physical 5a
apologizing 15d
appreciation, artistic 17a
approval 15b
architecture 17b; features App.17b
arguing 6d
art, fine 17b
artistic criticism 17a
artistic styles 17a
arts 17; jobs App.14b
automobiles 19c; parts App.19c

B

banking 14e
bathroom 8c
beach App.20a
beauty 11d
beliefs, political 25b; religious 13a
birds 24b, App.24b
birth 7b
boats 19b; travel by 19b
body, parts of 5b, App.5b; functions 11d
booking, holidays/vacation 20b
books 17c
broadcasting 18c
business 14

C

calculations 4d
calendar 3b
camping 20c
car 19c; parts App.19c
cause & effect 6d
character 6a, App.6a
chemistry 23b
chemical elements App.23b
children 7b
cinema 17e; film genres App.17e
civil service, jobs App.14b
clarifying meaning 15c
clothing 9c, 16c; fabrics 5f
colours/colors 5b
communicating 15
company personnel & structure App.14b
comparing 5e, 6d
compass, points of 2b
computers 15f, App.15f
conditions of work 14c
congratulating 15a
construction 14b; jobs App.14b
continents App.20a
cooking 10d
cosmetics 9b
countries App.20a
countryside 24a
crime 12d, 26
crime fighting 26c
criticism, artistic 17a
crockery & cutlery 8c
currencies App.9a

D

daily life 8
dance 17d
date 3b
days of week 3b
death 7c
decline, economic 14e

dentist 11c
descriptions 5; people 5a; things 5c
dessert 10c
dining out 10a
dining-room 8c
direction(s) 2
disability 11b, 12b
discrimination 12e
discussing 6d
diseases App.11c
doctors 11c
doctrines, religious 13a
drama 17e
drinks 10a
drug abuse 12d

E

earth 23c, 24a, 24e
eating 10d; eating out 10a
economics 14a, 14d, 14e
economy 14e
education 22; jobs App.14b
electrical goods 8b
elections 25b
electricity 23b
emergencies 11a
emotions 6b
emphasizing 6d
energy sources 23c, 23b
environment 24, 23c
equipment, sports 16c
evaluating 5d
examinations 22c
examples, giving 6d
expressing views 6d

F

fabrics 5f
family 7
farm animals 24c
farming 24c
feelings 6b
festivals, religious App.13b

films   17e; genres App.17e
finance   14d; personal 14e
first aid   11a, 11b
fish   10b
fitness   11d
fittings & fixtures   8b, 8c
flowers   App.24c
food   10, 9b; preparation
     10d; jobs App.14b
foodstuffs, basic   9b
fractions   4c
friends   7a
fruit   10c
functional words   1a
funerals   7c
furnishings   8b, 8c
furniture   8b, 8c
further education   22d

G

gardening   24c; tools
     App.8c
gems   App.9c
geography   24a
geology   23c
geometrical terms   App.4d
good-byes   15d
government   25; jobs
     App.14b
grammar   21b, 1a
growth, economic   14e
growing up 7c

H

handicapped   11b, 12b
health   11d;
health care, jobs   App.14b
herbs   10c
hesitating   15d
higher education   22d
hobbies   16a, App.16a, 20a
holiday   20, App.20a
holidays App.13b
home   8
homelessness   12c
horticulture   24c
hospital   11c; departments
     App.11c
hotel   20b
house   8
household   8b, 8c

household goods   9b
housework   8d
housing   8a, 12c
how much?   4
human body   App.5b
human character   6, App.6a
human lifecycle   7c
human relationships   7
hygiene   11d

I

ideology, political   25b;
     religious 13a
illness   11b, App.11c
industrial relations   14a
industry   14d, 14b; jobs
     App.14b
information technology   15d
insects   24b
interjections   15d
international organizations
     27c
international relations   27c
introductions   15a

J

jewellery/jewelry   App.9c
job application 14c
job interview   14c
jobs   App.14b
journalism   18
justice   26b, 26c

K

kitchen   8c

L

labour/labor relations   14a
language   21
languages   App.21a
language families   App.21a
leisure time   16, App.16a
length   4a
letter writing   15c, App.15c
life sciences   23a
life cycle, human   7c
listening   21b
literature   17c
location   2b
lounge   8c
love   7b

M

mail   15e
manufacturing   14b; jobs
     App.14b
marriage   7b
materials   5f
mathematics   4d;
mathematical terms   App.4d
meals   10a
meaning, clarifying   15b
measuring   4b
meat   10b; meat dishes 10b
mechanics   23b
media   18
medical science   23a
medical treatment   11c
meetings   15a
mental activity   6c
metals   App.23b, App.9c
military personnel   27b
military ranks App.27b
minerals   23c
money   14e, 9a, App.9a
months   3b
movement   2
movies   17e; genres
     App.17e
music   17d
musical forms   App.17d
musical terms   App.17d
musicians & instruments
     App.17d

N

nationalities   App.20a
newspapers   18b
nuclear physics   23b
numbers   4c

O

obligation   15c
oceans   App.20a
office   14b; personnel,
     structure App.14b
optician   11c

P

packaging   4b
parliament   25, App.25a
parties, political   25b,
     App.25b

VOCABULARY INDEX

parts of the body   5b,
   App.5b; animal App.24b
pastimes   16a, App.16a
pay *(work)*   14c
paying, for holiday/vacation
   20b
peace   27c
permission   15c
periods, artistic   17a
personnel   App.14b
pets   24b
photography   16c
physical sciences   23b
physics   23b; nuclear 23b
place   2
places of work   App.14b
planets   App.23c
pleasantries   15a
police   26c
politicians   App.25a
political institutions   App.25a
politics   25; ideology 25b
position   2
post   15e
poultry   10b
poverty   12b
precious stones   App.9c
prejudice   12e
press   18b
prison   26c
professions   App.14b
program(me)s, TV & radio
   18c
publishing   17c, 18b
punctuation   21c
punishment   26c

Q

qualifying *(reservation)*   6d
quantity   4, 9b

R

radio   18c
rail(road)   19e
reading   21b
regions, geographical
   App.20a
relationships   7
relatives   App.7a
religion   13
religious festivals   App.13b

research   23a, 23c; jobs
   App.14b
reservations, expressing   6d
restaurants   10a
retail, jobs   App.14b
road signs App.19c
road travel   19c
rooms   8b, 8c
routine   8b, 8d

S

school   22a, 22b, 22c,
   App.22b
science   23
scientific disciplines App.23a
sea   24b, 19b, seas
   App.20a; pollution 24e
seafood   10b
sealife   24b, 10b
seasons   3b
self-catering holiday   20c
self-service vacation   20c
senses   5b
services   App.9a; jobs
   App.14b
sexuality   12e, 7b
shape   4a
ships   19b
shoes   9c
shopping   9, App.9a; food
   9b; clothes 9c
sickness   11b
sights, tourist   App.20a
size   4a
social discourse   15
social services   12b
society & social issues   12
space *(universe)*   23c
speech   21b
sport   16b, 16
sports equipment   16c
stars   App.23c
stationery App.22b
stores   App.9a
strikes   14a
styles, artistic   17a
subjects, academic   22c, 22d
substances   5f
surprise   15b
sweet *(dessert)*   10c

T

telecommunications   15e
telephone   15e
television   18c
temperature   4b
thanking   15c
theater   17e
thought processes   6c
time   3; of day 3b
timepieces App.3b
toiletries   9b
tools   App.8c
tourism   20, App.20a
trade   27c
trains   19e
transport   19, means
   App.19a; jobs App.14b
travel   19, 2c
trees   App.24c
trial   26b

U

unemployment   12b, 14c

V

vacation   20; beach 20a
vegetables   10c
verbs   App.21b
views, expressing   6d
violence   12d, 26a, 27a, 27b
vocabulary   21a
volume   4b

W

war   27a, 27b
watches & clocks   App.3b
wealth   12b
weapons   27b
weather   24d
weight   4b
wild life/animals   24b,
   App.24b
word processing   15f
work 14b, 14c
workplaces App.14b
writing   21b; letters App.15e

X, Y, Z

zodiac   App.23c